Unnatural Death

Unsolved Murders and Mysteries

Unnatural Death

Michael M. Baden M.D. with
Judith Adler Hennessee

Unsolved Murders
and Mysteries

John Canning

timewarner
paperbacks

A *Time Warner* Paperback

This omnibus edition first published in Great Britain by
Time Warner Paperbacks in 2003
Unnatural Death/Unsolved Murders and Mysteries Omnibus Copyright ©
Michael M. Baden M.D., Judith Adler Hennessee and John Canning 2003

Previously published separately:
Unnatural Death first published in Great Britain in 1991 by
Sphere Books Limited
Reprinted 1991 (twice)
This edition published by Warner Books in 1992
Reprinted 1993, 1994, 1995, 1998, 1999, 2001
Reprinted by Time Warner Paperbacks in 2002
Copyright © Michael M. Baden, M.D., and Judith Adler Hennessee 1989

Unsolved Murders and Mysteries first published in Great Britain in 1987 by
Michael O'Mara Books Limited
Published by Futura Publications in 1988
Reprinted 1989, 1990 (twice), 1991
Revised edition published by Warner Books in 1992
Reprinted 1993, 1994 (twice), 1995
Copyright © John Canning 1987, 1992

The moral rights of the authors have been asserted.

A CIP catalogue record for this book
is available from the British Library.

ISBN 0 7515 3518 4

Printed and bound in Great Britain by
Clays Ltd, St Ives plc

Time Warner Paperbacks
An imprint of
Time Warner Books UK
Brettenham House
Lancaster Place
London WC2E 7EN

www.TimeWarnerBooks.co.uk

Unnatural Death
Confessions of a Medical Examiner

To Colonel Henry F. Williams,
New York State Police,
in appreciation for his legacy to the forensic sciences.

—MICHAEL M. BADEN, M.D.

To my daughter, Nancy.

—JUDITH ADLER HENNESSEE

CONTENTS

Introduction.................................... ix

1 Heroes and Conspiracies...................... 1
   The Price of Fame

2 The Education of a Medical Examiner 23
   Life and Death, Uptown and Downtown

3 Autopsy 33
   Anatomy and Destiny

4 History..................................... 48
   From Taxman to Medical Examiner

5 Manhattan Postmortem 58
   City Politics

6 Earthly Remains 77
   Identifying the Dead
      MIAs • Airline Crash • Algae Lady • Floater • Hair

7 Time of Death.............................. 90
   Biological Clocks
      John Belushi—Drug Overdose • Pinchos Jaroslawicz—
      Stone Cold • David Hendricks—The Pizza Connection

8 Crazy Quilt................................. 110
   Multiple Murders

Mary Beth Tinning—Where Have All the Children Gone?
• Joe Christopher—The Buffalo Slasher • Richard Kuklinski—The Ice Man

9   Almost Perfect. 140
    Without a Trace
        Catherine Fried—Burking • Carl Coppolino—Succinyl-
        choline • Dr. X—Curare

10 Close Calls 165
    Accidental Death
        Whitney Young—Nigerian Drowning • Dr. Josephine
        Wells Brown—Frightened to Death • Daphne Mellon—
        Youthful Indiscretion • S&M—Careless Love

11 Diagnostic Follies. 187
    Natural Endings
        Leonard Barco—Ordeal by Error • Claus von Bulow—
        Was It Insulin?

12 Attica. 207
    Who Did It?

Index 217

INTRODUCTION

Medical examiners are the only doctors whose patients are dead and therefore silent. They cannot explain why they died, so we have to find out in other ways. We are detectives of death—we visit the scene; we examine the medical evidence and the laboratory findings and put them together with the circumstances and the patient's medical history. Through the autopsy, we make the body speak to us. Deciphering the message is an art as well as a science.

Our medical specialty is forensic pathology. We know about the three kinds of unnatural death—suicides, homicides, and accidents. We are trained to analyze traumatic injuries—gunshot and stab wounds, blunt force, and poison. Our work is different from that of hospital pathologists who autopsy bodies to study the ravages of disease. Our methods are different from those of doctors who care for the living and whose concern is more the treatment than the cause. We want to know how the knife went in, from above or below, and where the person who wielded it was standing; which bullet hole was the entrance and which the exit and where the shot came from. Medically, these things may be irrelevant, but in a courtroom they are extremely significant in deciding the cause and manner of death and reconstructing how it happened. The kind of autopsy we do is called a medical-legal autopsy.

Forensic pathology is an untaught specialty, a stepchild of the medical profession. After medical school we get our training as apprentices in a medical examiner's office. There is even confusion about our title. In some states we are called coroners, but in most parts of the country coroners are not doctors. They tend to be undertakers and tow-truck operators who got into the business because they could transport bodies. They hire doctors to do autopsies. These doctors are untrained in forensic pathology and often make mistakes. People are accused of murder and go to trial based on those mistakes. Others escape detection, and still others go free for lack of strong medical evidence. The United States has no systematic, comprehensive method of certifying death. There are fewer than four hundred full-time forensic pathologists in the entire country, not nearly enough to handle the number of deaths that fall within our province. Of the two million deaths a year in the United States, 8 percent are unnatural. (In younger people, up to age thirty-five, the figures are higher—more than half are unnatural.) All the obvious homicides are autopsied; most accidents and suicides are not. Death certificates often list the wrong cause of death.

Medical examiners (MEs) frequently see things no one else sees, the deaths that need not have happened, the failures of society. As public doctors, our findings should be used to make public policy; instead, we are too often viewed as Cassandras, telling people things they don't want to hear. It was an ME who first drew attention to the problem of battered children. MEs know that alcohol is a silent partner in almost half of all unnatural deaths. It's an underlying cause, as in drunk driving, so it isn't written on the death certificate. It is there in small plane crashes and in boat accidents and accidents in the home. It is commonly present in suicides and deaths by fire.

In the public sphere, MEs see ways to prevent death just as other doctors see ways to prevent disease. Part of our job is to identify new diseases, like AIDS, before they become epidemics. We also see the results of unsafe technology, the flaws in design that cost lives. Airplane seats were designed with metal bars attached to the bottom of the chair to hold suitcases and keep them from sliding backwards. During crashes, people's feet were being cut off at the ankle. One New York City ME kept a "centipede," a large tray of these feet. The danger was pointed out to the pathologist the FAA sent to observe autopsies. The bar was redesigned so that it didn't cut feet.

These techniques need not be confined to the dead. In Europe, clinical forensic pathologists are on call to hospital emergency rooms where they use the same methods of analysis with the living as with the dead. Here, with the exception of rape kits, we have been slow to take advantage of what forensic science can offer.

The case of Tawana Brawley, the black teenager who claimed to have been abducted and taken into the woods where four white men allegedly raped her for four days, might have proceeded along different lines if a clinical forensic pathologist had been available at the hospital when she was brought in. Brawley, who was missing for four days in November 1987, was found in a plastic garbage bag behind the apartment building her family had been evicted from two weeks previously. Her body was smeared with feces, and "Nigger" and "KKK" were scrawled across her chest. She was brought to a hospital emergency room in Wappingers Falls, a small community in upstate New York. The situation was complicated by the fact that Brawley refused to allow the hospital to use the rape kit at first, and five hours elapsed before any evidence was taken. During that time, the attendants washed her. Even so, the photographs, the analysis of her clothing, the vaginal swabs, and the hospital and laboratory reports, which I later reviewed for the attorney general, contradicted her whole story.

If, as Brawley said, she was repeatedly raped by different men for four days, there should have been some evidence of it. There was no semen. There was not even a bruise. If the rape took place in the woods, there should have been traces of earth or pine needles or grass or leaves on her hair and clothes. There was no evidence that she had been in the woods. But there was evidence that she had been somewhere else. The FBI lab, which analyzed the feces on her clothes, found dog hairs in it. The dog hairs belonged to a pet dog that lived two apartments away from where Brawley was found. The racial slurs were also open to question. I had seen similar writings before which were self-inflicted. They had certain things in common: they were a political statement; they were written on a surface that was easily accessible to the victim, and their imprint was neither painful nor disfiguring. When these elements are present, such writing is virtually always done by the central character in the drama.

The circumstances were also strange—that Brawley would be brought to a place that had once been home and where her abductors would risk being seen and identified. There was no indication that she had been hurt or that a crime had been committed, as a grand jury would later determine, but her story was distorted and politicized by her advisors who sought to turn it into a paradigm of racial injustice. To a large extent, they succeeded. Because correct forensic procedures had not been followed immediately, there is still doubt: a great many people who don't believe Brawley's story still think *something* happened and that the system didn't work for her.

Forensic pathology is a profession with an untapped potential, one that is not properly appreciated. But it is also a profession that is enormously gratifying—it offers the adventure of detection, the excitement of discovery, the satisfaction of searching for the truth. It is a profession I have loved since I watched my first autopsy thirty-four years ago.

MICHAEL M. BADEN, M.D.
JANUARY 1989
NEW YORK CITY

1

HEROES AND
CONSPIRACIES

THE PRICE OF FAME

HEROES AND CELEBRITIES are not always granted the comfort of resting in peace. The price of fame is often a posthumous role in a conspiracy theory. When Marilyn Monroe died of an overdose of barbiturates, a small industry sprang up to prove she had been murdered. The brevity of Pope John Paul I's reign—he died suddenly after only thirty-three days in office—inspired stories of a murderous cabal that silenced him before he could put into effect threatening changes. Bobby Kennedy is said by some to have been killed by a guard who was standing near him and not by the wild shooting of Sirhan Sirhan. After J. Edgar Hoover's death, presumably of natural causes, there was talk of murder. Joan Crawford's death (she was signed out as a heart attack) drew whispers of suicide. The famous and infamous, the celebrated and notorious, do not bleed and die the way the rest of us do. They have scenarios, intricately plotted dramas. Buried villains still stalk the earth, hidden in other guises, and news of their obscure ends in faraway villages only brings disbelief. In 1979 Dr. Josef Mengele, the "Angel of

Death" at Auschwitz, drowned in Brazil, where he was living under an assumed name. He was identified unequivocally through his teeth, but many people still think he is alive. There are reports of sightings and offers of a reward for the "real" Dr. Mengele.

In this, the century of the spy, deaths are scrutinized with a view to the plotter behind the curtain, the stranger in the shadow. The hero cannot be undone by a single assailant—an oversized life demands a memorable death, one not accorded other mortals. There must be a plot to bring him down. Amelia Earhart, on the last leg of a flight around the world, disappeared in the Pacific Ocean somewhere between New Guinea and Howland Island, her next stop. It was 1937, and dark tales of espionage circulated: she was really a spy on a reconnaissance mission and the Japanese caught her and tortured her (in fact, some people think she is still a captive). What happened was more mundane. She got lost and ran out of gas. She had removed a heavy antenna from her plane. Without this device, she failed to pick up radio signals that would have directed her to Howland Island.

Even when an autopsy is done, the speculation doesn't stop. On the contrary. Marilyn Monroe's autopsy findings were used as evidence that her suicide was a murder. It was considered highly suspicious that there were no barbiturates in her stomach, which is where they are usually found after a suicidal overdose. Instead, they were only in her bloodstream. This was taken to mean that she couldn't have swallowed the pills; therefore, she must have been injected. An injection presupposed a second person. But this is jumping to conclusions. The process of absorbing liquids into the bloodstream works faster in some people than in others. Alcohol, barbiturates, and water could all have been absorbed after Monroe lost consciousness and before she died. It is possible that the toxicologists did not examine the stomach contents as carefully as they might. They were not as sophisticated then as they are now, and it's difficult to say what they might have missed.

People assume that most autopsies are done properly, that only the ones they hear about have been botched. The distinction is really between natural and unnatural death. Most natural deaths are autopsied competently or not at all. It is the autopsies of unnatural deaths that are performed ineptly, but few people know. Only those of public figures are made public.

After the assassination of Martin Luther King, Jr., the question arose whether James Earl Ray had committed the murder all by himself. Ray was carrying too much money when he was finally caught, and he was thought to be too dumb to have managed such a complex job and escaped all by himself. Dr. Jerry Francisco, the Tennessee medical examiner in Memphis (who also oversaw Elvis Presley's autopsy), waited to get permission from Coretta King to do the postmortem. When there is a murder, permission should not be required. The interests of society demand an autopsy.

Even after he was given permission, Francisco appeared overwhelmed by respect and did less than he should have. The bullet went through King's jawbone and into his neck, but Francisco didn't trace the gunshot track, which is normal procedure. Nor did he attempt to identify the black material in the wound. The material became a source of much speculation. It could have been powder grains, which would have meant that King was shot from up close, by someone standing less than a foot away. Ray was about one hundred yards away. It was like a rerun of the John F. Kennedy assassination, with the possibility that there was a second shooter and Ray was the patsy: Ray shot and missed, and someone standing next to King on the second-floor balcony of the Lorraine Motel shot him at close range.

The theory didn't work. Ten years after King's death, as part of my work on the congressional Select Committee on Assassinations (I headed the medical investigation into King's death), I sent a slide with the black stuff to McCrone Associates, a laboratory in Chicago that specializes in identifying particles. Under an ordinary microscope, with the light coming up from below, smoke, soot, carbon, and lead all look alike. They are just black spots, with no distinctive structure. The lab identified the black stuff not as gunshot powder but as lead. Lead is exactly what it should have been if it came from Ray's gun. Ray had shot King with a .30-06 soft-nosed hunting bullet. The tip of a soft-nosed bullet is lead, and when it strikes bone it breaks apart, giving it greater killing power.

In three of the "crimes of the century"—the kidnapping and murder of the Lindbergh baby, the murder of Sir Harry Oakes in 1943 in the Bahamas, and the assassination of John F. Kennedy—the autopsies, which were acceptable according to the standards of the day, were forensic disasters. The Lindbergh baby's death was attributed to a fractured skull. Years later I went over the evidence for a symposium, "Forensic Science, Then and Now," a fifty-year review of the profession given by the American Academy of Forensic Sciences. The fractured-skull diagnosis was wrong for two reasons: there was no fracture, just separation of the unfused skull bones which is normal in all babies, and there was no brain damage. It's the brain damage, not the fracture, that would cause death. The baby was probably smothered at the time of the kidnapping to keep him from crying out and alerting the family and the nurse who were all in nearby rooms.

Sir Harry Oakes, one of the richest men in the world and a confidant of the Duke and Duchess of Windsor, was discovered lying in a burning bed on his back with a bludgeoned skull. The body had been moved after death—the dried blood on his face ran up from his ears toward his nose, defying gravity. Nobody noticed. The duke, in his capacity of governor of the Bahamas, oversaw the investigation. Oakes's killer was never identified. His son-in-law was accused and tried but found not guilty.

It isn't that a well-done autopsy would have solved these murders. Conspiracies don't show up in autopsy reports, and anyway, there seems to be a need to tell stories about the lives and deaths of famous people. But an autopsy clears up the physical questions surrounding the death. We can see what happened and what didn't. It's part of the process of finding the truth.

Where bungled autopsies are concerned, President Kennedy's is the exemplar. After his death it was inevitable that conspiracy theories would arise and proliferate, but there would not have been so many errors and distortions to feed on if the autopsy had been done properly. From the beginning it was surrounded with confusion and secrecy and papered over with an enormous concern for appearances. Suspicion was created simply from the way it was managed. It opened the door to grassy knolls and second gunmen and whatever theory anyone wanted to present. It fed a conspiracy industry that mixed together the FBI, the CIA, the Mafia, the Russians, and the Cubans in a monster plot that was the culmination of our Cold War fantasies. The country could accept the myth of the Lone Ranger but not its underside, the lone assassin.

Our European counterparts in forensic medicine, more cynical and sophisticated about the uses of power than we, were skeptical of the clumsy way the Kennedy autopsy was handled. They thought it was sinister, that the clumsiness had to be officially sanctioned. At the very least, such carelessness revealed a lack of desire to find the truth. Taking it one step further, the autopsy could have been part of the conspiracy—it was deliberately sabotaged to destroy evidence.

American assassination buffs developed elaborate theories but were hampered in trying to prove them. The Kennedy family controlled access to the evidence, which was kept in the National Archives, and rarely granted anyone permission to view it, a policy that generated even more suspicion. The privately owned Zapruder film of the assassination (the main pictures available) was endlessly analyzed, sequence by sequence. Conspiracy devotees enhanced and blew up each frame; a shadow of a shadow became a face behind a tree, dark figures lurked on the fringes. They saw that Kennedy's head moved backward instead of forward after he was shot. If the bullet came from behind, they reasoned, from the Texas School Book Depository Building where the killer, Lee Harvey Oswald, was shooting from, then the impact would have forced the head forward. Since the head moved backward, they said, JFK was shot from the front, which meant there were two shooters, one from the grassy knoll. This theory is not unreasonable; it's just wrong. They left out of their calculations the acceleration of the car Kennedy was riding in. Beyond that, the body simply does not react that way. The force of the bullet would just as likely cause Kennedy's head to move forward as backward. It's not predictable.

In 1977 Congress set up the Select Committee on Assassinations to resolve these and other vexing questions. I was asked to take charge of the forensic pathology investigation, and I assembled a panel of eight other medical examiners. I thought nine of us would have more credibility than one. Among us, we had performed over 100,000 medical-legal autopsies. (Other panels investigated nonforensic areas—the Cubans, the Mafia, the photographs, etc.)

Even at the very beginning in 1963, there were rumblings within the community of medical examiners that the autopsy was a disaster, and that Commander James J. Humes, who had done it, was not trained for it. In fact, he had never autopsied anyone with a gunshot wound. The leading critic of the autopsy was Dr. Cyril Wecht (who later served on my committee), the coroner/ME of Pittsburgh. Wecht was forthright, outspoken, and saw no virtue in being diplomatic in this matter. It was a secret autopsy done by a man who was not competent for the job, he said, but he didn't get any points for saying out loud what his peers knew. His complaint looked like sour grapes, and many forensic pathologists, even though they agreed with him, thought him irresponsible and self-serving for making it. In contrast, Milton Helpern, the highly respected chief medical examiner of New York City and the soul of diplomacy, suggested in an interview that the government should have called in competent MEs to assist Humes. Some of the leading MEs in the country were in Baltimore, Philadelphia, and New York. In fact, Earl Rose, the Dallas coroner, was a trained forensic pathologist. As a result of the interview, Helpern thought, his name was removed from a list of lecturers to the Armed Forces Institute of Pathology (a federal training program for pathologists).

After the assassination, Kennedy was brought to Parkland Hospital where he was pronounced dead. There are television clips of Earl Rose, standing at the door of the hospital like Horatius at the bridge, saying no to the Secret Service men, no, they couldn't remove the body, and the Secret Service men telling him to get out of the way or he would be run over. They almost had a fistfight.

The Dallas coroner had jurisdiction over the body. Murder was a state crime. Legally, Kennedy should not have been moved, but in this situation other considerations overrode the legal ones. At that early stage, no one knew who had shot the President or if Lyndon Johnson was also in danger. The Secret Service wanted LBJ out of Dallas and back in Washington. Mrs. Kennedy also wanted the body out and refused to leave without it. In the end, the Kennedy entourage physically pushed Rose out of the way and rushed to the airport. They were worried that the Dallas police might chase them. They knew they were taking the body illegally.

No forensic pathologist has ever examined the body of the President. We did our investigation by reviewing the medical and autopsy reports, the photographs and X rays and clothing. It had not occurred to the Warren Commission (which was set up shortly after the assassination to investigate it) that a forensic pathologist could contribute anything to the proceedings. Among its illustrious members—Chief Justice Earl Warren, former CIA director Allen W. Dulles, Representative Gerald R. Ford, and others—there was no one who had any appreciation of forensic medicine and the mysteries it could clarify. They were unaware that there were two kinds of autopsies, the usual hospital one and the forensic one, or that it mattered that Commander Humes didn't know the difference between an entrance wound and an exit wound. They didn't know the difference, either. They thought a pathologist was a pathologist, and one could do as good an autopsy as another. And so, many of the questions that the Warren Commission thought it had answered in 1964 were still unresolved in 1977. Our job was to answer them: to pinpoint where the bullets had entered and exited, and to trace their trajectories. Did they come from behind, where Oswald was, or from the grassy knoll in front? From above, or from ground level? Could a single bullet have gone through both Kennedy and Governor John Connally and emerged "pristine"? How many shots were fired? Was Oswald the only shooter?

In doing the investigation, we literally had to begin at the beginning. The variety of conspiracy theories had called into question every bit of evidence, including the body itself. According to one scenario, during the plane ride from Dallas to Washington the entrance wounds were altered to look like exit wounds in order to confuse everyone about the direction of the shots. According to another, the original autopsy report, photographs, and X rays had all been stolen from the National Archives and replaced with fakes. I wondered at the vast numbers of people that would have been required to carry out all these tasks and the extraordinary combination of luck, competence, and intelligence, so lacking in all other human endeavors, that would have been needed to pull off these delicate and complex conspiracies in secret—and have them remain secret.

Our first order of business was to determine whether the photographs and X rays were indeed those of President Kennedy. A number of doctors had treated JFK, and they supplied us with his old skull X rays. They matched those in the archive. Lowell Levine, our forensic dentist, identified them from the teeth. The family balked at having X rays of the head published in our final report. That distinctive Kennedy jaw was the source of some anguish—it looked too much like him, they said. We compromised. In the published report, the lower part of the jaw, showing the teeth, is blocked out. To my knowledge, this was the only thing the family censored. The report itself was published as written.

As the archive gave up its secrets, we realized that everything wasn't there. Kennedy's brain, which had been removed during the autopsy and placed in the archive, was missing, and so were the microscopic slides of tissues, and the paraffin blocks in which tissue is hardened. They had simply disappeared. We didn't think anyone had made a deliberate effort to mislead us or destroy evidence—the most important things, all the photographs and X rays, were there. We thought perhaps the missing material had been buried with the President at Arlington, but an exhumation was out of the question. The family had not been enthusiastic about this investigation. It was just a painful reminder. The location of the missing items is still a mystery, but their disappearance is not particularly sinister. Memorabilia of the famous have a way of vanishing into doctors' private collections. That is what happened to Einstein's brain. In the 1950s, Martin Luther King was treated at Harlem Hospital for a stab wound in the chest. In 1978, when we tried to get his medical records and X rays for the committee, they were missing. The administrator had put them in a safe, but somehow they had disappeared.

Kennedy's body was brought to Bethesda Naval Hospital at about 7:35 P.M. on November 22. Commander Humes, the chief pathologist, was not sanguine about doing the autopsy. He knew he had never done one like it before. Why not request help? I asked him. He explained that he couldn't—he was low man in the hierarchy, and he had to follow orders; in the military, you don't tell generals and admirals that you are unqualified for the job. And he had been reassured that Colonel Pierre Finck, the head of wounds ballistics at the Armed Forces Institute of Pathology, was coming to assist and observe. Finck, he figured, knew about bullet holes.

Colonel Finck, it turned out, had never done an autopsy involving a gunshot wound, either. For almost a decade he had been in charge of reviewing the records of U.S. military personnel who had died of gunshot wounds. Two people who were not professionally trained in what they were doing were watching each other. Finck didn't offer guidance because it never occurred to him that Humes needed any. When Finck didn't speak, Humes thought he was doing the job right.

Humes was also getting other signals. He understood, he told us, that he wasn't really supposed to do a full autopsy. He was just supposed to find the bullet. (Everyone thought the bullet that had hit the President in the back was still in his body.) This idea was conveyed so obliquely that Humes couldn't explain exactly how he knew. Somehow, he absorbed it from the FBI and the Secret Service. They hadn't given him any orders. Talking to him was like talking to the people who did the Vietnam body counts—they didn't have to be told what was wanted. It wasn't necessary to spell out anything for Humes. It was apparent that the body had been brought to Bethesda against the coroner's objections, to accommodate the wishes of the family. Humes understood, he told us, that the Kennedys were not interested in having an autopsy done. He also knew that religious Catholics tend to be opposed to autopsies. And he was not in a position to press the issue.

The room was chaotic. Generals, admirals, and cabinet members milled around, shocked. Humes, a mere commander, seemingly had no control of his own autopsy room. He was there to please his superiors. He felt it was beyond his powers to describe the wounds and decided to rely on photographs. "The complexity of these fractures and the fragments thus produced," he wrote in the autopsy report, "tax satisfactory verbal description and are better appreciated in photographs and roentgenograms which are prepared." The photographer was there, the corpsman who usually took pictures of damaged hearts and cirrhotic livers and other diseases. He was snapping away when he caught the attention of an FBI agent, who came up to him and asked for his clearance. "Clearance?" said the corpsman. "This is my job." The agent took away his camera, exposed all the film, and threw him out. (The exposed film is in the archive.) "We've got our own man taking pictures," the FBI agent said. The FBI photographer, who had clearance, was in the same quandary as Humes. He had never taken autopsy pictures before and was untrained in photographing gunshot wounds. His pictures showed it. A proper photograph would have shown the injury first as it was and then cleaned off, next to a ruler to give perspective on its size and position in the body. None of his pictures clearly defined the entrance or exit wounds. The photographs of the body's interior were out of focus. You have to know at what level you want to shoot—the chest is deep. He didn't take pictures of any internal organs. These are the pictures Humes proposed to rely on, his own descriptive powers having failed him.

Given all these ambiguities and conflicting purposes, the autopsy itself was woefully inadequate. Before the President was buried, no one, either in Dallas or in Washington, looked at both sides of the body, front and back, and realized that a bullet had entered the back and exited the throat. The people in Dallas never turned Kennedy over and never saw the back wound. Humes didn't figure things out until after the President was lying in state in the Rotunda.

The President arrived at Bethesda with a massive head wound, a back wound, and a throat wound. Humes, who was stymied, did not call Dallas to find out which hospital medical procedures had been performed that had bruised or altered the body before it arrived at Bethesda. Therefore, he did not know that a tracheostomy had been performed through the exit wound in the throat. Dallas thought the President had been shot in the throat and was trying to help him breathe. Humes saw the entrance wound in the back, but he didn't connect it with the throat wound, where the bullet had exited. (As it happened, this was the so-called "pristine" bullet that went on to wound John Connally, but no one knew that until later.)

Humes took X rays to see if the bullet was still inside the body. Nothing showed up on the X rays, and he told the FBI the bullet had entered the back, gone in a few inches, and then fallen out of the same hole it entered. But bullets don't do that. As a bullet passes through the body, the track it makes collapses on itself. The bullet can't back out. He couldn't understand what had happened to the head bullet, either. (The Connally bullet was found on a stretcher in the hospital. The Kennedy head bullet was found on the floor of Kennedy's car in front. It had struck the windshield strut and broken in two.)

It took Humes about two hours to do the autopsy. He spent the rest of the night (from midnight to 5:30 A.M.) helping the mortician embalm the body and put the skull together. The autopsy should reasonably have taken the better part of a day. A complicated one can take eight hours, and this one was complicated. The autopsy is not finished until you work out the bullet tracks along with the exits and entrances. Humes explained that he was in a hurry, that the family was waiting for the body.

Humes took notes of his autopsy findings, but he didn't stay to write the report. He'd been in the morgue since 7:30 the previous night (Friday, November 22), and at 5:30 A.M. he was exhausted. He also had to take his daughter to her confirmation on Saturday morning.

When he returned on Saturday afternoon, he noticed there was a problem with his notes. They were stained with blood. Humes was a fastidious man; he cared about appearances, and the blood disturbed him. He remembered having visited Abraham Lincoln's birthplace in Illinois and seeing an antimacassar that had been taken from Ford's Theatre. It had bloodstains on it, and Humes thought how unseemly it was for Lincoln's blood to be on public view. He was deeply concerned about the Kennedy family's feelings and told the committee, "The original notes which were stained with the blood of our late President, I felt, were inappropriate to retain to turn in to anyone in that condition. I felt that people with some peculiar ideas about the value of that type of material, they might fall into their hands." There was only one thing to do, and he did it. He burned his notes. The missing notes added to the paranoia, the belief that there had to be a conspiracy.

That afternoon Humes did what should have been done when the body arrived at Bethesda—he called Dallas. He spoke to Dr. Malcolm Perry, one of the doctors who had attended Kennedy in Parkland Hospital, and learned about the tracheostomy through the bullet hole in the throat. The light dawned. He hadn't known there was a bullet hole in the throat at all. He'd thought it was just a tracheostomy. He now realized that the tracheostomy incorporated the exit wound, and he understood that he hadn't been able to find the bullet because it had gone into Kennedy's back and out his throat. But by then it was too late to trace the bullet track, so Humes tried to figure it out from memory. The Warren Commission drawing shows it starting high on the back and moving downward and out the throat. It is wrong. The X rays and photographs show the wound to be lower on the back and the track slightly upward. Fifteen years later at our interview, Humes excused himself by saying he didn't have any photographs of the autopsy to refer to.

Humes worked on the autopsy report from Saturday afternoon until about 3:00 P.M. Sunday, doing the best he could under difficult circumstances. It is not clear what facts he used from his original notes. Since he wrote the final report after talking to Dallas, he incorporated some material that he didn't see with his own eyes. The result was an autopsy report filled with errors, sins of omission and commission. Bullets weren't tracked, the brain wasn't sectioned, the measurements were inaccurate, the head wound wasn't described. The weights and measures of body organs made no sense. The liver was down as weighing 650 grams—one and a half pounds—which is too light to sustain life. An adult liver weighs a little over three pounds. Other organs—the pancreas, the prostate—were not described at all. The collarbones weren't separated from the breastbone to permit an examination of the neck organs. The entire neck area was undisturbed by the autopsy, which is one reason why Humes couldn't trace that bullet track. He didn't shave any hair from around the head wounds in order to examine them. The wounds were photographed through the hair.

One of the things that had haunted the President was his Addison's disease. Over the years, rumors that he was debilitated by it had surfaced and been denied. It was a well-kept secret, and the family wanted it to remain one. In the early 1960s, public officials had an easier time keeping secrets. The concept that the press had the right to know every intimate detail of a President's life was not yet in vogue. Civilians, such as the medical people at Parkland Hospital, couldn't be controlled, but the military could be trusted.

Addison's disease is an atrophying of the adrenal cortex, the glands that make cortisone, a hormone that regulates the electrolyte balance of sodium and potassium. An imbalance causes progressive weakness, weight loss, and death. At one time the disease was fatal; now you take cortisone to replace what your body cannot manufacture. Cortisone causes odd fat deposits—an upper-back hump, full cheeks. Kennedy had them both, but Addison's disease is not mentioned in the autopsy report, nor are the adrenal glands. It is standard procedure to describe them. I asked Commander Humes about it when he came to Washington to testify before the committee. Even then, fifteen years later, when it no longer mattered, his feelings of respect were so strong that he refused to comment for the record about Addison's disease. The family didn't want any mention of any diseases that might be present, he said. However, several doctors had treated Kennedy for Addison's and taken X rays of his pituitary gland, the gland at the base of the skull that controls the adrenals. He had had a number of sets of X rays taken. The doctors had also written reports. The adrenals were very tiny—the disease had atrophied them.

Perhaps the most egregious error was the four-inch miscalculation. The head is only five inches long from crown to neck, but Humes was confused by a little piece of brain tissue that had adhered to the scalp. He placed the head wound four inches lower than it actually was, near the neck instead of the cowlick.

Despite all these errors and for the wrong reasons, Humes came to the right conclusions—that Kennedy had been shot by two bullets from behind, one in the head and one in the back. They were in the wrong place and badly tracked, but he got the two most important things right.

In reconstructing the events, we were hindered by not having all the evidence we needed to work with. We had X rays of some things, pictures of others, X rays and descriptions of still others. We also had Kennedy's clothes. The shirt and jacket each had a round bullet hole in the back. The pictures of the President were unfocused, but helpful. They showed the burn of an "abrasion collar," a redness on the skin surrounding the entrance wound, in the same place where the clothes were torn. That was the entrance wound. In front, the throat wound had been distorted by the tracheostomy (an ordinary exit wound pushes the skin out), but the clothes again saved the day. There were slitlike tears on the tie and shirt collar that were typical of an exit wound. Exits look like little cuts.

For the head wound, we enhanced the X rays and saw the entrance perforation on top of the cowlick. Pictures of the wound yielded more when viewed through a stereopticon. In three dimensions they showed the oblique lines (beveling) on the bone in the back of the skull that an entering bullet makes. Only the top part—the cerebrum—was injured by the bullet track, which couldn't have happened if the bullet had been four inches lower. We also used a little common sense. Humes had placed the wound four inches below where it was, but the cowlick was right in the center of the FBI photograph. A photographer tries to center his picture.

We reconstructed the exit wound at the throat from X rays of the skull and skull fragments and photographs of a single piece of bone which came to be called the Nieman-Marcus fragment. Three skull fragments had been retrieved from the limousine, brought to Washington, X-rayed, and later vanished. The fourth, measuring about two by one and a half inches, was found a few days after the autopsy by a premed student walking his dog in Dealey Plaza, where the shots were fired. He took it home to his father, a doctor, who knew what it was and had it photographed. At a party, the photographer couldn't resist talking about it, and the story got back to the FBI. Agents swooped down on the premed student, who was saving the fragment as a souvenir. He had it wrapped in a piece of cotton in a Nieman-Marcus box. It later disappeared from the archive, along with the other fragments, but the photographs of it were good enough for purposes of reconstructing the skull.

There was no evidence that anything had hit the President from the front.

Near the end of the hearings, John Connally came to Washington to testify. One of the last and most baffling problems was the mystery surrounding the magic bullet, the bullet that went through two people—into Kennedy's back and out of his throat; into Connally's back (he was sitting in the jump seat with his back to Kennedy) just above his right armpit, injuring his lung and fifth rib, and exiting in front below his right nipple, then into his right wrist near the thumb, through the radius bone above the wrist and out of the undersurface of the wrist, and finally part way into his left thigh and out. It was a very acrobatic bullet. Connally was convinced that it never happened, that he was shot with a separate bullet entirely.

The bullet was an Italian 6.5 millimeter, for a Mannlicher–Carcano rifle—a military, not a civilian, bullet. In conformity with the Geneva Convention rules of civilized warfare, military ammunition is made with a full metal jacket. The idea is that the bullet will not break up inside the body but go through it, causing less pain and suffering. Police ammunition is usually not jacketed. It is soft enough so that when it hits a body the nose of the bullet flattens, slowing it down. It doesn't go through the body and hit someone else. An unjacketed bullet could not have performed the way this metal-jacketed one did. It was able to accomplish so much because it went through soft tissue. In its passage through Kennedy, it did not strike bone. Once inside Connally, it struck a very thin bone—a rib—which did not slow it down significantly. The only bone of substance it struck was Connally's right wristbone, after which it was almost spent and barely managed to penetrate Connally's left thigh. It was found on a stretcher at Parkland Hospital.

Believers in the existence of a second shooter on the grassy knoll called it the pristine bullet, indestructible, but it was damaged; it is flat on one side. The FBI ballistics examination concluded that the bullet matched Oswald's rifle, but this did not satisfy the conspiracy buffs. They scoffed at such a simplistic connection. Of course it matched, they said; it was planted on the stretcher to mislead everyone into thinking Oswald was the lone assassin. It had the right markings for Oswald's weapon, but it really came from the firing range where he had honed his marksmanship; it had not been fired in Dealey Plaza. We had to resolve that question.

First, had the bullet burrowed into Connally's thigh bone? If it had, it couldn't have leaped out and fallen onto the stretcher. In one of the X rays of Connally's leg, there is a tiny sliver of metal adjacent to the femur. Everyone concluded the obvious— that the bullet had come in and hit the bone. But a bullet that goes two inches deep and into bone doesn't suddenly decide to reverse itself. (Humes made the same mistake with JFK. He thought the bullet in the back had retraced its steps and fallen out. It was this same bullet.) It can't just drop out of the same hole unless it is very close to the surface. From one of Connally's

X rays, it looked as if the bullet was next to or in the thighbone. But the X ray was a lateral one, a side view, and you can't see depth on it. In the archive is another X ray, a front view that shows the sliver is clearly not in bone. It's just under the skin. It did not hit the femur. The bullet, its energy gone by then, only penetrated the first layers of skin. Only half an inch of it went in. The penetration was shallow enough for it to have fallen out and landed on the stretcher.

Next, was the Connally bullet the same one that had been found on the stretcher? A tiny fragment of bullet was removed from Connally's wrist in Parkland Hospital and put into the archive. We took it, together with the bullet from the stretcher, and sent it to a special laboratory in California. The lab does neutron activation analysis, a technique for finding trace amounts of heavy metals that is so sensitive it can distinguish between two bullets on an assembly line. The trace metal content in the bullet found on the stretcher and the fragment from Connally's wrist matched perfectly. It was a copper-jacketed military bullet with a core of 99 percent lead and insignificant amounts of strontium, arsenic, nickel, platinum, and silver. As small as they are, these traces are like fingerprints.

There was one last thing about this bullet that I could only resolve by firsthand observation. According to Connally's medical records, the bullet struck him nose first in the back and left a vertical scar. I thought the records were wrong. If it was the same magic bullet, it would have gone in sideways—with the length, not the point, first. After leaving Kennedy, it would have lost its power and become a tumbling bullet, and tumbling bullets rotate. When they finally strike, they strike edgewise. I needed to examine Connally.

In 1978, John Connally was running for the presidency. He came to Washington to testify before the committee and agreed to let me examine his scars in his suite at the Mayflower Hotel. He was an impressive-looking man with a presidential air, a man who behaved as if he had important things to do. His manner was affable and confident. Connally wasn't too happy with the whole enterprise. I was a stranger; why should I be allowed to examine him? He had given permission, yes, but it was awkward. Amenities, formalities, had to be gone through. His wife, Nellie, was there, and an aide, Julian Reed. I mentioned the name of a good friend in Corpus Christi, an offshore-oil man, who was also a friend of Reed's and a contributor to the campaign. The social connection made things less uncomfortable when I asked Connally to take off his clothes.

He removed his shirt. There it was—a two-inch-long sideways entrance scar in his back. He had not been shot by a second shooter but by the same flattened bullet that went through Kennedy. I wanted to see the thigh wound, but I had to let it go. I could not bring myself to ask him to take off his pants. The Corpus Christi friendship was not close enough for that, and Connally was in a hurry—he had a plane to catch.

Connally remained unconvinced. He had been in Dallas, and he knew. He said he heard a shot, turned partly around, and then he was shot. This could well have happened if the first shot missed both him and Kennedy (Oswald fired three times), but Connally thinks the first shot hit the President and the second hit him.

The following day, I testified that there had been one shooter, Oswald; three shots from behind Kennedy; and two wounds. There was no entrance wound in front. The President had been killed by a lone assassin. Forensically, we had proved it beyond a doubt.

G. Robert Blakey, the chief counsel of the Committee on Assassinations, tended to agree with Connally—he didn't think a single bullet could do that much damage. All along he had questioned and poked at every point of proof as we brought it in, as he should. I thought he was only playing devil's advocate at first, but he had a theory of his own and he wanted support for it.

Blakey came from a background of investigating organized

crime, and came to believe there was a conspiracy. He had been immersed in the Mafia for years. He had written books about it—*Racket Bureaus,* and three volumes of *Perspectives on the Investigation of Organized Crime.* The Mafia was his life's work, and the committee became important in furthering that work. In 1981, two years after the hearings, he published *The Plot to Kill the President.* (His coauthor, Richard N. Billings, the editorial director of the committee, was chronicling our progress in 1979.) Blakey believed there were two shooters, Oswald in the book building and an unknown on the grassy knoll. If there were two shooters, the assassination had to be defined as a conspiracy, and he had a theory that linked it to the Mafia. Blakey's only hard scientific evidence came from a Dallas police department tape which belonged to a motorcycle cop. The cop had inadvertently left his radio on transmission at the time of the shooting. The tape at police headquarters had been saved because it had another homicide report on it. Early on, I had listened to it and found it indecipherable. To my ears it was valueless. All of a sudden, when the investigation was almost over and it was clear we weren't coming up with any forensic evidence that suggested a conspiracy, Blakey resurrected it. He wanted a second review of the acoustical evidence.

First, he brought in a group of acoustics experts who were famous in Washington for having worked with the Nixon tapes. They couldn't make anything out of this one. Then he called in a pair of acoustics professors from Queens College in New York. They interpreted the static on the radio and announced they heard three definite gunshot sounds and a 70 percent definite fourth. The probable fourth shot came one second after the third. The total amount of time for the four shots was eight seconds. It was physically impossible for Oswald, with the rifle he used, to have fired four shots within that time, which meant there was a second shooter—and a conspiracy.

The science of acoustics had even more to reveal. From the sound vectors—the pattern of the sound waves—the experts said they could tell the direction of the bullets, and the sound vectors were going straight to Kennedy's head from the grassy knoll. I listened to the tape, too, but all I could hear was static. Or possibly backfire.

Blakey was very impressed. The hearings were being broadcast live on public television. Each night, the committee staff prepared for the next day's testimony. I would sit down and explain my opinions, and the staff would try to knock holes in them. It was like an informal doctoral examination. There were no surprises, but there was no script, either. I had already testified, but Blakey scheduled me to go on again, following the acoustics professors. He asked me if I could say that my forensic evidence was consistent with the acoustical findings. "Consistent with" is one of those catch-all phrases that means something could be possible. It is used a lot in our profession, especially on the witness stand when evidence can be interpreted in more than one way. All Blakey wanted me to say was that a grassy-knoll bullet might have struck the President. I didn't believe that. Forensically-speaking, I was certain that absolutely nothing from that grassy knoll had hit the President.

On the final day of the hearings, just before I was due to testify, Blakey decided we were running out of time and scratched me. I have always thought that there would have been enough time for me if I had been more in tune with the acoustics experts.

The acoustics theory won the day and became the basic scientific evidence for a conspiracy. The committee decided that 70 percent was a high enough margin to suspend disbelief in a fourth shot. The members' willingness to do so indicates that they had other compelling reasons—nonmedical ones—and without the acoustical evidence they wouldn't have been able to support the conspiracy idea. The members were not particularly knowledgeable about the forensic evidence. Before I testified, I was asked by an aide to distribute a series of questions to them so they would know what to ask me to look good on camera.

The committee ended its deliberations with a hybrid theory. It concluded that three shots were fired from behind by Oswald, that two of them hit Kennedy and one missed him; and that a fourth bullet was fired by an unknown assailant from the grassy knoll and also missed him. The committee voted to pass its findings along to the FBI with a mandate to search for the second shooter. The FBI listened to the tape too, but couldn't get past the static. It rejected the mandate.

The verdict on the assassination is unchanged. On the twenty-fifth anniversary of Kennedy's death, the same old conspiracy theories were dragged out, dusted off, and presented to the public all over again, as if our investigation had resolved nothing. People went on thinking what they wanted to think.

2

THE EDUCATION OF A
MEDICAL EXAMINER

LIFE AND DEATH, UPTOWN AND DOWNTOWN

MY CAREER BEGAN almost without my realizing it, and years
went by before I became aware that I had chosen it. I had never
heard of forensic medicine before going to medical school. I
planned to be an internist and follow in the footsteps of my
Nobel Prize–winning mentors, Dickinson Richards and Andre
Cournand at Bellevue Hospital. But doctors, like everyone else,
go where their personalities and emotional needs lead them. The
confident, aggressive ones usually go into surgery. A dispropor-
tionate number of future psychiatrists have emotional problems
in medical school. Pathologists and researchers prefer academic
medicine—they would rather relate to microscopes and other
doctors than talk to patients. Forensic pathologists are comfortable in the limelight and enjoy talking to the public. We have
to be articulate. We bear witness. Our tradition is to give testimony in court. There's an early, unwitting job description of a
forensic doctor in the account of the death of Julius Caesar by
Suetonius, the gossip. After Caesar was stabbed, says Suetonius,
he was examined by a physician named Antistius. Antistius then

went to the Forum and told the assembled Senators that Caesar had twenty-three stab wounds, one of which was fatal.

I liked the public side of it. The excitement and the immediacy of it appealed to me. Every morning on the radio there were stories of murders, of plane crashes, of violence in the night, and I would go to work and see the results in front of me. More than anything I liked the instant gratification that came from doing an autopsy and knowing the diagnosis right away. Once, while I was still a student, we zoomed up the East Side Highway to Harlem in a police car. The cop drove on the wrong side—he headed north on the south drive. It was the most amazing thing, as if the Red Sea were parting in front of us.

I liked the reporters and the television cameras. The fact that they were covering my work added importance to it, an extra dimension. The visibility counterbalanced the low esteem in which we were held by the rest of the medical profession. Forensic pathology was filled with misfits. It was considered a dumping ground for incompetents, a field that alcoholics descended into, a refuge for doctors who couldn't make it in the real world.

Anatomy fascinated me. As a medical student I was drawn to the morgue at Bellevue because the bodies were there. The autopsy room was a huge cavernous space with long windows and a twenty-foot ceiling. It was not air-conditioned. The elements of pathology that excited me were all there in my first visit—the mystery, the thrill of discovery, the rigor of research, the connection with public health, the talk with respected medical advisers. When I came in, a group of doctors was standing on one side of this enormous room while Milton Helpern, the chief medical examiner, stood on the other, doing an autopsy all by himself. The body was a thirty-five-year-old man who had died of what everyone feared was smallpox. The other doctors wouldn't go near the body. It was a matter of caution. We had all been immunized. I walked over to look. The case was unique even then. This was 1955, and the last smallpox illness in the city had been in 1947. It was essential to diagnose it quickly.

It was clear how important the ME's office was, what a profound effect it could have on public health. If the disease was smallpox, the whole city might have to be immunized.

Helpern permitted me to assist him, and when it was over he sent me to the library to research old articles in dusty journals from the 1880s that compared smallpox to similar diseases and explained how to tell them apart. Certain forms of chicken pox, I learned, could look like smallpox. I talked to the chairman of the pediatrics department, who had done work on fatal chicken pox in children.

When the microscopic tissue studies that Helpern had prepared came back, we found out that the man had an underlying lymphoma and was getting cortisone treatments for it. His immune system had been knocked out by the lymphoma, and the massive doses of cortisone made him more susceptible to other infections. (Cortisone in smaller doses does not have this effect.) The man had hemorrhagic chicken pox. Because of his immunosuppressed state, he died of it, just as AIDS kills today.

Helpern adopted me and became my mentor. After a major plane crash he took the time to explain things to me and encouraged me to do autopsies with the professionals. He liked the old European concept of the professor with a retinue of students learning from him and beholden to him. For years no medical student had cared about the medical examiner's office, and suddenly there I was, caring. He was short of people—not many go into this field—and he needed all the help he could get, but that didn't matter; I was very taken with the whole thing, and with the way he was taken with me.

All during my years in medical school and as a resident, I moonlighted in the ME's office. I saw that the process of death investigation mirrored society, that money and power played the same role in death as in life. Helpern sent me on all kinds of cases. One night he sent me to the Plaza Hotel to sign a death certificate. There, at a black-tie fund-raising dinner to benefit

Presbyterian Hospital, in a ballroom full of prominent doctors, two of whom were flanking her at the table, a woman had died.

A tablemate had asked Helpern to smooth the way for removal of the body. The doctors thought it was a heart attack. Two of them were sitting with the body in a back room (it would have been unseemly to abandon it to a waiter), and they wanted it taken to a funeral parlor as soon as possible so they could get back to their table. According to the law, the body could not be removed without a death certificate, and none of the doctors there could issue one. If the woman had died of a disease, the doctor who had treated her for it could have issued a certificate, but she hadn't even been under treatment. The death had been sudden, and only someone from the ME's office could sign the certificate.

The dinner was still in progress when I arrived. The woman, who had been a big contributor, lay on a makeshift table. She wore a long, glittering silver lamé dress. I thought there was a possibility that she had choked on a bolus of food (the French call such a death a "café coronary"; it looks like a heart attack but it's really food), but her tablemates disagreed. The two things that people have the most trouble swallowing are steak and shrimp. People with bad teeth try to get around the difficulty of chewing them by swallowing bites whole. One of the doctors said no, definitely not; she had started with her vegetable and potato; and she hadn't even gotten to her meat yet, and besides, she had a history of heart disease. What had happened was very clear to them. They didn't need to know any more than they already knew. She had been eating and talking, and all of a sudden she couldn't talk, and then she slumped forward and fell into her food. The other doctor, a retired professor of surgery, had stuck his finger into her mouth and examined her throat and found no obstruction. I told them I wouldn't do a full autopsy, but I had to examine her neck to make certain she hadn't choked on her food. They were upset, but they agreed.

They had no choice. The funeral director was waiting to take her out.

I had no equipment with me. I had called the office on the way home. The maître d' got a small kitchen knife, and I made an incision near the Adam's apple. A big bright green broccoli florette was lodged in the airway, blocking it. In his effort to help, the surgeon had just pushed it in farther. He had been drinking, I noticed, and hadn't been careful enough. Nobody congratulated me on my diagnosis. "When can we get the body released to the funeral director?" they wanted to know.

When I finished, I drove to the South Bronx. A call had come earlier to go there, but Helpern had wanted me to take care of the body at the Plaza first. The dinner guests were important people, and he didn't want them to be inconvenienced. In the Bronx there was a dead baby. A single cop sat in the hallway, reading a book, waiting for me. No car was parked on the street to show the way. The inequalities of life continue into death. On Park or Fifth Avenue, the police send three or four cars. You always know exactly where to go. In the South Bronx, a single car drops the cop off. He calls in when the doctor is finished and is picked up.

The cop let me into the apartment as if he owned it, as if the people who lived there didn't exist. They hardly noticed. They were a lively family—even though it was close to midnight, the mother and her four small children were up and running around. There were no tears. The room was small and musty. Wiring hung from the ceiling, patched together; the electricity was stolen from the apartment next door. The dead baby lay in an old crib. There was a pink Princess telephone—Welfare paid for it—and across the room in a corner, the perfect skeleton of a small rat. An odor of decaying food rose from the sink, littered with half-eaten TV dinners. I couldn't find anything wrong with the baby. The ME's office sent the morgue wagon for the body. At the autopsy the next day, the lungs were heavy and filled with fluid, bacteria, and white blood cells. The baby had died of untreated pneumonia.

On another nocturnal excursion, I visited a man in his seventies whose Lower West Side apartment was on the top floor of a four-story walkup. It was a natural death. Most of the deaths we investigate are natural. There just isn't any other doctor around to sign the death certificate. At first I thought he might have been murdered. The apartment looked as if it had been ransacked. Drawers were open; clothes were strewn across the floor. The police had done it, looking for identification. The man was lying in bed wearing a white polo shirt, black pants, and slippers and socks. Under his shirt was a peculiar-looking belt with zippers on the underside. I said to the cop on guard, "Hey, he's got a money belt." I had never seen anyone wearing one before. The cop was surprised. "Gee whiz, Doc, I missed it," he said. I unzipped it and found $40. "List it in the inventory," I told him. He was grateful. Cops get demerits for overlooking things at the scene.

Later, in the office, when I was telling the MEs the story, they laughed at my naïveté. By not questioning the amount, I may have legitimized a theft. Who carries only $40 in a money belt? When someone dies alone, it's open season on his possessions. People tramp in and out of the apartment—the Emergency Medical Service, the cops, the mortuary personnel, the ME. The cops search for a medical history, the name of the doctor, the names of the next of kin, and during the extensive rummaging, things of value—cash, jewelry, stamp collections—disappear. It's rare that the relatives even know that anything is missing or, knowing, can prove it. Traps have been set and people have been caught, but it still goes on.

I was surprised at how little sorrow there is for the dead. So many of our clients are drug addicts or alcoholics, and the families have already used up their grief, or written the person off. A twenty-four-year-old woman was brought in, a heroin overdose with needle scars and fresh puncture marks. They represented years of family disruptions, of tears and rage and despair. Her father, a professor, came down to identify her. He sat in the lobby in his dark blue suit reading the *Wall Street Journal,* totally uninvolved, oblivious to everything around him. When I spoke to him, he assumed the attitude of a man who had come for a job interview. He looked at his daughter and said yes, that's my daughter—is there anything else? She had died for him a long time ago. He signed the paper and left.

I also remember a woman in her twenties with a husband in his seventies who had died suddenly. They lived in an expensive apartment with very little in it except a collection of pornographic books. They had been married less than a year. The wife was distraught, in tears. The police had already interviewed her and the neighbors when I arrived. She told them he had died in his sleep of a heart attack. They were satisfied. I didn't see any injuries to the body or evidence of pills or drugs. Everything seemed in order. The funeral director was on his way over. She wanted the body cremated.

The next evening I saw her again in a French restaurant. She was the center of attraction at a party, joyful and radiant. The other tables were sedate; hers was lively. The noise caught my attention. She was in the middle of a laugh when she saw me; she stifled it and nodded. Then she whispered to a friend and the table quieted down. I felt a twinge, but the husband had already been cremated.

My first homicide had little to do with forensic medicine. It was a crime-and-punishment case, a tale of vengeance and power. In 1963 I was still a resident at Bellevue trying to make up my mind about my medical career and still moonlighting nights and weekends at the ME's office. They let me do everything except murders. Murders were too important for a novice. But this time, when the call came at 2:00 A.M., the ME in charge didn't feel like getting out of bed, and he asked me to go in his place. I was on duty anyway. It was a big vote of confidence.

The case was a shootout at the old New Yorker Hotel, at 34th

Street and Eighth Avenue. Police cars surrounded the entrance, their lights flashing. Television cameras were there, and reporters interviewed me. There had been a huge manhunt for this killer. Upstairs, Frank Falco, the dead man, lay on the bed in his shorts, his head and chest riddled with bullet holes. The Trantino case, as it came to be known, became a *cause célèbre* and is still reverberating.

On a hot August night, Falco and his partner, Thomas Trantino, had held up a bar in Lodi, New Jersey. Two cops responded to a call for help but were overpowered. Falco and Trantino were sadistic and looking for thrills. They ordered the cops to strip and perform fellatio on them, and at the moment of orgasm they shot the cops in the head. Afterward, they danced. The police force never forgot and never forgave.

They found Falco a week later. They surrounded his room; one came in through the door and another through the window from the fire escape. They told me they were on the verge of arresting him but he resisted; they thought he had reached for his gun, and they had to shoot him. Then they saw he just had a Coke bottle.

Two days later, the second gunman, Thomas Trantino, gave himself up. His lawyer told the judge that he was afraid the cops would kill him. In due course he received a life sentence. During twenty years in prison he reformed, found religion, educated himself, and became a model prisoner. In 1985 he was scheduled to be paroled. The friends and family of the cops and other members of the force were outraged. They insisted Trantino had crossed so far beyond the boundaries of human behavior there was no way he could ever come back; he would have to be shut away forever. They told the parole board that a criterion for parole is restitution, and the only way Trantino could make restitution was by restoring the dead to life. The board rescinded the parole. In the winter of 1988 he came up for parole again. The cops got a huge crowd of people out in the freezing cold to rally and demonstrate. Members of one family went on television and said that since Lodi they had felt sick every day of their lives, thinking about what had happened to their loved one. Jail was the only vengeance they could get, and they didn't want to relinquish one second of it. The scene at Lodi was "a sea of blood," one cop recalled at the rally. "An eye for an eye, a life for a life . . ." Trantino is still inside.

The Trantino case was one of those that made me believe my work was important, but my peers in medical school told me I would waste my life, that real doctors didn't become medical examiners. Their arguments worked like reverse psychology. When I went out at night I knew that I was doing something that mattered. And if other well-trained competent doctors avoided it, perhaps that was one more reason to go into it. The two halves of my life, the hospital and the morgue, intersected with the death of a drug addict I was treating at Bellevue.

Addicts get infections of the heart valves—endocarditis— from dirty needles. They inject bacteria or fungi which float around in the bloodstream looking for nice warm nooks and crannies to nestle in and grow. The heart valves, which are constantly opening and shutting, are among their favorite places. If they settle on the right side of the heart, they form colonies and clusters, move to the lungs, and cause abscesses; if on the left, where the aorta and mitral valves are, the clusters can break off and be carried to any part of the body, including the brain. This is what had happened to my patient. A cluster of bacteria broke off and went to his brain. He had a stroke and woke up with the right side of his body paralyzed. He told me about shooting up drugs, so I was able to figure it out. Otherwise, the condition is hard to diagnose. Most of these cases didn't survive, and he was not expected to. He needed months and months of intravenous penicillin and a lot of luck. Finally, he graduated from a wheelchair to a cane, and walked out of the hospital. It was a major triumph for me. Everyone congratulated me—I was a hero; I had beaten the odds.

I saw him again two days later, lying on a table in the ME's office. He had lost his tolerance for drugs in the hospital, misjudged the amount, and overdosed. Treating him with penicillin hadn't been enough. We had to prevent such a thing from happening in the first place. Deaths like his should be used to educate people about the perils of drugs.

At some point I realized I was spending weekends and holidays and all my free time in the ME's office. I had chances to practice other kinds of medicine—radiology, surgery, dermatology—but I didn't pursue any of them. I was working in the ME's office because it was what I liked to do. I could make a difference there. I had a vision of practicing medicine in a way that would touch the lives of thousands of people, that would improve the lot of humankind rather than just individuals. There's a Latin inscription on the marble wall of the ME's office: "Let conversation cease. Let laughter flee. This is the place where death delights to help the living."

Without that dimension, it's just a charnel house.

3

AUTOPSY

ANATOMY AND DESTINY

AT AUTOPSY I am always aware of the capriciousness of life
and the random nature of death—an explosion, and someone
is in the wrong place at the wrong time; a car crash, and a few
seconds earlier or later would have made all the difference.
Thornton Wilder explored this idea in his novel, *The Bridge of
San Luis Rey,* about five people in Peru who were precipitated
into the abyss when an ancient bridge collapsed. "Why *those*
five?" he asked.

Death marks the end of the physical body, but the body tells
the story of its works and days at autopsy; sometimes a whole
biography is there in the cast and color of blood and bone, the
wounds and scars gathered in a lifetime. We can't see the last
image on the retina, but we can see what was eaten, breathed,
injected. The way people die is a reflection of the way they live.
Barring accidents and acts of God, most people who are killed—
thieves, drug addicts, adult victims of domestic violence—live
in such a way that they attract violence. Most murder victims
unintentionally court death by putting themselves in dangerous

situations. Those of our clientele who die of gunshot wounds frequently have old bullets inside them, from previous adventures. Many of our suicides have old scars on their wrists from past failures.

The rich die differently from the poor, the ignorant from the educated. Suicide is favored by the upper classes, who turn aggression inward, against themselves; homicide is more prevalent among the lower classes, who turn it outward, against others— which is one reason we are so fascinated when a Jean Harris kills. It is out of character, privilege degrading itself.

We see the way people have lived, the marks life has left on them. In the 1950s we used to see corset lines. Older women of good breeding died with indentations on their liver from the constant pressure of whalebones. As far as we could tell, no harm was done. Prostitutes have scarred fallopian tubes from repeated bouts of gonorrhea. In men, the same scarring narrows the lining of the urethra. Tattoos enjoy high favor among the antisocial population. Something like one quarter of drug addicts and an amazing number of people who are murdered are adorned with them. They are not the sentimental hearts-and-roses kind that were so popular among sailors in World War II. They are homemade, often designed in jail by a friend. They have a smudged quality, and tend to be a monochromatic blue-black—the supply of colored pigments in jail is small. "Born to lose" and "I don't believe in friends" are popular expressions of philosophy, and so is the bravado of "Kill me, I've never died before," with a bullet hole through it. They are helpful in identifying people.

Every autopsy is a surprise. We never know what we'll find inside. The human body is a machine based on chemical principles. Even knowing those principles, I feel an enormous wonder and awe at the body and its ability to function in the face of terrible odds. So many things can be wrong, so many abnormalities and diseases can be present, and yet we go on living. When I was a medical student, I assisted a venerable pathologist, Dr.

Benjamin Morgan Vance, at an autopsy. The body was riddled with cancer of the pancreas. It had spread all over. I watched, fascinated by what President John Adams once called "This physical disgrace of human nature"—cells gone wild, destroying others. I marveled at how this man had been able to survive so long. Dr. Vance cut through the pancreas and showed me a bullet that was lodged in it, in the middle of the cancer. The bullet had killed the man. He had been shot in a holdup. He had more cancer than we normally see in people who die of it. It was genetics and the vagaries of the body that had kept him alive.

Deciding most causes of death is a process of exclusion. Seldom are the signs quite so obvious as they were in the time of the guillotine when Madame Defarge knitted a stitch for every head that dropped. Most of us die from a long-standing condition, one which many people have, but to which they have not succumbed. Usually, MEs choose the most likely cause and set aside the others. The choice may get us into trouble with those who have a vested interest in the death. Political, financial, and sentimental interests all have their own imperatives. This was the situation when Elvis Presley died, officially of heart disease. Elvis had had an enlarged heart for a long time. That, together with his drug habit, caused his death. But he was difficult to diagnose; it was a judgment call. After he collapsed, he was rushed to the hospital. Jerry Francisco, the Tennessee ME, supervised the autopsy and took tissue samples for toxicology. He found a pharmacopeia—codeine, barbiturates, amphetamines, and tranquilizers. None by itself was at a lethal level except for codeine, and then only for a nonaddict. Elvis was an addict. Was it the heart or the drugs that killed him? The doctor who did the autopsy thought it was drug abuse, but Francisco, who issued the death certificate, called it heart disease. Whether or not it was also a cover-up can be debated. Heart disease was a popular diagnosis with Elvis's fans. As far as Memphis is concerned, its favorite son was not a junkie and did not die a sordid death.

A few years after Elvis's death, when details of his drug capacity were seeping out to the public, Geraldo Rivera consulted me about a television exposé of how Elvis overdosed. I thought there was room for doubt, that it was not quite so simple. Rivera was not happy with my conclusions. He wanted a hard-edged, no-nonsense statement that Francisco's diagnosis was a cover-up. My opinion was too ambivalent for him; it didn't make for good television. He found another doctor who agreed with him.

The standard American autopsy begins with a Y incision, a cut from each shoulder to the pit of the stomach, and then a straight line down to the pubic bone. Another incision is made across the back of the head. When the body is sewn up and dressed for viewing, nothing shows.

It takes about two hours to do an uncomplicated autopsy on a person who died of a stroke or a heart attack. Bullet wounds take longer. Mafia killings always take more time because of the number of bullet holes. We have to check each injury to see whether it contributed to the death.

The autopsy is the final proof that we are not all born equal. Some people are born with wide coronary arteries. Where arteries are concerned, the bigger and wider they are, the longer the life span. Wide arteries that are clogged with plaque still have more space for the blood to flow through than narrow ones. Newborn babies have already developed signs of the arteriosclerotic plaque they will die of sixty or seventy years later. The plaque is a combination of cholesterol, fat, and calcium, and looks pale yellow. George Bernard Shaw knew the secret of long life. When asked to explain his longevity, he is said to have responded that he owed it all to choosing the right grandparents. He lived to be ninety-four.

It is widely believed in some quarters that jogging and exercise help to diminish plaque and prevent heart attacks, but it has never been proved. This unwarranted assumption developed in 1958 after Clarence De Mar, "Mr. Marathon" of Boston, died of cancer of the colon four days after his seventieth birthday. He was autopsied, and magazines published pictures of his arteries, which were almost plaqueless. Doctors who jogged considered the activity to be a fountain of youth, and prescribed it for longevity. Twenty-six years later, Jim Fixx, the darling of the running crowd, put a crimp in this theory by dying at age fifty-three of a massive heart attack. He had a hereditary predisposition—his father had died at age forty-three of a heart attack. Fixx had an enlarged heart, and two of his arteries were clogged enough for bypass surgery. He had been jogging for seventeen years.

We think of the body as symmetrical—two arms, two legs, two eyes, two ears—but it isn't. The right lung is bigger. There are three lobes of lung on the right side and only two on the left, to make room for the heart. The liver presses on the right kidney, so the left kidney is bigger. The left testicle normally hangs lower than the right. If the right one hangs lower it's an abnormality caused by a tumor, an artificial testicle, or situs inversus, a condition in which everything in the body is reversed.

After seeing a lot of insides, we can usually tell if something is wrong. The normal liver has the texture and color of the calves' liver in the supermarket, but it is thicker. An alcoholic's liver looks like pâté—yellow with the fatty consistency that is so desirable in goose liver. A scarred liver indicates cirrhosis. Nodules form like roadblocks which prevent the blood from flowing through the liver. Cirrhosis is a nutritional disease. In Third World countries it is caused by starvation. In the United States, where hunger is on a different level, almost all of it comes from alcoholism, but not all alcoholics have damaged livers. Those who manage to eat decently while drinking copiously can die with a healthy liver.

The two kidneys weigh the same as the heart, about three quarters of a pound. A damaged kidney is usually smaller than it should be. Kidneys age like people. As the arteries harden, the kidneys become shriveled. Other organs also show their age. The thyroid acquires nodules, the lungs accumulate soot, the arteries harden. The ovaries, like the kidneys, become wrinkled and smaller.

Strangulation shows up in a fractured windpipe. We see hemorrhages in the neck caused by squeezing against the Adam's apple or hyoid bone, which is just above it. We also see tiny pinpoint hemorrhages in the whites of the eyes. Those are from burst capillaries. Strangulation allows blood into the head from the artery in back of the neck but prevents it from getting out, thus raising the pressure.

The brain has a soft consistency, like firm junket. It is the only organ that is enclosed in a rigid structure. It floats in fluid to protect it from banging against the skull. If the brain is bruised, we can tell from the position of the bruise whether the person was hit on the head or fell to the ground and struck his head on the pavement. If he was hit on the head, he has a bruise on the scalp, a fracture immediately under it, and a bruise on the brain under that. The injuries are directly beneath each other, and the wound is called a coup injury. If the back of the head strikes the pavement in a fall, there is a bruise on the back of the head and a fracture under it, but the bruise on the brain will be on the front, not beneath the others. The brain's momentum drives it against the front of the skull. This is a contra-coup injury.

There are three traditional signs used to determine how long a person has been dead—algor mortis (the temperature of death), livor mortis (the color of death), and rigor mortis (the stiffness of death). They are not precise. The sooner we get to the body, the more accurate we are. Circumstances modify the numbers: heat, cold, exercise, and drugs can hasten or slow the process of decay and confuse the time and cause of death.

Rigor mortis begins to show two hours after death and takes twelve hours to peak. When the body dies, some cells live longer than others. They keep chemically active for a while, which is why we can do transplants. (Contrary to popular belief, the hair and fingernails do not continue to grow after death.) Rigor is first noticeable in the muscles of the face and eyelids, and then spreads slowly through the body to the arms and legs. The stiffness remains for twelve hours and gradually disappears. After thirty-six hours, the body becomes soft again.

Livor mortis has to do with gravity and also develops in a time sequence. It begins after the heart stops mixing the plasma and red cells together. In the eight hours after death, the red cells settle like the sediment in a bottle of wine. As they settle, red color appears on the skin beneath. It takes an hour or two for the color to become noticeable. After eight hours, the red cells break down and squeeze out of the capillaries into the body. The color then becomes permanent. If a person dies in bed lying on his back, the color would normally be found on his back. If he has lividity on the front part of his body, we know he has been moved—he may have died inconveniently in the wrong house, or he may have been murdered.

The third major sign is algor mortis. After death, when oxygen is no longer fueling the body and keeping it warm at 98.6 degrees Fahrenheit, the temperature falls by about 1 degree each hour.

The autopsy includes routine toxicology tests for common causes of death in our times—from alcohol, cocaine, barbiturates, and other drugs that people use for pleasure or to do away with themselves. There is a misconception about lethal combinations of drugs and alcohol. It is not the combination that kills, but the amount. By itself, each one can be lethal. Barbiturates slow down breathing. Taken in large enough amounts, they stop it entirely. It is surprisingly difficult to overdose on most tranquilizers. Robert McFarlane, former national security adviser, tried it with twenty or thirty Valiums, but that wasn't nearly enough. He would have had to take at least two hundred pills to kill himself. The hospital he was taken to didn't think it necessary to pump his stomach. McFarlane was never in any serious danger; he just needed twelve hours to sleep off the effects of the tranquilizer. He was perhaps doing what many failed suicides do—crying for help. (Wrist cutting is often used as a distress signal. Many people slit the small veins on the inner wrist and miss the large arteries, which are on the side where the pulse is. Bleeding is slow, and there is enough time to go to a hospital to be saved.)

Arsenic, strychnine, cyanide, curare, and other exotic poisons are often overlooked, and tests for them are too expensive to perform routinely. Rarely can we tell from the autopsy that poison is present. We are suspicious—or should be—because of the circumstances. Cyanide is easy to find if we are looking for it. Any reader of mystery stories knows that it has an odor of bitter almonds. The odor lingers even at the autopsy, but there's a catch—not everyone can smell it. The ability to smell it is genetic, and only 40 percent of the population have the right genes. For those with the wrong genes, cyanide provides two other clues—it turns the skin and blood dark scarlet, and it corrodes the stomach. Cyanide prevents oxygen from being distributed to the body. It kills by suffocation.

Of all the exotic drugs, cyanide is the one most associated with spies and international intrigue. As a suicide pill, it acts rapidly. Hermann Goering avoided hanging by chewing on one, and Gary Powers, the U-2 pilot who was shot down over the USSR, also carried one. In the end, Powers decided it was easier to face the Russians than eat the cyanide.

Mysteries seem to attach themselves to cyanide. During Watergate, a mini-conspiracy grew up around Dorothy Hunt, the wife of E. Howard Hunt, Watergate plotter, CIA man, and writer of thrillers. While trying to land at Chicago's Midway Airport, Mrs. Hunt's plane nose-dived into a row of bungalows, and she was killed in the fiery crash. At the autopsy, cyanide was found in her lungs and blood and in those of the pilot and six other passengers. The discovery gave rise to wild rumors that she had been carrying $2 million for a White House payoff, and that she was poisoned to prevent it from being delivered. The story was an invention, a symptom of the times. The cyanide was real, produced in the fire from burning plastics in the plane.

Cyanide has been put in everything from Tylenol capsules to Kool-Aid. As a gas it is the most effective poison for causing mass death. Only a few gases can kill a lot of people quickly. The air dilutes most of the others. In the Bhopal chemical disaster, it was cyanide gas that was released inadvertently; and cyanide was the active ingredient in Zyklon B, the gas used in Nazi concentration camps.

Strychnine also acts quickly, but not as fast as cyanide. Unlike cyanide, it is painful. It's like an electrical wire gone wild, with sparks going off in all directions, disrupting the orderly progression of nerve impulses. The body goes out of control and into convulsions, arching backward, and the muscles of the face contort into the unmistakable *risus sardonicus*—sardonic grin. The convulsions prevent breathing. After death the muscles relax, and we don't see any of this agony on the autopsy table. Without a toxicology report we can't tell if it's strychnine. If the victim has taken it in the form of rat poison, we see little seeds in the stomach. Rat poison looks like sunflower seeds. The seeds are coated with the poison. The first time I saw them they were in the stomach of an old woman. Her daughter, who lived with her, said she had been depressed and had had convulsions before she died. Others knew of her depression, too. I sent the police back to her apartment to find out what she had been eating. They found the seeds in a half-empty cardboard box. We weren't sure whether it was a suicide or whether she was near-sighted. It could also have been a murder. You can never be certain with a poisoning. The scene and the circumstances count just as much as the autopsy. We finally decided it was a suicide because of her depression.

Arsenic, colorless and odorless, also known as "inheritance powder," has a venerable history. In the Middle Ages, kings and princes had tasters, but if the taster was part of the plot he could take small amounts of arsenic and build up a resistance to it.

The Borgias favored it, and it is thought that Rasputin was an arsenic eater. Arsenic acts slowly. Four to seven hours after it is taken, it causes diarrhea and stomach pains. It used to be mistaken for cholera, a fairly widespread disease. It kills by dehydration, by unbalancing the ratio of salts to water in the body, and by shock. It is invisible on the autopsy table. In the eighteenth and nineteenth centuries, people baked it into cakes and fed it to their rich relatives. One London husband whose numerous rich wives died one after the other was suspected of having poisoned them. Scotland Yard exhumed their bodies and found arsenic. The man went to the gallows proclaiming his innocence, and years later, a curious student of toxicology tested the soil where the wives were buried and found that it was full of natural arsenic. The poison could well have seeped into the coffins. Did he or didn't he? the student wondered. It was too late to ask.

Curare, one of the rarer poisons, is lethal only when injected into the bloodstream, not when eaten. It paralyzes almost all the muscles, including the ones that control breathing. Edgar Allan Poe used this effect to enhance the horror of his story, "The Premature Burial," in which the victim was almost buried alive. He was paralyzed, but his mind was clear—he knew what was happening and that he couldn't call for help. Curare is undetectable except by chemical analysis. Two similar drugs— Pavulon and succinylcholine—are widely used in the operating room to decrease the amount of heavier, life-threatening anesthetics. They relax muscles. They work quickly and their paralyzing effects disappear quickly, properties which also make them ideal for murder.

In 1975, the FBI asked me to investigate a series of deaths at the veterans hospital in Ann Arbor, Michigan. The FBI has no resident medical examiner and does not usually get involved in murder—that is a matter for each state—but the hospital was on federal property. In a period of six weeks during July and August, thirty-five patients—an incredibly high number—had episodes of near-fatal cardio-pulmonary arrest. It seemed like an epidemic. All of them were on IVs.

Rescue from this temporary muscle paralysis consists of artificial respiration for a few minutes until the paralysis wears off. But it has to be done quickly. Two nurses were most proficient at it. Again and again they dashed in in the nick of time and performed valiantly. Only five patients died.

Four bodies were exhumed and autopsied. Nothing unnatural showed up, but tissues were sent to the FBI crime lab. They found Pavulon.

The patients' charts showed that one or the other of the same two Filipino nurses—Leonora Perez and Filipina Narcisco—had been on duty during every crisis. They were put on trial. The defense raised $90,000 in the Philippines and here. The Philippine government considered the trial important enough to send an observer. About twelve thousand Filipino nurses worked in the United States.

Perez and Narcisco were found guilty of poisoning six patients. The prosecution theorized that they were trying to dramatize the need for more nurses and chose this method of alerting the world. The nurses had no comment, but they had a champion who proved stronger than the U.S. system of justice. Imelda Marcos, then at the height of her powers, paid for part of the defense. Imelda claimed that the case was an extension of an unfair U.S. immigration policy and the nurses were victims; that the charge against them was trumped up to keep Filipino nurses out of the United States.

Perez and Narcisco spent less than a year in jail. Months later, the federal judge who had heard the case unexpectedly came down with a new ruling: upon further examination of the record, he realized he had permitted errors to take place. One of the assistant U.S. attorneys, for instance, had spoken to the press in a biased manner, he said. He set the guilty verdict aside and ordered a new trial. It never took place. I was told that Imelda was threatening to make trouble over the American bases in the

Philippines, and the national security took precedence over the Pavulon victims.

More obscure than curare is ricin, a vegetable poison that comes from the castor oil plant. Like arsenic, it's a masquerade poison. Its symptoms are easy to confuse with those of a viral or bacterial infection—abdominal pain, nausea, cramps, convulsions, dehydration. It irritates the intestinal tract, causing the red blood cells to break apart and preventing them from carrying oxygen to the heart and brain. Death comes from an electrolyte imbalance. Ricin made international headlines in 1978 when Georgi Markov, an important Bulgarian defector and BBC broadcaster whose news programs were beamed to Sofia, was stuck in the leg in the middle of the day on Waterloo Bridge. The mechanism was very James Bond—a platinum-and-iridium pellet tinier than a pinhead, injected through the tip of an umbrella. The killer hailed a cab and vanished. Markov lingered for four days with the undiscovered pellet in his leg, and then died. No one in the hospital knew what the illness was. It took a medical examiner from one of the British intelligence services to find the pellet and figure out which poison it was. Meanwhile, across the Channel in Paris, another Bulgarian defector, Vladimir Kostov, had had a similar run-in with an umbrella two weeks before. Kostov was ill for a few days with stiffness and fever, but he recovered. By chance, his pellet had lodged in muscle in his upper back, away from major blood vessels.

Shortly after these revelations, a Bulgarian diplomat with the UN collapsed at his East 86th Street hotel in New York. The Bulgarians thought his death might be retribution for their excesses in London and Paris. According to protocol, diplomats who die in their embassies are off limits to MEs, but they are not entirely free of restrictions. Foreigners need permission to take a dead body out of the country, and for that they need a death certificate.

I had no trouble getting into his hotel room—it was his residence, on U.S. soil. He was lying on the floor, as if he had just collapsed, and he had a bruise on his cheekbone. It looked like a typical heart-attack injury. After a heart attack we often see such bruises on the nose, chin, or cheekbones—the prominences. If you fall while you are conscious, you put your hand out instinctively to protect your face. If you collapse during a heart attack, there is no time for that. It is so quick, you can be unconscious or dead by the time you hit the floor. We took him to the ME's office with a physician-observer from the Bulgarian consulate. The consulate insisted on the observer, and I would have insisted if they hadn't. One reason for the autopsy is to anticipate and answer any questions that might arise, the main one in this case being whether or not the diplomat had been murdered.

At the postmortem we saw that his arteries were clogged with plaque and his heart was scarred, evidence of an old attack. He also had fluid in the lungs, another clue to heart disease. Nothing in the hotel room pointed to violence. The scene was innocent— the door was locked from the inside, there was no sign of a struggle, and there were no drugs. His body showed no puncture marks. We did the toxicology anyway, just in case, but found nothing.

The exotic poisons are mainly used on special occasions by people who have embarked on extraordinary enterprises. In accidents and suicides, the most common poison by far is carbon monoxide. It is one of the suffocating poisons. Almost all of the people who die in fires die of carbon monoxide inhalation. It combines with the hemoglobin in the red blood cells, preventing them from absorbing oxygen. Finding it at an autopsy is easy— the skin and blood turn cherry-pink. The color is a warning that other people may be in danger. One of my early cases was a man who had died in his Upper West Side tenement and been brought to the ME's office. His skin was cherry-pink. We interviewed the family. Yes, the father had been throwing up, the son said, and the same thing had happened to him, the son, the day before. He had gone to Presbyterian Hospital and been treated for stomach pains. He was not the only one. More than half a dozen people in this same tenement building had gone to Presbyterian to be treated for stomach pains, and two of them had died. One was an eighty-year-old man with heart disease. The other was an alcoholic. Nobody in the hospital had checked for carbon monoxide. Nobody knew that carbon monoxide turned the skin cherry-pink. We reported it to the police. During the summer, work had been done on the heating system in the basement of the building, and the flues hadn't been rehooked properly.

Technology has changed the use of these poisons and other ways of killing. There are fashions in death as well as in life. After 1952, would-be suicides could no longer turn on the gas and put their head in the oven. In that year, natural gas displaced illuminating gas (a combination of carbon monoxide and hydrogen) in American homes. It was cheaper. Natural gas is not poisonous to breathe. Since then, automobile exhaust has replaced illuminating gas and the garage the oven. Other poisons have been supplanted by barbiturates, which were not widely available until after World War II. They are used for suicide, rather than murder, as far as we know. For murder, all poisons, old or new, suffer from an inherent limitation—a primitive delivery system. The person who administers the poison—the murderer—has to be physically close to the victim.

The advent of the heavy plastic garbage bag has made it easier to dispose of dismembered bodies and has increased the number of them. In the old days, when a murderer cut up a body to get rid of it, he put the pieces in a steamer trunk and shipped it to an imaginary address in Florida. Once in Florida, the trunk sat unclaimed in the railroad office. After a few days it started leaking and began to smell, and someone noticed. Now, the danger of discovery is less. A killer can saw a body or hack it to pieces, put the pieces in four or five bags, and distribute them along the highway. No one will pay the slightest attention. People take the garbage out all the time. The plastic bags retain fibers and fingerprints, but are themselves untraceable.

Whatever the elaborations on unnatural death, the basic autopsy hasn't changed for a century, and the body reacts to injury in the same ways. Even with the latest technology, we have the same problems we have always had—how long has the body been dead? Was the baby alive when it was born? Was the victim drowned or put into the water after death? Was the death natural or unnatural?

4

HISTORY

FROM TAXMAN TO MEDICAL EXAMINER

THE OFFICE OF the coroner (once called the crowner) is first described in 1194 during the reign of King Richard I of England. It was an office essential to running the kingdom, the place where death and taxes came together. The coroner was partly a taxman, and the dead were a means of raising revenue that might otherwise have eluded the grasp of the king. Suicides were of particular interest. Because of the terrible stigma of suicide and the laws against it (it was considered self-murder), families tried to hide it from the authorities. According to the church, a suicide could not be buried in hallowed ground, and according to secular law, the property of a suicide was forfeit to the crown. The coroner's office ferreted out suicides and claimed their property for the crown, acting as a sort of primitive royal insurance company to help keep the king solvent.

The coroner is mentioned in the churchyard scene in Shakespeare's *Hamlet,* where the gravediggers wonder how it can be that Ophelia, who committed suicide, is being buried in hallowed ground. The first gravedigger explains: the Crowner has ruled that Ophelia did not go to the water; the water came to her, and that made all the difference. The second one observes, "If this had not been a gentlewoman, she should have been buried out o' Christian burial."

The idea that doctors or medical knowledge could be useful in investigating death had yet to make a mark on the system. The coroner held inquests and based his decisions on common sense. His most important qualifications were loyalty to the king and social status. He was a landed aristocrat and was not paid. Presumably, he was above corruption and would have been insulted by an offer of money.

As time went on, the nobility relinquished its monopoly, and the office lost status. The coroner became a minor county officer who ranked slightly higher than dog catcher. In the early eighteenth century, he was paid twenty shillings for every inquest, Parliament having realized that the opportunity to demonstrate loyalty to the king was not a sufficient reward. At the time the office was exported to the colonies, its prestige was at a nadir in England.

In the colonies, as elsewhere, autopsies were forbidden by religion, but every so often there was an exception, in the interest of a higher good. Autopsies could be performed in Massachusetts once every four years for the purpose of teaching medical students, but the body had to belong to a criminal. The first record of an autopsy being performed in a murder investigation was in Maryland in 1665. A man named Francis Carpenter was accused of killing his servant, Samuell Yeoungman. The autopsy showed a skull fracture and hemorrhage around the brain. Carpenter had beaten Yeoungman with a club, and he died two days later. The verdict, handed down by a coroner and six jurors, none of whom was a doctor, was that Yeoungman had died because he hadn't gone to a doctor. It was not an auspicious beginning.

In the eighteenth century, the connections were becoming clearer between the way people lived and the state of their internal organs. In England, Sir Percival Pott examined men with cancer of the scrotum and found the disease confined to those who had been chimney sweeps as children, twenty years before. They practiced their trade naked, and they didn't bathe much. Sir Percival correlated the cancer with the chemicals in the soot.

In medical circles, the autopsy was becoming important both to teach and to treat disease, but in the popular mind it remained what it had always been—a ghastly punishment, the equivalent of being drawn and quartered. William Hogarth immortalized the idea of the autopsy as the ultimate torment in a sequence of panels, *Four Stages of Cruelty.* In the first, small boys are torturing dogs, cats, and a bird. In the second, one boy now grown is whipping a horse that has fallen in the street, and in the background another is beating a sheep. In the third, the central figure has progressed to slitting the throat of a girl. In the fourth, it's all over for him—he's on the autopsy table being dissected for the edification of assembled medical students. A dog is eating his entrails.

By the French Revolution, medical schools had begun to develop, and their need for cadavers was supplied by an enterprising new breed of body snatchers known as resurrectionists. Working at night, they "resurrected" the body from its earthly grave and sold it to anatomists, as Jerry Cruncher did in *A Tale of Two Cities.* Someone from the grieving family would come the next day and find that the ground had been dug up. Families were forced to hire graveyard sitters. They sat for three days, after which time there was sufficient decomposition to foil the grave robbers.

There were never enough bodies, and a thriving black market sprang up. Medical schools competed with each other to get them—the biggest and richest schools bought most of the bodies. Prices skyrocketed. At the University of Edinburgh's school of anatomy, Professor Robert Knox paid ten guineas per body, and two legendary Scottish ghouls named William Burke and William Hare saw a way to earn money. When they couldn't rob graves they suffocated the living, using a technique which came to be known as "burking"—putting a hand over the nose and mouth and sitting on the chest. It leaves no signs. Burke and Hare were found out when a medical student came to class one day and saw his girlfriend on the autopsy table. They stood trial for fifteen murders. Hare, the brains of the operation, turned king's evidence and got out in a few years. In 1829 Burke was hanged and given the ultimate punishment—he was autopsied. The children of Edinburgh perpetuated their memory in a poem:

> Burke's the butcher,
> Hare's the thief,
> Knox the man that buys the beef.

Knox continued his career as a noted anatomist.

After Burke and Hare, grave robbing peaked as a profession. In 1832 it became legal to buy unclaimed bodies. The great Victorian urge to understand and categorize everything in the whole world began changing prejudices, and more dissections were done. Coroners, however, were still ordinary local folk, untrained to do their job. A reformer, Dr. Thomas Wakley, crusaded to require coroners to be doctors, but his contemporaries, especially the coroners, were satisfied with the status quo. The unsuccessful search for Jack the Ripper in 1888 finally forced Scotland Yard to rethink the dismal state of death investigation. Murders often went unreported. The bodies were just buried. There were no death certificates, no general sense of who was dying or of what, natural or unnatural. Knowing that coroners could not be relied on to explain the cause of death, the Yard started using hospital pathologists in murder cases. They only knew about disease, but they were better than the coroners.

Things came together with the Crippen murder case, which

was not only one of the highlights of 1910, but a triumph for forensic medicine—pathology, toxicology, and the microscope combined to convict the killer.

Dr. Hawley Harvey Crippen murdered his wife of over seventeen years, Cora Turner, with an overdose of hyoscine (a drug that induces twilight sleep; today it is called scopalamine), after which he cut her apart at the joints and buried the pieces in the cellar of their house. To the Scotland Yard pathologist, Crippen's method of disposal gave him away. It was obvious that the killer knew anatomy. Not many people were aware that an entire skeleton could be disarticulated with a scalpel by cutting through the tendons that hold the joints together. But not all of Turner was there, and at first the body could not be identified. The head and arms and some of the organs were missing, and there was no way to tell the sex, or that it was really Turner. Crippen maintained that his wife was alive and the body in the basement was someone else. Turner was flamboyant and good-looking, and he thought she had run off with one of her many lovers. But there was a scar on the pelvis, and Turner's friends, who were convinced that her husband had murdered her, said she had had a hysterectomy.

The strongest evidence against Crippen was circumstantial. He had used his own name when he bought the hyoscine, and he had wrapped the parts of his wife's body in one of his pajama tops. At the trial the microscope was the main attraction. The issue was the scar. The defense claimed it was nothing but a fold in the flesh. Bernard Spilsbury, who was Scotland Yard's first full-time forensic pathologist, put some of it under the microscope and showed that it looked different from normal tissue. William Henry Willcox, the toxicologist, found hyoscine in the tissues and made crystals of it, which the jury could also look at under the microscope. It was the first time such evidence had been used in a courtroom.

It took the jury only twenty-seven minutes to find Crippen guilty. It's hard to say whether they were more impressed with the microscope or the evidence. He was hanged a month after the trial.

Across the Atlantic, forensic medicine in America was still in a backward state. In most places, coroners were politicians, nominated to balance a political ticket, like vice-presidents. New York City established the office of the medical examiner in 1914 after a series of scandals and disreputable incidents that brought discredit to the profession. Under Tammany Hall, the old coroner system had become corrupt. The coroner was paid by the body, but there were not enough of them to satisfy his income requirements. It was not unknown for him to pull a body from the river, issue a John Doe death certificate, and then throw it back again. And again. The coroner got $11.50 per body to look at it and say it was dead. For $10 he would provide aid and succor to the grieving family by declaring a suicide to be a natural death; for the grand sum of $50 he would declare an inconvenient homicide to be a natural death and ensure that no incriminating records would pop up later to embarrass the killer. In one rowdy episode, an unclaimed body was seen in the East River floating between Brooklyn and Manhattan. The coroners for each borough rowed out to the middle of the river and whacked each other with oars until one of them lost his balance and fell into the water. The winner hauled in the dead body, trussed it up, and rowed back to shore, as hundreds cheered. Such spectacles did nothing to advance the integrity of the profession, and in 1914, a reform mayor, John Purroy Mitchel, defeated Tammany, and replaced the office of coroner with that of the medical examiner. He made it a civil service job, based on merit. For the first time, the chief ME had to be a physician and a pathologist trained in doing autopsies. Applicants were required to take a written exam and perform an autopsy. In February 1918, Dr. Charles Norris, the head of Bellevue Hospital Laboratory, assumed office as the first chief ME.

The rest of the country continued the old ways. There is still no national system of death investigation in the United States.

Every state has a different method, and most don't use trained forensic pathologists. The system in each community depends on historical accident. Usually a given system has changed gradually, sometimes unavoidably, forced by events that exposed its flaws.

In Oklahoma City in the 1960s, the event was the indictment for murder of the son of a very substantial citizen. George Cole, who was in his late teens, and two of his college friends, out for fun, picked up a twenty-four-year-old man and got into a brawl with him in a parking lot. The man, John Wallace, who had two children, fell down dead. The hospital pathologist who did the autopsy diagnosed death from a brain hemorrhage caused by a punch received in the fight, which made it a homicide. He described the ruptured vessel as having an aneurysm in it. But he had misinterpreted his findings. At the trial it came out that the aneurysm had probably started to blow out before the fight, while Wallace was in a bar. He had a headache from it; he was disoriented, acting peculiarly, and he started the fight. When he fell down, it was because of the aneurysm, not the fight. He died of natural causes.

There were headlines in the newspapers, and Cole's father complained that his son had been indicted for a nonexistent murder because of an untrained pathologist. Soon, Oklahoma established an ME's office headed by a forensic pathologist, but the state shied away from funding it. The ME was forced to use the facilities at the local hospital, which infuriated the hospital's staff. Decomposing bodies came in and stank up the place. In an act of desperation, the ME autopsied one of them in the field outside the hospital to make the point that he needed more money. He got it.

Lack of money was also a problem for Dr. Norris, New York City's first chief ME. A big, imposing man with a gray Vandyke beard, Norris was a wealthy aristocrat for whom it was out of character to beg and grovel for bigger budgets. He supplemented the salaries of the doctors and secretaries on his staff with his own money. Doctors earned $2,000 to $3,000 a year.

Norris died in 1935. His successor, Thomas A. Gonzales, who was chief until 1954, had no trouble attracting doctors, even at such abysmal salaries. During the Depression, when doctors were often paid in kind, if at all, $3,000 a year looked very attractive. Later, after World War II, they were locked in by golden handcuffs—their pensions and benefits.

Milton Helpern was chief ME from 1954 to 1974. The job was easier then than now. In the early 1970s, when practically everything became politicized, MEs began to get into trouble. The public noticed when people died in police custody. Before, blacks and other minorities had few civil rights. People had always died in police custody, but there had never been regular public outcries about it, the prevailing view being that they were the bad guys and the police were the good guys. If MEs diagnosed those deaths in custody as heart failures, we enraged the families. If we said they were due to excessive force, we enraged the cops. So it was that an office that started as a twelfth-century branch of internal revenue became a center of municipal power struggles.

These days it's a rare ME who manages to stay out of trouble for any length of time and still maintain his independence. The job is an unhappy combination of science and politics, two disciplines that do not mix well, and the result is inevitably controversy. MEs are not team players. Over the years there is a buildup of cases in which the ME has been too independent to suit the tastes of the politicians, prosecutors, defense attorneys, and insurance companies. He makes enemies in powerful places. The child of an influential family dies of an overdose and the family does not want the cause on the death certificate. The wife of a politician commits suicide and the husband wants it declared a natural death. Truth is not the criterion. If we do our job right, one group of people or another will be offended, and we can become a political liability in the next election. Thomas Noguchi of Los Angeles was brought down for reasons that had nothing to do with his competence and so were two of the best MEs who served with me on the Assassinations Committee, Cyril Wecht of Pittsburgh and Werner Spitz of Detroit.

The Los Angeles County Board of Supervisers tried to fire Noguchi twice, once in 1969 for allegedly praying that two 747s would collide so he would have a lot of bodies to autopsy. After litigation he was reinstated, but in 1982 he was demoted from chief and transferred to a teaching job with higher pay. He became a professor of pathology at the University of Southern California. This lateral move took place after Noguchi made public his findings that William Holden's death was directly connected to the actor's alcoholism. Frank Sinatra and other influential friends of Holden's objected strongly. Noguchi had no right, they said. But it had always been Noguchi's policy to release the cause of death. It is a public office. Most MEs do the same.

Wecht ran for county commissioner and other political offices and antagonized a lot of politicians during his campaigns, one of whom was the sheriff of Allegheny County (which includes Pittsburgh). The sheriff investigated Wecht's coroner's office and accused him of using county facilities for outside work. Most MEs do outside work to supplement their income. Salaries run about $80,000—less than half of what pathologists generally make around the country. Wecht had been providing services quite openly to other counties at their request. He also had a private practice. In his defense, he claimed this work benefitted the county—medical students, doctors, and lawyers watched him perform the autopsies and learned from them. After the charges were raised, he ran for the U.S. Senate and was defeated. He now teaches, writes, and consults.

Spitz was forced to retire when the director of the health department charged that he was "not a team player," and dredged up a fifteen-year-old contract he had made to do autopsies in another county. The contract had previously been approved. The director also said Spitz took things from the office that did not belong to him. The list was leaked to the press, and when he left in September 1988, one newspaper story read: SPITZ STEALS PENIS. The penis in question had been kept in a jar on exhibit in the little museum attached to the ME's office. It had been put away in a closet temporarily.

My turn came, too.

5

MANHATTAN POSTMORTEM

CITY POLITICS

BECOMING THE CHIEF medical examiner of New York was a fulfillment. I had worked in the ME's office for eighteen years; I had studied and apprenticed for it. I had published, done research, taught, and testified. I had had gubernatorial and mayoral appointments, and been named to the Select Committee on Assassinations. My mentor had been one of the few qualified full-time forensic pathologists in the U.S.—Milton Helpern.

I envisioned the office as independent, scientific, apolitical. Pure. Robert Morgenthau, the district attorney of Manhattan, saw it as an arm of the DA's office, with a malleable ME doing his bidding. But if the DA needs a rape in order to prosecute, should the ME somehow find evidence consistent with a rape? If the police say their prisoner died of a heart attack and not a choke hold, should the ME oblige with a death certificate that says cardiac arrest? What is really wanted is an elastic man, one who will stretch and bend his findings to suit the DA's needs and the political climate. Truth and excellence play no part in this arrangement. Numbers are what count, getting convictions for the DA, and the ME's office exists for that purpose. Its own purposes are always subordinate to somebody else's agenda. The DA and his numbers look good for a while, but the ME is degraded and his work suffers. The office succumbs to creeping corruption, a little bit here, a little bit there, until it begins to resemble the old coroner system it replaced.

Perhaps it wasn't surprising that I lasted only a year.

I was sworn in on August 3, 1978. When I inherited the office, nine doctors were responsible for 6,500 autopsies per year. I hired eight full-time board-certified forensic pathologists (there were only about 150 of them in the whole country) and a serologist. They worked for low salaries (our budget was only $2.8 million), but the job offered psychic income, professional gratification. There was enthusiasm, interest; we had research projects going on, and medical students flocked to us. I had great plans. We were going to lead the country in a renaissance of forensic medicine.

I thought the office should be involved in environmental medicine. After all, we are public health doctors, and we had a unique opportunity to set up research programs. We were the only ones who were autopsying healthy people. The hospitals had all the sick ones. Our clients had been hit by a car or gotten into a knife fight; they were fine except that they were dead. I started to save the tissues of normal people to use as a comparison, a baseline, for future measurements. I was inspired by the mercury scare. High levels of mercury were reported to have been found in swordfish, but what had actually been found was a more accurate testing technique. New technologies set new standards, and there is nothing to compare them with. According to my measurements, the level of mercury was the same as it had always been.

A similar problem existed with radioactive contamination. In March 1979, one of the nuclear reactors at Three Mile Island almost melted down, and everyone started measuring the levels of radioactive iodine. The trouble was, nobody knew exactly what those levels had been before. Nobody had monitored the amounts normally present in people's bodies. Scientists had tested cows and milk and grass, but not people. I worked out an arrangement to collect and test tissues with Merrill Eisenbud, a professor at the Institute of Environmental Medicine at New York University, and Richard Coumbis, New Jersey's chief toxicologist. New Jersey has an inordinate number of cancer cases for its population. We planned to get a big freezer and stock it with specimens—livers, bone marrow, and blood—to find out the normal levels of radioactive iodine or strontium or PCBs or dioxin. I thought our freezer would serve as an early-warning system. I saw the office as a place of life, where the living could benefit from our knowledge.

At the end of my first year, on the morning of Friday, July 13, 1979 (my daughter's birthday), I supervised the autopsy of Carmine Galante, the Mafia boss who had been gunned down in a restaurant the day before, and then went to City Hall to see Mayor Koch. He was warm and friendly. My year of probation was almost over, he explained (that confused me; it was a six-month probation and it was over), and he had asked the five New York City district attorneys and my boss, Reinaldo Ferrer, the health commissioner, for letters evaluating my performance. Such letters were standard procedure, he assured me. Four of the letters were complimentary but he'd gotten two negative ones, and he wanted me to answer them so he would have my replies on file. It was just pro forma. One letter was from Ferrer; the other was from Robert Morgenthau, the Manhattan DA.

It disturbed me that Ferrer, my boss, had sent a critical letter. Only two months before, he had praised me in a speech. Morgenthau didn't worry me particularly. In my view we were not natural allies; he and I were supposed to check and balance each other. Should I talk to him? I asked Koch, thinking that the matter could be disposed of easily. Koch thought that was a terrible idea. Whatever I did, he specifically did not want me to talk to Morgenthau. The letter was confidential; he did not want Morgenthau to know he had shown it to me. My reply in writing was to be equally confidential, just for his files. I took both letters back to my office.

There were twelve complaints, four from Morgenthau and eight from Ferrer. Some criticized my administrative abilities (sloppy), others my judgment (bad), and others my attitude (uncooperative). I was also accused of mishandling five cases.

I sent two letters answering the complaints back to Koch and met with him again on July 31. Our second meeting was more formal than the first. He told me he couldn't live with a situation in which the chief medical examiner lacked the confidence of the most important district attorney in the city, and he was demoting me. I would no longer be chief. He also had a second letter from Morgenthau. He had given my confidential reply to Morgenthau's first letter (which was also confidential) to Morgenthau, and Morgenthau had answered it. Now Koch gave Morgenthau's second letter to me. It was an elaboration of his first. Koch himself wrote nothing.

Among Ferrer's administrative charges:

1. I had hired four associate MEs who sold their houses and came to New York before getting Ferrer's approval. This cost the Department of Health over $200,000 and created havoc with the budget.

I replied that I didn't have the power to hire anyone without authorization. Ferrer had approved the hiring. One of them was his neighbor in Westchester whom he had asked me to hire. No one had a house to sell.

2. He had requested but not received a detailed analysis of the structure of the MEs office.

I had sent him a seventy-page analysis.

3. It had taken me six months to review all services for which fees might be charged (such as giving a copy of the autopsy report to the family) with an eye to raising the price.

This was correct. I hadn't done it fast enough.

4. I had left the city without informing him or the mayor of my whereabouts.

This was false. I had not.

5. I had illegally requested the records of a former methadone patient from Beth Israel Hospital, violating federal laws on patient confidentiality.

We were investigating the death of a man with a ruptured spleen who could have been murdered or could have died of a preexisting disease. We requested the medical history on his spleen, not his records on drug use. Ferrer had gotten it for us.

Morgenthau had four charges altogether, two of them about my administrative techniques:

1. My office had lost two knives and a pair of pants that were evidence in a murder case.

We had indeed misplaced them. We couldn't find them for three months. "It is difficult to assess what effect the loss of the evidence will have on the trial," Morgenthau wrote. But we had found the evidence before it was needed for the trial—we had found it even before he wrote the letter.

2. I had kept Laura Drega, one of the assistant DAs, waiting for forty-five minutes, and when I finally got around to seeing her, there was another person in the room.

I had kept her waiting. The MEs office was outnumbered—there were nine of us and about two hundred assistant DAs, many unfamiliar with the ME's office. Drega was relatively inexperienced with homicide and was unfamiliar with autopsy reports. The other person in the room had been an ME who was supposed to be there.

Three years later, when I sued Koch for wrongful dismissal, Drega, who is now a judge in Brooklyn, was working for Elizabeth Holtzman, the Brooklyn DA. We subpoenaed her, but she was too busy and said she was not going to answer the summons. The judge was outraged that a lawyer would ignore a summons. He telephoned her, but she turned him down too. Finally, he sent two federal marshals to bring her in, with instructions to use handcuffs if necessary. She arrived without the handcuffs. It took us two days to get her to court in order to testify that I had kept her waiting for forty-five minutes.

The remaining five complaints charged me with mishandling five cases. Four of them had been inherited from my predecessor. They were either unfinished or had been reopened during my tenure.

People v. *Levine,* one of Morgenthau's cases, was a stabbing and strangulation death on the Lower East Side. The assistant DA wanted the ME to say it was also a rape. The killer, David Levine, had broken into a neighbor's apartment to burgle it. He thought Miriam Weinfeld, the woman who lived there, had left for work, but she was late that day; she was still in the shower, and she surprised him. She came out and found him and he killed her. Within hours of her death, Levine was caught buying things on her credit cards. The evidence against him was strong, but it was also circumstantial. Robert Warren, the assistant DA, who was on his first homicide case, thought it was a rape and also thought the jury would be more likely to convict if it was. The body was found nude and covered with a bloodstained blanket. The serology report stated that acid phosphatase was present in the vagina. Semen contains acid phosphatase, and Warren assumed this was evidence of semen. But acid phosphatase is ubiquitous. Broccoli and cabbage have large amounts of it, and so do snails. It is commonly present in the vagina. Without sperm and certain chemicals found in semen, its presence meant nothing. One other factor ruled out rape. Weinfeld was a virgin. Her hymen was intact.

The acid phosphatase disagreement had reverberations. Morgenthau accused me of having flippantly remarked to Warren and others at a conference that the victim was "putting snails up her vagina," and the snails would account for the acid phosphatase. Warren professed himself to be outraged by my vulgar utterance, although, at the time, he kept his feelings a secret. Later, at my trial, no one could be found who had heard me express this opinion, and several people who had been at the conference told television reporters that I had never said it. Warren had to back down. At the trial he took the position that I said it as we passed each other in the hallway when no one else was there. I had never said it.

Before the Levine trial, Dr. Josette Montas, the ME who had done the autopsy, asked me to have a conference with Warren to discuss the phosphatase business. She was caught between us and wanted guidance on how far she could go with saying it was rape. Could the penis have gone in maybe an inch? Half an inch? I said no, there was no sexual penetration. At Levine's trial for murder, the prosecution asked Montas if her findings were "consistent with" rape. She said yes. Levine's defense lawyer didn't have the presence of mind to ask her if her findings were also consistent with its not being rape. Levine was convicted and put away.

This sort of creative justice undermines the entire system. The important thing here is winning, and if truth and fairness are stretched in the process, so be it—it's just a slight bending of the facts, a little embellishment. Everyone knows the killer is guilty. If the ME can say the victim was raped as well as strangled, or dead for four hours instead of two, the DA will be absolutely certain to get a conviction. Otherwise, there's a chance the killer will get off. The end justifies the means. Most MEs do it, and the DA gets his conviction. But it is compromised testimony, and the lie casts a shadow on the truth.

In this instance there may have been extra pressure to stretch the truth, to correct a past mistake. It was very important that Levine be jailed. A few years before, he had been a suspect in a burglary. Levine had arranged for a friend to hold up the grocery store where he worked. The owner had a gun and shot the friend dead. The police found a note in Levine's handwriting setting up the robbery in the friend's pocket. The note was the principal evidence against him. Morgenthau's office lost the note, and the police had to let Levine go. If they hadn't lost it,

Levine would have been in jail and Miriam Weinfeld would still be alive.

Then there was the Willie Welch case. Morgenthau claimed that I had failed to provide an autopsy report for ten months, an excessively long time, which prevented his office from prosecuting the case. In their quest for the file, his staff reported dozens of unreturned phone calls, which caused much annoyance. I wrote in my letter that most of them were returned. The DA's office had no central message taker, and people never got their messages. Ten months is indeed a long time to delay issuing an autopsy report, but the delay was unavoidable and had no connection with prosecuting the case. Morgenthau didn't need the autopsy report to present the case to the grand jury. He just needed the cause of death, which he had in the death certificate.

The Welch case had begun under my predecessor, Dominick DiMaio. Willie Welch, a twenty-two-year-old black man, was found dead in his apartment on the Bowery on New Year's Eve, 1977. The body was autopsied by Dr. Yong Myon Rho, who found the cause of death to be drugs and alcohol. No one claimed the body, and Welch was buried in potter's field.

A few months later, Welch's roommate, David R. Gordon, walked into a police station, overcome with guilt, and confessed to strangling Welch. The cops found him less than convincing, but he was persistent. He confessed again and again, on the telephone and in person, compulsively, obsessively. Nobody wanted to hear it.

In September, shortly after I became chief, he began threatening to kill a cop to get attention. I didn't think a threat to kill a cop could be ignored. I looked at the autopsy records. The on-the-scene photographs were suggestive of strangulation—Willie Welch had a scarf wrapped around his neck. I thought Gordon might be telling the truth, and I ordered Welch's body exhumed.

The neck organs were in a plastic bag inside the body, as they should have been. The windpipe (the hyoid bone, just above the

Adam's apple) had been fractured. Ninety-nine percent of the time, a fractured windpipe means strangulation. I sent the autopsy report to Dr. Rho so he could reevaluate his original findings. Rho was reluctant to deal with it. He was upset. I had contradicted him. I didn't press him. That was the reason for the delay. Morgenthau won his case against Gordon anyway. I was the main witness.

The three other cases I was accused of bungling were on Reinaldo Ferrer's "poor judgment" list. One was the Robert Soman suicide. Ferrer wrote in his letter that I "was slow and unresponsive in implementing" an agreement to change a cause of death. He was misinformed. I had never agreed.

The Soman death occurred on Dominick DiMaio's watch. In May 1975, Robert Soman, a physically healthy fifty-seven-year-old man, jumped out of a twelfth-story window in the middle of the night. It was an obvious suicide. He had been depressed for months, and he had to climb over chairs to get to the window. He could not have fallen out accidentally. There was a lot of insurance. The policy provided that the family could not collect if he killed himself within two years. The two years were not up. The family hired a large and prestigious law firm and sued DiMaio to change the cause of death.

The law firm had many things to recommend it, one of them being that it had close ties to the city administration. It had been the city's counsel in an SEC investigation, and a relative of the deputy corporation counsel (one of the city's lawyers) was in the firm. I had not been informed of this. When the case was called, an unusual thing happened. No one from the corporation counsel's office appeared in court to defend the ME and his diagnosis. The hearing was rescheduled five times, and each time no one from the city appeared to defend the cause of suicide. Finally, the judge ruled that the city had defaulted and ordered the medical examiner to change the cause of death from suicide to accident. By then, a year and a half had passed, and I was the medical examiner. I did not think the court could order me to change the truth to a lie. It would be like calling a gunshot wound a stab wound. If I caved in, I would be expected to do it the next time and the next. I also thought the whole case had the appearance of a political payoff. In any event, they didn't need me. The family won by a default judgment.

Arthur Miller was another of the cases on Ferrer's "poor judgment" list. Arthur Miller was a black leader in Brooklyn who got in the way of a traffic ticket and two nervous cops. He died of a choke hold in a police car. According to Ferrer, my big mistake lay in issuing a "premature autopsy report" and changing it the next morning. "His conduct further exacerbated an understandably tense situation," Ferrer's letter said. I assume he was referring to the cause of death. Nothing else was issued. The autopsy report, which was not premature, was not changed.

Two white cops had stopped a young black man in his twenties for a traffic violation. It was early evening. While they were writing the traffic ticket, neighbors and friends started to gather around. They became a small crowd. The cops got a little flustered with all these angry black people shouting at them that they were picking on a kid. Then Arthur Miller, in his mid-thirties, the kid's older brother, arrived. Unknown to the cops, Miller was a hero of the community, a former amateur boxer, and a man who worked with the police to help neighborhood children. He was also licensed to carry a gun. In what may have been the most unfortunate gesture of his life, he raised his arms to calm the crowd; his jacket opened, and the nervous cops saw he had a gun in his belt. They jumped him, dragged him into the car, and drove to the precinct. When they arrived, he was dead. The cops said they thought it was a heart attack.

In a case like this—a police confrontation—any deaths have to be investigated immediately. Special care has to be taken because of the power of the authorities to cover things up. You need as objective a finding as possible, a finding that is above reproach. It fell to Dr. Milton Wald, the deputy chief ME of Brooklyn, to do the autopsy. Wald wasn't sure how to handle it; he didn't know what to do about listing the cause. We worked it out on the telephone.

"Everything is normal," he said. "I can't find a cause."

"Are there any marks on his neck?" I asked.

"Yes, bruises."

"Any hemorrhages in the eyes?"

"Yes."

"Any damage to the windpipe?"

"Yes; there are hemorrhages in the neck muscles."

"Well," I said. "Isn't this neck compression? With an arm or a nightstick?"

"You're right," he said, "but our policy is to say 'pending further study' until the commotion dies down, or to say 'psychosis with exhaustion.' "

Psychosis with exhaustion is an ME euphemism designed to exonerate the police and pacify the family and draw a polite curtain of silence over the events. It means that the person in custody started acting crazy and died while being subdued. His heart couldn't take the exertion of his psychotic behavior. That way, his death was really his own fault.

I did not think psychosis with exhaustion was the way to go. I'd been through situations like this during the 1960s, and I knew the best thing was the truth, delivered as quickly as possible, before the anger started to simmer. We would just inflame the situation by lying about it. I told Wald to say that the cause of death was compression of the neck. He did.

The Miller family didn't think they would be treated fairly. Even before we were finished with our autopsy, they hired their own pathologist to do a second one. He was very surprised to see that our cause was not psychosis with exhaustion, and he confirmed our findings. The community calmed down. Koch called to tell me what a wonderful job I'd done, and sent me a spontaneous letter of commendation. The letter later became a source of embarrassment to him when I sued the city. He had forgotten about it. Ferrer's charges said that my irresponsible behavior could have made a potentially violent situation worse. When Koch was shown the commendation he nearly fell off the witness stand, but he recovered his aplomb quickly—if Reinaldo Ferrer, his health commissioner, said he was wrong, then he had to be guided by that, Koch said.

Ferrer's last accusation, also in the "poor judgment" category, was that I publicly and indiscreetly discussed the death of Nelson Rockefeller and "included a number of details not previously presented in such fashion as to indicate that the governor had died during sexual intercourse." I was supposed to have disclosed these details during a speech titled "The Functions of the Chief Medical Examiner's Office," which I gave at Lenox Hill Hospital in the month following Rockefeller's death. My entire presentation, said Ferrer, was focused on the governor's death. Somehow, this public indiscretion remained a total secret from the media, which were slavering for details on Rockefeller's death. Not a single word of it appeared in the press.

Ferrer, who was not present during my speech, learned of it from Dr. John Finkbeiner, a Manhattan oncologist at Lenox Hill. Finkbeiner, who said he was sitting in the back of the auditorium, apparently heard something entirely different from what I said. My sole reference to Rockefeller was a response to a question from the audience. One of the Lenox Hill doctors asked if the hospital should have issued a death certificate. Should Rockefeller's death have been reported to the ME? I explained that the hospital has the right if the patient is under the care of his own doctor. If you die at home or in the hospital, and your doctor has been treating you for the disease you die of, the ME doesn't come into it at all. The hospital or the doctor signs the death certificate, and it remains a private matter. Finkbeiner's version, which he later testified to, was lengthier. He had not heard me say anything about sexual intercourse, but he said he had heard me describe the autopsy and stomach contents. He said I had told the audience that Rockefeller had eaten two meals, the remains of which were still in his stomach. Finkbeiner did not know that there is no way to count the number of meals eaten from the stomach contents. Besides, Rockefeller was never autopsied.

These charges were doubly painful to me because I had done everything I could to have Rockefeller's death dealt with properly. I had thought there should be an autopsy. He had died suddenly at night in his townhouse/office near the Museum of Modern Art. He was working on a book with his young assistant, Megan Marshak. The gossip was ferocious.

I was at a conference in San Diego at the time. The office was inundated with calls. Half the reporters in New York had suspicions to impart: that Rockefeller had really died in Marshak's apartment and was subsequently dressed and carried over to his townhouse; that this need to observe the proprieties had caused a delay in getting the ambulance and could possibly have cost him his life; that it wasn't just a scandal, a crime had been committed and covered up. Some people thought he had actually died five hours before. Part of this speculation was the Death of a Great Man Syndrome—how could Nelson Rockefeller die a natural death? He wasn't even sick; his annual checkups always described him as being healthy.

By the time I found out he was dead, the body had already been moved to the family compound in Pocantico Hills in Westchester County. The family did not believe in drawing things out. I had to decide whether there was enough information to get it back against their wishes. The funeral director was calling, requesting permission to cremate. Because of the finality of cremation, the ME in New York City, as in many other jurisdictions, must approve all cremations to make sure that nothing serious, like a murder, has been overlooked. If the body has been moved, the custom is to get the approval from the place where the death certificate was issued.

I called Rockefeller's physician, Dr. Ernest R. Esakof, who had issued the death certificate. Esakof told me that Rockefeller hadn't been as healthy as everyone thought. In the last few months he had been treating him for hypertension and heart disease. The family hadn't wanted anyone to know. The fact that Esakof was treating Rockefeller for the condition he died of—heart disease—took the case out of my jurisdiction completely. We had no legal basis to do an autopsy. Cynics thought that the family pulled strings in order to avoid one, but the family didn't have to; they had a right to their privacy. Rockefeller was not an ME's case, and he was not removed from my jurisdiction because of privilege or because he could get away with anything he wanted, even after he was dead.

Still, I thought it would be the better part of prudence to have an autopsy done. Without one, the questions would continue to be asked and the stories would never end, just because he was a Rockefeller. I told Esakof about all the calls we were getting, all the suspicions. Look at President Kennedy, I said. The more mystery there is, the more people speculate. Wouldn't Mrs. Rockefeller want to put all the questions to rest? Esakof told me that Mrs. Rockefeller had consulted with Henry Kissinger and other advisers and decided against an autopsy. By the time he called me back, the body had already been cremated.

After Koch demoted me, I sued the city for wrongful dismissal and reinstatement. The chief ME is the highest civil service position in the city, and according to the law he can be removed only for cause, such as incompetence. The mayor should not be in a position to hire and fire the chief ME at will. It interferes with the ME's ability to act independently and turns the job into a political appendage. Koch had demoted me arbitrarily, without a hearing, on the basis of two secret letters. It was like a Star Chamber proceeding. In 1982, three years after my demotion, we went to trial.

During my career, some people had racked up grievances against me, and the trial gave them a chance to cash in. One of the people who testified was John A. Keenan, a former assistant DA and a friend of Morgenthau's. Back in 1968 Keenan had asked me to omit writing "drug addict" on the death certificate of a man who had died of a gunshot wound. We had a policy about that: we made a notation on the back of the certificate, which was used to compile public health statistics. Keenan didn't want the jury to know the dead man was an addict. If he looked attractive to the jury, then the killer would look that much worse. The principle was the same as in the Levine non-rape case. It was just helping things along a little. I thought it was nonsense and said so. Keenan did not appreciate my position. Fourteen years later he went on the stand to support Morgenthau's charge that I was derelict in returning phone calls to his assistants. When he had been an assistant DA, he said, I hadn't always returned his phone calls promptly, either. In the middle of the trial, Keenan came into good fortune. While he was testifying, it was announced that he had coincidentally been elevated to judgedom. That made him a colleague of Judge Haight, who was the sitting judge at my trial.

Morgenthau's performance as a witness was marred by his embarrassment and discomfort at being there. He found himself unable to answer questions about normal procedure and the general mechanics of things, and he kept contradicting his depositions, blaming the stenographers for the discrepancies. The stenographers were furious. He didn't seem to understand how the grand jury process worked. He complained that he couldn't prosecute in the Welch case because he didn't have the autopsy report soon enough to show to the grand jury—but the grand jury is never shown the autopsy report.

Koch was his usual confident self on the witness stand. He went out of his way to praise me, saying what an excellent pathologist I was, but excellence was really not the point. "Dr. Baden's temperament was such that he couldn't work well within the system," Koch said. The main thing was that his chief ME had to get along with the most important DA in the city.

After he testified, Koch came over to shake my hand. It was just a charade after all, and no hard feelings, he seemed to be saying.

I won my case and Koch was ordered to reinstate me, but he and Elliot Gross, whom he appointed to succeed me, appealed. Gross, the former chief ME of Connecticut, had been Morgenthau's choice from the beginning, but Koch had preferred me. They won. The court adopted Koch's argument that the job of chief ME was too important a position for the mayor not to control, and that the mayor should have the right to hire and fire at will. Ironically, Koch was able to use this ruling later to fire Gross.

In 1981, I took a two-year leave of absence from New York City and worked in Suffolk County. In 1986, Governor Cuomo's director of criminal justice asked me and Lowell Levine, a forensic dentist, to organize the New York State Police Forensic Sciences Unit, to be on call and solve forensic mysteries. The majority of counties in the state had coroners, not MEs, and they needed help.

The problems with the New York City ME's office continued after I left. The Tennessee Williams diagnosis was difficult. Williams, who was seventy-two years old and a lifetime user of alcohol and barbiturates, died at the Hotel Elysée in Manhattan on February 25, 1983. Gross found a long, thin rubber medicine bottle stopper in his mouth and attributed his death to it: Williams choked on it, he said. However, it was not wide enough to stop up Williams's airway. In fact, it was not even *in* his airway. It was in his mouth. He had been drinking and had overdosed on barbiturates. The press kept calling Gross for the toxicology report, and he kept saying the work wasn't done yet. He had sent Williams's tissues to the lab under another name. The lab people knew what he had done, but they didn't know which name he had used. Gross explained that he was worried about foul play: because of Williams's celebrity, he wanted to ensure that the lab didn't leak anything to the press. This behavior was labeled cautious and discreet by some; others considered it paranoid. Six months later, after the press had lost interest, Gross quietly issued another cause of death, taking into account the secret toxicology findings—that Williams had swallowed enough barbiturates to cause death.

Another embarrassment was the Michael Stewart case, a long-drawn-out scandal with shrieking headlines which still remains a festering sore of racism. Stewart, a young black man who was caught spraying graffiti, was beaten and subdued by the transit police. He was taken to the hospital in a coma and kept alive for eleven days. The doctors noticed neck injuries when he was brought in. Gross did not identify them at the time of the autopsy.

After the autopsy, Gross held a press conference and announced that Stewart had died of cardiac arrest and that there was no evidence he had been injured. I believe this diagnosis encouraged the transit police to deny they had beaten and subdued Stewart. A few days later, the toxicology report came back from the lab. Toxicology had found alcohol in Stewart's body, and Gross blamed the death on too much alcohol. After conferring with other experts, he decided the cause was traumatic injury to the cervical vertebrae, the implication being that Stewart did it to himself, having fallen down while drunk. This is another form of psychosis with exhaustion. At the trial of the transit police, there were two competing causes of death, which meant that Morgenthau had to bring in outside MEs to clarify matters for the jury, a humiliating state of affairs for the DA of Manhattan. Dr. Brian Blackbourne, chief ME of Massachusetts, testified for Morgenthau that the cause of death was a choke hold. He was the only one to say so. Many people, including me, had believed all along that the cops had cut off Stewart's air supply with a nightstick, and he had gone into a coma from which he never recovered. (There had not been a single diagnosis of a choke hold death by cops since Arthur Miller's death in 1978.) Morgenthau lost the case. There were too many conflicting causes of death. Since then, the family has brought a civil case against the city and Gross for violating Stewart's civil rights.

These blunders culminated in the notorious preppy murder

case, in which Jennifer Levin and Robert Chambers, two children of privilege, went to Central Park in the middle of the night to have sex, and Jennifer Levin wound up dead. Chambers said he accidentally grabbed her around the neck and squeezed during rough sex. It was a complicated case, but it was assigned to a junior ME whose inexperience led her into errors and omissions. She did not search the body for fibers and hairs. She mistook bruises for bite marks on Levin and called in a dentist who agreed with her. Morgenthau held a televised press conference using the bite marks as an example of the viciousness of Chambers's attack. The marks were ordinary bruises. Levin's damp clothes were put in a plastic bag, where they acquired a coat of mold that made it impossible to use them for evidence or for the lab to do blood, semen, and saliva tests. The ME work was so careless that Morgenthau again had to pay outside experts to testify for him. This time Werner Spitz, chief ME of Detroit, came. It cost the city almost fifteen thousand dollars.

Chambers pled guilty to first-degree manslaughter and got five to fifteen years, but it was a plea bargain, incorporating other charges of burglary and fraud. Five to fifteen is what he might have gotten for only one of the other charges.

For whatever reason, Morgenthau was just as unhappy with Gross as he had been with me. Gross suffered a similar fate to mine—Koch fired him in 1987. Ironically, a few months later, an assistant DA in Morgenthau's office called me in as a consultant on the Carl Andre–Ana Mendieta defenestration case.

They were both sculptors. Andre, at fifty, was well established; his thirty-six-year-old wife, Ana Mendieta, was on her way up. The marriage was in trouble. He was a womanizer, and she was gathering evidence for a divorce. He was brawny; she was tiny. They were both heavy drinkers and fiercely temperamental. She went out the window and landed on the roof of a grocery, thirty-two floors below their Greenwich Village apartment, at about 5:30 A.M. A doorman thought he heard someone crying, "No, no, no, no," followed by a loud crash. The police labeled it a homicide rather than a suicide or an accident. They had no confession, no eyewitnesses, and no other real evidence. The ME confirmed what the cops told him. The DA, however, assumed the ME had independent medical evidence to support his findings. Even the police thought the ME had something more, something of his own to add, when he agreed with them. He didn't. Apparently, he just adopted their version. Nobody from the ME's office visited the scene. There was blood under Mendieta's fingernails and a scratch on Andre's face. Did she scratch him? No one knows. When they moved the body, they didn't protect her hands.

The autopsy established that Mendieta was alive when she went out the window. A body bleeds more if it is alive on impact, and she had inhaled blood into her lungs. Beyond that, very little could be proved. Was it suicide? Suicide does not come out of a vacuum. There are red flares in advance. Mendieta had no history of suicide attempts. Did she fall? Was she pushed? The injuries are the same if you jump, fall, or are pushed. On the other hand, if she jumped or was pushed she would have landed at different distances from the building. In an accidental fall, the body is usually nearer the wall. Mendieta's body was found fifteen feet away from the side of the building, more consistent with a jump. There was no evidence of a struggle in the apartment near the window. But finally, it was impossible to say what the manner of death was. There just wasn't enough information.

After the ME called it a homicide, the DA's office decided to bring a case, but they had very little evidence. Andre was acquitted. His wife's relatives and friends are still convinced that he threw her out the window.

6

___

EARTHLY REMAINS

IDENTIFYING THE DEAD

THERE ARE ONLY so many ways to identify a body. The great majority are identified visually, by family members. Failing that, the best, most effective way is also the simplest: by comparing X rays of bones or dental records to the body. In a tragedy such as the *Challenger* explosion, the Air Force had provided another way to identify some of the astronauts. The Air Force keeps a record of footprints and it had those of the four astronauts who were in the service. Flyers wear thick shoes that give extra protection to the feet in a crash or a fire. Even if feet are sheared off, they can be reunited with the right body by toxicology and immunology tests.

Even without the footprints, identifying the astronauts was easy. There were only seven of them, and each differed in age, sex, or race from the others. Everyone knew who they were. Two were women and five were men. One of the men was black and one was Oriental. The capsule they were in broke apart on impact with the water. It was found two hundred feet down with four bodies still in it. Two other bodies were nearby, but the seventh had vanished. Days later, when the searchers were about to give up, they finally found it. They hooked a long chain between two scallop boats and ran the chain along the bottom of the sea. The remains were well preserved. They were far below the sun line, where there are no bacteria and no algae.

In wars and mass disasters, identification is not always so easy.

In the summer of 1985, the Army released the remains of Lieutenant Colonel Thomas T. Hart, who had been missing since December 21, 1972. He had been one of fourteen men in an AC-130 shot down over Pakse, Laos. The site, the first one the Laotian government had permitted Americans to excavate, was known to the Army, which has a list of all the places where planes went down during the Vietnam War. Ann Hart, the pilot's widow, who lived in Pensacola, Florida, had gone to visit the site with a delegation of families of the missing in 1982. She had seen pieces of bone scattered around, and had even picked up a humerus (armbone) fragment. Looking at all these chips and at the destroyed plane strewn across the landscape, she was convinced that her husband was dead. He could not have survived the crash.

The bones were gathered up and identified at the Central Identification Laboratory of Hawaii (CILHI), one of three military mortuaries in the United States. Remains from Asia are sent there. In 1985, CILHI issued death certificates. Mrs. Hart was not at all certain she could trust the identification. Before accepting the remains, she wanted an anthropologist to look at them. Dr. Michel Charney, a forensic anthropologist at Colorado State University, looked inside the casket and saw little bits and pieces, bone chips and fragments, that could have been almost anything. Among them was the humerus fragment Hart had picked up. Charney said there was no way anyone could be identified from those chips. Hart started a lawsuit against the U.S. government.

Meanwhile, in Oklahoma City, a similar story was unfolding. Major Hugh Fanning and his electronics warfare officer (or gunner) were shot down over North Vietnam in their two-seater fighter plane on October 31, 1967. The Vietnamese returned the remains as if they were a single person. CILHI opened the pouch and saw that it contained a mixture. All the teeth matched the gunner's dental records. But CILHI also assigned some of the other remains to Fanning. Considering the circumstances of the death and the site of the crash, it was reasonable to do so. The fractures on all the bones looked like the kind of high-impact injury that comes from a plane crash.

Katherine Fanning, the widow, had doubts about the procedure. After all this time, how could anyone tell her that her husband's remains were indeed her husband's? She asked the Marine major who was the case officer assigned to help the family through the system. The major, in an effort to put her mind at ease, fudged. He said it was a dental identification. Fanning was buried.

In 1985, Katherine Fanning read about the Thomas Hart case, and all her doubts revived. She requested the Pentagon to send her husband's personnel file. In the folder was a black-and-white diagram of a skeleton. The parts that were recovered were inked in. All portions of the skull and teeth were untouched. Fanning had the remains disinterred, and Clyde Snow, a forensic anthropologist, and Fred Jordan, the chief ME of Oklahoma and a forensic pathologist, looked at them. It was clear there was no biological way to identify them.

The Pentagon was exceedingly upset by this finding. CILHI investigated and concluded that the real mistake was the case officer's kindness—he had inadvertently misled Fanning. She might not have been satisfied if he had told her the identification was made on the basis of the circumstances, but it would have been true. Fanning was not appeased and sued.

MIAs and their families are sacred. They also have a powerful lobby in Congress. As the scandal and outrage grew, the Army was confronted with the necessity of having to do something about it.

The director of anthropology at CILHI was Tadao Furue, a Japanese who came to America after World War II. During the U.S. occupation of Japan, he worked at an American military base studying anthropology and doing identifications. He had a reputation for being a miracle man—he could make identifications from bones that no one else could. Furue handled the MIAs from Southeast Asia. It is slow, unrewarding work. Of 2,413 men missing and unidentified in Vietnam, over twenty-three hundred are still missing. About five hundred of these are known to have gone down in the South China Sea, and may never be recovered. Others were allegedly seen being captured alive and were never accounted for. Every so often the Laotians have permitted the U.S. to go into the jungle and excavate the site of a plane or helicopter crash. In addition to having a record of where all planes were last seen, the Army has the number on the plane's tail and the names of the crew.

Before the scandal became unmanageable, the Army called in three consultants: Ellis Kerley, a forensic anthropologist in charge of the anthropology department at the University of Maryland; Lowell Levine, the forensic dentist who would later identify Josef Mengele from his teeth; and William Maples, an anthropologist from Florida. (Maples and Kerley are part of the roving New York State police forensic unit that is codirected by Levine and me.) They reviewed Furue's work to find out how the identifications were made and were very critical. In their opinion, Furue's identifications were unsupportable. Short of witchcraft, there was no way he could produce the results he claimed. It appeared that he first looked at a downed plane's passenger list for vital statistics—names, heights, weights. He would then pick up a piece of bone and say, This is a white Caucasian male, five feet eight—and lo, there on the list was an MIA who fit that description. It was like Roald Dahl's short story "Taste," about the gentleman who was so clever at guessing the labels on wine bottles. He got it right all the time because he peeked.

Furue denied it. He explained himself very simply—first he looked at the bones in an unbiased manner, and then he looked at the list.

There are charts and formulas that were drawn up after World War II, ways to measure bones so as to determine height, weight, sex, and race. The tables establish the relationships, but in order to use them, you have to have some information to begin with. To get something you have to give something. The charts are of little value with the bone fragments that Furue was so successful with. Fragments can be assigned to a particular person only if they fit into a bigger bone or if they look the same as the skull and match the age, sex, and race.

Kerley is now Scientific Director, and Levine and Maples are permanent overseers of CILHI and sign off on each identification. In 1987 the Army invited various visiting forensic scientists to lecture and suggest ways of improving the identification process. I was one of them. When I got there I found a public relations ossuary—an exhibit for junketing politicians. In a large room, skeletal remains were spread out on ten tables. Ribs and clavicles, femora and humeri, tibiae and vertebrae were arrayed in splendid order. It was neat, clean, and unreal.

The staff was lopsided—eight anthropologists, one dentist, and no pathologist. It was clearly anthropological territory. They spent their days matching every bone against the list of the men still missing in Vietnam, but it was apparent that the only bodies being identified were the ones with teeth. For all their numerical superiority, the anthropologists were operating at a distinct disadvantage. They were missing a very important piece of equipment—an X-ray machine. The identification of bones requires comparing old X rays with new ones, looking at fracture lines, picking up the grooves and shapes that are unique, the little trabeculae (curlicues) that make up the bone structure. They didn't have the old X rays, either.

I recommended that they get an X-ray machine and add a pathologist to the team, but even so, other military procedures sometimes undercut the entire MIA operation. One policy called for shipping dental records in the same plane as their owners. If the plane crashed, the records were destroyed. In 1985, after a crash in Gander, Newfoundland, that killed 248 soldiers and burned their records, the military developed a new policy. Now, medical records are duplicated and stored in Monterey, California. When the *Stark* was hit by an Iraqi missile in the Persian Gulf in 1987, identification of the thirty-seven sailors who were killed was much simpler—there was no need to rely on the records on the ship. However, in another self-defeating policy, the Army destroys medical records and X rays after six years, which makes it almost impossible to identify the missing after that time. Military X rays used to be stored in the National Personnel Record Center in St. Louis, Missouri, but there was a fire in 1973. Eighteen million records were demolished. Since then, whenever a dead soldier's records are missing, the excuse is that they were lost in the St. Louis fire. It gives everyone an out.

In October 1988, Ann Hart and her family were awarded $632,000 for having suffered severe emotional distress. The Fanning case was still pending.

On June 24, 1975, Eastern Airlines Flight 66, from New Orleans to Rome with a stopover in New York, delayed its takeoff about fifteen minutes because a VIP, a prominent surgeon at Tulane Hospital, was late. There were high winds at JFK that day. Eight minutes before Flight 66, a Boeing 727, arrived, the pilot of an Eastern jumbo jet decided it was too risky to try to land and flew off to Newark. The next plane, a Flying Tiger DC-8, was cleared for approach to the runway, but the pilot thought the wind shifts were too unpredictable. He almost crashed. Eastern Flight 66 came in right after. The pilot decided to land. When he was about twenty feet off the ground, he got caught in the wind shear. The plane dropped suddenly, the right wing hit a light stanchion, and the plane crashed. Of 124 people on board, 113 died. Seven people were injured and four walked away unscathed. All of the survivors were sitting in the rear of the plane.

Late in the afternoon the ME's office heard about the crash on the radio. The announcement of a mass disaster is like an invitation to a party. Within an hour all roads leading to the scene are jammed, voyeurs mingling with off-duty cops—anyone with the remotest excuse converges on it. Politicians come to be interviewed. Fire engines and ambulances line up. Extra cops hang around. The terrible secret about all this activity is the looting. It is always blamed on the local population, but it is only in remote areas that they are the first on the scene. At a busy airport, the first people on the scene are those whose job it is to rescue the living and protect the bodies of the dead. At the Eastern crash, the first arrivals were the Port Authority police, the local police, and the firemen, followed by EMS, doctors, nurses, morticians, and nearby residents. The amount of looting was immense.

Regarding looting, the relatives of the dead are in an impossible position. The firemen, the police, and the local residents all rush in to try to save the living. It is very difficult to ask someone who came to resuscitate your spouse if he took her jewelry and wallet. There is no recourse and no way to accuse anyone or even prove that anything was stolen. You could say that your mother had a diamond ring that she always wore and that it was missing, but you couldn't say you had actually seen her wearing it that day, or that it hadn't come off her finger at the moment of impact.

Flight 66 was a rich flight. One survivor said that he had put $10,000 into his wife's purse that morning. The purse was found. The money was gone. Bishop Iveson Nolan of the Episcopal Diocese of New Orleans was on the plane in all his majesty, wearing the accoutrements of his office, his gold-and-amethyst ring and cross, and a gold wristwatch. The bishop's body was found intact, but his jewelry had vanished.

For the medical examiner, the main thing is to identify the bodies. The easiest way to begin is with personal property and the airline passenger list, which has a seat number for every passenger. At the untouched scene, we can see patterns of injury and the relationships of bodies to body parts, enabling us to work out exactly what happened. Arms and legs are near the torsos they belong to, and people are close to their property. But there seems to be a universal instinct at work after a plane crash, an urge to line up the bodies neatly and an illusion that doing so is helpful. After the Eastern crash the police gave each body a consecutive number, removed all valuables from the bodies, and put the wallets and jewelry into individual manila envelopes. The envelopes were sent to the police property office so that nothing could be stolen. (At this point, there was not much left. It looked like a planeload of paupers.) In the process of safeguarding the property, they removed all remaining identification from the bodies. By the time we arrived at the scene, having fought rush-hour traffic, the bodies were covered with sheets and lined up on the tarmac under a hastily constructed yellow tent.

Most crashes occur on landing or takeoff, and the impact is worst in front. First-class passengers are mangled. Those in the mid-section of the plane suffer fewer injuries. Assuming a fire has started, death is likely to be from smoke inhalation and carbon monoxide poisoning. People in the rear have the best chance of staying alive. Flight attendants, who are usually seated backward, sustain the fewest injuries. Even in first class, they are not nearly as damaged as the passengers are. The passengers suffer skull fractures and whiplash from the sudden deceleration. If the seats faced backward, people would be supported by the chair. But the FAA doesn't think there is enough evidence to turn the seats around, and the airlines don't think the public would accept it.

In a mass disaster, most people are identified from their fingerprint and dental records. Almost everyone has dental records. One of the victims was a Syrian who had grown up with nomads. Through our embassy and theirs, someone was found to go by camel to the remote village where his dentist and dental chart were. On the chart, certain teeth were missing. That was enough to make the identification.

If fingerprints and teeth fail, we try bones. The body has 209 bones, and any one of them can be used for identification. We ask the family to bring old X rays to the office, and we then take another one of the same bones in the same position. Once, hospitals kept X rays that dated back to the early 1900s, but no longer. X rays contain silver. The efforts of the Hunt brothers, Nelson and Bunker, to corner the silver market in 1979–80 pushed up the price of silver, and with it the intrinsic value of X rays. Hospitals, which are perennially short of money, emptied out their X-ray vaults.

We made a preliminary identification of the Eastern pilot and copilot from their uniforms. They had absorbed the full brunt of the crash. Livers, lungs, and hearts extruded from their bodies. The pilot's chest was crushed. The parts were like a jigsaw puzzle—I could fit them back together with the torn aorta. (I also did blood tests to prove it was the correct heart.) He had severe hardening of the coronary arteries. I asked the FAA for his records, and why he had been permitted to fly. His cardiac exams, which are required every six months, were superficial. He hadn't been given any of the stress tests which are used to pick up heart disease. His union didn't permit sophisticated cardiac analysis. Most pilots spend years achieving their position, and by the time they are ready to ferry around giant planes, they are in their fifties and sixties, the period of their peak earnings. It is also the peak period of heart disease. According to the black box, the copilot, whose heart was normal, was at the controls at the time of the crash. It is usual for them to trade places. Some pilots like to land and others like to take off. But it always haunted me—was there any special reason why the copilot was flying the plane?

In April, 1976, the headless, handless body of a woman was found floating in Greenwood Lake which borders the Appalachian Trail between New York and New Jersey. She had a peculiar gash under her left breast, and was covered with green algae.

The body was slim and athletic, so the ME who did the autopsy thought she was in her twenties. He also thought she had been dead for about three weeks. Most people who are dumped in New York are young—they are the ones who are involved in drugs and alcohol and passion and violence. The troopers put out posters and made broadcasts asking if anyone of that age was missing, but no one came forward to claim the body. After six days, two troopers, Dan Reidy (now retired) and Jimmy Curtis (now chief of security at Fort Knox) brought the body down to the city in a coffin to show me. The ME who did the autopsy was a hospital pathologist, and they thought this case was too complicated for him to handle.

He had gotten her vital statistics wrong. She was about fifty-five years old. She had the calcium deposits in her cartilage and the bone spurs on her spine that come with age, and her ovaries had atrophied. An ovary is about the size of a walnut. As it gets older, it becomes shriveled like a prune. There were band-saw cuts on the torso. Band saws are what butchers use. They leave a clean wound. The remains of a fruit-and-vegetable meal were in her stomach. As Sherlock Holmes would have divined instantly, the peculiar gash was made to remove a scar that was distinctive enough to identify her even without her head and hands.

It was the first time I had seen a green body. I scraped some algae off the torso and went to a biologist recommended by the Museum of Natural History. Under a microscope, he identified two generations of algae—fresh green from this year and dead from the year before. So the woman had been dead for at least a year and a half.

Dan Reidy reported the new description to the newspapers, and the radio stations picked it up. The next day the troopers got a call from a woman who said the body was probably her sister, Katherine Howard of Elmont, New York, and she was certain Katherine's husband had killed her. Did her sister have any distinguishing characteristics? we asked. Yes; she had a scar under her left breast. The woman hadn't seen her sister for two years. The last time they had been together they had eaten a meal of fruit and vegetables.

One phone call had established the identification and had provided a lead on the killer.

The husband, Wilbur Howard, who was in his sixties, was known by the police to be a minor criminal. He had reported his wife missing in August 1975. The police had given him a polygraph test, which he flunked, but without a body they were helpless. He lived in a big house in Nassau County and had a workbench, a band saw, a boat, and a station wagon—all the equipment he needed to murder his wife, dispose of her body, and suffer none of the consequences. The carpeting in the station wagon had stains that looked like blood, but they didn't test out. The carpeting had been washed with detergent, which chemically alters blood, so we couldn't be sure.

Wilbur Howard was very cool. He said he thought his wife had run away. There had been ill feeling between them, but that proved nothing. He had no reason to be nervous. The body was unidentifiable. We couldn't even find any X rays to prove that the torso was his wife's. But we did have feet. We disarticulated one of them, and a trooper found a podiatrist in Elmont who recognized the toes. He was 90 percent certain the foot belonged to Katherine Howard, but he had no X rays. Everything matched—the foot, the scar, the last meal, and the amount of time she had been missing—and there was nothing we could do. In frustration, Reidy asked Howard to help him close the book on it, to put a confession in his will and lock the will in his vault. When he died Reidy could close the case.

Two years later he died of a heart attack in Maine. Given his past record, the state troopers wanted to make sure he wasn't scamming for the insurance. Reidy identified the body. It was the right man. Reidy went to his lawyer to open the safe deposit box. There was no confession. The body is still officially unidentified.

Sometimes the method used to hide an identity boomerangs and becomes a means of identification. A man's body was seen floating in the Hudson River and washed up on the Jersey riverbank. Even though the border between New York and New Jersey is a line in the middle of the Hudson River, there's an old tradition that supersedes the maps. For purposes of dead bodies, the border is the high-tide line on the Jersey side. Anything washed up below it is considered to be New York City property. More often than not, it comes from New York, and we send a morgue wagon over to pick it up. If it were on the beach beyond the high-tide mark, it would be New Jersey's problem. I always had the feeling that the custom in New Jersey was to push the body back in.

This particular body had been weighted with ropes and chains, but something had broken, and the body had risen to the surface. All but one of the fingertips—an index finger—had been destroyed by decomposition, and the remaining finger was charred. Fire acts in a peculiar way. It destroys, but it also preserves, the way tanning leather preserves the skin. The prints on the finger were still clear, but one fingerprint by itself was not enough to make an identification. There was no way to tell the man's race from the color of his skin—after we die, we all turn black—but the hair was Caucasian. From the extent that his molars were ground down, the man appeared to be in his sixties. The only other thing I found was a badly healed fracture of the right hip.

I had the body of a white male, five feet ten, 160 pounds, with a bad hip. The bad hip suggested a limp, and the missing persons bureau in New Jersey had a report of a lost husband with a limp. The wife told us he had fractured his hip in Leavenworth Prison twenty-five years before, and after that it was easy. Leavenworth had an X ray. It was the same person, and he was an upper-echelon mafioso. (We had thought he might be, from the ropes and chains. The Mafia is very predictable.) We got his finger-prints from Washington for the final identification. His one print matched.

In May 1979, a woman's leg came in from the Hudson River. It was shaved and had well-manicured toes. A few days later, I was giving a lecture and one of the people attending it, a detective from Toms River, New Jersey, mentioned that he'd had a torso for three months and couldn't identify it—it was a young woman who was wearing underpants that had strands of hair on them. The hair belonged to a number of different people. We don't see many dismembered young women in New York. There was a strong possibility that it was the same person.

We yielded jurisdiction. By tradition, whoever has the heart gets the rest of the body. The cut end of bone on the leg matched the irregularly cut part on the torso. Both pieces seemed to be equally decomposed. It turned out to be Theresa Ferrara, one of the people who had been involved in the $8.5 million Luft-hansa heist at JFK airport. She was a hairdresser. That's where the hair had come from.

7

TIME OF DEATH

BIOLOGICAL CLOCKS

ALGOR, RIGOR, AND livor mortis, the three cardinal signs that have traditionally pointed to the time of death, do not always perform precisely for us. The circumstances surrounding the death, the environment, whether it was hot or cold, whether the victim struggled or took drugs—these things can hasten or slow the process of decay and modify the numbers. Putting them all together is usually more an art than a science. Such was the case when John Belushi died in Los Angeles. Had he been alone, the exact time might not have been so important. But Cathy Smith, his Canadian friend and drug groupie, had been with him, and they were doing drugs. The time of death was critical in establishing whether Smith had given him his final injection, the one that killed him. The police investigation trailed off, which is customary in these circumstances. Deaths like Belushi's happen every day. An addict wants drugs and someone provides them. It's a consensual situation, and the provider is only technically guilty of a crime. DAs rarely go after these people. They don't have the resources. But when a case becomes notorious, they are forced by public opinion to do something. Cathy Smith forced their hand. She sold her story of the last hours of John Belushi to the *National Enquirer* for $20,000. When the police came to see her, she fled to Canada.

Belushi had been on a drug binge for four days, shooting up with Smith all around Los Angeles. On the night of March 4, 1982, he was sitting at a table at On the Rox, a bar on Sunset Boulevard, waiting for Smith. After she arrived with a bag of drugs, they shot up in the owner's private office. At about 2:00 A.M., Belushi, Smith, and a friend, Nelson Lyons, left for Bungalow 3 at the Chateau Marmont Hotel, where Belushi was living, for a drug-shooting party. In the course of the night, Robin Williams and Robert De Niro arrived and left at different times. Shortly after 3:00 A.M. Belushi felt cold and wanted everyone out. Lyons, who was the only other person there, left. According to Smith, she gave Belushi his last injection at 3:30 A.M. It was a speedball, a combination of cocaine and heroin, to calm him. He was paranoid and agitated from his days of cocaine. He didn't know there was heroin in the injection. She was trying to bring him down, to cure a cocaine high with a heroin low, which is part of the folklore of drugs. It doesn't work. Smith and Belushi then showered, and she sat on the edge of his bed while he lay on it, talking about scripts and movie deals. He was still cold, so she turned up the heat and went into the living room. At 7:45 A.M. she heard him coughing and brought him some water. He went to sleep. At 10:15 A.M. she left him alive and sleeping and drove to a bar to bet on a horse. At 12:30 P.M. he was found dead by his exercise instructor. The Emergency Medical Service arrived at 12:35. Smith returned at 1:45.

I was called in by the Los Angeles DA to evaluate the time and cause of death. Later, I was asked to testify before the grand jury as the principal scientific witness. Dr. Thomas Noguchi, former chief coroner/ME of Los Angeles, who would normally have filled this role, had been removed from office in one of his periodic quarrels with the powers that be. The DA didn't want to rely solely on Dr. Ronald Kornblum, the acting chief coroner (he was since made chief), who hadn't had as much experience with drugs as I had had in New York City. Belushi's wife, Judy Jacklin, also asked me to investigate. After reading the *Enquirer* article, she wanted Smith charged with her husband's death.

The autopsy report didn't point to one drug or the other as the cause of death. Under Canadian law, giving someone drugs is not an extraditable offense, but murder is. The Los Angeles DA would need very persuasive evidence that Smith caused Belushi's death before the Canadians would allow her to be extradited.

According to the EMS, police, and autopsy reports, Belushi was found with a little stiffness around the jaw, which is where rigor begins. EMS had difficulty placing an airway in his mouth. Rigor would have taken an hour or two to set in, putting the death between 10:30 and 11:30 A.M. But I couldn't rely on the rigor by itself. Rigor sets in more rapidly if you are very active before death. I looked at the lividity. The coroner had examined Belushi and taken photographs of him at 4:37 P.M. The pictures show a definite purplish color on Belushi's back (he was lying on his back when he was found), and the skin blanched when it was pressed. That kind of color is about right for six to eight hours after death. In two more hours, the color would be permanent—there would be no blanching. According to the lividity, he died between 8:30 and 10:30 A.M., earlier than the rigor would indicate.

The coroner also took Belushi's temperature at 4:37 P.M. It was 95 degrees. Figuring that the body temperature drops one degree per hour after death, he would have died at about 1:00 P.M., half an hour after the exercise instructor found him dead. Obviously, something was wrong. At 12:35, when EMS arrived, rigor had already started. But there were reasons for the temperature reading to be off. Belushi's weight accounted for some of the difference. He was overweight, and the amount of fat around the body organs affects the rate of temperature loss. The thinner you are, the faster you become cold. Belushi's body would have cooled at a slower rate than normal. Cocaine also raises the body temperature. Cocaine makes you hyperactive. If you are taking a lot of it, you are wired; the muscles shiver and quiver. Belushi's temperature may have started out as high as 100 or so, a little higher than the 98.6 degrees that all our calculations derive from. From his temperature, he couldn't have been dead before 10:30 A.M. It would have had to be lower than 95 degrees.

From the mortal signs, the time of death ranged from 8:30 A.M. to 1:00 P.M. Rigor put death at 10:30 to 11:30 A.M. Livor put it at 8:30 to 10:30, but rigor ruled out the earlier time. And so did algor. Death at 8:30 A.M. was too early for Belushi's temperature to be as high as 95 degrees by 4:37 in the afternoon. It should have been lower by then. All of the possibilities could be taken into account with a death at 10:30 A.M., give or take an hour. But what was the cause of death?

According to the autopsy report, Belushi had an enlarged heart and a swollen and heavy brain that weighed about 1,620 grams. Fourteen hundred grams is normal (about three pounds). It is common in a drug overdose for the brain to have more fluid in it than usual, but this condition is not enough by itself to cause death. The effects of the drugs were unmistakeable, however, and there was no other cause to compete with them. Toxicology found very large amounts of cocaine in Belushi's organs and a level of morphine (the breakdown product of heroin) in his bloodstream that was beyond lethal. He had enough of both drugs in him to kill two people. But which one actually killed him? The physiological signs of a heroin overdose were there: fluid in the lungs and froth in the windpipe, mouth, and nose (the airways). In a sense, a heroin overdose is a drowning from fluid that has seeped out of the blood vessels. A cocaine overdose doesn't have those effects. Death from cocaine is uncommon. When it does kill, it kills by causing arrhythmia—the heart stops and starts periodically, or it beats too fast. Either way, blood isn't pumped to the rest of the body. Cocaine kills quickly, within half an hour. Many of the cocaine deaths that I have seen were brought on by swallowing large amounts of it while the police were breaking down the door to the apartment, or by smuggling it internally. Coke mules swallow little condom balloons to get the stuff into the country. If the balloons break or leak en route, one or two grams is enough to cause death.

Heroin is the opposite of cocaine. Death from a heroin overdose comes on gradually. Heroin depresses the brain so much that the brain forgets to give the signal to breathe. Within the hour you lapse into a coma and remain unconscious, going into a deeper and deeper coma. When the coroner examined Belushi, he still had more than twice a lethal level of morphine, the breakdown product, in his blood. (Heroin is a mixture of morphine and acetic acid, which is one of the components of aspirin.) Given that amount, Belushi would have died within two hours of being injected. If Smith's 3:30 A.M. speedball injection was the final one, Belushi would most probably have been dead by 5:30 A.M. Yet, Smith said he was alive and talking at 7:45 A.M., and none of the cardinal signs squared with death at such an early hour. The signs placed his death close to 10:30 A.M. (give or take an hour). There had to be a later injection, and it had to have been given to him at about 8:30 A.M. in order for those signs to start developing at 10:30 A.M. By her own word, Smith was still in the room with Belushi at 8:30 A.M. She didn't leave for the bar to place a bet until 10:15 A.M.

Smith told a second story to the police, changing some of the times in her *National Enquirer* story. She told the police that Belushi had taken a shower at about 6:30 A.M. (not after the 3:30 A.M. injection), and that at 9:30 (not 7:45) she gave him a glass of water. Her second story confirmed that the 3:30 A.M. injection was not the last one and could not have caused the coma. If you are slipping into a coma, you don't take a break for a shower and then slip back into it. If the 3:30 injection didn't contain enough heroin to cause Belushi's death, there certainly wasn't enough to put him back to sleep after the shower. Once he was awake and moving around, the drug would begin to wear off.

One last sign completed the picture of a heroin overdose. At the postmortem, there were 750 cubic centimeters of urine in Belushi's bladder (1000 cc is a little more than a quart). That much urine produces a very distended bladder. Our bodies make 1-2 cc a minute. Belushi hadn't urinated for hours. A person who was sleeping normally would have felt uncomfortable, but a person in a coma wouldn't have known he was uncomfortable.

Smith would not admit to giving Belushi an injection after 3:30 A.M., but the medical evidence was against her. So was the fact that no one else was in the bungalow with Belushi at the time the later injection was given. She served fifteen months in jail for involuntary manslaughter. She got out on March 17, 1988, and returned to Canada.

On September 20, 1977, the day he disappeared, Pinchos Jaroslawicz had a business appointment with two Israelis, Shlomo Tal and Pinhas Balabin. Jaroslawicz was a diamond cutter who worked in the block-long diamond district on West 47th Street, between Fifth and Sixth avenues. He was seen walking into the building where Tal had his small office-workroom just down the block from his own, and knocking on the office door. Nobody saw him leave. He didn't come home for dinner that night or the night after. Half a million dollars' worth of small diamonds vanished with him.

On West 47th Street they worried that his disappearance was part of a plot to destroy the diamond business along with the Hasidic Jews who ran it. There had been other episodes, other disappearances and murders. Since the beginning of the year, $3.5 million worth of jewelry and stones had been stolen in sixteen robberies. There was a Puerto Rican connection—three diamond merchants had been killed there, and a courier had run off to San Juan carrying stolen diamonds. Only a few days before, a missing diamond merchant had been found in the East

River. From the X rays of his stomach, it looked as if he had swallowed a packet of diamonds. And now Pinchos Jaroslawicz was missing. An Orthodox Jew, he dressed in a black frock coat and hat and wore a beard and ringlets. He was well known and respected in the community, a family man with a two-year-old daughter. No one had a word to say against him. But he was gone, and so were the diamonds. Was he as upstanding as he seemed to be?

The diamond business was more than just buying and selling stones—it was a way of life, a culture, built on trust. Millions of dollars in stones changed hands every day without anyone asking for a receipt. The community had an unwritten rule about guns. No one carried them. Buyers and sellers did business on a handshake, not even bothering to write itemized lists of the stones they traded in. This trust eased the flow of diamonds around the world, and it was being threatened. Was this another Puerto Rico courier case? Was there a gang of thieves killing couriers for their diamonds? What would happen to the trust? Without it, everything would be destroyed.

The police searched Tal's workroom several times and found nothing. Balabin, who had his own office, claimed ignorance. The police put out an international alert for Pinchos Jaroslawicz. By now he could be anywhere. A week later, two cops saw a 1972 Buick station wagon parked at the edge of the Grand Central Parkway in Forest Hills, Queens. They banged on the window and found Tal curled up on the floor, asleep.

Tal had several variations of his story, but the basic line was that two masked men with guns had pushed their way into his workroom, killed Jaroslawicz by hitting him on the head with a two-by-four, and stolen the diamonds. Tal was terrified that they would kill him too, so he agreed to hide the body and keep quiet about the whole thing.

After that, it got a little murky. According to one of Tal's versions, five days after the murder the two masked men kidnapped him, drugged him, and drove him around Brooklyn, Queens, and Nassau County for three days. They spent one night at a motel. The next thing he knew, the two cops were knocking on his car window. In another version, the two men telephoned him and ordered him to meet them, and out of fear for his family, he agreed. Either way, he wound up drugged on the highway.

Tal took the police to his office, where the body was hidden in a plastic bag. Jaroslawicz, who was six feet tall and very skinny, was tied up tightly in the fetal position and folded into a very small space—a wooden, boxlike affair, two feet high, two feet wide, and three feet long. The box was under the workbench. It had no bottom.

The police were immediately suspicious of Tal's story. To begin with, his former life in Israel did not inspire confidence. He had a record of car theft, and Balabin, his partner, had one for drugs and grand and petty larceny. But aside from their checkered past, how could Jaroslawicz have been killed eight days ago? He was in excellent condition, almost as if he had just been put there. His skin was a normal color, not green and decomposing, and there was no evidence of the bacteria which cause the body to bloat. Besides, they had already searched the workroom, and no one had been there. The body had to have been brought there later.

Dr. Yong Myun Rho, deputy chief ME, was put in charge of the autopsy. He knew there would be a lot of publicity on this case, but he was unprepared for the extent and intensity of it. To Dr. Rho, a courteous and gentle man, saving face was very important. A public disagreement was unseemly, regardless of who was right. He was taken aback by the anger of the ultra-Orthodox rabbis who made no such distinctions between public and private disagreements and were more concerned with what God thought of them than with the needs of the New York City municipal establishment. The rabbis thought that Jaroslawicz had suffered enough. It was indecent to cut him up now after all he had been through; let the dead rest in peace. More important, autopsies were against their religion. They were determined not to leave without the body. They crowded into the lobby of our building and the street outside, a small army in black frock coats and beards, threatening to sue Dr. Rho if he touched the body. He was afraid they would hurt him physically, and he asked me to do the autopsy. I went outside to talk with them.

I understood their anxiety. I had been through this before. I tried to explain to them that when there is a homicide, we are mandated by law to do an autopsy. It will help to find the killer. They were not interested. They told me that Jaroslawicz's cousin, a well-known medical malpractice lawyer, would sue me if I touched Jaroslawicz. It was a delicate situation, but there were ways around it. A little diplomacy was required. Even though we were obliged to do an autopsy, they had redress. They could go to court to prevent it, and I could promise them that I wouldn't do anything until they got a court order. This had been my approach through the years—to advise families of our legal obligations and their options, and not to appear in the role of the villain.

But there was a catch. Without an autopsy or a court order, I couldn't issue a death certificate. Not having a death certificate was a serious problem for them. According to Jewish law, the body had to be buried with no undue delay by sundown. And I knew perfectly well that there was no way they could get a court order to prevent the autopsy in that amount of time. It takes days. In fact, even if they went to court, it would be highly unlikely that a judge would issue such an order. This was a murder, after all. So a ruling would probably go against them.

To smooth ruffled feathers, there was one other suggestion I could offer—that I do the minimum autopsy required by law. The minimum autopsy required by law is a full autopsy, but there was no need to go into details. It was not that we were simply lying and disregarding their rights. There were many other cases when I compromised by making a smaller incision, not only for the rabbis but for any family requesting it. And we don't take specimens for teaching purposes from these bodies. I also promised that I would do the autopsy under strict Orthodox Jewish rules. They were very skeptical of this—what did I know of Orthodox rules?—so I told them they could have a rabbi present to watch and make sure we were not doing anything improper. The Orthodox believe that God puts you back together, but He has to have all the pieces. Not only is the autopsy disturbing; there is also the possibility that some of the blood can be lost.

Rather than wait to go to court, with the near-certainty of losing, the lawyer, Jaroslawicz's cousin, arranged for a rabbi pediatrician to watch. Rabbi doctors are more like doctors than rabbis. They think like doctors. In the autopsy room we understood each other; we had the knowledge, the rites of passage, the common bond of helping a patient, and all these things became more important than race or religion. Your identity is with your professional group, not your birth group. The rabbi doctor knew that I had to do a full autopsy. He understood what "the minimum necessary" was.

The game we had been playing was the game of saving face. The rabbi pediatrician was there to save face for the community. My job was the public health; I dealt with the rabbis over and over again, and I needed a good relationship with them—I didn't want to offend them.

For twenty years, Rabbi Edgar Gluck, the Hasidic Brooklyn Orthodox liaison, and I had been building a relationship of confidence in each other. He knew I wouldn't do an autopsy if it was unnecessary—if, for instance, the person died in an automobile accident. For the rabbis, the main purpose was to ease the family's grief and to let them know that they, the rabbis, had done the best they could. We all knew that the law was the law, that there were certain things I was bound to do. It was like a scene from an old play that we rehearsed anew each time. Gluck would negotiate about the autopsy, and we would say we had to do it. He could then tell the family that he had gotten the best compromise he could. I could tell the family that we had spoken to Gluck and we had done the minimum necessary, according to the law. We would all get what we wanted and needed. The family wanted to know they had done everything that was in their power to do. That was all God could ask of them. And if we went ahead and did the autopsy in spite of their objections, it was not their fault. They had nothing to feel guilty about. They had protested, and they had been heard.

At about noon I did the autopsy on a paper shroud so that no blood was lost. The shroud and even my gloves went back into the body. It doesn't matter if you put extra things into the body as long as you don't lose blood. God will know what belongs and what doesn't. The rabbis in their black frock coats and hats and side curls still surrounded the building like sentinels of death. Three hours later they left with the body of Pinchos Jaroslawicz, in time to bury him before sunset.

Jaroslawicz had died of suffocation, and as Tal had said, he had also been hit on the head with a two-by-four. He had a fractured skull and a bruise on his brain under the broken bone. After he was unconscious, he was put into the plastic bag and tied so that his feet were down. He had lividity on his lower legs, on the lower backs of his thighs, and on his lower abdomen. There was no sign of his having been moved, or his position changed. The lividity could only have happened the way it did if he had been in that position continuously since he died.

For someone who had been dead a week, Jaroslawicz looked very good. There was no decomposition. The critical thing was the cold. He was in a plastic bag without insulation, lying on the cold tile floor, and the temperature was the same inside as outside the bag. It was too cold for bacteria, which don't usually grow in the body when the temperature is less than 40 degrees Fahrenheit. When the body dies, two forces struggle to control it—decomposition and mummification. In the desert, mummification wins—you lose fluid and dry very rapidly, and the bacteria can't get started. In the frigid zones (or in a snowbank), the wet cold keeps the body hydrated and the bacteria out. In Tal's workroom, the plastic prevented Jaroslawicz's body from drying, and the cold tiles stabilized it.

The discovery of Jaroslawicz's body was a terrible embarrassment for the cops. How could they have overlooked him when he was under their noses, so to speak, all the time? They were worried about the fun the press was going to have with them. The first thing they had to do was polish their image. They could think about the killer later. This wasn't just a little local murder—diamonds were an international business; other couriers had disappeared and police around the world had been looking for Jaroslawicz. They couldn't have overlooked him, it just wasn't possible, and the proof of his not having been there was the lack of decomposition.

Having gone that far, the next step led them straight into a logical swamp. If Jaroslawicz wasn't there, then he had to have been killed somewhere else and brought back, in which case he had been dead for only two days (the last search had been two days before). The logistics were perhaps bizarre but possible. In order to return Jaroslawicz to Tal's office, the kidnappers would have had to break into the building with the dead body, always carrying it carefully in the exact position in which it was found to preserve the lividity, and place it under the bench.

But why would anyone want to do such a crazy thing? Not only that, this sort of behavior was inconsistent with good criminal practice. It made no sense for Jaroslawicz to be discovered at all. Without a body, the killers were beyond reach. But even if they were mad enough to take such a risk and lucky enough to pull it off, the existence of the body prevented them from exploiting the fears on Diamond Row—that Jaroslawicz was involved in an international conspiracy and had absconded with the diamonds and broken the code of the street.

The police did have one point. The critical question was the time of death, and from the lividity alone there was no way to be absolutely certain that Jaroslawicz had really been dead for a week. When a body is kept cold, it can look as if it has been dead for just a day. But we had a new technique for determining the time of death—the potassium eye fluid test. The test measures changes in the level of potassium in the eye fluid. In life, there is a small amount. After death the red cells break down, and the potassium in them enters the vitreous fluid very slowly. The level rises predictably. This happens regardless of temperature. There was enough potassium in Jaroslawicz's eye fluid to account for his having been dead for eight days.

The police were not very happy with this development. They wanted us to confirm that Jaroslawicz had been there only since the last search. They didn't even want to believe that the potassium test was valid. I had to get John Coe, the chief ME in Hennepin County (which includes Minneapolis), the man who developed the technique, on the phone. Coe told the police captain that I wasn't making it up.

I asked the captain in charge of the investigation if I could talk to the cop who had looked under the bench. It turned out that nobody had looked. They had thought the space was too small. I could see why. For a big man, Jaroslawicz had been a very small bundle.

Seven months later at Tal's trial, the courtroom was filled with Hasidim, all in black, the same men who had threatened Dr. Rho and had tried to prevent the autopsy. When I finished testifying that Jaroslawicz had been hit on the head with a two-by-four and suffocated and that Tal had had the opportunity to do it, they burst into spontaneous applause. As much as they hadn't wanted me to do the autopsy, they also didn't want this SOB to get away with breaking the code. Tal was convicted and went to jail. The diamonds were never found.

The diamond district became quiet after this flare-up. The wave of robberies and murders stopped. The vanished courier who had run off to San Juan was forgotten. We analyzed the X rays of the merchant who had been found in the East River to see if he had swallowed anything. If you are carrying diamonds and someone is after you, swallowing them is the natural thing to do. Small opaque whitish spots showed up on the stomach X ray. I invited the New York State commissioner of corrections, who had come down to consult with me, to watch while I opened the stomach. If the white spots were diamonds, I wanted a witness. They weren't. They were little globs of barium. The merchant had had an esophagus problem of some kind and had taken a barium test. The diamonds were gone.

The case had an ironic postscript.

A few years later a doctor in a Queens hospital called me. A newborn baby had died of a rare disease—its bones hadn't developed properly from cartilage. The parents didn't want an autopsy—there was no reason why they should—but the doctor had visions of glory. The X rays showed strange abnormalities that had never been reported or been described in the literature. Undeveloped bones was a brand-new syndrome.

I told the doctor he might get the Nobel Prize for it, but the parents had the right to say no. It was a little more complicated, he said; the mother had taken a new kind of medication when she was pregnant, and the medication could have caused the baby's condition. It could be another thalidomide scandal. That made an autopsy legitimate, and I explained to the family that it could help other people. They agreed.

The doctor was the same rabbi pediatrician who had watched me autopsy Jaroslawicz. Now he was a treating physician. His research was sponsored by the March of Dimes Birth Defects. He was going to write a paper, and he wanted everything on that body tested for everything. The results were all negative. He was not able to connect the child's condition with the drug. He would have to do many more autopsies before he could begin to make any connections.

Very little interferes with the law of the digestive process. It is not precise to the minute (no biological process is), but within a narrow range of time it is very reliable. Within two hours of eating, 95 percent of the food has moved out of the stomach and into the small intestine. It is as elemental as rigor mortis. The process stops at death.

On November 8, 1983, the bodies of Susan Hendricks and her three children, Rebekah, Grace, and Benjamin, were found hacked to death in their house in Bloomington, Illinois. They had been chopped with an ax and sliced with a knife. Blood and gore splattered the walls and ceiling of the room the three children were in. The wife's room was less messy. She had been covered with a blanket before being hacked. The police theorized that she saw it coming and pulled up the covers. David Hendricks, the husband and father, said he had been out of the state for a few days on a business trip when it happened.

On November 3, Hendricks, the president of CASH Manufacturing, had told his secretary he was going on a sales trip to Wisconsin and neighboring states, and was planning to leave the following midnight and drive all night. Hendricks, who had an associate degree in orthotics and prosthetics, was in the backbrace business. He had patented the cruciform anterior spinal hyperextension (CASH) orthosis and ran a mail-order business selling it. His secretary later testified that she was somewhat surprised. This was the only time she could remember his mentioning a departure time, and in fact, the whole trip was a little out of the ordinary—he usually flew when covering long distances.

David and Susan, who had been married for ten years, were members of the Plymouth Brethren, a nondenominational religion of puritanical tenets. Its adherents lived unadorned lives, denying themselves the temptations of civilization. Divorce was not permitted except for reasons of adultery or abandonment. If adultery was suspected, members of the hierarchy investigated and decided on the punishment, which could be shunning or silencing or excommunication.

On the afternoon of Friday, November 4, the day David was to leave, Susan went to a baby shower and David took the children to a pizza parlor for dinner. They arrived at 6:30 P.M. and ordered a medium vegetarian pizza and a pitcher of root beer. The dough and cheese were covered with sliced mushrooms, green peppers, olives, tomatoes, and diced onions. The place was connected to an amusement area with rides and games, and the children played there before and after dinner. They ate between 7:00 and 7:15 P.M. By 9:30 P.M. they were home and in bed. Susan returned about 10:30. David told the police he kissed them all goodbye and left about midnight. He traveled through Illinois and Wisconsin and by morning he was making sales calls, some of which had a strange, dreamlike quality. He told some buyers he hadn't brought samples of his brace with him; he told others that he was on an extended vacation and just wanted to see people who were using or planning to use the brace. Later, the police found both models of his brace in his car.

David called home frequently, trying to reach Susan, but no one answered the phone. He didn't know what to think. He called neighbors and in-laws to tell them he couldn't get an answer at home, and where was Susan? No one was worried. The area they lived in was singularly free of crime. He even called the police and asked them to find out if there had been a car accident. Maybe Susan was in the hospital. The calls finally created a stir, and at 10:30 P.M. on November 8, about half an hour before he returned, neighbors and police found the bodies.

The police were suspicious of the scene. It had a staged, faked look. A chest of drawers was tipped forward and drawers were pulled out, but the frenzy of the killings did not match the neatness of the drawers. They tested for hair and blood samples and latent fingerprints of strangers, but all they found were the hand, palm, and fingerprints of David and Susan on the inside of her checkbook. There was no telling when they had been made—paper preserves prints for a long time. The handles of the ax and butcher knife, which were found with their blades neatly aligned at the foot of one of the children's beds, were wiped clean. There were no bloodstains on David, his clothes, or his car. As odd as it seems, the murderer would not necessarily have been spattered with blood. The body bleeds surprisingly little from the first blow. When the ax hit the head, the blood seeped into the mattress. There are no major arteries in the head and therefore no gushing fountain. The mess comes from "flyers"—blood and tissue are flung on the walls and ceiling as the weapon is waved around for the next blow and the next. If the murderer did get bloody, he could easily have showered and disposed of his clothes along the highway.

David did not go into the house. He was taken to a neighbor's, where the police questioned him for a little over an hour, and then to the station house for more questioning. The next evening a reporter asked him whether the house had been burglarized, and he replied, "They [the police] said that some things looked like some things were taken." But his remark only deepened the suspicions of the police. None of them could remember saying any such thing. How could he know the scene was suggestive of burglary unless he had set it himself? No evidence supported an alien axman theory. They needed evidence to break his alibi, something that would prove he was in the house at the time of the murders.

I was asked to go over the reports and look at the stomach contents.

The children had finished eating at 7:15 P.M. The food should have been digested by 9:15 P.M., two hours later, but the vegetables looked freshly eaten. Digestion of the onions and mushrooms had not yet begun. All of the samples were the same, without eccentricities. Not only the amount of food, but the condition of it was the same for all of them. They all had died at about the same time, and it had to have happened shortly after they got home, less than two hours after eating. This put their father on the spot. (As he learned more about the digestive process, David changed his story slightly, moving his time of departure back toward 11 P.M. The earlier he left, the less likely it was that he could have killed the children, but he couldn't make it early enough.) If the children had been alive at 11:30 P.M.—the time David said he left—or even 10:30, when Susan returned, the pizza would have been completely digested. Susan's stomach contents—crudités, cheese, crackers, and cookies—were also undigested. None of them was alive at 11:30.

The DA was convinced, and during the investigation he found a motive—a crisis of faith. David's growing sexual needs clashed with the constrictions of his marriage and religion. He was trying to create a new and freer life-style but could not break the moral and emotional chains of the old one. Susan was a quiet, unattractive, dowdy woman who wore neither jewelry nor cosmetics. David was her match in plainness, but two years before her death, at the time his business became successful, he changed his appearance from an overweight, greasy-haired, ill-dressed figure to an attractive man—he lost forty pounds, bought clothes that fit him, and had his hair styled minus the grease. He explained the changes on purely practical grounds: he lost weight for health reasons, and someone gave him a free coupon to get his hair done. But the police found a parade of molested back-brace models who had a different explanation—a story of a gradual slide into temptation. The brace was designed to be worn over clothes, but in the spring of 1981 David began telling his models it was necessary to take off their clothes for accurate measurements—first their tops and then everything.

He told one model that nude fittings were standard procedure. She wore a hospital gown under the brace, open in back, and he marked her back with a felt pen. Then she reversed the gown, and he marked her breasts. He was perspiring and couldn't look her in the eye, she said, and she rebuffed him. He told her he was a good Christian, and his wife couldn't find out, and maybe he could take her to Kentucky in his airplane.

At a convention in Phoenix he masqueraded as a doctor and told a model to take off her leotard and bra. He started to massage her back and left breast, but she got nervous and quit. He told another model to take off all her clothes. She wrapped herself in a towel and he asked her to open it. He then made marks beneath her breasts and told her she could drop the towel entirely. She had a medical problem, he said, scoliosis, a condition he could correct temporarily by massaging her spine into alignment. Later that evening they went out. He spoke of his religious conflicts. He had been reared in a very religious household and had studied the scriptures, but now he was having serious doubts about his beliefs. He also told her he had had several affairs, but he thought his infidelity was harmless as long as his wife did not find out. Driving back to town, they stopped to admire the lights of the city from a mountain overlook. He tried to kiss her, but she wasn't interested. At the hotel, he offered to pay her for the modeling and the sightseeing, but she refused. He hugged her and apologized.

At the trial, David explained his behavior by denying some of it, especially the parts about his religion and his wife (even if he was outnumbered, it was his word against the models', after all), and announcing a new development in his business—a universal brace and size chart. The body-hugging brace fittings and felt markers were part of this new idea. He had to make measurements.

Both sides spent lavishly on forensic experts. The prosecution imported four, of which I was one, and the defense called five, including Earl Rose, who had been in Dallas on November 22, 1963. He testified that there were big time variations in the breakdown of food. Those on the defense side sought to muddy the digestive waters. In their view, the digestive tract had ways and means of its own that softened the rules. As the system gurgled along, food moved through in its own good time and for its own reasons, and there were too many eccentricities for anyone to say with certainty how long it took. You could only give an estimate. Exercise in particular modified the time, and the fact that the children had been so active in the amusement area almost definitely slowed the process.

It is true that there are conditions under which the clock is disturbed. Exercise and emotional state can make a small difference—less than an hour. Certain extraordinary situations—the prolonged terror of a kidnapping or rape—would slow digestion considerably, but we were not talking about that. The fact that the digestion of all three of the children was the same confirmed their time of death beyond a 95 percent certainty. The defense was trying to emphasize the 5 percent possibility.

The jury found David guilty of murdering his family, but he appealed the verdict. He disputed the motive the prosecution attributed to him—he hadn't gone to bed with any of the models, he said, and without having been unfaithful he had no reason to kill his wife. And the surfeit of medical examiners debating the inevitability of digestion raised a reasonable doubt about the timing.

He lost the appeal.

8

CRAZY QUILT

MULTIPLE MURDERS

In serial murders, the random factor inspires the most fear—the idea of a wandering murderer, moving from community to community, unknown to all. Anonymous killers are the most difficult to find. There are all kinds, from Jack the Ripper to Son of Sam, and we don't really know how many of their murders are solved. They have us at another disadvantage—many of them operate across state lines, while we are confined to our own territory. The FBI has begun to profile the deaths by computerizing the murder method and the victim's characteristics, but catching multiple murderers still depends mainly on good police work. Most of those who are caught know their victims, and their methods fall into patterns. The role of the ME is to confirm the victims—that is, to certify that they *are* victims of a particular killer—and to find the pattern.

People didn't begin to get openly suspicious until after the ninth child died. Before that, the doctors ascribed the deaths to pneumonia or sudden infant death syndrome (SIDS) or an "inborn error of metabolism," which is a euphemism for bad genes. How else could they explain so many dead children in one family?

In January 1986, shortly after Governor Cuomo announced the formation of the New York State forensic unit, Chief Richard E. Nelson of the Schenectady police department called us on our first official case. He had had a series of nine deaths over fourteen years, all children of Mary Beth and Joseph Tinning. Some of them were crib deaths, but it didn't look right to him, it felt funny, and he thought that the doctors might have made a mistake. Maybe the children had inherited some terrible genetic flaw, but what about the adopted one?

Jennifer was the first to go. Jennifer was a meningitis baby. She died in January 1972, after having lived only nine days. Meningitis is a natural cause, but the disease was older than nine days. Jennifer had been born with it, which is not a common occurrence. It is a disease that comes from bacteria—from shooting heroin with dirty needles, or from a botched self-abortion. Sympathy poured out for Mary Beth Tinning. What a terrible thing it was to lose an infant like that. At least she still had two other healthy children, Joseph, two years old, and Barbara, four years old.

Fifteen days after Jennifer's death, Mary Beth Tinning brought Joseph to the Ellis Hospital emergency room with a quilt wrapped around his head. He had suddenly stopped breathing. He'd had a seizure and suffered brain damage from lack of oxygen. The hospital kept him for ten days, thinking it was a viral infection, and discharged him with medicine to prevent further seizures. Later the same day Tinning brought Joseph back to the emergency room. The medicine did not seem to have worked; he had had a convulsion at home. He was DOA.

No autopsy was done at the hospital. The death certificate lists the cause of death as "cardiorespiratory arrest" due to a seizure disorder, which means that the heart and lungs have stopped functioning. This is what happens to all of us when we die. It is a "wastebasket diagnosis," made in the absence of any true findings.

In March, six weeks after Joseph's death, Tinning brought Barbara, her other child, to the hospital. Barbara was lethargic after a convulsion. The hospital wanted to keep her, but Tinning said no. An hour and a half later she returned with an unconscious and barely breathing child who could not be revived. Barbara was autopsied—nobody was sure what happened—and declared to have died of Reye's syndrome. Reye's syndrome, which later came to be connected to aspirin, was first described by Ralph Douglas Kenneth Reye, an Australian. The symptoms include liver enlargement and brain swelling. Barbara did not have either. Reye's syndrome is another wastebasket diagnosis. Some cause of death had to be put on the autopsy report.

In less than two months, Tinning had lost three children. She had no more left. Enormous sympathy flowed out to her. She became famous in Schenectady; people stopped her on the street to commiserate and offer condolences. She became pregnant again, and in November 1973, Timothy was born. Timothy lasted for nineteen days. Tinning found him in his crib semiconscious, blue, and making odd gurgling noises. She picked him up, but it didn't help. He was DOA at Ellis. Again no autopsy was done. The diagnosis was SIDS.

SIDS, or crib death, only happens to babies who are less than a year old. The baby stops breathing for absolutely no reason that anyone can fathom. No cause has ever been found. There are a lot of theories about it—occult viral infection, milk allergy, hormonal infections, stuffed nose. Most babies are nose breathers, and over half of crib-death babies have colds in the days preceding their death. But SIDS babies don't make noise. They don't gurgle and they don't turn blue. They are just found dead. The only known treatment for or prevention of crib death is to hold the baby. Babies that are picked up don't die.

Crib death looks a lot like suffocation, except that suffocation causes blueness. There is no damage. In suffocation, the lungs stop while the heart continues to pump the residue of oxygen in the body until it runs out. During that time—about five minutes or so—the baby can be resuscitated.

Nathan was born on March 30, 1975, fifteen months after the death of Timothy. At the age of three weeks he ran into trouble. Tinning brought him to St. Clare's Hospital in an ambulance, unconscious and cyanotic (blue). He was having difficulty breathing. Noting that there was blood around his nose and mouth, the hospital transferred him to Albany Medical Center, which is larger, newer, and technologically superior. Albany thought it was pneumonia. The doctors suggested that Tinning could use a little psychiatric help to get her through this time of trouble, but she refused. Nathan stayed in Albany for over a month and recovered. He returned home in May. In September he was gone. Tinning brought him to St. Clare's dead. She was driving the car and heard him gurgle, just as Timothy had, and he was blue. St. Clare's did an autopsy and signed Nathan out with acute pulmonary edema, which is yet another wastebasket diagnosis. Tinning was left without any babies again.

Mary Frances was born three years later, in October 1978. The following January she was brought to St. Clare's, having almost succumbed to SIDS—Tinning said she caught it just in time, picked the baby up, and did mouth-to-mouth resuscitation. Mary Frances had been lying on her back in her crib for five minutes. The doctors, completely in the dark, sent Mary Frances to Boston Children's Hospital for a workup.

After two days, Tinning signed out Mary Frances against the hospital's advice. The hospital ruled out a metabolic disorder and, failing all else, recommended an apnea monitor. An apnea monitor is a machine that is kept by the baby's bed with leads to its chest. It has an alarm that goes off if the child stops breathing. Not even the apnea monitor could save Mary Frances. On February 20, Tinning brought her to St. Clare's in an ambulance, dead. Mary Frances had been just fine until 7:15 that morning, when her mother looked in on her. At 7:30 Tinning heard the alarm going off, but by the time she got to Mary Frances's room, it was too late. Dr. Janet Christman, the pathologist who did the autopsy, found nothing. "There must be an inherited lethal lesion, probably in the heart," she wrote. She didn't test the chromosomes, but everything else had been ruled out. There was no lesion. The death certificate said SIDS. Mary Frances was four months old, the right age for it. She was number six.

Jonathan was born nine months later, in November 1979. Instead of three umbilical blood vessels—two arteries and one vein—he had only two; he was missing one artery. However, his chromosome studies were normal. St. Clare's and Boston did workups and found no congenital abnormality. On February 12, Tinning brought him to St. Clare's cyanotic and not breathing. The doctors found what they thought might be an aberration in the way his body handled urea. Five days later he was back home, but not for long. On February 20 he was readmitted in a coma. At wit's end, St. Clare's sent him to Albany Medical Center, where he lived for two more days. The autopsy was unclear about the cause of death. It was a possible pneumonia, with a question mark. It was a definite cardiorespiratory arrest.

But they still had Michael.

During this long stream of ghastly misfortune, the Tinnings had decided to adopt a child. Six babies born to them had died inexplicably, and everyone thought it was a genetic disorder. If they adopted, the jinx would be broken; there would be no question of an evil inheritance. In 1978, sympathetic agencies found Michael for them. He was eight months old. In February 1981, Tinning brought him to the hospital, vomiting after a fall. The hospital treated him for gastroenteritis and sent him home. A week later, Tinning was driving in the car with him when he was taken ill. She went to the doctor's office, sat down, and calmly waited her turn. It took about ten minutes for the doctor to get to her. She explained that something was wrong with her child, who was out in the car. The nurse ran out, but Michael was dead when she got there. Nobody blamed her.

Dr. Robert L. Sullivan, the chief ME of Schenectady, thought Michael's death might be due to pneumonia and sent tissues to the toxicology lab. He instructed the lab to "rule out suspicion of homicide." Sullivan was the first person to show suspicion. He was not suspicious enough. "Rule out" means consider the possibility, do the tests, and rule it out or not, as the case may be. Toxicology ruled out poisoning only.

Tami Lynne, Tinning's ninth child, was born in August 1985. She lived for four months before being found "unresponsive" in her crib by her mother. There was blood on the pillowcase. An autopsy was performed and the initial diagnosis was SIDS. This was the third SIDS diagnosis.

About three babies in a thousand die of crib death. The odds against two crib deaths in one family are enormous. The odds against three are astronomical. A pathologist who was consulting with the police, initially told me he thought the cause was an "inborn error of metabolism," but there is no such condition that could have affected the adopted child. There is no known genetic disease that can cause sudden death in healthy children. An "inborn error of metabolism" means an enzyme problem, and people get sick from it; they don't die suddenly from it.

Tinning herself was immune to criticism. Throughout all these devastating losses, social workers were sent to help her through her ordeal. Social workers have a conceptual problem with this kind of tragedy. They assume their role is to be an advocate for the bereaved family, not the children. After every death they came to comfort Tinning, who thrived on the attention. Instead of being questioned by the police, she got sympathy from the social workers. The doctors were equally sympathetic. All the death certificates reported natural causes. Nobody wanted to ask hard questions. Tinning became a sympathy junkie. She was the woman who lost the babies.

Through the years, a variety of causes of death were invented to take care of suspension-of-disbelief situations like this. Until 1961, when Dr. Lester Adelson, the ME of Cleveland, wrote "Slaughter of the Innocents," an article about forty-six murdered children, certain thoughts were too monstrous to think. It was not within the realm of social possibility that a parent would intentionally hurt a child, and doctors were reluctant to put in writing that such behavior existed. Instead, there were an inordinate number of deaths from vitamin deficiencies and a great many falls and unexplained accidents.

Now we have brand-new syndromes to account for the inexplicable and the unthinkable. Ondine's syndrome (or curse) is one that has to do with metabolism. (Ondine was a water nymph said to have caused the man who loved her to sleep continuously.) During sleep we take in less oxygen, and the amount of carbon dioxide in the brain rises. At a certain point, the rising level of carbon dioxide warns the brain that it is running low on oxygen and had better take a breath. In theory, in Ondine's syndrome the warning doesn't reach the brain, and it forgets to signal the body to breathe. A recently discovered syndrome is the "shaken-baby syndrome," also known as "infant whiplash syndrome," based on the fact that an infant's head is very big for its body and the neck muscles haven't developed enough to support it. Shaken-baby syndrome is a sort of death by inadvertence: the baby is shaken too hard (entirely by accident), and dies with hemorrhaging in the retina and the back of the brain. If we look carefully, we can usually see where something hard has made contact with the top of the baby's head. Even now, doctors simply don't want to believe that such things go on. Not only were the doctors and hospitals in Albany and Schenectady blind; Boston Children's Hospital, which is connected with the great teaching institution of Harvard and whose staff ought to have known better, did nothing but suggest an apnea monitor for Mary Frances, who was the second SIDS diagnosis.

MEs tend to be intimidated by the social network of SIDS organizations around the country. They have a strong lobbying group and have raised tens of millions of dollars to support research. The guilt and anguish of SIDS parents is terrible to face. They become furious if the ME asks the normal skeptical questions: Was there any plastic around? A dog bite? Suffocation? Sometimes there are accidents; it isn't really crib death. A plastic cover was left in the crib, perhaps. I've found babies under the mattress, the children of drug addicts. There's a lot of denial. SIDS organizations often try to discourage the investigation of these deaths as murders. They admit grudgingly that a real suffocation is possible occasionally, but it's not fair to disturb the other grieving parents. Smothering infants, however, is a repetitive crime. It is one of the few homicides that is repetitive, along with child battery and rape/murders.

Police Chief Nelson of Schenectady got the Tinning records for me. There had been no inquiry whatever. Each death by itself could have been explained away innocently, but not if it was viewed as part of a cluster. Two of the children, Joseph and Timothy, had not been autopsied. The police had been utterly incurious—not only had they not questioned Mary Beth and Joseph Tinning, they had never interviewed their neighbors, friends, or family. The social workers who were sent in lieu of the police found no evidence of child abuse or neglect; there was none to find.

I looked at the pattern. The death of Jennifer, the first baby, was different. All of the others had died of natural causes. She was the only one who had actually had a disease. Jennifer looked to be the victim of a coat hanger: Tinning had been trying to hasten her birth and had only succeeded in introducing meningitis. The police theorized that she wanted to deliver the baby on Christmas Day, like Jesus. She thought her father, who had died while she was pregnant, would have been pleased. Jennifer had disappointed her—she was born on December 26.

According to the records, none of the babies had been found dead in his sleep, the sine qua non of crib death. I ruled out SIDS right away. Tinning said she had picked up one child as it was turning blue, and it died in her arms—but no baby dies of SIDS while being held. The way to prevent SIDS is to pick up the child. Several of the Tinning children had turned blue—in the car, in her arms, in the crib; she brought them to the hospital cyanotic. If a baby is unconscious but alive, SIDS is ruled out. Turning blue is a sign of suffocation—the lungs stop and no oxygen reaches the cells. Nothing happened while the children were in the hospital. The single constant factor in all of these deaths was the presence of Mary Beth Tinning.

Mary Beth Tinning spent over a decade making and losing babies. During all that time the only response she got was a form of encouragement—sympathy, understanding, and compassion. That seems to be the main thing she was after. At family gatherings she considered herself the star, and she would leave in a huff if the rest of the company did not render homage. We looked for other, less frivolous motives, like insurance, but could fine none.

Tinning's husband had not escaped her lethal attentions, either. In 1974 he was rushed to the hospital with barbiturate poisoning. He was a man who did not take barbiturates. His wife admitted that she had added them to his cereal. She was having an affair with a minister at the time, and somehow could not juggle two men. But Joseph Tinning, as laid-back as his wife was strong-minded, did not feel that his marriage had been destroyed by this attempt to annihilate him, and bore his wife no ill will. He still supports her.

After the pathologist, the police, and I discussed his "inborn error of metabolism" theory, he concluded that Tami Lynne had died of suffocation, not SIDS, and a policewoman was sent to interview Tinning. She told Tinning a number of things that should have been said before, in particular that her stories were not consistent with the autopsy findings. Tinning started to confess. She confessed to the attempted murder of her husband and to smothering Tami Lynne, Timothy, and Nathan—and then it began to get late and she went to sleep. The next day, her lawyer told her not to say anything else.

After her confession, everyone—hospital staff, doctors, neighbors, social workers—came forward claiming to have been suspicious all along, but not enough to have done anything about it. Tinning had told people that her children had congenital heart defects, a reasonable story.

The Schenectady DA determined that he could charge her with Tami Lynne's death, but it was necessary to reexamine the remains of Nathan and Timothy before making a finding. We exhumed Nathan's body. It had nothing wrong with it. He was healthy but dead, a state that was in line with smothering. We ran into a little trouble at the exhumation of Timothy. There had been a mixup. The coffin contained the remains of another child. The parents had been grieving at the wrong grave. Tinning was indicted for the last death, that of Tami Lynne. She was tried, convicted, and is appealing. The rest of the case is in limbo, awaiting further developments.

The confusing thing about the .22 caliber killer (who later came to be known as the Buffalo Slasher) was his versatility. Serial murderers repeat themselves, favoring a certain weapon, a particular approach, a style. The Slasher used several weapons—guns, knives, hammers, screwdrivers—which drew attention away from his style. He left a pile of victims, all but one of them black men and that one a dark-skinned Hispanic, and that threw the police, too. Racism was the obvious inference, but the real pattern was more subtle than that.

The first killings took place on September 22 and 23, 1980. Four black men, three in Buffalo and one in Niagara Falls, were shot at close range with a sawed-off .22 caliber rifle. They had no connection with each other. The killer simply walked right up to them on the street and pulled the trigger. The gun was hidden in a brown paper bag whose purpose was also to catch the shells.

He got away clean in Buffalo, but he was almost undone in Niagara Falls. He was a stranger there, unfamiliar with the streets, and after the shooting a crowd of people started to chase him. They almost caught him, but he got away in his sister's car, driving across one of the bridges that connects Niagara Falls with Buffalo. His escape was not without a trace. As he fled, he dropped the shell casing from the bullet, a fact that was reported in newspaper accounts of the killing. The .22 caliber killer never struck again.

Two weeks later, a new orgy of violence erupted. Two black cabdrivers in Buffalo were found dead on successive nights in an isolated wooded section near the water. Their hearts had been cut out. The newspaper headlines were unnerving, although people tend to forget that in a grisly crime like this, the victim is dead before his heart is removed. But a maniac was loose, and it looked as if he had declared open season on black men. There was talk of a white conspiracy: white cops and a white DA were investigating the killings, and a white ME had done the autopsies. The ME didn't provide much information—she wasn't even sure of the weapon—and the blacks thought she was covering things up. Unfortunately, Buffalo's black chief ME, Dr. Justin Uku, was on vacation visiting his family in Nigeria. As the hysteria level rose, people began to see a nationwide conspiracy to kill black men. The Buffalo Slasher could be responsible for most of the unsolved murders of black men not only in Buffalo, Rochester (where four people were shot), and New York City, but also in Atlanta, where the entire city was hysterical over a series of child murders. Even a succession of choke hold deaths committed by the police in Los Angeles was considered part of the plot.

After the heart murders there were fears of a riot. Michael Kelly, the assistant DA in charge of homicides in Erie County, asked me to reautopsy the two cabdrivers before they were buried. It was 1980; Koch had already demoted me and in the process had unwittingly bestowed on me a reputation for being objective. After doing the postmortems, I sat down with the families. Previously, they had been ignored, and they didn't think they were getting the whole story. I explained the findings, and they were satisfied that at least a proper investigation was being done.

After the second postmortem, a picture of the killer began to emerge. One of the cabdrivers had been stabbed in the back of the head with a screwdriver, an act which requires a great deal of strength. The skull of the other cabdriver had been fractured with a small square-faced hammer. Both had been stabbed many times in front, and cut through the sternum (breastbone). There were different kinds of cuts on the bodies. Some were like stab wounds from a knife, and some—very sharp—looked as if an instrument like a linoleum cutter had been used.

In order to accomplish all this, the killer not only had to have been carrying a small hardware store, he had to know anatomy. It's not easy to remove an organ like the heart—or any organ— unless you know what you are doing. The average untrained murderer doesn't know that he has to cut laterally between the ribs to get to the chest cavity. Once there, the heart is not just sitting around in plain view; it is surrounded by a sac to protect it, and the sac has to be cut separately before the heart can be reached. This was a killer who knew. The hearts were surgically detached from their connecting blood vessels without unnecessary tearing of the sac. The procedure is to separate the ribs (not break them) and reach in blindly, knowing exactly what you will find. The choice of weapon, which combined both sharpness and heft, was knowledgeable. I thought perhaps our man was a hunter.

He also had to be endowed with enough self-confidence to go hand-to-hand with his victims. Nobody sits there and allows himself to be jabbed in the head with a screwdriver. I thought I saw a pattern. Because of his swagger, his brazenness, and his ability to work in such close quarters, I thought the .22 caliber killer was the same person as the Buffalo Slasher. Although the method was different, the killer needed the same physical assurance to walk up close to his victims and shoot them. He knew he was stronger and quicker than they and could deflect any blows they might try to deliver. The two cabdrivers were not novices, either; they knew their way around the streets, and each had an arrest record. The pattern wasn't the weapon, it was the fearlessness, the confidence in his ability to handle himself. Most murderers don't exhibit those qualities. They prefer an arm's-length relationship. They don't want their victim to be in a position to grab at them.

In December, a few days before Christmas, a series of random slashings took place in New York City. The killer ran up to people on the street (and one in the subway) and stabbed them with a knife. He killed four people that way—three black men and one dark-skinned Hispanic—all strangers to him and to each other. Two others were also stabbed, but they lived.

In Buffalo, Michael Kelly, the assistant DA who had first called me in, and Ed Cosgrove, the DA of Erie County, also thought the Buffalo killer and the New York Slasher might be the same man because of the combativeness, the bravado. Another detective, Sam Slade, considered by his colleagues to be the best homicide detective in New York State, thought that psychologically, using a knife was an upgrading in self-esteem, an escalation of personal daring. It was more courageous than a gun; it was face-to-face combat.

But this was the third shift in weapons, and no one could be certain. Slade connected the slashings and the shootings, but the cabdriver deaths were too crazy. Was this the same man who cut out hearts? I thought it was. I argued that people change methods in midstream when they have good reason to do so. Look at the Atlanta child murders—all of a sudden the victims were turning up undressed, because the killer had read that the police were getting fiber evidence from their clothes. The .22 caliber killer switched because he was afraid the police were getting too close to the gun. Why wouldn't he switch again if he felt threatened?

One way to find out more was to look at the autopsy reports of the five people who were stabbed to death in New York City. Kelly asked and was turned down. The files were locked up, unviewable, he was told by Elliot Gross. Gross refused to open them without permission from Robert Morgenthau. He didn't think there was any connection anyway, and neither did Morgenthau.

Regardless, a state trooper was dispatched to Gross's office. He was thrown out. Throwing out colleagues is simply not done. It comes under the heading of professional discourtesy. Even if it was a wild-goose chase, a sister agency had a right to see the files. Kelly and Cosgrove tried to win over a high-ranking police official, a New York City deputy chief of detectives, but he thought the connection was absurd, too. He went so far as to leak it to the press, the subtext of his story being ridicule: look at these hicks from upstate trying to get publicity; they think they can enhance their importance by associating with us. Neither the official nor the reporters mentioned that Buffalo's 75 percent rate of solved homicides is higher than New York City's 65 percent, which is below average. (The national "solve" rate is about 70 percent.)

Getting the records from the city turned into a battle of the DAs. Morgenthau got into it, echoing the upstate hick line. Cosgrove, who happened to be president of the New York State District Attorneys Association, was angered by the high-and-mighty tone and finally convinced Morgenthau to let us see the files.

Even after we had permission, the graciousness level stayed below the freezing point. Gross wouldn't let the reports out of his office. Kelly and I had to sit there and read through them under the watchful eye of his assistant MEs. He had five of them. It was almost as if they were afraid we would steal something. Gross himself sat at the head of the big conference table, bristling like a porcupine. It was very uncomfortable. At the time, I was deputy chief ME in Queens and under Gross's jurisdiction, but I was in his office under other colors, as a consultant to Buffalo and a colleague of Kelly's.

But none of this mattered. The minute I saw the photographs I knew. It was obvious that one person had done the killings. All of the New York City stabbing victims looked alike. They were young brown-skinned men with thin moustaches, and they could have been brothers to the .22 caliber victims in Buffalo. In a random selection it would have been extraordinary if two of them had looked alike. None of Gross's five people had noticed the resemblance. Each of them had autopsied only one case. Also, I had the advantage of having seen the upstate victims. It was really an accident that I noticed the faces at all. Wounds are what we examine, not faces. It just happened to hit me.

We felt satisfied with our connection, but it wasn't enough to establish definitely that the Slasher was also the .22 killer. Detectives had found four shell casings (the paper bag had not been foolproof) at the scenes of the shootings, and they had .22 caliber bullets that had been taken out of the victims. They had no gun, but the gun could be traced through the bullets.

Bullets can be identified by their size (.32, .38, etc.) and by the number of lands and grooves they have. While a rifle or handgun is being made, an instrument is fitted into the barrel to rifle it—that is, to make spiral grooves in it. The raised surfaces between the grooves, called lands, put a spin on the bullet (necessary for accuracy). The rifling pattern is imprinted on the bullet as it passes through the barrel when the gun is fired. Every type of gun—every Colt .38, say—has the same number of lands and grooves spiraling in the same direction—left twist or right twist. But there are also microscopic markings made on the bullet as it comes out of the barrel, tiny imperfections that are unique to each gun. Ballistics specialists use them to match up the bullet with the gun it was fired from.

Sam Slade, the homicide detective, took charge of the bullets. He sent them to the FBI crime lab for an analysis of the lands and grooves. The lab reported that the bullets could have been fired from five possible makes of weapons. Four were handguns and one was a rifle. Slade also had shell casings, and the casings bore the imprint of the firing pin, which strikes the back of the bullet. Knowing the imprint, the process of exclusion was easy. Slade got illustrations of firing-pin marks from all five gun manufacturers, and was able to eliminate three of the weapons. The remaining two, a handgun and a rifle, were both made by the Sturm Ruger gun company in Southport, Connecticut. From the company's specifications, the murder weapon had to be a .22 rifle. Slade knew from witnesses that the .22 killer wasn't walking around with a rifle slung over his shoulder. The gun had been hidden in a brown paper bag. That meant the barrel had been sawed off.

In January 1981, a strange story wafted its way to Buffalo from Fort Benning, Georgia. Private Joseph C. Christopher, a white soldier, was arrested for attacking a black soldier with a paring knife. The victim was brown-skinned and youthful and had a thin moustache. Christopher was put into the stockade, where he tried to emasculate himself with a razor blade, after which he was transferred to the base hospital. There he began to unravel and confessed to a nurse that he had killed blacks in Buffalo and New York City, that he "had to" do it. The nurse reported it, and the police immediately connected him with the Buffalo Slasher.

They traced his itinerary, and he was in the right places at the right times. He was the sort of person who kept things, and he still had a bus ticket dated December 19, 1980, from Fort Benning to New York City, where, on December 22, four people were killed with a stiletto. He was on his Christmas furlough. He had continued on to Buffalo, arriving on either Christmas Eve or Christmas Day. While he was there, a black man was stabbed to death at a bus stop, and the next morning another one was killed in the same way in Rochester, eighty miles away. Several other blacks in Buffalo survived stabbing attacks.

Slade got a warrant to search the house in Buffalo where Christopher lived with his mother and sisters. His mother had converted the living room into a shrine, with candles burning under a picture of his dead father. Christopher was born and raised in an Italian neighborhood by a dominant father and a passive mother. His father was a maintenance worker with the Buffalo sanitation department. His mother was a registered nurse. He had three sisters, two of them older than he. He adored his father, Nicholas, an outdoorsman and a hunter, who taught him to shoot. In 1976, when Christopher was fourteen, his father died, and Christopher inherited his gun collection.

In the basement of the house was a workshop. Slade found screwdrivers and hammers and a single bullet that had misfired. The bullet and shell hadn't separated. It matched the firing-pin imprint on the cartridge that Slade had picked up at the scene. Christopher's father also had a hunting lodge forty miles southwest of Buffalo, which Christopher had helped him build. They went there to shoot. On the grass near the house Slade found two spent cartridges. They also matched. The lodge was an armory. He found .22 caliber ammunition, a gun collection, and the sawed-off barrel of a .22 rifle—but not the rifle. The weapon was missing.

Christopher made a videotaped confession to his psychiatrist, admitting to the shootings in Buffalo, the subway slashing in New York, and the murder of the two cabdrivers. A confession alone is not enough—people often come in off the street and confess to all sorts of crimes they may or may not have committed— but Christopher knew things that only the killer could have known. He knew that the second cabdriver had been killed with a screwdriver, and he knew about the saplings. The body of the first cabdriver had been hidden in a wooded area, and saplings had been cut down to cover it. The police hadn't been able to figure out what tool the murderer had used to cut the trunks.

On the videotape, Christopher mentioned in an offhanded way that he had chopped down the saplings with a small hatchet.

Christopher's friends were stunned by his confession. The woman he had once lived with said she couldn't recognize him from the newspaper accounts. "The Joe Christopher I'm reading and hearing about is not the Joe Christopher I knew," she told the *New York Times.*

Other friends, black and white, confirmed that Christopher was singularly ordinary. He had worked as an unarmed guard and as a maintenance man; he liked to hunt and fish (his greatest passion was the outdoors); he was neither angry nor violent nor a racist. In fact, he socialized with blacks and worked with them in the home improvement business. In 1978, two years before the killings began, for no particular reason his life began to fall apart. He broke up with the woman he had been living with and quarreled with his black coworker and friend. He moved back into his mother's house. He fell asleep at his security job and was sacked in 1979. Friends say he started drinking. It was almost as if he had made a conscious decision to shut down his life, or that cycle of it, and go into hibernation. In September 1980, one week before the .22 caliber killings began, he enlisted in the Army. He didn't have to report to Fort Benning until mid-November.

What was his motive? Although Christopher felt compelled to confess, he had no such compulsion to explain himself. He was different from the normal serial killer. He didn't quite fit our preconceived ideas of what he should be. He wasn't killing for fun or for money or even for sex; and he was killing blacks despite the fact that he had black friends. He didn't seem to be killing for hate. He could be one of the hallucinating psychotics, like Son of Sam, the select few who hear God or the devil telling them to kill. He could also be a sexual sadist, a killer for whom the real purpose is a show of physical superiority and aggression. Studies show such people to be outwardly friendly. They have no criminal record before they start their career in murder.

Often there is a conflict with their adult sexuality. Their family and friends are invariably shocked. In these situations, the victim is significant. The victim represents something.

The Army has a theory, a riff on guilt and shame and a sexual conflict that could not be resolved. The Army thinks Christopher is gay. He was friendly with black soldiers, but his relationships had another dimension—he performed fellatio on them in the stockade in return for extra food. He also made a pass at the captain of the stockade. The Army thought he was physically attracted to a particular type (thin, with a moustache), but he knew the men were off limits. So he tried to destroy the thing that was tempting him. By killing them he proved he was macho, like his father. Joining the Army was part of the need to be macho, too, to meet his father's expectations.

The prison psychiatrist, who observed him briefly, thought the truth about Christopher might be simple racism. He had trouble getting along with some of the blacks in prison. But the psychiatrist does not have much information. No effort is made to study the minds of prisoners, to learn what made them killers, and to try to prevent it in the future.

Christopher's trial in Buffalo proceeded without exploring his motives. He was convicted of the three Buffalo .22 caliber shootings, and in New York City he was convicted of the four slashings. Morgenthau apologized to Michael Kelly.

Christopher was not tried for the shooting case in Niagara Falls or for killing the two cabdrivers. Everyone is backing off from those. The method of killing the cabbies was too crazy to risk a trial. If a court should rule that Christopher was mentally incompetent, his other convictions might be questioned and the findings overturned. As things stand, people are safe enough from him. He was put in prison for four murders and can't be considered for parole until 2099. In prison he lives in special housing to protect him from being attacked by blacks. Meanwhile, he was diagnosed as a schizophrenic and is deteriorating.

He is isolated, a loner, and doesn't talk to anyone. He won't even permit blood to be drawn for medical tests.

One other loose end is still dangling. The police never found the sawed-off .22, and it bothered them. Maybe it was at the bottom of the Niagara River, thrown out of the car while Christopher was escaping from the crowd, but maybe it wasn't. Would Joe Christopher throw away his father's gun? More likely he would have hidden it, cherished it. Could he possibly have buried it in his father's grave? It was an intriguing idea. Rumor has it that gravediggers went to the cemetery in the middle of the night and surreptitiously dug up Nicholas Christopher's grave. It is fairly easy to do—you just take off the topsoil with the grass, all in one piece, and then lay it back on the ground when you are finished. The metal detector they brought along picked up a long metal object, and they were elated—they thought they had finally found the gun. But they hadn't; it turned out to be a flower holder.

Richard Kuklinski was a free-lance scammer, a man of many deals, whose business interests included cars, food, and guns. He liked to spray cyanide in people's faces. ". . . there are people . . . all over the country that have died from something . . . that wasn't natural, let's put it that way," he told an undercover agent. An imposing bear of a man, he had the energy and vitality required to keep all his deals going; at the same time, he had taken the precaution of learning about the ME trade. He knew that cold storage was the solution to the alibi problem—if he froze a body for a year or two and then defrosted it, no one could tell the time of death. The police dubbed him the Ice Man (his personality, too, was cold, calculating, icy), but he also kept up with other aspects of forensic medicine, arranging his schemes with our vulnerabilities in mind. He knew that MEs rarely suspect cyanide, and he knew which foods would hide the taste of it. His family was ignorant of his line of work, but they lived a gambler's life—one day they were rolling in money and the next they were broke. His business associates had a way of disappearing after they met with him.

George Malliband of Huntingdon, Pennsylvania, was his first known victim. On January 31, 1980, Malliband left home with $27,000 and met Kuklinski in his office in Emerson, New Jersey. Kuklinski owed him $35,000 from a previous deal, and that, added to the $27,000, made a $62,000 deal for Malliband. Kuklinski was selling him pornographic videos and blank tape at a profit, and Malliband planned to resell them for an even bigger profit.

The day after the meeting, Malliband's brother Donald received several nervous phone calls from him, saying he was afraid Kuklinski was "setting him up." Nobody ever saw or heard from Malliband again. Four days later, he was found in a fifty-five-gallon drum in Jersey City with four gunshot wounds in his chest. His family told the police that while Kuklinski was setting up the deal, he called Malliband fifteen times. On the strength of the phone calls, the police started sniffing around Kuklinski, but they found nothing.

The second scam—a rerun of the videotape deal—was more ambitious. On July 1, 1981, Louis Masgay put together $95,000 in cash, hid it in a secret door panel of his car, and left home to meet Kuklinski in a diner in Little Falls, New Jersey. Masgay was at a pitch of excitement. Kuklinski had been playing him on a string, something he did to perfection. His entire MO was based on the psychology of anticipation. He made numberless phone calls to his mark, luring him on, stirring up his greed and playing on his fear that the deal might fall through. He escalated the amount of cash he needed before the deal could be done. The final twist was withdrawal—not delivering and not delivering until his mark was in a state of high tension. He'd done a particularly fine job on Masgay. In June, the month before this final meeting, Masgay had left his home in Forty-Fort, Pennsylvania, five times to meet Kuklinski, and Kuklinski had stood him up each time. Each time Masgay had been carrying over

$50,000. Now he was frantic to consummate the deal. He had become obsessed with it. He was expecting to make a huge profit, and his family thought that Kuklinski had prevailed on him to bring even more money this last time. On July 1, the day of the meeting, Louis Masgay vanished. That same day his abandoned car was found; the secret panel had been ripped open and the money was gone.

Two years later, in September 1983, Masgay's body was found in Rockland County, New York, wrapped in plastic bags and wearing the same clothes he had worn on the day of his disappearance. Like his predecessor, he had been shot, but he had only just begun to decay. He looked fresh, as if he had died the day before. When the ME did the autopsy, he noticed ice in the tissues. Kuklinski had miscalculated slightly—the plastic wrapping had kept the cold in, and the body had been found a little early, before the ice had melted completely. Masgay was identified from his fingerprints, after which the police were able to connect him with Kuklinski through the toll phone calls. They later found a witness (a convicted murderer) who had worked for Kuklinski in his rented warehouse in North Bergen. The warehouse contained an industrial freezer, an abandoned well, and other amenities. The witness had had occasion to go into the freezer and had seen Masgay hanging there, but had decided not to mention it to anyone lest he end up keeping Masgay company.

Kuklinski was aware by now that the police were interested in his affairs and became more cautious. For his next victim he assumed the name of Charlie Brown. On April 29, 1982, Paul Hoffman, a pharmacist, went to meet him with $25,000. This time the bait was a hijacked shipment of Tagamet. Tagamet is a prescription drug to ease the pain of ulcers. It was the most frequently prescribed drug in the country. The going rate was $36.00 for 100 tablets. Hoffman was going to buy it for $9. Like Masgay, Hoffman became obsessed. His wife and son and partner remember him getting calls and then, after talking about the deal, becoming irritable and frustrated, fearful that it might not go through. On the few occasions when they picked up the phone, a man named Charlie Brown was on the other end. The police traced the toll calls to Kuklinski. In five months, Kuklinski had called Hoffman forty-five times. After April 29, the day they were to meet, the calls stopped.

Hoffman and his station wagon both disappeared. A year later, the car was found in Kuklinski's rented warehouse, where he stored and moved cars for his auto-theft business. Hoffman's body was never recovered, but the police think they have a good idea of what happened to it. The people who rented the warehouse after Kuklinski left noticed a foul odor coming from the abandoned well, which had been capped with cement. The police went down, but all they saw were some plastic bags and other debris. The well narrowed and fed into an underground stream, and they could follow it no farther.

Bits and pieces of evidence were gradually piling up against Kuklinski. There wasn't nearly enough to arrest him, but two of his associates, Daniel Deppner and Gary Smith, hadn't been so clever at covering their tracks. On December 17, 1982, the police issued a warrant for Deppner, charging him with stealing cars. Smith's warrant was out already, charging him with stealing checks and cashing them. They searched Smith's house, where both men lived, but the two of them had already run to Kuklinski, who hid them in various New Jersey motels—the York, the Liberty, the Skyview—and fed them.

It wasn't long before Kuklinski began to worry about their stability. He couldn't hide them indefinitely, and Smith, in particular, had a weak personality. If he were caught he would not be tough enough to withstand the pressures; he would make a deal to save his own neck and be a witness against Kuklinski. With Deppner assisting, Kuklinski killed Smith in Room 31 of the York Motel. It was a two-step operation—first the cyanide and then the lamp cord. Kuklinski, who was supplying the food, cooked meals at home and brought them to the motel in a Teflon

Dr Baden explaining the trajectory of the bullet that struck President Kennedy's head to the Select Committee on Assassinations, U.S. House of Representatives, in 1979.

Photograph of President Kennedy showing the emergency tracheotomy made to help him breathe, at Parkland Hospital in Dallas. The incision cut through and obscured the exit wound in his neck. (*Jack Fox*)

The entrance wound in the back of President Kennedy's head from the first shot that hit him. The wound fragmented his skull.

Diagram reconstructing the entry points and trajectories of the two gunshots to the head and upper back of President Kennedy.

A 1979 enhancement of the 1963 X-ray of President Kennedy's head (taken before the autopsy), showing the path of the bullet. The white spots are fragments of the bullet that entered the back of his head and exited above his right ear.

The first page of the official 1963 autopsy report, prepared by Col. James J. Humes. The organ weights are incomplete or erroneous, and the diagram of the bullet tracks is inaccurate.

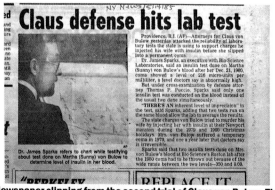

NY News/5/4/85

Claus defense hits lab test

Providence, R.I. (AP)—Attorneys for Claus von Bulow yesterday attacked the reliability of laboratory tests the state is using to support charges he injected his wife with insulin before she slipped into a permanent coma.

Dr. James Sparks, an executive with Bio-Science Laboratories, said an insulin test done on Martha (Sunny) von Bulow's blood after her Dec. 21, 1980, coma showed a level of 216 micro-units per milliliter, a level doctors say is abnormally high.

But under cross-examination by defense attorney Thomas P. Puccio, Sparks said only one insulin test was conducted on the blood instead of the usual two done simultaneously.

"THERE'S AN inherent level of imprecision" in the test, said Sparks, adding that two tests run on the same blood allow the lab to average the results.

The state charges von Bulow tried to murder his wife by injecting her with insulin at their Newport mansion during the 1979 and 1980 Christmas holidays. Mrs. von Bulow suffered a temporary coma in 1979, and one a year later that doctors say is irreversible.

Sparks said that two insulin tests done on Mrs. von Bulow's blood at Bio-Science's Boston lab after the 1980 coma had to be thrown out because of the wide range between the two levels—350 and 0.08.

Dr. James Sparks refers to chart while testifying about test done on Martha (Sunny) von Bulow to determine level of insulin in her blood.

Newspaper clipping from the second trial of Claus von Bulow. The defence attorney successfully challenged the laboratory findings of insulin and convinced the court that Sunny von Bulow's coma had not been caused by insulin.

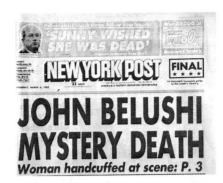

The most mysterious thing about John Belushi's death was the hour it took place. In establishing the time of death, we were able to identify the person who caused it.

On the night of their murder, the Hendricks children ate a mushroom, tomato, green pepper and onion pizza for dinner. At autopsy the amount of undigested pizza in their stomachs was critical in establishing the time of death and the guilt of their father.

The Italian restaurant in Brooklyn where Carmine Galante, head of the five Mafia families of New York, was shotgunned to death while eating lunch with his henchmen. It has since become a Chinese restaurant.

Close-up of Carmine Galante, just after he was killed, lying on his back on the ground, his cigar still clenched in his teeth.

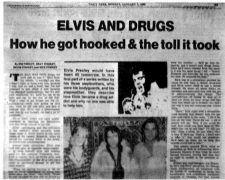

Top. The cause of Elvis Presley's death was the subject of much conjecture. The coroner finally decided it was heart disease.

Bottom. Reports leaked out that heart disease wasn't the whole story of Elvis Presley's death — that he had at least ten different prescription drugs in his body.

Photograph of an anonymous girl with shaved hair who had been shot in the head. The entrance wound, on top of the head, is round and surrounded by soot, revealing it to be a contact wound. The exit wound, to the right of it, has no soot or abrasion.

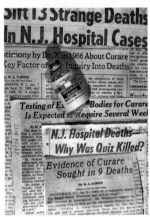

A small bottle of curare, the exotic poison used by 'Dr. X' to kill his colleagues' patients in the hospital.

Drawing of the entrance wound in the right side of the jaw and the trajectory of the bullet through the body that killed Dr. Martin Luther King Jr.

Marilyn Monroe in death. This picture was taken after autopsy and it is the pathologist's work which caused the face to sag. Before the procedure, say those present, the lifeless Marilyn remained beautiful.
(*This photograph was first reproduced in GODDESS by Anthony Summers, Sphere Books 1986.*)

pan. Smith liked hamburgers, which made things a little difficult—as Kuklinski later observed, you can't sprinkle cyanide on hamburgers; nobody would eat them with white stuff all over them. So he had to mix the cyanide into the ketchup. The purpose of the cyanide was mainly to knock Smith out (people have been known to survive doses of cyanide), preparatory to the main event—strangulation. No adult will permit himself to be strangled without putting up a fight, and Kuklinski was not interested in a physical struggle.

They put Smith's body under the bed, which had a wooden platform frame and box springs. The York Motel, which is just across the Lincoln Tunnel from Manhattan, had a high turnover rate. In December the rooms were warm; the heat was turned up to 80 degrees. Beneath the bed in the closed space it was about 100 degrees. Smith stayed under there for four days, during which time the room was rented more than a dozen times. The maid, who changed the sheets occasionally, complained about the smell, but the spring was on top of the body and she couldn't see under the bed. Smith was finally found on December 27.

The Bergen County ME who did the autopsy couldn't find the cause of death, but Dr. Geetha Natarajan, New Jersey assistant ME, saw a ligature mark around the neck, a furrow about as thin as an electrical wire from a lamp. She also observed that the beans in the stomach were charred at one end, and concluded that they were probably homemade. What restaurant would serve burned beans? Kuklinski had been right. No one looked for cyanide. There was no reason to.

During their ten-day motel shuffle, Smith and Deppner had called their wives frequently. Before his death, Smith told his wife, Veronica, he was afraid for his life. Deppner told his, Barbara, everything—that the three of them stole cars and transported them out of the state and ran chop shops. He called her before and after killing Smith, and told her how it was done, and that he thought he, too, was becoming dispensable. Barbara tried to save him: she told the police the story and asked them to protect him. In January 1983, the month after Smith's body was found, the police started looking for him. They wanted him for burglary, car theft, and stealing car parts. He was still broke and dependent on Kuklinski, who was still moving him from one motel to another under assumed names and feeding him. Kuklinski decided he had to go.

In May, a man riding a bicycle on Clinton Road in West Milford, New Jersey, near Passaic, saw a large bird—he thought it was a turkey buzzard—lift off and fly away. He went closer and saw a plastic garbage bag with a human head sticking out of it. It had a bushy, reddish Fu Manchu moustache and was missing four front teeth. The left arm was also sticking out. The body was inside two green garbage bags that were taped together in the middle. The police found motel receipts and private phone numbers in a pocket. The site was about three and a half miles from the Blazing Bucks Ranch, a property Kuklinski had an interest in. At some time in February, Kuklinski had asked his daughter's live-in fiancé, Richard Patterson, to help him get rid of something in the woods. Patterson was agreeable, but after catching a glimpse of what he was getting rid of he decided this was not the sort of family he wanted to marry into and relocated to Florida.

Dr. Natarajan did the autopsy. She found processed meat—hot dogs or Spam—and the same curiously burned beans in Deppner's stomach as she had found in Gary Smith's. She also saw a ligature mark on the neck and thought the cause was strangulation. From the way the body was discovered and from the lack of any other cause—no gunshot wound, no stab wound, no blunt force, no heart disease, no brain damage—it had to be murder. Her conclusion was based partly on instinct and partly on experience—the way we all operate. But her office didn't think this exclusionary process was strong enough to call the death a murder and thought the ligature mark could be an artifact of decomposition. Natarajan was certain enough of the ligature mark to call the manner of death a homicide, but signed it out as "cause undetermined."

At this point the police had a stack of murders and a chief suspect but no hard evidence and no witnesses. Someone had to go undercover to smoke out Kuklinski. Kuklinski had been dealing in weapons, promising buyers guns for cash, and this opened the door to the Feds. The Bureau of Alcohol, Tobacco, and Firearms wired one of its agents, Dominick Polifrone, and sent him in. Polifrone started hanging around one of Kuklinski's favorite bars. They met in September 1986, and in the course of establishing his credentials, Polifrone had to get up and punch someone.

Most of their conversations took place at the Vincent Lombardi truck stop on the New Jersey Turnpike, known as a favorite hangout for dealmakers trying to score. Polifrone's fellow agents sat in a car nearby, recording. Kuklinski kept wanting to talk in the bathroom, and Polifrone was never sure if he was on to him. He always refused. His fellow agents couldn't prevent Kuklinski from killing him in a bathroom.

It took a few weeks for the deal to take shape. They sparred back and forth, each offering a challenge, each trying to fool the other. Kuklinski was interested in cocaine. Polifrone said he could handle that—he could sell Kuklinski a kilo for $31,000. He would get it from a "rich kid." (The rich kid was really Paul Smith, another agent.) To make sure that Kuklinski knew he was a cold-blooded businessman, Polifrone suggested that they kill the kid and split the money—Polifrone would set him up and Kuklinski would waste him. Polifrone said he was looking for guns, "heavy steel." That was no problem for Kuklinski. He had a supplier who could get machine guns, grenades, silencers, plastique, everything—and all of it Grade A NATO stuff.

Kuklinski discoursed on the advantages of cyanide—"It's quiet, it's not messy, it's not noisy . . . there's even a spray mist around . . . you spray it in somebody's face and they go to sleep. . . ." He was a throwback to the old Murder, Inc., crowd.

He described a test murder he had committed on the street, just walking along in a crowd with a handkerchief over his nose and spraying a man. The man collapsed and died, and everyone thought he'd had a heart attack. "The best effect is to get 'em in the nose, they get it in the nose, and they inhale it," he said. But he wasn't married to this method—if Polifrone wanted to give him a contract, he could do it with lead, steel, anything.

Kuklinski also boasted that he had used cyanide to kill other people, and had outwitted the police—they had been watching him since 1980 and couldn't pin anything on him. He'd even frozen a corpse to confuse the time of death. He told Polifrone how he put someone in a fifty-five-gallon drum (no names were mentioned), and described his one-two method of killing with cyanide and strangulation. Polifrone knew that Kuklinski wouldn't be telling him all these secrets unless he was planning to kill him. The only question was when.

The deal finally began to come together in October at a truck stop in Ridgefield, New Jersey. Kuklinski sold Polifrone a first-quality handgun with a silencer for $1,100 (a sample of future attractions) and agreed to kill the "rich kid." He would do it with poison. (". . . why be messy?" he said on the tapes. "You do it nice and calm.") But Polifrone would have to supply the cyanide—ever since his regular supplier, Paul Hoffman the pharmacist, had disappeared down the well, his cache had dwindled. After this act of bonding, they would do the arms deal. Polifrone would deliver the money, and instead of getting guns, he would get killed.

They worked with beepers. Kuklinski beeped Polifrone to ask if he had "the big package" (cocaine) and "the little package" (cyanide) yet—he was ready to buy. Polifrone wasn't ready to sell yet—there had been an incident of tampering with Lipton Soup in a grocery store, and things were tight. Would Polifrone like to meet Kuklinski's armaments friend? No, Polifrone definitely would not. (It would be two against one, and prearranged meetings were dangerous. Other things could be prearranged, too.)

On December 17 they met at the Lombardi truck stop. Polifrone brought three scrambled egg sandwiches and a jar of quinine—a cyanide look-alike—to put on them. They would meet the "rich kid" at a motel (Polifrone had already pointed him out to Kuklinski) and socialize a little. After lunch they would take his cocaine and strangle him. The strangling was just to make sure. For all his cavalier attitude about cyanide, Kuklinski did not seem to know the exact amount needed to kill—less than 200 milligrams, or the contents of one capsule.

Kuklinski took the sandwiches and went home, promising to return with a van, a drum and sealer, gloves, and whatever else was necessary to dispose of the body. But the police were too nervous to let it go any further. They weren't sure what surprises he might be cooking up—for all they knew, a couple of men with guns would suddenly appear and blow Polifrone away. They gave Kuklinski ten minutes to doctor the rich kid's sandwich—and maybe Polifrone's, too—and then arrested him, charging him with five murders. His wife was in the car and a handgun was under the seat. They charged her with possession. (They never found out if Kuklinski had doctored one sandwich or two. The toxicologist at the New Jersey crime lab who tested the sandwiches put all three together and mashed them up. He found quinine throughout.)

The police had an impressive case. All along they had been generating leads and witnesses. They had a witness who saw Hoffman's car in the warehouse and another who saw Masgay's body in the freezer; they had the ex-fiancé in Florida and Polifrone's tapes and the quinine sandwiches; they had Barbara Deppner's recital of her husband's confession. But it was all circumstantial, without any hard medical evidence. No cyanide had been found in the bodies. The defense took the tack that Kuklinski had invented the stories on the tapes—he hadn't really poisoned anybody; it was all just "puffery," macho bragging. There was also a problem with Deppner's cause of death. Natarajan had picked up the ligature marks on his neck and called it murder. She hadn't considered cyanide. The body was too decomposed to find it, and if you have one cause you don't look for another. With no cyanide and a death by cause undetermined, the case against Kuklinski was weakened further. Had Kuklinski been lying? The state attorney general asked me to take a separate look before the trial to see if his taped confessions squared with the evidence.

Listening to the tapes, I thought Kuklinski knew too much. He couldn't have made up the stories if he hadn't done just what he said. His knowledge was too detailed. The irony of it was that if he hadn't strangled Smith and Deppner, no one would have thought of murder. Smith could have been left on top of the bed and been called a drug overdose or a suicide in a motel.

The defense was saying that no cyanide was found in the bodies, but the absence of cyanide didn't mean they weren't given it. After a few days you can't find cyanide in a body. That's one of the reasons it's such a good murder weapon. It breaks apart into carbon and nitrogen. The distinctive odor of bitter almonds is only discernible on a fresh body; it is lost as the body decomposes. But the cyanide didn't become entirely invisible—it showed up in the lividity. With the advantage of knowing the history of the case and seeing the pictures, I realized that Smith and Deppner both had patches of skin with the peculiar shade of red that comes from cyanide poisoning. They both had the lividity, and they both had marks around their neck. This was the proof, and it was entirely consistent with Kuklinski's stories to Polifrone. He had been telling the truth.

When I took the witness stand for the prosecution, some of my cyanide testimony was on the order of a double negative. The lividity proved that it *could* have been cyanide, I said (without the toxicology I couldn't be more definite), so you couldn't say Kuklinski was not telling the truth. It was convoluted, but the jury agreed with it. They found him guilty of murdering

Smith and Deppner, and he was sentenced to life. The minimum time he has to serve is sixty years.

Kuklinski wasn't tried for the other three killings. A second trial would have cost the state too much money, time, and effort. Instead, the DA used it as a bargaining chip. He wanted Kuklinski to plead guilty to the deaths of Malliband, Masgay, and Hoffman so he could close the cases. It looks sloppy and incompetent to have a lot of unsolved murders clogging up the books. Kuklinski agreed (including the missing body of Paul Hoffman). In return, the DA promised to leave his wife and children alone. His wife had been charged with illegal possession of a gun (it was in the car when the police caught him), and his son had been caught with marijuana. The charges were dropped.

Kuklinski still has one last secret. No one knows where he disposed of Hoffman's body. At first he told the police he would show them, but then he backed off. You never know when you might need a card to deal with. He still has something they want.

9

—

ALMOST PERFECT

WITHOUT A TRACE

A PERFECT MURDER is like a perfect scam—only the killer, the mastermind, knows how it was done or even that it happened. There is no suspicion and no investigation. For us, "perfect" murders are those that are difficult to prove from an autopsy. They are deaths for which we can find either the cause or the manner but not both. In smothering (or burking) which leaves no sign, we cannot be certain it happened. In drowning or falling from a height, we cannot determine whether it was an accident, suicide, or homicide. Often, we have to rely on clues at the scene not present in the autopsy room.

At a defenestration there are two scenes, the one upstairs and the one downstairs. Downstairs is the mute body. Upstairs are all the things it can no longer tell us—a suicide note, the signs of a struggle, one window that looks cleaner than the others. At one scene I found a bloody hat with a long cut across the top. I pieced together the dead man's skull bones, and there on his crown was the impact of a meat cleaver. His roommate confessed. They had fought over drugs; the roommate had killed him and thrown him out the window. The apartment was nine stories high, and he thought the injury would be hidden in the general mess of the impact. It could have been. But he wasn't very lucky, and he forgot something. He forgot to get rid of the hat.

Drowning deaths also need interpretation. On the surface it seems obvious—you drown because you are inhaling water instead of oxygen. But the lungs also fill with fluid in heart failure and in drug deaths. When the heart stops pumping, water accumulates in the lungs and froth forms in the mouth. As we saw with John Belushi, the same thing happens in a heroin overdose—fluid seeps out of the blood and works its way to the nose and mouth. We have to look for other clues. Generally speaking, if we find what looks like a drowning on a rooftop, we know it's drugs. If we find it in an elderly person at home with digitalis pills, it's heart failure.

The air-conditioning was turned up high and the house was freezing when the nude body of Paul Fried was discovered on July 23, 1976. Fried, a prominent Philadelphia gynecologist, was lying face down on the bedroom floor of his house near Rittenhouse Square. His nose was bloodied and there was a blood-stained pillow over his head. He was sixty-one years old. His wife, Catherine, was in her thirties, and they had been married for only a year. She had been worried that something like this might happen, she told the police. Her husband was an alcohol and barbiturate addict, and he had become suicidal. That very morning she had gone to Dr. Robert Brotman, a psychiatrist, to talk about ways to help him. She had been calling the house and couldn't get an answer and, apparently nervous about what she might find, had asked the psychiatrist and Ruth Kennedy, her business partner, to come with her.

The police found a note on the bedside table. The handwriting was shaky and a little difficult to read. It looked like a name—Flower, or maybe Glower?—and a phone number. From the number they figured out the name—Glauser. Glauser was Paul Fried's accountant. And under the name was the word "pills." They interpreted it as being a suicide note. Suicide notes are seldom neat, literate essays. If there's a dead body and the scene looks innocent, the police interpret the death as a suicide. There's always a subjective evaluation of what happened, an instant perception of the scene. If it looks natural or accidental, you make the rest of your judgments in that light. If you believe the distraught spouse, you give him or her more credibility.

It took ten years to establish that Paul Fried had been murdered.

On the strength of Catherine Fried's story, Dr. Halbert Fillinger, the assistant ME, did only a limited examination. He was usually more careful, but he was persuaded it was a sleeping-pill overdose, just as Catherine had said, and he sent the stomach contents to a lab for chemical analysis. Even before the results came back, he issued the death certificate—drug overdose, suicide.

Calling the death a suicide triggered alarm bells for Fried's three daughters from his first marriage. They would have accepted a natural death, but suicide was unthinkable. Carlie, the eldest, couldn't believe such a thing of her father. He would never commit suicide. His father had killed himself, and Paul regarded it as a contemptible weakness, a disgraceful act. Furious, the daughters went to Fillinger's superior, the chief ME of Philadelphia, Marvin E. Aronson. The family can always appeal the cause of death, and Aronson could have been expected to sit down and go over the records with them. They wanted a full autopsy. But Catherine, who knew Aronson socially, had asked him to hasten the removal of the body from the ME's office to a funeral home. He did, and she had it embalmed, even though she was planning to cremate it. The children got an injunction to halt the cremation and hired Milton Helpern to do a second autopsy, over Catherine's objections. (After he finished, Catherine's fit of urgency passed. She left the body unclaimed in the ME's office for over six months before cremating it.)

Helpern, who had only a few more months left to live, had become a little fuzzy, but he performed with brio. He described pinpoint hemorrhages in the eyes and bruises on the neck, but did not think they were particularly significant. In a fifteen-page report, he discoursed eloquently on the human body as "a museum" of pathological exhibits—he found hardening of the arteries of the heart and kidneys, benign tumors in the adrenal glands, lumps in the thyroid—but none of these, except for the hardening of the heart arteries, was life-threatening. He waxed poetic about the aging of the body, the changes and abnormalities in all of us as we grow older. And he finally decided that Paul Fried had died of natural causes. Aronson changed the death certificate to "cause undetermined," and the children felt much better. The stigma was gone. The case was finished.

About a year later, Jerald Sklar, a good-looking, intelligent former teacher who had been working in Catherine Fried's employment agency, contacted the Philadelphia office of the FBI and offered to make a deal. He would tell the FBI about three murders it didn't know about, and in exchange, he wanted a new career. He wanted to get into the Federal Witness Protection Program; he wanted a guaranteed income, and he wanted the FBI to get him into Harvard Law School. (If he had known a little more about the law, he might have tried to make a different kind of bargain. He thought he had immunity.)

Sklar confessed to hiring a killer to get rid of two business associates of his friend Michael Melvin Selkow, an underworld hustler and con man. Selkow owed them a lot of money and was not prepared to pay it. The third murder he knew about was Paul Fried's. He knew that Catherine had sat on his face and smothered him. She had told him about it. She had put a pillow over her husband's face and braced it with her knees and held down his wrists with her hands. She enjoyed it so much, she told Sklar, that she had the best orgasm she ever had in her life.

Catherine had never planned to kill her husband. All along she had been trying to get someone else to do it for her—first Selkow and then Sklar. Sklar had introduced her to Selkow in June 1975, a month before her marriage, telling her he had Mafia connections. Intrigued, she began an affair with him and gave him $2,000. She was planning to spend the weekend of the Fourth of July with him, but at the last minute she stood him up and flew off to Las Vegas to marry Fried. It was the third marriage for each. The day before the wedding, they signed individual prenuptial agreements, each renouncing all rights to the other's property. (As Paul's wife, Catherine would legally have been entitled to one third of his $450,000 estate.) On her return, she phoned Selkow to tell him the marriage was only a temporary interruption of their affair. She didn't plan to "live out the marriage," and in fact it had not been consummated. She and Paul were going to keep it a secret and maintain separate residences.

Two weeks after the wedding, Catherine showed Selkow some bruises which she said Paul had inflicted on her, and asked him to murder Paul. Selkow declined, but offered to bring over a hit man from Italy for the sum of $25,000. Catherine gave him a down payment of over $9,000.

On his side, Paul had not been idle. He told his lawyer that Catherine refused to sleep with him, and a few weeks after the wedding he had divorce papers served on her.

Weeks went by, and the arrival of Selkow's hit man kept being delayed. Catherine vacillated. It occurred to her that Selkow was ripping her off, and she decided to cancel the hit man. Selkow told her the cancellation fee was an additional $6,000. She sent him a letter ending their affair. Belying her tough, Lady Macbeth exterior, she wrote, "I'm grateful for the attention you gave me and am pleased to have paid for it. I felt so lonely and alone that I would have—that I would gladly have paid you a million dollars for half the attention you gave me. . . . I know that I'm not good company, nor a good screw, and all I can say is thank you." She thought the $9,000 down payment would cover the $6,000 cancellation fee.

Catherine and Paul reconciled. She and her two daughters from a previous marriage lived with him in his townhouse, trying to make a go of it. It was an uneasy truce, frequently shattered by bitter arguments. They fought over money constantly, verbally and physically. Neighbors said they were both black and blue, a pair of battered spouses.

Early in 1976, Catherine and her daughters moved a few blocks away to an apartment on the twenty-sixth floor of a luxury high rise, but she and Paul remained on their roller coaster. A few months later she found him injured at home, his face bruised, his speech slurred. In the hospital he confessed to his doctor that he had been drinking and doing drugs, and later he tried to destroy the hospital records. Two months before the murder he fell down the stairs of his townhouse and broke a small bone in the back of his neck. This time he stayed in the hospital to dry out. While he was resting and recuperating, Catherine and Selkow, a man she couldn't stay away from, broke into Paul's safe and stole $6,000 (no connection to the $6,000 cancellation fee; it just happened to be there) and her original prenuptial agreement. They left his. When Paul got out of the hospital, she cared for him in her apartment.

By now it was June 1976. The year of marriage had been a year of violence and disappointment. Catherine had had enough, and she tried again to have her husband murdered. This time she went to Jerald Sklar, who was working in her employment agency. In the presence of Ruth Kennedy, her partner, she begged him repeatedly to help her. It was really very simple. All she wanted him to do was push Paul off her twenty-sixth-floor balcony. The police would think it was a drunken accident. She would let Sklar take some of the art in Paul's collection—it was valuable stuff—in partial payment. Sklar didn't find the offer tempting enough, and she sweetened the pot with $50,000. He turned her down. She didn't have $50,000, he said. She didn't have it right now, she told him, but she would get it from the estate after he did the deed.

Things became critical in July. Neighbors called the police to break up a fight. Catherine, screaming that she would kill Paul, had to be physically restrained. On another occasion, after Catherine had gone to work, Paul telephoned his nurse. Catherine had been hitting him in his neck fracture, and he wanted to go back to his own house. Soon thereafter, the doorman called Catherine at work—Paul was moving out with his suitcase and some appliances, trying to load his car. Catherine grabbed Sklar and ran home through the streets, shoving people out of her way as she ran. How dare he take things out of her house! She confronted Paul   the sidewalk, where they had another of their hitting and shoving matches. Again the police arrived, and again she threatened to kill Paul, who now had less than forty-eight hours to live.

Back at the office, Catherine threw a set of keys at Sklar and harangued him all afternoon to kill her husband. She could talk of nothing else. Sklar continued to refuse, but prudently kept the keys long enough to have duplicates made. (On the weekend after Paul's death, when the house was empty, he and Selkow used the keys and cleaned out the place. Catherine was enraged. They had received payment for a job they hadn't done.)

The next day Catherine finally realized that nobody was going to do it for her, and began constructing a smoke screen. She spent most of the day on the telephone with doctors and lawyers, seeking advice about her poor alcoholic, drug-ridden doctor husband—how to help him, places to dry him out, ways to handle him. She called Dr. Robert Brotman, chief psychiatrist at the outpatient clinic at Jefferson Hospital (the same hospital where Paul taught), asking to have Paul committed involuntarily—he had hit her, he was refusing to seek treatment for his drug and alcohol habits, and he was suicidal. Brotman, who had never seen either of them professionally, agreed to talk to her in his office at 9:00 the following morning. More reluctantly, he agreed to interview her husband at home.

That evening she visited Paul to feed him. She poured a big glass of liquor for him and brought it up to his bedroom. She made a last-ditch effort to enlist Sklar's services, but he refused. (Those who later prosecuted the case were not entirely convinced of his innocence, but there was no proof.) Later in the evening she returned, bringing a hamburger for Paul's dinner, and invited a neighbor to come in with her. Still later, at about 2:30 A.M., she returned once more, this time silently and alone. She had created something of a cover for herself with the first two visits—Paul was alive both times when she left. The third time she suffocated him. Before leaving she rolled the body onto the floor and took the phone off the hook. She also had the presence of mind to remove $7,000 from the safe.

At 9:00 the next morning, Catherine kept her appointment with Brotman. From his office she called Paul, but the line was continuously busy. She was fearful that something had happened, and Brotman agreed to go back with her. He later said it was an odd request, and it took him a long time to realize he had been set up. Brotman pronounced Paul dead. The police were not suspicious—there was no forced entry, no sign of trauma—and Catherine explained about Paul's history of drug and alcohol abuse. He'd been popping pills all week, she said, and he was suicidal.

All of this was Sklar's story. Catherine had confessed to him, not to the police. If Ruth Kennedy hadn't been in the office to hear some of it, no one would have paid any attention. Sklar's word alone would have been almost worthless. Until his bombshell, the possibility of murder hadn't occurred to anyone. It is unusual for a woman to strangle or suffocate a man—or for a man to strangle another man, for that matter. Almost all strangulations between the sexes are men strangling women. Catherine was five feet three and weighed 105 pounds; Paul was five feet seven and weighed 151 pounds, but he was wearing a neck brace, which would have limited his ability to move his head, and he was woozy from painkillers, which slowed down his reactions. Physically, it was entirely feasible. But Clifford Hanes, the Philadelphia DA, wasn't sure he really had a case to prosecute. He was having trouble reconciling the two different autopsy findings—first suicide and then natural causes—with the newest cause, suffocation by pillow. He asked me for my opinion.

The body had been cremated, so I reviewed the records and photographs. And I saw that Milton Helpern's report had unwittingly described suffocation—pinpoint hemorrhages in the eyes and bruises on the face and neck. Pinpoint hemorrhages typically appear with manual strangulation, but they are not necessarily always there with smothering. They can develop naturally if the body is lying face down, as Paul Fried's was. Essentially, they come from burst capillaries, and figuring out how the capillaries burst is a matter of context. It's judgment and interpretation and your sense of the scene, the physical condition of the rest of the body. It was suspicious to me that the body was found on the floor. Natural deaths tend to take place in bed. Even with a heart attack or a stroke, most people manage to get to a bed before collapsing. The toxicology report, which came back from the lab after the first death certificate had been signed (the one that gave alcohol and drug overdose as the cause), and which no one seems to have looked at, showed no alcohol and a very low level of barbiturates. Without barbiturates, there was no suicide. The report contradicted the findings of both suicide and accidental overdose. Paul had a bad heart, but Helpern's slides and photographs showed no evidence of a heart attack. However, given Paul's heart condition, he would suffocate faster if he was deprived of oxygen. Considering all these things, Sklar's tale began to assume a great deal of credibility, mainly because it was consistent with the autopsy findings. A confession that reflects the autopsy findings is highly believable. People who just make things up can't explain the medical evidence.

The prosecutor agreed with me, but he chose that moment to move into private practice. The assistant DA, Hal Rosenberg, inherited the case, along with his assistant, James Jordan. They were perfect contrasts. Rosenberg was emotional and enthusiastic; Jordan was cool and reticent. (Rosenberg later became one of the lead counsels against Johns-Manville in the asbestos cases; Jordan has since become a partner in a prestigious law firm.) Both of them were reasonably certain that Catherine was guilty, but they lacked hard cold evidence—a witness who actually saw the suffocation, say. The confession didn't even come from her— it was indirect, secondhand, something she allegedly said to someone else. They were relying on the statement of Sklar, a professional liar who had already confessed to two murders. The only real corroboration was the autopsy finding, and even that was not very strong. I couldn't say with absolute certainty that the cause of death was suffocation. I couldn't even say that a crime had been committed. The fact of the crime—the corpus delicti—has to be established by evidence other than the confession. Neither the confession nor other incriminating statements could be admitted into evidence until the corpus delicti had been proved. The judge would not let me take into account anything except the physical evidence of Paul's body. I couldn't discuss the scene or the possibilities. The only thing I could say was "consistent with suffocation."

Among Catherine's chief defense witnesses were the two medical examiners who had signed the conflicting death certificates—Halbert Fillinger and Marvin Aronson, now working privately. Few lawyers are prepared to examine MEs properly. They don't know the right questions to ask. And the ME, if he chooses, can hide behind medical terms and peripheral issues, stonewall, and intone gibberish, with no one the wiser. Rosenberg and Jordan did their homework. They laced into Fillinger and Aronson and demolished both causes of death—suicide and natural—and then I offered the signs of suffocation, subtle but visible. The jury came back with a verdict of guilty, but it doubtless had other reasons in addition to the medical ones for doing so. Jordan thought the heavy and brutish appearance of Michael Selkow, who testified that he and Catherine were lovers, was extremely helpful to the prosecution. The jury, he thought, wondered what kind of a woman would sleep with a man like that. It cast her in a bad light.

Catherine appealed and won on the ground that there was insufficient evidence of the corpus delicti. The case was sent back for a new trial. This time a different judge allowed me to take into account the circumstances and history, and I was able to say that Paul Fried had very likely been suffocated. Suffocation is never definite. Again, the jury found Catherine guilty, and again she appealed.

Jerald Sklar, who wanted to go to Harvard, was convicted of the two murders he said he'd hired a killer to commit for Selkow and is serving two life sentences. The jury thought he did them himself. Selkow fared rather better. After being caught in a drug deal, he allowed himself to be wired and used as a witness against his former associates. Catherine's passionate affair with him is on hold while she is in jail.

Poisons and drugs are also invisible killers, but they have one great disadvantage—the person administering them has to be physically close to the victim, which immediately puts him at the top of the list of suspects. Nevertheless, doctors gravitate toward them. They are easy to get, and a well-chosen poison quickly breaks down into its elements and may never be found at all. Drs. Carl Coppolino and Mario Jascalevich may well have counted on that when each of them embarked on his misadventure.

Carl Coppolino, a slim, dark, and attractive anesthesiologist at Riverview Hospital in Red Bank, New Jersey, was a successful womanizer who lived with his wife, Carmela, in nearby Middletown. Carmela, also a doctor, worked at Hoffman-LaRoche Pharmaceutical Company. While in his early thirties, Carl developed a heart condition and had to spend much of his time at home, living on compensation from his disability policy. (It was later discovered that he was secretly taking digitalis. Digitalis causes abnormal lines in electrocardiograms which are easily mistaken for heart disease.) While his wife was out working, Carl passed the time by having an affair with a neighbor, Marjorie Farber. Her husband, William E. Farber, was a fifty-four-year-old insurance executive and retired Army colonel. It was a hypnotic affair. Carl mesmerized Marge out of smoking, and she felt herself to be living entirely under his spell, her will bonded to his. With the knowledge of Carmela, who was a trusting soul, they took trips to Florida, Atlantic City, and San Juan. As Marge later testified, one day Carl said, "That man has got to go," meaning her husband. An anesthesiologist, Carl turned to an anesthetic for his weapon, and ordered a number of vials of succinylcholine from a drug company. (Later, when he was asked what he needed them for, he explained that he was doing cat experiments, but he hadn't kept any records of them.)

Succinylcholine is artificial curare. It is used during operations the way Pavulon is—to relax skeletal muscles. This makes it possible to administer lighter doses of other more dangerous anesthetics. A continuous IV drip of succinylcholine causes muscle paralysis, but a single injection doesn't last very long—the drug breaks down in the body without causing harm. Carl tried to get Marge to inject her husband, but she couldn't quite manage it, and he finally had to do it himself. The colonel hung onto life stubbornly, not believing that his time had come. Carl was forced to resort to smothering him with a pillow, but the colonel still refused to succumb. In the struggle, Carl strangled the colonel with his bare hands, although Marge did not see it. Later, one of her daughters came home and noticed that "Daddy looks funny." As instructed by Carl, Marge called Carmela, who signed the death certificate, giving coronary thrombosis as the cause. Nobody thought that anything was amiss.

Two years later, in 1965, Carl and Carmela and their two children moved to Sarasota, Florida. Marge already had property there, and she decided to move down and live on it. Carl asked Carmela for a divorce, but she refused. A few months later, in August, Carmela, who was insured, was found dead. Carl called an acquaintance, Dr. Juliette Karow, who lived nearby. He was in a peculiar position, he said, and there were niceties to be observed. His wife had just died of a heart attack, but he had qualms about signing the death certificate—it just wouldn't look right—and could Dr. Karow sign it? Dr. Karow signed Carmela out as a coronary occlusion. Carmela's father, Carmelo Musetto, who was also a doctor, was astounded to learn that his thirty-two-year-old daughter had had a bad heart. How do you know? he asked Carl, and Carl explained that it had showed up in Carmela's autopsy. He shipped the body back to New Jersey to be buried.

Until now, Carl had been doing very well. He'd gotten rid of two superfluous people with no suspicion attaching to him; and he was making a living, if an unconventional one. At this point he stumbled. One and a half months after Carmela's death he remarried, but not to his longtime lover, Marge. Marge was getting on. She was already past fifty, and he was only thirty-four. He married Mary Gibson, thirty-eight, whom he had met in Sarasota playing bridge. Marge, whose patience had gone unrewarded all this time, was devastated and started spreading the story. First she told Dr. Karow, then Dr. Karow's priest, who advised her to inform the FBI. Instead, she went to the sheriff and said that Carl had probably killed his wife the same way he had killed her husband, by injecting Carmela with succinylcholine. The sheriff called Vincent Keuper, the Monmouth County, New Jersey, prosecutor. Keuper was at a loss. He called G. Malcolm B. Gilman, the ME for Monmouth County. Gilman, who traced his ancestors back to the *Mayflower*, had a strong sense of history but a shaky concept of his job. He didn't know what to do, either. They called Helpern in New York. He would know what to do.

Meanwhile, Dr. Carmelo Musetto, who had moved to Sarasota to be with his grandchildren, went to the Florida prosecutor. Musetto had actually known since the funeral that there had been no autopsy and Carl had lied to him. The New Jersey undertaker who had buried Carmela had told him. He had been afraid to say anything for fear that Carl would prevent him from seeing his grandchildren. He later testified, "I was lost. I was a lost man," to explain his curious silence.

With two people raising the alarm (the word of Marge, a jilted woman, was not enough), the New Jersey DA decided to investigate. Helpern exhumed Carmela first. She had been dead only four months. The colonel had been dead two and a half years, and exhuming such long-buried bodies was rarely done then. I assisted Helpern in our Decomposed Room, which is about twenty by twenty-five feet and is specially ventilated. In the center are two steel autopsy tables with running water. Around the walls are glass cabinets with jars containing body parts; there are electric saws and other instruments. G. Malcolm B. Gilman sat on a stool and watched. Because of Marge's accusation, we looked for injections first. Without her, we might never have found anything. We went over Carmela with a magnifying lens. Mold covered her face (usually found in exhumed bodies) and preserved the skin underneath by absorbing moisture. The most common sites of injections are the fleshy parts of the body—the shoulders, arms, thighs, and buttocks. We found a puncture wound in the left buttock. It looked like a little anthill. Helpern cut through it with a scalpel and saw a thin hemorrhagic needle mark, a puncture that went down through the skin. Marge's jilted-woman ravings achieved instant credibility. There was no reason for the injection. And Carmela had no heart disease. The mark of the injection was clear, but it was unlikely that succinylcholine had worked any better on Carmela than it had on the colonel. The prosecutor theorized that Carmela had been lying on her stomach, possibly asleep, and Carl had caught her unawares. He sat on her, which prevented her from moving and interfered with her breathing. The injection paralyzed her, making it easy for Carl to smother her with a pillow.

Colonel Farber was in Arlington Cemetery. It was wet inside his coffin, and his uniform looked better than he did. The tissues in front of his neck had deteriorated, but we found fractures of his right and left cricoid cartilages, just under the Adam's apple—he had a fractured larynx, which in this instance meant manual strangulation. His heart was well preserved and showed no evidence of a heart attack.

Carl was tried twice, once for the colonel's death in New Jersey and once for his wife's in Florida. The colonel went first. The case for Carl's having killed him was stronger—manual strangulation and an eyewitness, Marge. Both times F. Lee Bailey defended him. Bailey was at his peak, dramatic and exciting, drawing publicity like a magnet. He had a tremendous presence, and commanded the courtroom. His defense was that Colonel Farber had died of heart disease. He had not been murdered and therefore Carl hadn't done it. The prosecutor had to prove the murder had taken place. He had no toxicological evidence for Marge's story of a succinylcholine injection, but he did have evidence of the fractured larynx, which was passed among the jurors.

Using the hell-hath-no-fury approach, Bailey demolished Marge. "This woman drips with venom," he said; her story was a web of lies, the rantings of a woman scorned. Then he dealt with Milton Helpern, who was unaccustomed to being dealt with. Helpern had made slides of the colonel's coronary arteries and was planning to show a few of them to the jury to prove the colonel didn't die of heart disease. Bailey thought the jury should not be deprived of the benefit of all seventy-five of them, and insisted that Helpern show every last one. Using an old, cumbersome projector, Helpern had to explain away all the abnormalities in the colonel's arteries, one after another—this narrowing doesn't matter, that spot is unimportant and had nothing to do with his death, on and on for over an hour. The slide show succeeded in convincing the jury that Farber had heart disease.

The larynx remained. Bailey found two experts who thought the fracture was postmortem, an accidental blow inflicted by a gravedigger's shovel. This was very questionable, considering that the colonel was in a coffin when he was dug up. True, the sides of the coffin and the outer box had collapsed, but the inner lining surrounding the colonel was intact. But Bailey pulled it off, and Carl was acquitted of the murder of Colonel Farber.

For the second trial, the murder of Carmela in Sarasota, Bailey was a little too sure of himself. He had asked for a change of venue, hoping for the big-city sophistication of Miami, but he got the wrong venue. He got Naples, Florida, which was even smaller and more rural than Sarasota. He spent a lot of time with reporters, flying around the state in his Learjet. Frank Schaub, the prosecutor, was his antagonist in every sense. Schaub was a slow, deliberate talker who dressed badly and shuffled when he walked. Bailey was quicksilver, electricity. They were like the tortoise and the hare.

In Carmela's case, there was no backup fractured larynx. The critical question was the presence or absence of succinylcholine in the body.

Helpern was certain that Coppolino was guilty. The prosecutor had looked into his background at Methodist Hospital in Brooklyn, where he had worked previously, and learned that he had left under unsavory circumstances. The police had traced anonymous letters to him. He had sent them to a nurse, threatening to mutilate her if she continued to work in the hospital. He was jealous that she was taking away his patients. The hospital, not anxious to be caught in a scandal, let him resign. Shortly afterward, he declared himself disabled from a heart condition and began to live on his disability insurance. After that piece of information, we thought we'd see if anything had happened to any of his patients. We found an inordinate number of operative deaths that had never been reported, but there was no way to prove anything. There are surgical deaths and anesthesiological deaths. When a patient dies during an operation, the surgeon may call it an anesthesiological death, and the anesthetist may call it a surgical death. The hospital, desirous of avoiding lawsuits, says as little as possible.

Given Carl's background, Helpern believed the worst and thought he could find traces of this virtually undetectable poison. The breakdown products, succinic acid and choline, are normally present in the body. You have to find an excess. Helpern's chief toxicologist, Joseph Umberger, found the products, and Helpern testified that the amount in Carmela's brain was larger than normal. But Bailey charged that the tests had been conducted in secret, and the results were wrong. Three of the toxicologists who had worked on them agreed with Bailey. Helpern forced them out. Did anyone really know the normal amount of succinic acid and choline in a brain that had been buried for six months? It became a question of which toxicologist the jury would believe. Bailey's man, Dr. Francis Foldes, who found only normal amounts of the breakdown, was chief of anesthesiology at Montefiore Hospital and an expert on the subject. He had introduced succinylcholine into this country. He was a German refugee and spoke with an accent. Umberger, a farm boy from Oklahoma, did not seem to take himself seriously. He dressed in baggy pants and tobacco-stained shirt and carried an ancient, bulging briefcase. He looked like an alien among the suits of New York. As he walked in, chewing tobacco, his briefcase overflowing, he stopped and winked at the jurors. They cracked up. He looked like them; they recognized him as one of their kind, and they believed him. Coppolino was found guilty and given a life sentence, but he served only twelve and a half years of it. Now, almost a quarter of a century has passed, and his heart disease seems to have disappeared with age, reversing the usual process. His license to practice medicine was revoked, but he found something else to do. He consults.

He reviews cases and finds doctors who serve as witnesses at trials. He has become an expert.

While Carl Coppolino was trying out his skills with succinylcholine, Dr. Mario E. Jascalevich, another charming solipsist, was working with curare. Jascalevich was an Argentinian, born in 1927 in Buenos Aires. During the 1960s he invented a surgical stapler that carries his name. With the exception of euthanasia deaths, his was the first significant case in which a doctor was tried for intentionally killing patients who were also strangers. He was accused of murdering the patients of other doctors in his hospital to make himself look better. As doubt grew about their abilities, the money they earned from consultations would flow to him.

From 1963 to 1968 Dr. Jascalevich was the chief surgeon and the only one with full privileges at Riverdell Hospital, a small private hospital in Oradell, New Jersey. He was not popular with his peers. Other doctors complained how grudging he was with help. When they needed to consult with him on surgical problems—the treatment for abdominal pain, or a blood clot— he either wasn't available or he didn't respond quickly enough. In 1966 the hospital board brought in another surgeon, Dr. Robert Briski, an osteopath. Briski was helpful, cooperative, and available when needed, and he brought in his own patients. For a time, the board was delighted. Then something odd began to happen. Inexplicably, Briski's patients started dying after simple, routine operations—gall bladder, appendix. It was embarrassing. Within a year his privileges were restricted to minor surgery, like hernias, with someone watching. Briski was shattered. He thought he was jinxed.

A few months after Briski joined the staff, and over Jascalevich's objections, the board had brought in another general surgeon, Dr. Stanley Harris, whose specialty was vascular surgery. Soon his patients started to die, too, at the incredible rate of two or three a month. Harris couldn't imagine what was causing all these deaths. The autopsy results were vague—the deaths were attributed to various postoperative complications or heart attacks. Suddenly they stopped, and he relaxed. Then early one morning the hospital called to tell him that another of his patients had died. He rushed over and noticed that Jascalevich was there. Jascalevich had been on vacation for several weeks. Harris, who was more tough-minded than Briski, realized that none of his patients had died during the time Jascalevich was away. And now, just days after Jascalevich had returned, someone was dead. There was a notation on the patient's chart that Jascalevich had visited him. Harris thought it odd. He hadn't been asked to, and there was no reason for it. Harris thought he was on to something. He looked through the records of his other dead patients, and sure enough, Jascalevich had visited every one of them before they died. The visits violated protocol. Harris went to Dr. Allan Lans, a member of the hospital's board of directors.

The Coppolino case was making headlines, and succinylcholine was on everyone's mind. Lans thought Jascalevich might have been using it. He and Harris and other members of the board confronted Jascalevich and opened his locker. Inside they found needles, syringes, and eighteen vials of curare. The vials were almost empty.

The next day the board took its suspicions to Guy Calissi, the DA. Doctors almost never bring charges against each other to outside authorities. They had to be very certain of Jascalevich's guilt for them to go this far. Calissi and his assistant, Fred Galda, seized the contents of Jascalevich's locker and questioned him. Jascalevich handled them with a combination of charm and threats. He said he would resign but not under a cloud and not if the newspapers picked up the story and made him look guilty. Everything had to be kept quiet. He had a perfectly innocent explanation for the curare. He experimented on dogs at a medical school and used curare as an anesthesia. For the rest, he stonewalled. People die of "an undetermined physiological reaction," he said of a dead child; it could happen to anyone.

Three months later, Calissi and Galda ended their investigation and cleared Jascalevich. They didn't check the dog story or make the connection with Coppolino and his cat story. Jascalevich resigned and Harris succeeded him. There were no more suspicious deaths.

Over the next ten years, rumors kept bobbing up about a terrible secret harbored by the hospital—that thirty or forty people had been murdered and it had been covered up. From time to time a reporter would look into it, but nothing came of it until 1975, when Myron Farber at the *New York Times* became intrigued. The odds were against him. It was not to the advantage of certain interests to reopen the case. The DA and his assistant had become judges; the hospital board of directors were community pillars, and the doctors who issued the original death certificates would want to defend their diagnoses. They would become allied with the defense. A new investigation would cast a cloud on all of them.

Farber found a secret source (he later went to jail to protect the source's name) who gave him access to the old records. He went to the medical school where the animal experiments were supposed to have taken place and learned that Jascalevich had never done any work there. It was all a lie. What was the curare for? He also got records from the DA's office. Twenty-five patients had died. Thirteen of them seemed more suspicious than the rest. The chart of each had a notation that Jascalevich had been their angel of expiration—he had visited them just before they took their last breath. None was a patient of Jascalevich's. Some of them were dying of serious illnesses—cancer, heart disease. Of the thirteen, nine looked most likely to have been helped into their graves—the deaths were sudden and not in keeping with the nature of their illness. There was no cause that could compete with poisoning.

Farber presented the findings to the Bergen County prosecu-

tor, Joe Woodcock, who asked me to review the cases for him.
The New Jersey MEs who would normally have done it were
compromised. Both Edwin Albano, the statewide ME, and Lawrence Denson, the Bergen County ME, had been among the
original investigators who had accepted the deaths as innocent.
Woodcock assigned a junior person to it, assistant DA Sybil
Moses (now a judge). The case had been lying around for a decade; nobody thought it would go anywhere.

There wasn't enough evidence to force an exhumation of any
of the patients, but five families agreed to it. It could not have
been done without their consent. Other newspapers got wind of
the story, but their ability to use it was limited—no one could
print Jascalevich's name because he had not been officially
charged and could have sued for libel. To protect his reputation,
the press referred to him as "Dr. X." Everyone involved in the
case knew who he was—everyone except the public who needed
to know the most.

The first body we exhumed was that of Nancy Savino, a four-
year-old child, buried for ten years. She had seemed to be recovering after having her appendix removed, but then had died suddenly. The hospital did an autopsy, but no one could explain
it. The death certificate said "cause undetermined."

The gravediggers went to the cemetery at 7:30 A.M., which
is the normal time to dig up bodies. The main reason is eco-
nomic. If the body can be dug up, examined, and returned to
its grave the same day, it costs less. It's also less harrowing emotionally for the family. Exhuming a body that is ten years dead
is a highly dramatic thing to do. Usually, an exhumation is done
a few weeks, or at most a year, after death, the time during which
questions about a case arise. It was winter. Snow was on the
ground, and fresh flowers lay at the headstones. The gravediggers used a backhoe to break through the frozen topsoil. It took
a couple of hours, but we were lucky. The casket had been put
into a cement vault which keeps water out. Nancy Savino's parents had also chosen a metal casket for her. It hadn't cracked

and it was still sealed tight. Cast-iron caskets were used in the Civil War. When some of them were opened up a century later, the bodies were still in good shape—some had recognizable features and even internal organs. Many of the uniforms were preserved, and were taken out and put in museums. Nancy Savino's gravediggers pulled up her casket with loops of heavy cloth, and we brought it to our Decomposed Room. Everything depended on the condition of the body. Would the specimens be good enough for the toxicology lab? Curare concentrates in the cartilage of animals, and in the soft tissues that are among the earliest to decompose. But Nancy Savino had been embalmed, so there was a good chance we would find something.

The room was crowded. There were toxicologists to take specimens, a stenographer, two mortuary dieners (assistants to the pathologist who do such things as sew up the body), a photographer, Joe Woodcock (the Bergen County DA), and Edwin Albano (the Jersey ME). Beneath the facade of rational scientific inquiry, old resentments smoldered. Albano felt his turf had been invaded, and he was miffed that he hadn't been put in charge. Maybe people were saying that his first decision had been a whitewash, but still—it was a Jersey case, and why was it being done in New York City? He felt slighted. Helpern thought the whole thing was ridiculous, that after ten years there would be nothing but a putrid mess and a bag of bones. The press was skeptical. It was an election year in New Jersey and Woodcock might be running for governor. This looked like a publicity stunt. Suspicion and bitterness still lingered from the decade-old Coppolino case. Dr. Richard Coumbis, now chief toxicologist of New Jersey, had been one of those fired by Helpern for questioning his findings on the amount of succinylcholine in Carmela Coppolino's brain. Helpern had been accused of making the finding in secret, and here was another exotic poison that might be there or it might not, who could tell? To counter all this distrust, I wanted the exhumation and toxicology done in the open, in full view with everyone watching. No sleight-of-hand and no mirrors.

The moment of truth arrived. We uncranked the lid of the coffin and slowly lifted it up. No one in the room had ever seen a body that had been in the ground for ten years. There was a collective gasp as the lid was raised. Nancy Savino was most remarkably well preserved. The pink crinoline dress she had been buried in was clean and crisp. It looked starched. A cross and a withered rose lay on her chest, exactly as her parents had described them. The dryness had preserved everything. The organs and tissues could be analyzed.

By previous agreement, I divided the tissues among several toxicology labs in New Jersey, Long Island, and California. The eyes are particularly important in looking for poisons. Eye fluid (vitreous humor) is a place where they remain preserved. The eye contains about a tablespoon of fluid, like a little bag of water. The eye itself is a hollow organ and the fluid decomposes very slowly.

Dr. Richard Coumbis, the most skeptical of the toxicologists, who had specifically requested an eye, was the first to find curare. (What you actually find, using the gas chromatograph and mass spectrometer, are the molecular building blocks of the poison.) Then all the labs found it. We exhumed the other four bodies and found it in all of them. In the most decomposed body it was in the spinal cord.

The trial was presided over by Judge William J. Arnold. It was his last case before his retirement, and an awkward one for him. Two of his fellow judges were the Bergen County prosecutors who were being criticized for absolving Jascalevich in the original investigation. He had a nervous rash on his hands. All during the trial he wore rubber gloves and kept picking at them. I could hear him plucking away when I was on the stand. Other difficulties plagued him. He had trouble remembering the lawyers' names. He frequently had his eyes closed and seemed to be napping. The prosecutor thought he was biased in favor of

Jascalevich and asked him to disqualify himself, an unusual move for a lawyer to make against the judge who holds the fate of a client in his hands. He refused.

After thirty-five weeks of testimony, it took the jury less than three hours to come back with an acquittal. The defense attorney, Raymond A. Brown, understood that in a long trial a relationship develops between the jurors and the defendant. He grasped the value of personal connections and paid attention to details. Jascalevich dressed well and said good morning to the jury. He was friendly; he thanked me for my testimony even though I was on the other side. He greeted witnesses and said goodbye to them and expressed his gratitude to them when they left, like a good host. He kissed several of the women in the courtroom. Jascalevich ran a clinic for people on welfare, and many of his clients, who were not working, packed the courtroom and applauded him. The jury was so dazzled by his performance that they later sent a letter to Albano, expressing their outrage that the good doctor's medical license had not been restored to him after the trial. Jascalevich had voluntarily surrendered it at the time of the indictment.

But there was good cause. The New Jersey Medical Licensing Board had been investigating him for other reasons. Apart from his indictment for killing five patients with curare, the board charged him with seven counts of malpractice, including operating for cancer on a patient who didn't have the disease, fraud, and neglect. These therapeutic misdemeanors took place at another hospital in Jersey City where he had operating privileges. In 1980 his license was revoked permanently.

But Jascalevich knew when he was ahead. He skipped the country in 1981 and returned to Argentina, leaving the insurance companies holding the bag for malpractice charges. Raymond Brown, the defense attorney who had done such a wonderful job for him, wasn't paid either. Dr. X died in Mar del Plata, Argentina, in 1984, at age fifty-seven. Riverdell Hospital changed its name twice after the trial, but anonymity eluded it. It finally shut down for lack of patients. People felt nervous about going there.

10

CLOSE CALLS

ACCIDENTAL DEATH

ON MARCH 11, 1971, Whitney Young, the executive director of the National Urban League, died in Lagos, Nigeria. He had been attending an Afro-American conference with Ramsey Clark, the former U.S. Attorney General, and Percy Sutton, the former Manhattan borough president, among others. He was swimming in the ocean in rough surf about one hundred feet from shore when he collapsed. His friends, who were standing on the beach, saw his arm go up and his head go down before he went under. Clark, who was swimming with him, pulled him out of the water. His friends worked on him for over an hour with his head lower than his feet, but it was too late.

Young was autopsied in a Lagos hospital. The doctor reported that he had died of a brain hemorrhage, and returned the body to New York in a wooden casket with a metal liner. The death certificate came with the body, along with a description of the death. By international agreement, all countries have to supply a document stating that the death was not caused by a contagious disease. People who die of something contagious, like yellow fever, in a foreign country, can't leave—they must be buried or cremated there.

The family was not satisfied with the diagnosis. After it became public knowledge, rumors began circulating that Young had been killed. Even though he had been swimming in plain view of the whole beach, the diagnosis of brain hemorrhage had raised the possibility that someone had hit him on the head. Why else would he have a hemorrhage around his brain? The causes of a brain hemorrhage could be unnatural as well as natural. He was a good swimmer, so drowning was unlikely. Maybe there was a cover-up.

Dr. Allan Dumont, the family physician, called me. He was a surgeon and professor at Bellevue who had been one of my teachers. The family wanted another autopsy. When I opened the metal liner, the body was in good condition, embalmed and dressed with the two traditional sutured incisions. The usual procedure is to take the organs out, inspect them, and dissect them. The Nigerians had touched nothing. All the organs were in place, just as they had been in life. A towel had been put beneath the skin to soak up fluids. The brain was congested and reddish, and I took it out. Except for the color, it was normal. There was no injury and no hemorrhage. The lungs were more difficult to call. You don't always see water in the lungs in a drowning, and when you do, the fluid is the same as the fluid from a heart attack. There's no label on it, indicating point of origin. But there was sand and seaweed in the windpipe and sand in the bronchi, which was very persuasive evidence to me that Young had inhaled water and drowned. He also had an enlarged heart and a history of high blood pressure. It was a very hot day in Lagos, and bad hearts get into trouble in extremes of weather. I thought the heat had brought on cardiac arrhythmia. If he had been at home in bed and been treated he would have survived it; instead, it precipitated his drowning.

I found out later how the Nigerian autopsy had been done. The doctor had misinterpreted the reddishness around the brain.

It was due to gravity, not a blow. Young had been lying on the beach with his head lower than his feet while his friends tried to save him. Blood rushed to his brain, making it look as if he had hemorrhaged. The Nigerians had also practiced the hands-off policy that goes into effect around the world when an important foreigner dies. Important foreigners get special treatment. Corners are cut for them, which often serves to make the death look suspicious whether it is or not. In this death there were political nuances and media attention to consider, as well as the family's feelings. The Nigerians were sensitive to all of it. First, they contacted the American embassy. The embassy was not anxious to have an autopsy done—families don't usually want one—and sent its own doctor, a general practitioner, to observe the Nigerian ME. The American didn't really understand what he was seeing, but he represented the family's interests, and his presence should have permitted the ME to do everything he needed to do. The ME, though, saw things from another angle. He considered himself to be working under the guidance of the Americans, and assumed that everyone would be happier if he did the minimum necessary. If he had done a full autopsy and come up with a reasonable cause, the family would have been satisfied. It was just a case of good intentions and bad communications.

Late one April night in 1988, Robert Travis, Jr., twenty-five years old, and his seventeen-year-old cousin, Larry Peters, Jr., drove to the big mansion on the hill, the estate in Cambridge, New York, where they worked, to steal a little gasoline. It was a lark, a Tom Sawyerish prank, no malice intended. Travis didn't have enough money to buy gas. He and his cousin were the kind of people the police called "mullies," or "dirtbags," or "woodchucks"—rural people who grew up poor and ignorant, who wore the same dirty jeans covered with oil stains day after day, people who were constitutionally unable to stay out of trouble.

The estate belonged to Dr. Josephine Wells Brown, a seventy-six-year-old retired radiologist. Her husband, also a doctor, was dead, and she lived alone in a three-story redbrick Georgian house with fireplaces at each end. The estate was in a remote area near Glens Falls, and was virtually self-sufficient—she grew food and had her own generator and a gasoline pump for the farm equipment. She was an animal lover and kept registered quarter horses. Antiques were one of her interests—the house was filled with them, and she ran an antiques shop on the property. Around town she was regarded as something of a character for being outspoken and demanding and for devoting herself so wholeheartedly to her horses, but she was well liked.

Dr. Brown kept the farm going with a combination of house servants and field labor. She hired hourly farm workers (the only kind available) from the local population. Travis and Peters and a third man, Mark Dickinson, did the yard and stable work and were not allowed into the house. Dr. Brown kept the inside and outside people carefully separated. On payday, the outside workers went to a wooden shed in back of the house that opened into the kitchen and were given checks. Dr. Brown didn't keep cash in the house. She was afraid. A few days before her death she confided to a friend that she was particularly afraid of Travis, whose nickname was Matches. In his youth he had once burned down someone's barn.

On this particular day, Travis and Peters, who was somewhat dim-witted, were working together on Peters's grandfather's tractor. Peters lived with his grandfather. Travis, in a spirit of fun, suggested that they find some excitement that night, that they go out and drink wine coolers and smoke cigarettes. This was an adventurous thing for them to be doing. Their lives were narrow and their days repetitious.

That night, Peters sneaked out the window and met his cousin. After buying orange wine coolers and cigarettes, Travis had no money left to buy gas and decided to siphon some from Dr. Brown's pump. It was another daring thing to do.

They drove to the farm in Travis's half-wrecked 1973 Chevrolet with its unmatched doors from different cars, rusting and filthy. They went halfway up the driveway that circled the house, turned off their lights, and stopped, fearful of being seen. Upstairs, lights were still on. They sat for an hour, waiting. After a while the lights went out, and they drove the Chevy in the dark around to the rear of the house where the gas pump and antiques shop were.

Dr. Brown had left the night lights on near the pump, and Travis thought he'd better turn them off. The car could be seen in the light. But he could only do it by turning off the circuit breaker, which was inside the wooden shed, and he was too short to reach it. While Peters waited in the car, Travis went to look for a stool or a ladder to stand on. He had something else on his mind, too—Dr. Brown's rifle. He knew she had one, and he wanted to steal it. It's unclear where he thought she kept it. From interviews with Travis, the prosecutor had the impression that he thought she kept it outside her bedroom door. Travis was ignorant of her habits, too. Dr. Brown was accustomed to sleeping for a few hours after dinner, and then getting up to wander around the house. She was a night owl.

Travis opened the door that led to the kitchen and saw Dr. Brown standing there in a pink nightgown, holding the coveted rifle. She had known they were there. She had seen the car but hadn't wanted to go outside and confront them. Her worst fear was coming true. "What do you want?" she said. Travis was so startled he instinctively struck out, punching her in the neck. She collapsed instantly. He searched for a pulse but couldn't find one and decided she was dead.

He sat there for a while, trying to figure out what to do. He hadn't meant to kill her, and in a way it wasn't really his fault; so maybe the best thing would be to destroy the evidence. Given his past experience, the way to do that was to burn down the house. He went back outside and told Peters that he had found Dr. Brown lying there dead, but he knew exactly what to do—

she had once asked him to burn the house down if he ever found her dead. Peters helped him torch the house.

Travis carried the body into the living room and laid it in front of one of the fireplaces. He found a gasoline container and poured kerosene and gasoline through the house, around the body, and all over the Oriental rugs. He had found some gloves, but even so he burned his hand. Arson is tricky. Gasoline evaporates at a very low temperature. After pouring it, if you wait a few minutes to light a match, enough vapor may rise to create an oxygen-gasoline mixture that explodes—a fireball. Often in arson cases, the cops' best leads come out of the local emergency room, where people with burns on their hands or faces have gone to be treated. A more experienced arsonist would have started the fire from a distance, using a rope or a cord, and he would not have waited long enough for the gasoline to evaporate.

With the house beginning to blaze behind them, Travis and Peters drove back to town to arrange their alibis. Peters sneaked back through his grandfather's window. Travis arrived a few minutes later. He called Mark Dickinson, the third field hand, and told him they were needed on a rescue mission: Dr. Brown had just telephoned him for help. The fire in her fireplace was getting out of hand and she needed him to put it out. He didn't want to go alone, and he would pick up his friend on the way.

The next day in Peters's school, everyone was talking about the big fire at Dr. Brown's place and how she had died in it. It was the most exciting thing to happen in Cambridge in ages. Peters went to the infirmary to have the bandage changed on an old injury, and even there it was the main topic of conversation. He was one up on everyone, and he contributed to the excitement by telling the nurse that he had been at Dr. Brown's house the night before. After hearing this electrifying piece of news, the nurse called Peters's mother, who called the sheriff, who called the DA, and before he knew what was happening, Peters was sitting in the DA's office being questioned. He spent the whole day telling his story, gradually getting himself in deeper and deeper. At first he said he had had nothing to do with it; he was only there because his cousin had asked him. But he was very suggestible, and by the end of the day he admitted that he had seen Dr. Brown dead before the fire started and had incriminated his cousin.

Dr. Wong Ham Lee, the local pathologist, did the postmortem at Glens Falls Hospital. Travis had made the mistake of assuming the fire would destroy all signs of Dr. Brown's death, but it isn't easy to destroy a body. Flesh doesn't burn spontaneously, and kerosene gets used up very quickly. If a lit match falls on dead skin, it will go out. In a fire, people die of carbon monoxide poisoning and soot inhalation. After they are unconscious or dead, they may be burned, but the fire has to be fueled by something other than skin—by clothing, or a wooden floor.

The first order of business was to identify the body. You can't automatically assume that the body in the building belongs there. Dr. Brown had patches of unmarked skin. She was lying on the floor on her back. The ceiling had collapsed on her front, burning her badly, but she was not burned on her back, on the places where her body was pressed against the floor and no oxygen reached. From the skin we knew she was white, which was a start. As always, the most reliable way to identify the dead woman was through X rays and teeth. One particular tooth had had extensive root-canal work done on it. It was conclusive.

As is routine in a fire death, Dr. Lee tested for carbon monoxide. Finding none, he concluded that Dr. Brown hadn't breathed in any poisonous fumes and was dead when the fire started. But he also saw soot in the windpipe, which meant exactly the opposite—that she *had* breathed in smoke and was therefore alive when the fire started. So it looked like an accident—death from smoke inhalation. But there was also her head to consider. It looked as if she had a subdural hemorrhage around the brain, meaning that Dr. Brown had been hit on the head and died of a fractured skull and brain injury. That made her death a murder. Murder meant arson—she couldn't have died and then started the fire after she was dead. But the fire marshals had looked for accelerants and found no evidence of arson. When accelerants like gasoline and kerosene evaporate, they produce hydrocarbons (compounds made of hydrogen and carbon) that have a low molecular weight. But when wood burns, it produces heavier hydrocarbons. The marshals could find only the heavier hydrocarbons, and concluded the fire was an accident.

All this added up to complete confusion. Every sign pointed to something different. Travis had confessed, but the police were having a hard time believing him. His confession did not bear out Lee's finding of soot inhalation. They dug out Travis's file and found the barn burning, but they hesitated. The police are very reluctant to say a death in a fire is murder because arson is hard to prove, and they have to prove arson to prove murder. The fire marshals went back for a second look. Part of the problem with hydrocarbons is their volatility. They are hard to find. The winds just blow them away. This time the marshals looked under the rug, in clothing, in corners, and found low-weight gasoline hydrocarbons. It was arson.

Now the police had to find out whether Dr. Brown was dead when the fire started. Travis said yes and the subdural hemorrhage said yes, but that meant two different causes. The soot in the windpipe said no, but the lack of carbon monoxide said yes. Which was it? They called to run the findings by me—were they consistent with a possible homicide? I said they couldn't have it both ways—if they had soot they had to have carbon monoxide too. I reautopsied the body with Lee and found that the subdural hemorrhage was really an epidural hemorrhage—it was just under the skull. Dr. Brown had not been hit on the head. The injury was caused by the fire itself, after death. Fire has an immense destructive power. It tightens and tears the skin like a knife wound. It makes the blood in the bones boil so that they fracture and break apart. Part of the skull was found a distance away from the body.

I looked at the blood for the telltale pink of carbon monoxide.

It wasn't there. I looked at the lungs for soot and found none. Therefore, she had already been dead. The soot in the windpipe was a very small amount near the top and had been washed in after death. It came from the water the firemen had been pouring on the fire. Then I looked at the heart and saw a very severe case of hardening of the arteries. As a cause of death, that fit Travis's confession—he punched her and she collapsed and died. In cases of advanced heart disease, heavy physical exertion or a powerful surge of emotion, like rage or fear, can trigger a precipitous drop in the blood flow to the heart. The amount of oxygen being pumped kept diminishing until it was too little to keep her alive. The punch was the *coup de grace.*

At the autopsy, there was no evidence of the punch. All of Dr. Brown's injuries were due to the fire. Neither the police nor the DA was happy with my conclusions. My postmortem converted a simple homicide which pleased everyone into one that was complicated and difficult to understand. It was still a homicide—Travis's blow was responsible for her death—but it was indirect. It would have been easier to prosecute an obvious smash-on-the-head murder and a vicious killer.

The case is awaiting trial, and Peters and Travis are in jail. The lawyers worked out a plea bargain for Peters, but it fell apart. As one of the prosecutors said, he should be convicted of "public imbecility."

In the following story, which took place on Maui, the dates and some names have been changed to protect the family.

On the day of her death, Daphne Mellon spent most of the afternoon with her sister, Laura. They shopped at the Moon Bow boutique on Papalaua Street, where Daphne bought a black dress. Afterward they got a root beer at the McDonald's at the corner of Wainee and Papalaua streets. Daphne called her boyfriend, Matthew Privlin, and Laura overheard her telling him she would pick him up at 9:00 at the restaurant where he worked as a cook. That night Daphne drove her Toyota to Maui Community College, where she was taking a summer course in history. Her class ended at 8:30, and she planned to spend half an hour in the Kaoahumanu shopping center before meeting Matt. She never arrived. At about 9:30 or so, Matt called Priscilla Mellon, Daphne's mother, to tell her that Daphne hadn't shown up. He drank two bottles of beer in the bar and went home at 10:30, and then called again. He went to sleep at 2:00 A.M. Daphne didn't come home that night.

Early the next morning, Priscilla Mellon reported her daughter missing to the police. Shortly afterward, a stranger called to tell her that Daphne's wallet and car registration papers were scattered on the road in front of his house. Laura and Matt went. Driving along the Honoapiilani Highway, they saw Daphne's car parked on the shoulder. It was out of gas.

Daphne's partially decomposed body was found in the middle of a sugar-cane field on July 8, 1986. She was twenty years old and had last been seen alive three days before, leaving Maui Community College. If it hadn't been for the three teenagers who came to check on their marijuana plants, she would not have been discovered. Cane grows to a height of eight feet and is extremely dense. It wasn't due to be harvested for months.

After the body was discovered, Dr. Roger Kerris autopsied it and signed it off as "undetermined." Kerris was the ME of Oahu, but Maui didn't have an ME of its own, and every so often Kerris flew over to help. He couldn't find anything wrong—no disease, no injury, no sign of drugs or alcohol. There was semen in Daphne's vagina, but no indication of violence. Dr. Frank Bronson at the G.N. Wilcox Memorial Hospital and Health Care Center on Maui did the toxicology tests. He didn't find anything either. But Kerris didn't quite believe his findings. How could a healthy twenty-year-old woman have died of nothing? She was wearing very little—underpants and a shirt—and no shoes. Friends remembered that she had been dressed in a white ruffled shirt, a tie-dyed miniskirt, a sash, and sandals. And there was the matter of her car. It had been found a few miles along the road from the body, and the license and registration and wallet were found a few miles beyond that. Kerris thought the whole setup looked like murder, and the police thought so, too. She could have run out of gas and been picked up by her killer, who robbed her and got rid of her wallet at the nearest convenient place. Kerris didn't have any medical evidence to support his theory, but he wrote on the autopsy report that Daphne Mellon was probably raped and either strangled or suffocated.

(Not long after Daphne's death, Kerris returned to Louisiana, where he had come from. He was called back to Hawaii to testify in a battered-child case in which the defense claimed that the child's death from a fractured skull was unintentional: the baby had been dropped accidentally on his head. Kerris testified that a baby can't get that kind of fracture from being dropped on its head, and in an extraordinary lapse of judgment he told people that he had prepared for his testimony by getting some dead babies and dropping them on their heads. The babies had recently died from sudden infant death syndrome. Their parents had not been consulted about their participation in this experiment. In the ensuing pandemonium, Kerris fell from grace and was told that the demand for his services in Louisiana had diminished.)

Daphne's parents were distraught. They wanted the police to arrest Matt, but he had an unbreakable alibi. He had been working until 9:00, and the manager of the restaurant verified his story of sitting at the bar waiting for Daphne.

Matt and his mother and brothers had moved to Maui from Los Angeles after his mother's divorce. He had dropped out of school and gone to work to supplement her income. He and Daphne had dated on and off for two years, he told the police. They had had an affair, but she backed off when he offered to buy her an engagement ring. She was getting her degree at the University of Hawaii on Oahu. During the school year she slept with fifteen members of the football team and told Matt about it. He was fascinated. It excited him enormously. A central part of their relationship consisted of him asking her to describe the whole thing in graphic detail and her telling him. He would then get angry and say it was disgusting and she would cry. Then they would make up. The police were suspicious that he might have killed her in a fit of jealousy, but Matt had another candidate—Joseph Orami, a former classmate.

The night before her death, Daphne and Matt had gone to the Banana Moon disco at the Marriott Hotel. At around 10:00, Joseph had come to their table and said something crude about Daphne's body. Matt told him to buzz off. Joseph told the police that he didn't remember saying anything offensive, just "Hey, you got one nice old lady." Whatever it was that he said, the police didn't think he had killed Daphne. They gave him a lie detector test, and he passed. But because of the brief time of only half an hour (8:30–9:00) that Daphne was missing, the police thought a lot of people were lying. Matt, for one, might know much more than he was telling. He wouldn't finish his polygraph test and left the island because, he said, the police were pestering him.

The cause of Daphne's death remained a mystery for two years. In 1988 I was asked to evaluate several cases that the Maui police hadn't been able to solve. When I looked over the reports on Daphne, I picked up tantalizing hints of drugs that trailed off into nowhere. Daphne had bought $100 worth of cocaine from an acquaintance who worked at the Maui Horse Center, and a razor blade with cocaine residue was found in her car. The toxicology report was negative, so no one thought it mattered. One interview followed the thread—Detective Robert Tam Ho's talk with Alison Monk, one of Daphne's college friends. Alison had heard a rumor from Matt, who got it from someone he refused to identify, that Daphne had died at a party while freebasing cocaine. Her friends had panicked and moved the body to avoid being incriminated, not realizing that people would think it was murder. The police discounted Alison's story (where did this mythical party take place, and who was there?), but to me it rang true. It looked like the same old streets–of–New York kind of incident that I'd been dealing with for much of my career. In big cities the police call it "dumping," but wherever it happens it's the same thing. Someone overdoses unexpectedly in the wrong place, with the wrong people, and the body is an embarrassment. They don't have time, they don't want to be bothered with police procedures; these are not the kind of people to get involved in a sordid little episode, and they certainly don't want anyone to know they've been doing drugs. It's much easier to move the body somewhere else and go on with their lives.

Daphne's friends were amateurs, which is why the scene looked like murder. Amateurs always cause confusion. They don't realize the consequences of what they are doing. They had taken her body to the sugar-cane fields (an excellent hiding place) and then driven her car north and abandoned it when it ran out of gas. It could have been burglarized by anyone walking along the highway, who then discarded the wallet.

As for Daphne's wearing only a shirt and underpants, that reinforced the idea of a cocaine and sex party. Her shoes could have been left in the apartment where she died. There was no hyoid fracture, no sign of any violence—the only thing left was drugs.

Although the hospital toxicology tests were negative, I knew that I couldn't always believe everything I read in an autopsy report. The equipment at Wilcox Hospital, where the tests were done, was all right for analyzing urine, but not autopsy tissues. Without high-tech equipment, cocaine can't be found in a decomposed body. After death the enzymes continue to break it down, hydrolizing it into benzoylecgonine, which is even harder to find.

Now it was two years later, but I thought the ME's office might have saved the frozen tissues and body fluids. But the office was in disarray—nothing was left. I tried Wilcox Hospital.

Hospitals don't usually save this material for two years, but Daphne Mellon had been an unusual case for them. Wilcox normally did urine screening on addicts, and if there was any problem with the specimen, the addicts could always come back. Daphne was different—she was a murder, or so they thought. They rarely got the opportunity to examine decomposed tissues from a murder. There would be no second chance, and they had no authorization to throw out anything. So they saved it.

I mailed the fluids to Professor Randall Baselt, a forensic toxicologist and director of the Chemical Toxicology Institute in Foster City, California—a private lab that specializes in drugs in general and cocaine in particular. He found benzoylecgonine.

That gave us a cause of death but no satisfactory explanation of what had happened—only the whisper of a party that no one on Maui admits to having attended or even to knowing that it took place. Daphne's parents at first refused to countenance the idea of a drug overdose. The family was certain she had been murdered. To them, a murder was more comforting. A drug overdose was personal—to some degree it could be blamed on them. A murder was impersonal. A maniac was out there in the indifferent universe. Every time a young woman was murdered on Maui, they thought her killer might be the same one who killed Daphne, and they asked the police to investigate where he had been when Daphne died. Nothing ever turned up, and finally they became reconciled to the idea of a drug overdose. Priscilla Mellon was angry and bitter at Daphne's "friends," whoever they might be, who dumped her daughter's body so unceremoniously and left it to rot, just to save their own skins. But then one day a young woman was found on a beach on the other side of the island, and it started all over again. Mrs. Mellon called the police. Was there any possibility the same man could have killed Daphne?

Deaths during sexual misadventure are few in number and highly dramatic. They are almost always unintended. There are exceptions, like the man who had a heart attack while making love to his Electrolux, but usually it's a matter of being carried away by an overabundance of rapture and not noticing that the mechanism of joy has developed a kink. Risk taking is part of the thrill—the risk of tightening the rope, of being found out, of allowing yourself to be controlled by someone else. To an outsider, the deaths look like something else, like suicide or murder. The S&M practitioners and the solo performers who have rigged up elaborate contraptions to refine their pleasure look like the victims of a ritual killing carried out by a secret barbarian sect. Sometimes the scene has been dismantled and the victim dressed, making the death that much harder to explain, but under the clothes the body is bruised and bloody, and there are ligature marks around the neck that look like strangulation. The trappings confuse the issue and make it easy to misinterpret the manner of death—whether it is an accident, suicide, or murder.

The "suicides" are the adolescent boys—and an occasional girl—who have inadvertently hanged themselves while experimenting with new sensations. They have discovered that pressure on the carotid artery, cutting off the supply of oxygen to the brain, heightens the pleasure of orgasm. The closer they are to unconsciousness, the greater their pleasure. The idea is to ejaculate at the moment of tightest pressure on the neck, when the least amount of oxygen is getting to the brain, and to release the pressure just before losing consciousness. But something goes wrong with the escape device—the rope slips or the zipper gets stuck or the slip knot tightens—and they lose consciousness before they can disentangle themselves. They are found hanging in a private, out-of-the-way place—an attic or a basement. The great majority are signed out as suicides, which plays havoc with the statistics of teenage deaths, but that's another problem.

There is some question whether the parents are aware of what was going on and, given two impossible choices, if they prefer the stigma of suicide to the shame of an autoerotic death. When I was still working under Helpern, the parents of a Harvard student came to us. The Boston ME had declared their son's death by hanging a suicide, and they couldn't accept it. It was out of character. They had had a good close relationship with him, and if he had been depressed and miserable enough to kill himself, they would have known about it. The idea of not knowing was profoundly disturbing to them. They brought the Boston autopsy report, the police report, and the photographs of the scene to us. The evidence was in the pictures. The boy's fly was open, and there was a mirror and a copy of *Playboy* opened to the centerfold where he could see it. These are the universal artifacts of this particular scene. If it isn't *Playboy,* it's a similar magazine. He had put a piece of cloth between his neck and the rope so there would be no marks afterward and no one would know. Suicides don't worry about marks. His parents were relieved to learn the truth. Sexual experimentation was something they could live with.

There is a continuum in these affairs. Those who experiment with simple hanging often move on to more complicated arrangements with ropes and chains, weights and pulleys, dildoes and handcuffs. Unlike most of the people I see, their homes are filled with books—Freud, de Sade, Genet, von Sacher-Masoch. They are educated, successful professionals—more than any other group, doctors and lawyers seem to have an affinity for this sort of thing. I saw my first one when I was still a medical student—a lawyer found dead at home, wearing women's clothes. He had attached a dildo device to a bicycle, a long pink broomstick padded with foam rubber. As he got more and more excited and pedaled faster and faster he lost control of the situation and the device perforated his colon. We had no trouble calling his death: he was alone, and from the way he was dressed it was clearly an accident. Some of his neighbors knew about his proclivities.

The Sutton Place banker was more problematical. The police thought it was murder. He was a thirty-five-year-old vice-president of a French bank who lived in a luxury high-rise apartment on Sutton Place South. His coworkers hadn't been able to reach him and called the police. He had been dead twenty-four hours when they arrived. They found him spread-eagled on the bed, held down with leather straps attached to chains. His left hand was unstrapped, as if he had been trying to free himself when he died. A camera was set up with a remote switch and a floodlight. There was nothing in the room that looked as if it had killed him. The police thought it might be a ritual murder or that he had picked up a gay in a bar who had tied him up and killed him. There was a lot of camera equipment in the bureau drawer, but they couldn't tell if anything had been stolen. He also had a supply of marijuana, heroin, and amyl nitrite, also known as poppers or snappers. It's a fancy version of nitroglycerine. You squeeze the glass capsule to break it, then inhale, and the result, presumably, is a spectacular orgasm. It works the same way as hanging, by diminishing the supply of oxygen going to the brain. He had not been alone. Later, the police saw the note from his companion. "Dear Robert," it said, "What a wild kafkaesque evening. My telephone number is ———. Your move. Marilyn."

I didn't think his death had any connection with the leather and chains. He had no marks on his neck, just on his wrists and ankles. At autopsy, his lungs were filled with fluid. He could have been suffocated intentionally, but other than the fluid, there was no sign of it. Underneath the outlandish trappings, it looked like a normal heroin overdose, and toxicology confirmed that it was. Marilyn, the woman who wrote the note, was not prosecuted. All the paraphernalia belonged to him, and the doorman said he had a lot of visitors. He didn't die from his sex life, and the DA was satisfied that death was unintentional.

The most difficult of these cases to call are those involving S&M. The death is usually the result of a small miscalculation—but whose? Because S&M requires two people, there is a possibility that the mistake was deliberate. An internist who taught and practiced at a major New York hospital kept a diary and considered writing a book about his experiences, but was concerned that it might affect his practice. He knew he would have to deny his authorship, not out of shame but economics—he would certainly lose his license to practice if anyone unmasked him. And he didn't want to become a writer—he just wanted to write about *this*. "This is it, the sum and substance of my fantasies, lived, acted out, intended, aborted, and otherwise," he wrote. He worried about the bruises, the discolorations on his arms that his colleagues noticed at work. Fortunately for him, it was the skiing season, and they drew the obvious, if incorrect, conclusion.

The doctor was a masochist, obsessed with bondage fantasies, but the nurse he lived with was not a sadist. She loved him, and the thought of hurting him horrified her, but she also wanted to make him happy. It took him a long time to persuade her to cater to his desires. For her first full-fledged effort she hired a professional sadist, someone who provided physical pain for a living. One day he came home for lunch and the nurse had a surprise for him. They had experimented a little, so she wasn't entirely ignorant of the procedure. She put her favorite pillowcase over his head—the one with the lavender and violets—and slipped something down his back. As he fumbled to find it, she handcuffed his hands behind him. He went along with it, amused at her "childish games," but when she was finished with the preliminaries he had a chain around his neck, locked tightly in place, a gag in his mouth, and another tight chain between his legs, also locked in place. He was standing on a wobbly stool (a piece of furniture he could not remember seeing in the apartment before), his neck chain hooked to the ceiling, worrying about how dangerous it was—if the stool tipped over, he would hang himself.

She left the room and put some music on, a Vivaldi flute concerto. It enraged him. "How could she do that with me in here like this? She had gone off her rocker. I feared her return. What was next?" More chains were next, but he had to wait for them.

Waiting was part of the torture. She would leave for a while, come back and add something or hurt him in a new way, and leave again. He hung there, his wrists and fingers numb, the fight slowly ebbing out of him. Half an hour later she came back and chained his ankles together.

Her next return was more frightening. Standing behind him, she lifted the pillowcase and suddenly pulled a tight stocking over his head down to his chin. He couldn't breathe; it was pressed tight against his nose. Quickly she snipped a hole in it with a pair of scissors. He felt a trickle on his lips. Had she cut his nose? He couldn't tell. Then she wrapped adhesive tape around his face, mummifying him. "The heat was incredible. . . . I wanted out. . . . My jaw ached from the pressure on my chin. The pressure on my eyeballs made red kaleidoscopes. I knew if I choked on that damn gag the only thing to save me was a tracheostomy." She pulled a mask over his head and laced it up. Part of the pleasure is fear of the unexpected. The mask enhanced the sense of mystery and anticipation, the feelings of helplessness and submissiveness, of being at someone else's mercy. But she had overdone it. "I pushed with my tongue to move the gag forward. If I let that damn thing go further back it would cut off my air completely. My tongue was wedged below the gag. I felt it slipping backwards. Where was she?"

He realized that she hadn't spoken to him since she had first put the pillowcase over his head. "Was it she or had she gotten one of those crazy lunatics from one of the S&M clubs to take over for her?" He hung by his wrists, aching, numb, his genitals wrapped around with ropes and chains, his toes just touching the floor. The stool had been taken away. He heard a new record—"Strauss. Richard. Johann would have been too ludicrous."

He couldn't communicate with her, couldn't get her to pay attention to his needs. "I wanted to tell her that I needed to talk to her, that she was hurting me. . . . The first lash across my shoulders felt good. She landed a few good ones across the backs of my knees that burned like fire. I squirmed sensually with the warm glow that enveloped my back and butt. I began to enjoy myself. The thongs clattered dryly on the floor and the door slammed. She knew it."

Then she came back. "The first blow was like a knife. . . . Something was running down my back. Blood. It was cool. Aagh. . . . Another blow. My breathing was heavy. I tried to calm myself. My body shook. I let the pain envelop me. The redness of my mind suffused throughout me. The burning extended from my genitals to my fingertips. . . . A red kaleidoscope. I was going higher and higher. Maybe I was going to die. I didn't mind. I writhed with the redness, stretching and shrugging, feeling the burning skin fill my mind with redness. . . . The blood surged. An orgasm of relief. My mind cleared. I hurt. I smiled. I needed the pain to stay alive."

This first episode was in the summer. Soon the nurse learned what he liked and she herself became proficient at doing it. Their last game took place just before Christmas 1969. The doctor came home for lunch. The nurse put the gag and hood on him, handcuffed, chained, and whipped him, and let him stay like that, wondering what might happen next. While he hung there she ran out to Alexander's to pick up a Christmas present for him. When she came back he was dead. She unchained him, removed the mask and gag, put him in bed, and called the police.

The police sent him to us. They didn't see any signs of violent death—no knife or gunshot wounds—but they thought it could have been a drug overdose. He was thirty-five years old and had no history of illness. Until the age of forty, more men and women die of unnatural causes than natural—of suicide, accident, murder, or an overdose. I saw whip marks, ligature marks on the wrists and ankles, and hemorrhages in the whites of the eyes. The penis seemed scrunched and wrinkled. The mouth had abrasions inside, and there were also tears in the anus. All the organs were normal, and there was no sign of a heart attack or drugs.

After a body goes to the ME, a relative or someone close to the family has to make an identification and sign a form. The nurse came, and we discussed the findings with her. She was more comfortable talking to us as doctors than to the police. She had made her lover happy, and she didn't feel she had done anything wrong. She left the chains with us. They were a reminder of him. We reconstructed his death from her story. The gag was too far back in his throat. With a gag, you can breathe through your nose, but if it goes back too far it obstructs the entire airway. We sometimes get this kind of death when elderly people are robbed in their homes. The thief ties them up and gags them, thinking someone will come and rescue them, but the gag has been thrust too far back. By the time they are found it is too late.

The nurse told us the doctor had liked the first experience so much that she had begun doing it for him. The periods of isolation, of wondering what would come next, were part of the joy of it, and so was the music. When the police asked her why she had left him alone she said, "Because he looked like he was having such a good time."

I signed him out as "asphyxia during sexual bondage," and forbore to classify the death in one of our usual cubbyholes—homicide, suicide, natural, accident. It didn't seem to fit anywhere. It was *sui generis*. My job was to figure out the cause, not whether the death was intentional. That was the DA's job. And there was an opening for a criminal theory. A scenario of sexual jealousy could be developed, and a nurse who knew physiology could place a gag a centimeter too far. The DA decided it was a homicide—the nurse had contributed to the death by leaving the apartment. Even with the doctor's consent, she had an obligation to stay. The case seemed awfully flimsy to me. I thought he was just playing it safe—five years down the line no one could come back and say he had missed a murder. The grand jury decided not to indict. They thought it was disgusting and obscene, but the doctor and nurse were consenting adults; no one had been forced. The DA seemed satisfied with the decision.

11

DIAGNOSTIC FOLLIES

NATURAL ENDINGS

MANY OF THE cases I am asked to review hinge on the possibility of a mistaken diagnosis. In a murder, medical examiners who can't figure out the cause of death tend to go along with the police theory. Instead of arriving at their own independent conclusion, MEs just become rubber stamps. There is nothing deliberately dishonest about this. The police want to solve the murder, and the ME, mistakenly thinking he is there to serve them, adopts their theory. In murders between people who know each other, the police are usually right and no harm is done; but when they are wrong, lives are forfeit. Sometimes there is no murder, and a man is found guilty of a crime that didn't take place. This is what happened to Leonard Barco, a janitor for a toy store who was caught in the grindings of the system, unable to extricate himself.

On Sunday morning, April 28, 1985, Gail Morris, a thirty-year-old black woman, was found dead in the front seat of a rusted and abandoned red Volkswagen, together with a collection of beer cans and empty vodka bottles. She had lived in

Plainfield, New Jersey, and spent much of her time drinking with Leonard Barco, a forty-five-year-old black man who was married. Her blue snorkel jacket was lying across the roof of the car. Its presence led to her discovery.

To the police, Barco was the obvious suspect. He had been seen drinking with Morris the previous Thursday night. Her brother-in-law saw them Friday morning, and a friend saw them Friday night at a liquor store. No one else saw her alive after that.

On Sunday, the day Morris was found, the police took a six-page statement from him in which he confessed to fighting with Morris but not killing her. They had been together Saturday night, he said. She was drunk, he got more vodka, and they continued to drink together. She also took some pills. He stayed with her until about 11:00 P.M. and left after they fought about his going home to his wife. She picked up a broom handle that was lying on the ground and hit him with it. He hit her back.

On Monday, the ME of Union County, Dr. Gennaro Braga, who had held his job for over fifteen years, autopsied Morris. He saw marks on her neck and small bruises on her chest and back, but could not explain the cause of death. The police, who had already interviewed Barco, told Braga they thought he had killed her. Braga, who was not a pathologist, took their word for it, and even though Morris had no neck fracture, he decided she had been beaten and strangled. The death was now officially a murder.

Braga had interpreted his findings as being consistent with the suspicions of the police. As commonly happens, they told him what they wanted him to say, and he told them what they wanted to hear. But he disagreed with one thing. He didn't think Barco had gotten the time of death right. Barco had said that he had been with Morris on Saturday night and that she had been alive when he left her. Braga thought Morris had been dead for over twenty-four hours. This put the murder at about midnight of Friday the 26th.

On the strength of Braga's autopsy findings, the police arrested Barco and got a second confession from him. This one followed the line of Braga's interpretation. In it, Barco admitted to strangling Morris. He had been too upset to say so the first time they questioned him, he told Detective La Vigne—he got excited when a lot of people were around him—but he was telling them the whole truth now. He also became confused about the time he was supposed to have killed Morris. He switched from Wednesday to Thursday to Friday, but the police got him straightened out. Eventually, they convinced him he had killed Morris early Friday morning, not on Saturday night as he had originally said. He was remorseful. "I feel bad because I killed Gail," he said.

The police also thought they would have a stronger case if they could show that Barco had lied. In their report they noted that they found misstatements and discrepancies: in his first confession Barco said he struck Morris once; in his second, he struck her three or four times. To their way of thinking, they had caught him in a lie, which made him guiltier. Barco, unaware of the report, applauded the proceedings: he had been "treated like a man," he said; Detective La Vigne had been nice to him, but he did not like the other investigators.

The police had made every effort to fit the confession to the postmortem report, but a few facts didn't quite conform to it. The most glaring inconsistency was Morris's disappearance. She wasn't in the car during part of the time she was supposed to be dead. The car was parked near her sister's house, and her sister, Priscilla Diane Morris, saw it every day when she went out in the backyard to feed her Doberman pinscher. On Saturday, Priscilla's children were playing out back with a bat and ball, and the ball rolled under the car. Priscilla went under the car after it. As she later explained to the police, if Gail had been in the car, she would have seen her.

But if the case didn't all hang together, there was nobody else to pin the murder on. And it seemed reasonable for Barco to have done it. He languished in jail for eight months awaiting trial. At the end of that time, the public defender of New Jersey asked for my opinion about Morris's death. States that have capital punishment, as New Jersey does, also have legislative guidelines regarding its use. All murders are not equal. Someone has to decide whether the level of viciousness is enough to warrant the death penalty. In the past it was simpler—if the jury decided you were guilty, you were executed. Now there are nuances and calibrations. One way to measure the heinousness of the crime is by the pain and suffering of the victim. Was the victim conscious? For how long? The public defender wanted advice on whether the murder was heinous enough to sentence Barco to death.

When I looked at the evidence, I saw a number of discrepancies. Gail Morris had health problems that might have contributed to her death. She was a drug addict and an epileptic and had been hospitalized in the past for grand mal seizures. The hospital had given her medicine, but there was no evidence that she was taking it. Epileptic seizures can be triggered by alcohol, and if they are severe enough and last long enough they can cause death, but there would be no way to know whether that had actually happened. The bruises on her neck did not point to anything definite, either. They were just bruises, the kinds that are common to alcoholics, who often bump into things. Morris's windpipe was not fractured; there were no hemorrhages in her eyes. In fact, there was no evidence at all that she had been murdered. On the other hand, she had 0.46 percent alcohol in her blood, an amount high enough to cause death. She had probably overdosed on alcohol.

Other evidence put the time of death much later than Friday, and confirmed Barco's original story. The pictures of Morris showed unhatched maggot eggs in her eyes. Maggots have a reliable biological cycle. Their development from egg to worm to fly follows a predictable timetable. The stage and condition of those eggs was almost as good as having a clock. In my experience, flies deposit their eggs on people just after death or while they are unconscious. Between the time they are laid and the time they hatch, maggot eggs last less than twenty-four hours. Therefore, Morris must have been dead less than twenty-four hours when she was found on Sunday morning. If she had been killed on Friday, the eggs would already have hatched.

Rigor mortis also proceeds inexorably, and it told the same time as the maggot eggs. Rigor was extensive when Morris was found. It is at its stiffest twelve hours after death, and takes twelve hours to disappear. On Monday, when the body was autopsied, it was gone. Rigor could not have lasted from Friday night to Sunday morning.

Finally, there was the commonsense evidence of the blue jacket, the jacket that nobody stole. Morris's blue jacket was lying across the top of the car like a banner. In her ghetto neighborhood, a good blue jacket would not have lasted twenty-four hours—it would have vanished long before Sunday morning, when she was found. Morris was probably alive on Saturday and wearing her jacket.

Dr. Braga, who signed the autopsy report, did an extraordinary thing—he admitted to the judge that he had made a mistake. Few of us have the grace to apologize. He hadn't known about Morris's alcohol level. He had sent tissues to the lab, but he had not seen the results. Afterward, when the search continued for witnesses, people turned up who had seen Morris alive on Friday and Saturday. Barco was released from prison.

This story had a happy ending. The review system saved a man from the ultimate injustice. For the most part, it is the poor who get into this kind of trouble, but the cause—faulty forensic diagnosis—can be found on every level of society. Under different circumstances, Claus von Bulow, who had command of millions, had the same problem.

Claus von Bulow was accused of twice trying to murder his wife, Martha "Sunny" Crawford von Auersperg von Bulow, socialite and utilities heiress, with insulin injections. Between December 1979 and December 1980, Sunny was hospitalized three times in a coma. In the first episode at Newport Hospital, Dr. Janis Gailitis diagnosed her as having bronchopneumonia. He also noticed that she had low blood sugar. After she recovered, her New York doctor, Richard J. Stock, gave her a glucose tolerance test. Over a period of six hours, the test will show a high sugar level for diabetics and a low one for hypoglycemics. Sunny's sugar level went low. After four hours it was down to 23, and Stock diagnosed idiopathic hypoglycemia (low blood sugar of unknown origin, probably natural). The normal blood sugar level is considered to be between 80 and 120, but normal is what is normal for you. During exercise, a normal blood sugar of 100 can go down to the 20s with absolutely no ill effect. You don't get into serious trouble until it gets near zero. Sunny could manage very well at 23.

Early the following December when the von Bulows were in New York, Claus found his wife unconscious and rushed her to Lenox Hill Hospital. Her speech was slurred and she had a head injury, and Dr. Stock thought she might have a blood clot on her brain. But blood tests showed her pH to be very acid. Doctors pumped out her stomach, gave her fluids, and restored her electrolyte balance. Stock diagnosed "involuntary aspirin toxicity in the course of treating a severe headache." Sunny had overdosed on aspirin. She had taken at least sixty-five tablets, well above the lethal level for many people. Aspirin makes the blood acidic. The body's pH changes from alkaline to acid, preventing the enzymes from functioning properly. It is impossible to take sixty-five pills accidentally, without noticing it. Aspirin is not a cumulative drug. The pills all have to be taken within a short period of time.

The aspirin overdose was a failed suicide attempt. Nobody would say it, so Sunny wasn't offered counseling. Most of the successful suicides we see have already been seen by other doctors in the two or three months before their death. This was not just a cry for help like Robert McFarlane's, or a superficial wrist slashing. Most people would have died. There was no question of insulin.

The final hospitalization came three weeks later. On Sunday morning, December 21, Claus found Sunny unconscious on the marble floor of their bathroom at Clarendon Court, her Newport mansion. The window was open; it was 5 degrees Fahrenheit outside, and she was hypothermic—her temperature was down to 81 degrees when they got her to the hospital. It is rare to survive such a low temperature. The heart starts beating irregularly when the temperature falls to the mid-80s. Sunny was literally within minutes of death. Had von Bulow waited longer, she would have died. Judging from the way she was found and from the open medicine cabinet, the EMS people thought it was an alcohol and barbiturate overdose. The admitting doctors, who also considered her age and the fact that she had no history of illness, agreed. They took a blood sample and gave her a glucose test (this is one of the first things hospitals do when someone is brought in unconscious from unknown causes) and quickly learned that her blood sugar was 29. It was an abnormal finding, and they focused their entire attention on it. Usually, the hospital staff begins treating a suspected overdose right away, even before the lab results come back, but they were diverted by the glucose. Unaware that she functioned well with an even lower blood sugar level of 23, they thought that must be the cause of the coma. It was a misdiagnosis. Four hours later the lab phoned in the alcohol and barbiturate levels. The doctors discounted them. They were already working on the premise of low blood sugar.

They started her on an IV, which raised her glucose level. An hour or two later they drew a second blood sample, and the lab tested it for glucose. The glucose level was higher because of the sugar in the IV, but Sunny remained in a coma. The doctors asked the lab to test for insulin, but the lab technician didn't think it was necessary to test both samples and threw one out.

(Later, a great deal of confusion arose over which one of these samples was actually tested.) Insulin controls the glucose level in the body by "eating" sugar. If the sugar level is high, the pancreas produces more insulin to process it. If the sugar level is down at 29, where Sunny's was, the pancreas should stop producing insulin.

Sunny remained in a coma. The hospital lab sent the blood specimen to a more sophisticated lab in Boston, but something went wrong. The first time it got a 0.8 reading of insulin. The lab tested a second time, and the result was 350 units. (Ten to 20 units is normal.) Such a disparity usually indicates that something is drastically wrong with the specimen. The lab sent the sample to its main laboratory in Anaheim, California, to try a third time. A few weeks went by before the results came back. Anaheim got yet another number—216 units—and reported that number to the hospital. It seemed like a reasonable number. Intravenous glucose, such as Sunny was getting, can normally shoot the insulin level to over 216. No injection was necessary to arrive there. However, the high insulin level was used as evidence that Claus had injected Sunny. It was the scientific basis, the crux of the charge. An insulin level of 216 units is much too high to coexist with a blood sugar level of 29. It suggests insulin poisoning—unless the insulin and blood sugar are not coexisting at all, and the numbers come from two different specimens.

After being told that an excessive amount of insulin had put Sunny in a coma, the family became suspicious. Maria Schrallhammer, Sunny's fiercely loyal maid, who had been with her for twenty-eight years, remembered seeing insulin in a black bag. (Claus, who was very amusing, had been known to refer to her as "Mrs. Danvers," the housekeeper in *Rebecca*.) The black bag and its contents sat at the center of the case like some dark malevolent totem. It was of dubious provenance. Claus said it belonged to Sunny, but he thought that her son from her first marriage, Prince Alexander von Auersperg, had tampered with it. Alexander said it belonged to Claus. Everyone denied owning it. It was an orphan.

There were several sightings of it. Maria first saw the bag in a closet in Sunny's Fifth Avenue apartment and then again at Clarendon Court, on December 19, 1980, two days before her mistress was found unconscious. The bag was filled with drugs (including an exotic variety of Valium in the form of a yellow paste, not available in the United States), syringes, and several needles. Later, Maria saw a small glass vial of insulin. "Insulin, for what?" she asked, taking her suspicions to Alexander. He and his sister, Annie-Laurie, called Ala, hired Richard Kuh, a lawyer and former New York City district attorney, to conduct an investigation. They looked for the bag and found it a few weeks later in January 1981, inside a locked closet at Clarendon Court. There was no insulin in it. One of the needles had been used.

In the course of preparing for the trial, the prosecution tested the used needle and found that the outside of it was caked with insulin. This was interpreted as proof that it had been injected into Sunny, a conclusion that makes no sense at all. Needles don't work that way. After an injection, there is no drug left on the outside of the needle. The skin and tissues collapse over it as it is withdrawn, and wipe it clean. Traces of the drug remain in the inner bore of the needle, but not on the outside. In any event, the black bag and everything in it was tainted, having been handled by Claus's accusers before it got to the Rhode Island police.

Claus hired Herald Price Fahringer as his defense lawyer. Fahringer was the quintessential defender, tall, handsome, and silver-haired. His bearing was aristocratic, his tailoring impeccable. He had recently handled one of the Jean Harris appeals. He called me in to consult before the first trial.

When I looked over the records, I was struck by the amounts of alcohol and barbiturates. The alcohol level in Sunny's blood was 0.01 when she was brought to the hospital. This is low, but if you consider the rate at which the body absorbs and breaks down alcohol, it indicates a very high level in her blood when she collapsed at home. She had not drunk any alcohol from the time she lost consciousness in the bathroom until the time the tests were taken—a period of eight hours. The body burns up about 0.015 gram per 100 cc of blood every hour. That is one shot of whiskey or one can of beer per hour. After eight hours, her body would have burned up .12 gram—that is, eight drinks—and there was still some left.

She also had the equivalent of ten to twelve capsules of amobarbital in her blood, which by itself is enough to cause a coma. That level would also have been higher at the time of her collapse. But the hospital doctors looked at Sunny's condition from the point of view of treating it. If it wasn't dangerous, it didn't have to be treated. They didn't think she had enough amobarbital in her blood at the time she was hospitalized to be in danger. They didn't count back eight hours. And they were misled by the low blood sugar.

The alcohol and barbiturate levels and the aspirin overdose added up to a typical suicide attempt, the same kind I saw all the time in my job, except for the mansion and the marble floors. It reminded me of Edwin Arlington Robinson's poem about Richard Corey: he was "richer than a king," the envy of all the townspeople, but they saw only the superficial glitter; they didn't know anything about him. "And Richard Corey, one calm summer night,/Went home and put a bullet through his head." Suicide made sense psychologically, too. People who fail at suicide don't just give up—they keep trying until they succeed (assuming they are serious about it). Sunny tried twice—once with aspirin and then, three weeks later, with alcohol and barbiturates.

If I was wrong, if Claus had tried to murder her, he did it with barbiturates, not insulin.

I told Fahringer there was no insulin, that Claus was being tried for a murder attempt that had never taken place, and Sunny was in an irreversible coma because the doctors had misdiagnosed her. He might have grounds for a malpractice suit against the hospital, and I thought such a suit could strengthen his hand in the courtroom. But Fahringer did not believe it was his job to develop a malpractice suit. It was his job to see that Claus was found not guilty. He didn't go along with my suicide theory, either. In his view, there was no evidence of it, and he couldn't just come out of left field and claim suicide. No one in Sunny's family had ever suggested such a thing. More likely, Sunny was abusing drugs and kept taking larger and larger amounts and drinking more and more until she went into a coma. Even so, the general belief in the insulin theory was over-powering. It had been accepted by virtually everyone on its face value. In order to counter it and prove suicide, Fahringer needed extrinsic conditions—proof that Sunny was depressed or had been telling people that she didn't want to go on living. Other-wise, his credibility with the jury would dwindle, and so would his effectiveness.

Rather than gamble Claus's freedom against such high odds, Fahringer chose a two-pronged defense: Claus was innocent and it wasn't insulin poisoning, but if it was, there were other ways of explaining it, such as Sunny's abuse of drugs.

At the trial, he focused on the blood-test mixups. Altogether, there were two blood samples, two tests for glucose (one on each sample), and three tests for insulin. The first glucose test was taken when Sunny was rushed to the hospital in hypothermia with a blood sugar of 29. When the doctors took the second blood sample, Sunny was already being treated, absorbing sugar water from the IV. Her sugar level would be high, and the insulin level would have risen to meet it. So a high insulin level in the second sample would mean nothing. One of these blood samples was sent to the lab to be tested for insulin. One of them was thrown out. Which was which? The rest of the mixup centered on the three different test results for insulin and the fact that the lab had arbitrarily chosen the one that came out at 216 units.

The three different results invalidated the entire exercise. There was no way to know how much insulin Sunny had in her blood.

Fahringer didn't think he needed to belabor the three different laboratory results. It was enough that the lab had tested the wrong specimen for insulin. He interviewed the two hospital technicians who had handled the samples. One of them told him she thought she had thrown out the first sample (taken before the IV) and she agreed to testify to it, but she changed her story on the witness stand. Under oath she swore she did everything right—it was the second sample that was thrown out and the first that was tested for insulin.

Other things fell apart, too, for their own perverse reasons. Fahringer had bad luck with his witnesses. Joy O'Neill, a woman who had worked in an exercise salon in Manhattan (since closed), testified that Sunny came in often. They developed a friendship, and Sunny told her how she injected herself with insulin to lose weight. This story might have created a stir, but the salon's records, which the prosecution dug out at great effort, showed that Sunny had rarely gone there. Did the witness lie? Were the records wrong? Fahringer thought that Sunny's appointments were off the books for tax purposes, but the testimony undermined his case.

Two of the doctors that Fahringer relied heavily on were not persuasive with the jury. Dr. Milton Hamolsky, of Brown University Medical School, was pressed by the prosecution into admitting that he could not rule out an insulin injection as the source of Sunny's coma. The second doctor, John Thomas Carr, chief psychiatrist at Newport Hospital, diagnosed her as "neurotic and desperately in need of psychotherapy," and testified that she could be classified as suicidal. But Carr hardly knew her. He had gone to her room to interview her after her first coma, and had reached this conclusion after an acquaintanceship of about twenty minutes.

This ineffectual showing of the defense witnesses did not make much of a dent in the prosecution's case. Dr. Richard J. Stock,

Sunny's New York doctor who prescribed her sleeping pills and tranquilizers, testified against Claus. Stock had given Sunny the original glucose tolerance test and diagnosed idiopathic hypoglycemia. At the trial he said that Sunny's hypoglycemia was a nonserious disease, and she would not have gone into a coma from it. The coma had to be caused by an insulin injection. He had accepted the prosecution's numbers—the 29 glucose combined with the 216 insulin.

In addition to Stock, Stephen Famiglietti, the chief prosecuting attorney, lined up a team of Harvard Medical School professors to testify against Claus. They may have been brilliant at treating natural diseases, but they were out of their element when it came to diagnosing poisoning. They had no way of evaluating whether the lab tests made sense. None of them questioned the premise. They simply draped their opinion on the faulty structure of the insulin theory—that Sunny's low glucose and high insulin equaled poison.

Dr. Harris Funkenstein, a prominent Boston neurologist, testified that there could be only three possible causes for the coma—an insulin-producing tumor, a liver disorder arising from alcoholism, or exogenous insulin (injected from the outside). Having set up his own straw man, he then knocked it down: tests had established that neither of the first two causes applied; therefore it had to be the third. Funkenstein also thought the coma could have been "self-induced," as he delicately put it, but Fahringer stuck to his original plan and did not pursue this line of questioning. There had been no previous evidence of Sunny's injecting herself.

Dr. George Cahill, affiliated with Harvard Medical School and an expert on diabetes, also testified that injected insulin was the only possible explanation of Sunny's coma. Fahringer asked if he would still think the same thing if the insulin test was invalid, and Cahill replied that it didn't matter; it had to be insulin anyway because the sugar level was so low. Everyone lost sight of the fact that it was 23 during Stock's glucose test.

The doctors were equally uninformed about the levels of alcohol and barbiturates. Not having been trained in forensic pathology, they weren't suspicious enough and didn't have the background to ask the right questions; they didn't realize that the levels must have been very high when she went into a coma. Funkenstein dismissed the barbiturate level—it was too low to mean anything, he said. Cahill thought it was possible the barbiturates had contributed to the coma, but they couldn't have caused it—barbiturates have no effect on blood sugar. Therefore, it had to be insulin. None of the experts appreciated the significance of the earlier aspirin overdose.

By their testimony this clutch of prominent experts, unschooled in forensic medicine, gave weight and authority to a meaningless insulin test. They were presented with an assumption—that 29 glucose and 216 insulin meant that Sunny had been poisoned with an insulin injection—and they never questioned it. But Claus was very impressed with them. He identified with them socially. He sat there listening as one after another they put the noose around his neck and tightened it, and thought how admirable they were.

Later, during his appeal, I told him they were off the mark. "Oh, they were quite good," he said. "Yes," I said, "they were good but wrong." He looked puzzled. They were honorable men, didn't I understand? He regarded them as a connoisseur would, judging them on the basis of style, not substance. His sense of status completely dominated his code of values. Even though the doctors were wrong, he would be more likely to accept a false statement from a member of the club than the truth from an outsider. He had no animosity. I was not so dazzled. To me it looked like another case of the best and the brightest making a mess for everyone else to clean up.

I also thought that some of the main characters in the drama had something to protect, and might not be entirely unhappy if Claus were found guilty. Dr. Stock would be absolved of any problem that might arise from prescribing barbiturates. The hospital would be out from under a misdiagnosis and possible malpractice suit. The Harvard experts need never be questioned about the quality of their expertise. Sunny's children would avoid the stigma of having a mother who had tried suicide, and they wouldn't have to share her money with Claus. None of these matters was of overriding importance, but still, a guilty verdict would be convenient.

For its own reasons, the jury thought so, too. In March 1982, Claus was found guilty on two counts of attempted murder, based on Sunny's first and third hospitalizations. The aspirin overdose fell through the cracks.

Shortly after his conviction, Claus hired two new lawyers, Alan Dershowitz and Thomas Puccio. Dershowitz was in charge of finding grounds on which to appeal the verdict, which he did; after he won the appeal, Puccio handled the second trial. Like Fahringer, both lawyers were prominent if not flamboyant. They courted cameras and reporters and publicity. Dershowitz appeared frequently on Ted Koppel's *Nightline.* Puccio had just triumphed in the Abscam convictions, which sent a U.S. senator, among others, to jail for accepting a bribe.

Dershowitz gathered evidence to persuade the court that the first trial was legally defective and raised questions about the old evidence. Fahringer had laid the groundwork for an appeal by objecting in all the right places during the trial. He also helped to publicize Truman Capote's recollections of Sunny, which were used in the appeal.

Capote went on talk shows and gossiped about his friendship with Sunny. She drank a lot, he said, and she took drugs. He knew for a fact that she had injected herself with insulin in order to lose weight. This was not exactly new—Joy O'Neill, the woman in the exercise salon, had said the same thing—but O'Neill's evidence had been discounted, and her presence on the talk-show circuit would never have had the same fascination as Capote's did. Dershowitz understood that judges read the newspapers and are influenced by human as well as legal arguments.

While Dershowitz and Puccio were figuring out strategies, Claus called me. He had seen my name in Fahringer's records and wanted to talk about the medical and scientific evidence. I first met him at a working dinner in Sunny's fourteen-room Fifth Avenue apartment. Sunny was lying in a coma in the Harkness Pavilion at the Columbia-Presbyterian Medical Center. Two of Dershowitz's law students were working out of the apartment. Money was tight. The bulk of Sunny's $75 million estate was all tied up, and there was a strong possibility that Claus would never see the $14 million he was due to inherit on her death. The will didn't say anything about a coma. Meanwhile, he was living on the interest from a $2 million trust—$120,000 a year—and feeling squeezed.

Claus, always a gracious host, greeted me at the door wearing a smoking jacket. He mentioned that his daughter, Cosima, had attended the same school as mine, and joked about our notoriety: between us, we were keeping the *New York Post* in headlines, I with my fight with Koch and he with his attempted murder. The apartment was palatial, with marble floors, antique furniture, gilt mirrors, and a library full of leather-bound books that had an unopened look about them. Andrea Reynolds, Claus's Hungarian-born companion, was there, along with her third husband, Sheldon Reynolds, the television producer. Sheldon apparently had not yet read in the gossip columns that his wife was having an affair with Claus. Andrea, who had strong opinions, had taken it upon herself to coordinate the defense. She had a great deal of common sense and was very protective of Claus. His first batch of lawyers had let him down, she said, and she was anxious to develop the medical and scientific evidence. Claus was afraid it would get lost in the legal technicalities of the appeal.

Dinner was a tunafish casserole.

We had several dinner meetings, and I told Claus about my suicide theory at one of them. Even though he had everything to gain from it, he rejected the idea: "I don't think she would commit suicide," he said. He seemed to feel it would be worse for people to think that he had driven his wife to suicide than that he had killed her.

My role in the appeal was to evaluate the accuracy of the insulin levels which Fahringer had shied away from. Dershowitz and Puccio were high on it and had no qualms about trampling on Claus's delicate feelings. My affidavit had three themes: first, that insulin was not involved at all in Sunny's first episode in December 1979—her doctor in Providence, Janis Gailitis, had diagnosed bronchopneumonia; second, that Sunny was suicidal, and the aspirin overdose (the second episode) had to be a suicide attempt; finally, that Sunny had continued her suicide threat in the third episode, an alcohol and barbiturate overdose.

Dershowitz had a deadline for the appeal, and I worked to finish my affidavit on time. So did my associates, Dr. Robert Shaler, the serologist, and Dr. Leo DalCortivo, the toxicologist. After all the urgency, Dershowitz's assistants were in no hurry to pick up the documents. They were going to collect Capote's deposition first. I was a little miffed about this. I thought the gossip was trivial, and it disturbed me that Dershowitz was treating our work like second-class material. But it didn't matter. The judges overturned the verdict on a legal technicality, and the state decided to retry Claus.

At the second trial, which was televised, Puccio asked me to sit at the table with him when the prosecution experts testified. He wanted me to interpret medical and scientific evidence and tell him which questions to ask. Some doctors do this. I am uncomfortable doing it because it gives the jury the impression that I am an advocate, not impartial. I did agree to watch the trial on television at home, after which we would discuss his questions for the next day.

Puccio called me from Providence one Sunday, worried about an unsettling development. The prosecution claimed to have uncovered new evidence. Dr. Jeremy R. Worthington, a neurologist who had gone to Oxford and was on the consulting staff at

Newport Hospital, was being billed as a star witness against Claus. Worthington had seen bruises and scratches on Sunny at the hospital, the kinds of marks that looked as if they had been inflicted by another person. The prosecution had an inflammatory theory to match the bruises—that Claus had held Sunny down and injected her with insulin. He had first tried to knock her out with a barbiturate injection so he could inject the insulin more easily. Sunny tried to prevent him and they struggled, hence the bruises.

The theory was absurd. It was superfluous for Sunny to have two reasons to be unconscious. Why inject two drugs when one will do? The theory made more sense applied to a suicide than to a murder attempt. Suicides often use more than one drug, just to be sure. But Puccio was worried. The idea put a whole new sinister slant on their relationship, and Claus, who had been convicted once, was sinister enough already. He asked me to look over the hospital records to see if the theory had any merit and, if not, to see if it could be destroyed. He didn't want Worthington to testify.

There were several peculiar things about the theory. First, the bruises and scratches. It was not at all strange for Sunny to have marks on her body. Worthington had seen her the day after she had been admitted to the hospital. During those twenty-four hours, the hospital people would have tried to save her life; their efforts could easily have left bruises. They usually do. Just the act of lifting her onto the stretcher from the bathroom floor where she was found could have left bruises. But why was Worthington, a neurologist, talking about bruises and scratches? A neurologist knows about nerves. It was not within his professional competence to interpret Sunny's bruises as signs of a struggle—much less to take the leap and say that she was being held down and injected with insulin. He was being allowed to testify in an area outside of his expertise because court rules do not draw such narrow distinctions. The rules say that an M.D.

can testify on anything medical, whether he is board-certified in that area or not.

I also wondered why Worthington hadn't come forward before. Where had he been during the first trial? Surely the evidence of the bruises had been there then, too. I asked Puccio how the prosecutor had found him. It turned out that Worthington had found the prosecutor. He had volunteered his services. This was disturbing news. In my experience, witnesses who volunteer have to be doubly scrutinized because of possible conflicts of interest and yearnings for the limelight.

Even beyond these considerations, there was something strange about the whole thing. Why was this man, a neurologist, going to testify when the real expert on insulin was nowhere in sight? Where was the chief ME of Rhode Island, Bill Sturner, who knew about bruises and who had published papers on insulin poisoning and hypoglycemia? In the normal course of events, the prosecution would have called Sturner as a prize witness. Could it be that he had not been helpful to them? That he had not been able to corroborate the prosecutor's theory of insulin poisoning?

Worthington's curriculum vitae was a little unusual, too. On the witness stand he had testified that he had gone to college at St. Edward's School in Oxford and to medical school at the University of Bologna. The University of Bologna has a long, proud history. Its medical school, one of the oldest in Europe, was very prestigious during the Renaissance, but since then it had declined precipitously. Academically speaking, it wasn't in the same league as Oxford. Why had Worthington gone to such an undistinguished medical school where classes were conducted in Italian?

We called Claus. Claus knew everyone. He and Andrea Reynolds, whose marriage had by now disintegrated, had a room across the hall from ours at the Biltmore Plaza Hotel. Claus sauntered over, wearing an elegant gray silk robe. Claus knew Worthington. He also had a good friend who lived in Oxford and offered to call him. In addition, one of the legal assistants, Andrew Citron, called his brother Zachary who was studying history at Oxford, and offered him $50 to find out if Worthington had actually gone there. It was 9:00 A.M. in England, Monday morning, but we still had the rest of the night before having to appear in court. Zachary called the university records office. The school had no record of Worthington. Oxford University didn't even have a college named St. Edward's.

Later that morning, in a hearing with the judge (no jury) on Worthington's qualifications, he was asked again about his college, and this time he modified his original answer. St. Edward's, he explained, was an English public school in the town of Oxford. It had no connection with the university. He had not gone to college at all. Instead, he had lived in Italy for a few years, and then enrolled in the University of Bologna's medical school. Although he had taken two forensic medical courses there, the judge decided he was not qualified to discuss the origins of Sunny's scratches and bruises, and he was not allowed to testify. Bill Sturner, the ME who had been notably absent at the first trial, didn't testify in this one, either. Not having seen Sunny in the hospital and having no knowledge of her history, he was unwilling to say that her bruises were the result of a struggle.

Puccio relied on my affidavit and suggestions and argued to the jury's satisfaction that insulin poisoning was not the cause of Sunny's coma but that alcohol and barbiturates were, and that it could have been a suicide attempt. The black bag, which was a dramatic physical thing, lost its position as a centerpiece, and its influence waned. The jury brought back a verdict of not guilty and Claus walked out free, but the case had by this time moved into another realm, beyond a simple yes or no. Claus's world is still divided into people who think he was unjustly accused and people who think he got away with murder. It probably always will be.

12

ATTICA

WHO DID IT?

ALL THROUGH THE summer of 1971, unrest was building in Attica, a maximum security prison in upstate New York, and by September the prisoners had a pile of unresolved grievances. When the riot came, it was triggered by a small incident—a prisoner threw a can of food at a guard, and his privileges were taken away. The next day, Thursday, September 9, the riot erupted spontaneously in Cell Block A after breakfast. Prisoners from all four cellblocks (A–D) surged down the corridors toward "Times Square," the crossroads of Attica, where a guard stood at his post. The guard, William Quinn, slammed down the gates, but one of them had a faulty bolt, and the prisoners broke through. They beat Quinn and left him lying in a coma with a fractured skull. They took forty hostages.

The state police were called in. Led by Captain Hank Williams, a hulking three-hundred-pounder, they began retaking the cell blocks, fighting their way through with tear gas and guns. Before they could retake the fourth (D), and against Williams's advice, they were ordered to stop. The prison authorities were getting more and more worried about the hostages, and they lost their nerve. The decision was a mistake. In prison riots, the longer you wait, the more chance there is that someone will get killed. There are always enmities in prison. During a riot, when the prisoners are no longer protected by guards, people try to get even.

Russell G. Oswald, the commissioner of corrections, began negotiations. The prisoners set up committees and asked for help from outsiders they trusted. Tom Wicker, the *New York Times* columnist and author, was one; Louis Farrakhan, who later became the leader of the Nation of Islam, was another. The negotiators met with the prisoners in D yard, where there was also a complement of reporters and television cameras. The prisoners had twenty-eight demands, including better food and medical care. Oswald agreed to all but three of them. He refused to remove Vincent Mancusi as superintendent of Attica, he refused to grant total amnesty, and he refused to allow passage to a Third World country to those who wanted to go.

About fifteen prisoners were running the insurrection, led by Roger "Champ" Champen, Frank "Big Black" Smith, and Herbert X. Blyden. Most of the others in the cell block were supporting it. If they weren't, they at least knew enough not to say so—except for two of them. Barry Schwartz and his friend Kenneth Hess talked to one of the reporters covering the story, and Schwartz slipped him a note saying that not all the prisoners were in favor of the uprising. The reporter brought the note to the leaders, who accused Schwartz and Hess of betrayal. They were taken away and their throats were slashed—but not fatally. Schwartz was later seen leaning out the window with a towel around his neck, yelling for help. It was a brief reprieve. The other prisoners pulled him back in, and the leaders decided that he and Hess had to be killed. The next day the prisoners took Schwartz to an empty cell and laid him on a mattress on the floor. A circle of inmates handed around a knife and each of them stabbed him many times. They did the same to Hess in a different cell. It was a group effort; it made each inmate equally guilty of murder, and they were bound to silence in mutual defense. A third man, Michael Privitiera, was killed the same way. He was erratic and violent and was inciting fights among the prisoners. All three of the dead prisoners were white ethnics—two Jews and an Italian—outside the mainstream of prison culture, which was predominantly black ghetto.

On Saturday the 11th, William Quinn, the guard at the crossroads, died in the hospital. So there were four deaths, three of them not known to those outside the walls, before Attica was retaken.

By Sunday, the third day of negotiations, Oswald was increasingly frustrated by the lack of progress. Amnesty was the sticking point. The prisoners knew Quinn was dead, and they were insisting on a pardon. Oswald and Governor Nelson Rockefeller were more and more worried that the prisoners would kill the hostages. They were threatening to slash their throats. All of the observers could see that the prisoners were armed with knives and spears from the tool shed. Samuel Melville, a 1960s radical who was known as the Mad Bomber, was in there, and he was probably stockpiling Molotov cocktails. The prisoners had dug trenches in D Yard—it looked like the Western Front in World War I. The guards also thought the prisoners had guns.

On the morning of Monday the 13th, the prisoners turned down Oswald's final offer. Within minutes the troopers went in. They had wanted to go in all along, and Rockefeller finally agreed. It had lasted four days.

Rockefeller issued orders that none of the corrections officers were to join in the retaking of the prison. They were too emotionally involved. They had been humiliated by the uprising; they were angry at Quinn's death, and they wanted to save their fellow guards who were hostages. They would be looking for revenge. Some of them went in with the troopers anyway. Later, they said they hadn't heard the order. One of the hostages was shot in the chest and killed with a bullet from a handgun that belonged to a corrections officer.

Just before the troopers went in, a helicopter flew over the yard and dropped tear gas. The prisoners took eight hostages up to the catwalk overlooking D Yard, blindfolded them, and stood behind them, holding knives to their throats. They thought this would prevent any forcible retaking of the yard, but the troopers brought in sharpshooters, each aiming at a single prisoner on the catwalk. Other troopers charged into the yard, firing shotguns. The shotguns contained double-O buckshot, which has 9 or 12 pellets per cartridge. It is commonly used for riot control. The troopers fired rapidly for a few minutes. Then it was quiet. The prisoners surrendered.

Thirty-nine people died in the retaking of Attica. Thirteen were hostages. The rest were prisoners. Hank Williams, who led the state troopers, was unfairly made the scapegoat. He wasn't promoted for years.

The prisoners didn't have guns or Molotov cocktails after all. They did have knives and sharp instruments, and some of the hostages were cut. Early eyewitness accounts coming out of the prison confirmed what everyone expected—that the hostages were killed by the prisoners. The dead hostages were brought out wearing bloody blindfolds around their necks. The press and the assembled throng believed that the prisoners had behaved true to form and carried out their earlier threats.

No single mortuary was large enough to handle all the bodies, and they were sent to a number of different places in the Rochester and Buffalo area. The majority of them—nineteen inmates and eight hostages—went to Rochester, and the first medical news (as distinct from the eyewitness news) came from there. John Edland, the ME of Rochester, reported that everyone had died of bullet wounds. Most of the hostages had head wounds from double-O buckshot. That was how their blindfolds got bloody. None of the hostages had a slit throat. On Tuesday, Edland's story was in the newspapers. It was extremely unpopular with the guards.

Edland's analysis came as a terrible shock to Oswald and Mancusi, the superintendent. It was plainly beyond belief, and Oswald decided to get a second opinion. I was recommended to him, and I flew to Attica. The prison rose from the plains like a huge medieval fortress, with turrets and thirty-foot-high walls. The stench of tear gas emanated from it.

When I walked in, Oswald and Mancusi stared at me in dismay. They had expected someone older, more buttoned-down, someone more bureaucratic, like Dr. James Bradley, the official who had recommended me. I was thirty-seven, had long hair, and looked like a hippie. Bradley reassured them that I was not a wild man. Oswald, who was pained and concerned about the deaths, wanted the bodies of all thirteen hostages reexamined. He was certain there had been a mistake. He and Mancusi thought the hostages had been beaten and abused for days, and he had seen with his own eyes that the hostages' throats were cut. They had been up on the catwalk with knives at their throats and the troopers had gone in to save them. And now Edland was saying that the troopers had killed them. It made no sense. Oswald's first reaction to me was that there was a communist plot of some kind. Why else would Edland lie? He and Mancusi didn't want me to bother reautopsying the prisoners; they just wanted me to do the hostages.

The idea that Edland would be part of a communist plot did not seem plausible to me. He was known among MEs as a right-winger. He was also very good. I said I had to look at *all* the bodies, prisoners and hostages, and that to understand one death, I had to understand all of them. To do it properly, I had to reconstruct the scene, see where the bullets came from and where everyone was standing, find patterns of injury. I was not there to prove that Edland was a liar. If I couldn't examine all the bodies, I said, I would rather not do any. I would return to the city.

My response gave them an out. Mancusi, who had an us-against-them attitude, became very irritated with me. He didn't want it done that way, and he was quite ready to dispense with my services. Oswald thought about it, however, and decided I made sense. He said yes.

I stayed from Wednesday to the following Monday. I looked at the hostages first. Most of them were in funeral parlors, embalmed and ready for burial. The death certificates had been written. Some of those who had been on the catwalk had cut marks on the back of the neck and one had a stab wound in the stomach, but none of these injuries had caused death. Edland was right. They had all died of bullet wounds, and the shots had come from a distance. There was no powder or soot on the skin. One prisoner, who was in a tunnel in the yard, died of a shotgun blast to the left thigh—he bled to death. Judging from the three-inch spread of the double-O shot, the nearest weapon had been nine feet away. (Shotgun pellets spread about one inch per yard.) Six of the hostages had died of a single shot to the head, which looked odd, like an execution, but could be explained by their positions in the yard. One of the troopers had discharged his buckshot at a prisoner who was making a threatening gesture, and missed. From where he was standing, the pellets would wind up 150 feet away, spread out at head height. A group of hostages was standing in a circle blindfolded in just that spot.

By Tuesday afternoon, a controversy was raging over Edland's analysis. Was he deliberately misleading everyone? One of the funeral directors called a press conference. He could prove that Edland was lying, he said. The body he had prepared for burial had been beaten to death by a prisoner, and Edland had falsely said it was shot by the troopers. There was no bullet wound in the body. The troopers were being given a bum rap.

The funeral director also subscribed to the conspiracy theory. He thought there was a cover-up, that somehow "they" were trying to appease the prisoners. The community in general agreed that there was a plot to blame the deaths on the troopers rather than on the prisoners. The corrections people lived near the prison, and the community supported them.

I looked at the body of the guard who supposedly had died of a beating. His eyes were indeed blackened, and he had other bruises. I turned the body over. There was a gunshot wound in his back. The funeral director hadn't seen it. While he was preparing the body he had tipped it this way and that, but he had never turned it over completely. The guard looked as if he had been beaten, but the coloration of his bruises was faded. It had probably happened on the first day of the riot. In any event, he hadn't died of his bruises; he had died of the bullet wound. It was late at night when I found the bullet hole, and the funeral director was out. I telephoned him to come and look. He rushed over carrying his bowling ball. Then he went to the phone and called his wife. Honey, he said, don't say anything else to the newspaper reporters.

After doing the guards, I reautopsied the prisoners. They had not been identified. Each had a number. In his hurry, Edland had left some of the bullets in them. There was a question about one of them, Elliot Barkley. Arthur Eve, a black state assemblyman from Buffalo, who was one of the outside negotiators, claimed that Barkley, a leader of the uprising, had been deliberately killed by the troopers as punishment. During the four days, Barkley had been very vocal, criticizing the system on television. Some of the prisoners said they saw him alive after the retaking, but Edland's autopsy report said he died of a single rifle shot in the back. Eve and others interpreted this as an execution. When I reautopsied Barkley, I saw the single rifle shot, but it was a very big hole—too big for the bullet. The bullet had gone in sideways. It was a tumbling bullet (like the one that hit John Connally in Dallas); it had hit something else first, which meant it hadn't been meant for Barkley originally. When the prisoners realized that the execution couldn't have happened, they waffled about having seen him alive.

Within a few days after the surrender, there were charges of brutal retaliation, of prisoners being made to run a gauntlet of guards, of punishment and injury. The State Investigation Commission impaneled a grand jury, which came down with forty-two indictments against sixty-two prisoners, listing over twelve hundred charges, most of them centered around the taking of hostages. One prisoner, John Hill, was tried and convicted for killing Quinn, the guard. Over forty other trials were planned, but civil rights groups protested that all the indictments were against prisoners and none against the guards—the guards should have been indicted for their post-riot vengeance. Governor Hugh Carey, who was elected after Rockefeller's term, set up a commission to look into the charges of unfairness. The commission agreed that it was "selective prosecution," and on New Year's Eve, 1976, Carey decided to "close the book" on Attica. He pardoned seven inmates and commuted the sentence of John Hill.

Part of the fallout from Attica was the establishment in 1974 of a medical review board to monitor the deaths of prisoners. I've been a member since the beginning, and we have been able to change some conditions. Many prisoners were dying of what local doctors said were heart attacks. The guards had told the doctors so. (There are no prison pathologists. Bodies are handled by the local coroner. In the past, he did not autopsy most of them.) Investigating these deaths, we found the telltale signs of a choke hold—pinpoint hemorrhages in the eyes and bruises on the neck. Now, all prison deaths must be autopsied.

Other deaths were caused by the effects of tear gas. When prisoners became unruly, guards would put on masks, throw canisters of tear gas into their cells, and then, still wearing masks, go in and beat the prisoners. Inmates were dying from lung irritation and pneumonia. We succeeded in having a law passed forbidding guards to use tear gas unless it had first been approved by the superintendent. Since that time, there have been no deaths from tear gas.

Suicides were the principal preventable cause of death. Most of the suicides had given warning; they had threatened to kill themselves before they actually did it. We made the guards aware that the threats should be taken seriously and that counseling should be provided. With the knowledge that they are accountable, that someone is watching, the prison authorities have a different attitude. Medical care is better. We've cut down on the number of suicides and on all unnatural deaths.

Something positive came out of Attica: the kind of public service medicine that is a natural outgrowth of our profession. MEs all over the country should be similarly engaged, but such a policy is more the exception than the rule. The system has been failing for some time, undermined by the dearth of untrained MEs and the politics of death—the primacy of political over medical considerations. We should be trying to attract more medical students to forensic science. We should raise the salaries and status of MEs and banish their fears of being fired for meritorious service. We should encourage states to improve the quality of forensic science services and make them available to all on request. We are not doing any of these things.

These reforms are important, but by themselves they are not enough to turn the system around. Before anything can be done, there must be a change of attitude—a recognition that a problem exists and an appreciation of the value of forensic pathology.

INDEX

Academy of Forensic Sciences, 4
Adams, John, 35
Adam's apple, 38
Addison's disease, 14
adrenal cortex, 14
age, determination of, 37–38, 86
Albano, Edwin, 160, 161
alcohol, 2, 37, 39, 73, 190, 195–96
    in von Bulow case, 193, 195–96,
        199, 203
algor mortis, 39, 90, 92–93
amobarbital, 196
amyl nitrite, 181
anatomy, asymmetry of, 37
Andre, Carl, 75–76
Ann Arbor, Mich., veterans
        hospital in, 42–43
Antistius, 24
apnea monitor, 113–14
Armed Forces Institute of
        Pathology, 7, 9–10
Arnold, William J., 162–63
Aronson, Marvin, 142, 149
arsenic, 40, 41–42, 44
arson, 172
arteries, coronary, 36, 37–38
aspirin, 192, 196
Attica prison, 207–15
autoerotic death, 178–80
autopsies, 36–39
    incisions for, 36
    Judaism and, 97–100
    natural vs. unnatural death and,
        3
    past restrictions on, 49

public opinion of, 50
time required for, 36
toxicology tests included in,
        39

Bailey, F. Lee, 154
Balabin, Pinhas, 95, 96, 97
barbiturates, 2, 39, 46
    in von Bulow case, 193–204
Barco, Leonard, 187–91
Barkley, Elliot, 213
Baselt, Randall, 178
Belushi, John, 90–95, 141
benzoylecgonine, 177–78
Bhopal chemical disaster, 41
Billings, Richard N., 20
Blackbourne, Brian, 74
Blakey, Robert G., 19–21
blood sugar level, in von Bulow
        case, 192–206
Blyden, Herbert X., 208
bodies:
    decomposition of, 100–101
    determining age of, 37–38, 86
    disposing of, 46
    identification of, 77, 78–82,
        84–86, 88–89
    jurisdiction of, 88, 89
body snatchers, 50–51
bones, identification of, 81, 85
Bradley, James, 211
Braga, Gennaro, 188–89, 191
brain, 38, 93
Branson, Frank, 174
Brawley, Tawana, xi–xii

Bridge of San Luis Rey, The (Wilder), 33
Briski, Robert, 157–58
bronchopneumonia, 192
Bronson, Frank, 174
Brotman, Robert, 141, 146–47
Brown, Josephine Wells, 168–73
Brown, Raymond A., 163
Buffalo Slasher, 119–29
bullets:
    full-metal jacket and, 17
    identification of, 124
    reversing of, 12, 17
    tumbling, 18, 213
Burke, William, 50–51
"burking," 51

cabdrivers, Buffalo, 120–22
cadavers, black market in, 50–51
Caesar, Julius, 23–24
Cahill, George, 199, 200
Calissi, Guy, 158–59
capital punishment, 190
Capote, Truman, 201
carbon monoxide, 45, 172–73
Carey, Hugh, 214
Carpenter, Francis, 49
Carr, John Thomas, 198
Central Identification Laboratory of Hawaii (CILHI), 78–79
Challenger, 77–78
Chambers, Robert, 75
Champen, Roger "Champ," 208
Charney, Michel, 78
chicken pox, 25
chimney sweeps, 50
choking, 26–27
cholera, 42
Christman, Janet, 114
Christopher, Joseph C., 125–29
cirrhosis, 37
Citron, Andrew, 206
cocaine, 91, 93–94, 177, 178
Coe, John, 102
Cole, George, 54
concentration camps, 41

confessions, corpus delicti and, 149
Connally, John, 8, 12, 16, 17–19
    author's examination of, 18–19
Connally, Nellie, 19
contra-coup injury, 38
Coppolino, Carl, 150–57
Coppolino, Carmela, 150–52, 153–54, 155
coroners, x
    historical role of, 48–49, 53
    scandals involving, 53
corpus delicti, 149
corruption, ME office and, 55, 58–59, 64–65
corsets, 34
cortisone, 14, 25
Cosgrove, Ed, 122, 123
Coumbis, Richard, 60, 161, 162
coup injury, 38
Cournand, Andre, 23
crashes, airline, 82–84
Crawford, Joan, 1
crib death, *see* sudden infant death syndrome
Crippen, Hawley Harvey, 52
Cruncher, Jerry, 50
Cuomo, Mario, 73, 111
curare, 40, 42, 161
Curtis, Jimmy, 86
cyanide, 40, 136, 137–38

DalCortivo, Leo, 203
death certificates, 25–26, 69
death(s):
    cell life after, 38
    determining cause of, 35
    determining time of, 38–39, 90, 92–93, 102, 106–107, 129, 190–91
    fashions in, 46
    social class and, 27, 35
    unnatural, U.S. rate of, x
    see also specific kinds of death
De Mar, Clarence, 36
De Niro, Robert, 91

Denson, Lawrence, 160
Deppner, Barbara, 133–34, 137
Deppner, Daniel, 132–34, 138–39
Dershowitz, Alan, 201–203
diabetes, 192
diamond business, 95–97
Dickinson, Mark, 168, 170
digestion, death and, 106–107, 108
digitalis, 151
DiMaio, Dominick, 65, 66
diplomats, death and, 44–45
"Dr. X," *see* Jascalevich, Mario
Drega, Laura, 62
drowning, 140, 141
drug addicts:
    infections of, 31
    tattoos on, 34
drugs, 90, 92, 93–95, 141, 150
    alcohol and, 39
    see also poisons; *specific drugs*
Dumont, Allan, 166

Earhart, Amelia, 2
Eastern Airlines Flight 66, 82–86
Edland, John, 210–11, 212
Eisenbud, Merrill, 60
endocarditis, 31
Esakof, Ernest R., 70–71
Eve, Arthur, 213
evidence, vanishing, 9
exercise, heart attacks and, 36–37

Fahringer, Herald Price, 195,
    196–99
Falco, Frank, 30
falling, 140
Famiglietti, Stephen, 199
Fanning, Hugh, 79
Fanning, Katherine, 79
Farber, Marjorie, 151–52, 153
Farber, Myron, 159
Farber, William, 151, 154–55
Farrakhan, Louis, 208
Federal Bureau of Investigation
    (FBI), 42–43
Ferrara, Theresa, 89

Ferrer, Reinaldo, 60–61
    charges against author by,
        61–62, 66–70
Fillinger, Halbert, 142, 149
Finck, Pierre, 9–10
Finkbeiner, John, 69
fire, 45, 88, 170–72
Fixx, Jim, 37
foreign countries, death in,
    165–66, 167
forensic pathology, ix, 23–24
    beginnings of, 49, 51–52
Four Stages of Cruelty (Hogarth),
    50.
Francisco, Jerry, 3
Fried, Catherine, 141–50
Fried, Paul, 141–50
Funkenstein, Harris, 199, 200
Furue, Tadao, 80–81

Gailitis, Janis, 192, 203
Galante, Carmine, 60
Galda, Fred, 158
garbage bags, plastic, 46
Gibson, Mary, 152
Gilman, G. Malcolm B., 152–53
Gluck, Edgar, 99–100
Goering, Hermann, 40
gonorrhea, 34
Gonzales, Thomas, 55
Gordon, David, 65–66
grave robbing, 50–51
Gross, Elliot, 73–74, 75, 123

Hamlet (Shakespeare), 48–49
Hamolsky, Milton, 198
Hanes, Clifford, 148
Hare, William, 50–51
Harris, Jean, 34
Harris, Stanley, 157–58
Hart, Ann, 78
Hart, Thomas T., 78
heart attacks, 45, 141
    exercise and, 36–37
Helpern, Milton, 6–7, 24–25, 55,
    58, 143–44, 154, 161

hemorrhages:
  epidural vs. subdural, 172
  pinpoint, 38, 68, 143, 148
Hendricks, David, 104–109
Hendricks, family, 104–107
heroin, 91, 94, 141
Hess, Kenneth, 208
Hill, John, 214
Ho, Robert Tam, 176
Hoffman, Paul, 131–32, 136, 139
Holden, William, 56
homicide:
  social class and, 34
  "solve" rate and, 123
Hoover, J. Edgar, 1
Howard, Katherine, 87
Howard, Wilbur, 87
Humes, James J., 6, 8, 10–14, 15
Hunt, Dorothy, 40
Hunt, E. Howard, 40
hyoid bone, 38
hyoscine, 52
hypoglycemia, 192

Ice Man, *see* Kuklinski, Richard
infant whiplash syndrome, 116
infections, drug addicts and, 31
insulin, von Bulow case and,
  191–206

Jacklin, Judy, 92
Jaroslawicz, Pinchos, 95–103
Jascalevich, Mario E., 157–64
jogging, 36–37
John Paul I, Pope, 1
Johnson, Lyndon, 7
Jordan, Fred, 79
Jordan, James, 149–50

Keenan, John A., 71–72
Kelly, Michael, 120, 122–24
Kennedy, Bobby, 1
Kennedy, Jacqueline, 7
Kennedy, John F., assassination
  of, 3, 5–22
  acoustic evidence about, 20–21

Addison's disease and, 14
autopsy report on, 13–15
autopsy report on, errors and
  omissions of, 10–12
conspiracy theories about, 5–6,
  8, 19–20
final verdict on, 22
missing evidence and, 9
Nieman-Marcus skull fragment
  and, 16
"pristine bullet" and, 8, 12, 13,
  16–18, 19
Select Committee on
  Assassinations' conclusions
  about, 19
Kennedy, Ruth, 141, 147
Kerley, Ellis, 80–81
Kerris, Roger, 175
Keuper, Vincent, 152
kidneys, 37
King, Coretta, 3
King, Martin Luther, Jr., 3–4,
  9
Knox, Robert, 50–51
Koch, Edward, 60–61, 68–69, 71,
  72–73, 75, 120
Koppel, Ted, 201
Kornblum, Ronald, 92
Kostov, Vladimir, 44
Kuh, Richard, 195
Kuklinski, Richard, 129–39
  evidence against, 137–38

Lans, Allan, 158
La Vigne, Detective, 189
Lee, Wong Ham, 171–72
Levin, Jennifer, 75
Levine, David, 63–65
Levine, Lowell, 8–9, 73,
  80–81
Lindbergh baby, 4
liver, 37
livor mortis, 38, 90, 92
looting, disasters and, 83–84
lungs, 37
Lyons, Nelson, 91

McCrone Associates, 3–4
McFarlane, Robert, 39, 193
maggots, 190–91
Malliband, George, 130
Mancusi, Vincent, 208, 211–12
Maples, William, 80–81
Marcos, Imelda, 43
Markov, Georgi, 44
Marshak, Megan, 70
Masgay, Louis, 130–31
medical examiners:
   history of office of, 53–54
   lack of standardization of,
     53–54
   mayor's power over, 71, 72–73
   political pressures and, 35,
     55–54, 58–59, 64–65,
     214–15
   role of, 110, 187
Mellon, Daphne, 173–78
Mellon, Priscilla, 174, 178
Melville, Samuel, 209
Mendieta, Ana, 75–76
Mengele, Josef, 1–2
meningitis, 111
mercury scare, 59
Miller, Arthur, 67–68, 74
military medical records, 83
Mitchel, John Purroy, 53
Monk, Alison, 176
Monroe, Marilyn, 1, 2
Monteas, Josette, 64
Morgenthau, Robert, 58, 60–61,
    71–72, 74–75, 123
   charges against author by,
    62–66
morphine, 93
Morris, Gail, 187–91
Morris, Priscilla Diane, 189
Moses, Sybil, 160
multiple murders, 110, 119–20
Musetto, Carmelo, 152, 153

Narciso, Filipina, 43
Natarajan, Geetha, 133, 134, 138
National Enquirer, 91, 92, 94

National Urban League, 165
natural gas, 46
Nelson, Richard E., 111, 117
New York State Police Forensic
    Sciences Unit, 73, 80, 111
New York Times, 159
Nightline, 201
Noguchi, Thomas, 56, 91
Nolan, Iveson, 83–84
Norris, Charles, 53, 54

Oakes, Harry, 4
Ondine's syndrome, 116
O'Neill, Joy, 198, 201
operative deaths, 155–56
Orami, Joseph, 176
Oswald, Lee Harvey, 6, 8
Oswald, Russell, 208, 209, 211
ovaries, 38, 86

Patterson, Richard, 134
Pavulon, 42–43, 151
Perez, Leonora, 43
Perry, Malcolm, 13
*Perspectives on the Investigation of
    Organized Crime* (Blakey),
    20
Peters, Larry, Jr., 168–70, 173
pituitary gland, 14
plaque, arteriosclerotic, 36
Playboy, 180
Plot to Kill the President, The
    (Blakey and Billings), 20
Plymouth Brethren, 104
Poe, Edgar Allan, 42
poisons, 40–43, 44–46, 150
   see also drugs
police, theft by, 28, 83
police custody, deaths in, 55
Polifrone, Dominick, 135–37
potassium eye fluid test, 102
Pott, Sir Percival, 50
Powers, Gary, 40
"Premature Burial, The" (Poe), 42
Presley, Elvis, 35–36
prison deaths, 214

prisoners, psychiatry and, 128
Privitiera, Michael, 209
Privlin, Matthew, 173, 175–76
psychosis with exhaustion, 68, 74
Puccio, Thomas, 201–204, 206

Quinn, William, 207, 209

Racket Bureaus (Blakey), 20
radioactivity, standard levels of, 59–60
rape, evidence of, xi–xii, 64, 175
Ray, James Earl, 3–4
Reed, Julian, 19
Reidy, Dan, 86–88
restitution, parole and, 30
resurrectionists, 50
Reyes syndrome, 112
Reynolds, Andrea, 202, 205
Reynolds, Sheldon, 202
Rho, Yong Myun, 65, 66, 97–98
"Richard Corey," 196
Richards, Dickinson, 23
ricin, 44
rigor mortis, 38, 90, 92, 191
Rivera, Geraldo, 36
Riverdell Hospital, 157–58, 164
Robinson, Edwin Arlington, 196
Rockefeller, Nelson, 69–71, 209
Rose, Earl, 7, 108
Rosenberg, Hal, 149

sadomasochism, 179, 180, 181–86
Savino, Nancy, 160–61, 162
Schaub, Frank, 155
Schrallhammer, Maria, 194–95
Schwartz, Barry, 208
scopalamine, 52
Scotland Yard, 42, 52
Select Committee on Assassinations, 3, 6
  Kennedy assassination reconstructed by, 15–19
Selkow, Michael, 143–45, 150
serial murders, 110, 119–20

sexual bondage, *see* sadomasochism
shaken-baby syndrome, 116
Shaler, Robert, 203
Shaw, George Bernard, 36
Sinatra, Frank, 56
Sirhan, Sirhan, 1
situs inversus, 37
Sklar, Jerald, 143, 145, 147–48, 150
Slade, Sam, 122, 125–26
"Slaughter of the Innocents" (Adelson), 116
smallpox, 24–25
Smith, Cathy, 90–92, 94–95
Smith, Frank "Big Black," 208
Smith, Gary, 132–34, 138–39
Smith, Paul, 135
smothering, 140, 148
Snow, Clyde, 79
social class, death and, 27, 34
Soman, Robert, 66
Spilsbury, Bernard, 52
Spitz, Werner, 56–57
Stark, 82
Stewart, Michael, 74
Stock, Richard, 192, 198–99, 200
strangulation, indications of, 38, 147
strychnine, 40, 41
Sturner, Bill, 205, 206
succinylcholine, 42, 151, 157
sudden infant death syndrome (SIDS), 110, 112, 113, 115, 117–18
Suetonius, 23
suffocation, 51, 112–13, 118
suicide, 1, 2, 76, 141–42, 196, 204
  adolescent, 179
  attempted, as cry for help, 39–40
  early laws regarding, 48
  by gas, 45, 46
  social class and, 34
  stigma of, 48
Sullivan, Robert L., 115

Tagamet, 131
Tal, Shlomo, 95, 96–97, 102
Tale of Two Cities, A (Dickens), 50
tattoos, 34
testicles, asymmetry of, 37
theft, police, 28
thyroid gland, 37
Tinning, Barbara, 112
Tinning, Jennifer, 111, 117
Tinning, Jonathan, 114
Tinning, Joseph, Jr., 111–12, 117
Tinning, Joseph, Sr., 111, 118
Tinning, Mary Beth, 111–19
Tinning, Mary Frances, 113–14
Tinning, Michael, 114–15
Tinning, Nathan, 113, 119
Tinning, Tami Lynne, 115, 118–19
Tinning, Timothy, 112, 113, 117, 118–19
Trantino, Thomas, case of, 30–31
Travis, Robert, Jr., 167–70, 172, 173
Turner, Cora, 52

Uku, Justin, 120
Umberger, Joseph, 156
United States, death in, x

Vance, Benjamin Morgan, 35
veterans hospital, Ann Arbor, Mich., 42–43

von Auersperg, Prince Alexander, 194
von Bulow, Claus, 191–92, 194–97, 200–206
von Bulow, Martha "Sunny" Crawford von Auersperg, 191–206

Wakley, Thomas, 51
Wald, Milton, 67–68
Wallace, John, 54
Warren, Robert, 63–64
Warren Commission, 7–8
Watergate affair, 40
Wecht, Cyril, 6, 56
Welch, Willie, 65–66
Wicker, Tom, 208
Willcox, William Henry, 52
Williams, Hank, 207, 210
Williams, Robin, 91
Williams, Tennessee, 73–74
Woodcock, Joe, 160, 161
Worthington, Jeremy R., 203–206
wrist cutting, as distress signal, 40

X rays, 81–82, 85

Yeoungman, Samuell, 49
Young, Whitney, 165–67

Zapruder film, 5–6
Zyklon B, 41

Unsolved Murders
and Mysteries

CONTENTS

Editor's Note 7

WHO WAS THE MURDERER?

Dr John Bodkin Adams *Colin Wilson* 9
Janice Weston *Fenton Bresler* 18
The Lindbergh Baby Kidnapping *Henry Lester* 23
William Herbert Wallace *Colin Wilson* 31
Adelaide Bartlett *Colin Wilson* 40
Lizzie Borden *Henry Lester* 50
Tony Mancini *Colin Wilson* 59
The Axeman of New Orleans *Henry Lester* 67
The Ordeal of Jeremy Cartland *Brian Mariner* 76
Jack the Ripper *Colin Wilson* 85
'Zodiac' *Henry Lester* 96

WHAT HAPPENED TO THEM?

Freddie Mills: A Puzzle *Fenton Bresler* 106
The Prime Minister Disappears *Colin Wilson* 113
The 'Dingo' Baby *Colin Wilson* 121
Donald Crowhurst *Alan Wykes* 128

IDENTITIES: TRUE OR FALSE?

The Riddle of Rudolf Hess *Jock Haswell* 134
The Tichborne Claimant *Michael Hardwick* 144
Was Chessman the Red Light Bandit? *Colin Wilson* 152
Oscar Slater *Colin Wilson* 160

ACCIDENTS

The Great Bombay Explosion *Michael Hardwick* 168
The Moorgate Crash *Alan Wykes* 176

ENIGMAS OF AIR AND SEA

Korean Airlines Flight 007 *Richard Garrett*   183
Royal Tragedy at Eagle's Rock *Richard Garrett*   192
A Red Eagle Falling *Michael Hardwick*   201
The *Lusitania Richard Garrett*   209
The Haunted U-Boat *Colin Gumbrell*   217
Who Mined the *Maine*? *Michael Hardwick*   227
Robert Maxwell: Was he Murdered? *John Canning*   235

Select Bibliography   252
Index   254

EDITOR'S NOTE

'Truth will come to light; murder cannot be hid long.' Thus said Launcelot Gobbo in *The Merchant of Venice*. But though murder can seldom be hidden the murderer can be – and frequently is – as exampled by some of the accounts that follow.

The crime of murder has always exercised a horrid fascination over the minds of men. 'Thou shalt not kill' has seemed to many to be the starkest of Mosaic injunctions. But an extra chill is added when the crime is unsolved. Could the murderer strike again? Might he be sitting next to one in the bus or underground? Indeed, might one even have met him within the past few days?

Edgar Lustgarten has written of the spell amounting almost to obsession which the Wallace case exerted over the celebrated dramatic critic James Agate, who believed the weight of evidence for and against Wallace's guilt to be exactly evenly balanced. At the end of one of their many discussions on the matter Lustgarten asked Agate to adopt the theory that Wallace was innocent. What sort of person would have committed the crime?

'A genius,' replied Agate flatly. 'A brutal, bloody fiend – and a genius.'

'I wonder whether he reads the stuff written on the crime,' Lustgarten said, 'and sometimes talks about the case among his friends.'

'That,' said Agate sombrely, 'is the most shocking thought of all.'

Research on this case has turned up new findings, discussed in a following chapter, so that the evidence is not perhaps quite as baffling as it once was, but Agate's reaction strikes a reciprocating chord.

The mystery surrounding Robert Maxwell's death is one where the balance of possibilities again is so finely drawn as to defy any definite solution. The persuasive hypothesis of suicide is contradicted by the gigantic optimism and resolution of the man; the very plausible theory of death from natural causes is counterbalanced by the opinions of three Israeli doctors and two respected French pathologists which point to murder. The case truly fulfils

Winston Churchill's dictum used in another connection of 'a riddle wrapped in a mystery inside an enigma', and is set to run and run.

However, murder or possible murder is but one facet in the kaleidoscope of the unsolved. There are areas of speculation hardly less intriguing. Is it really possible that a modern prime minister could have been a spy for a foreign power? Might the prisoner in Spandau not have been Rudolf Hess, and did his death have sinister overtones? Could Caryl Chessman, in San Quentin's Death Row awaiting execution for more than a decade and afforded every legal facility to establish his case, have been innocent after all? On the face of it such questions may seem far-fetched, even absurd, and yet there is solid, well-researched evidence which supports these suppositions.

What is not in doubt is that the subjects discussed in this book will be focal points of controversy and passionate argument for years to come. Indeed, some of them have already survived undimmed the battering of time.

Our modest hope is that the ensuing essays will provide a modicum of light rather than heat for the debates.

My thanks are due to the contributing authors for a happy collaboration, to Georgie Evans for editorial assistance, to Sarah Coombe for illustration research, and to my paperback editor Alice Wood for guidance and help with this new edition.

John Canning

WHO WAS THE MURDERER?

DR JOHN BODKIN ADAMS

'Scotland Yard's murder squad is to investigate the suspected mass poisoning of wealthy women in Eastbourne during the past twenty years. Because the vast extent of the murder suspicions is not yet known they will start by examining the wills of more than 400 m⸱ ⸱ and women who died in the town, and their investigations may uncover the most sensational episode in British criminal history.'

This strange little paragraph appeared in the *Daily Mail* on 22 August 1956 – strange because it is obviously accusing some person, or persons, of mass murder, while it at the same time admits that the inquiry has not yet even begun.

The 'mass murderer' was an unprepossessing fat man named Dr John Bodkin Adams, and the *Mail* paragraph marked the beginning of his trial – not his trial in a court of law, but his trial by the British press. What followed is, in itself, one of 'the most sensational episodes in British criminal history . . .'.

'It is expected,' added the *Mail* as an afterthought, 'that the names of twenty-five people will be picked out as possible victims of a maniac.'

Bodkin Adams certainly looked as if he had been specially cast for the role of maniacal mass murderer, with a figure like that of Sidney Greenstreet, the urbane villain of *The Maltese Falcon*, and plump, pendulous cheeks that made him look like a rather sinister baby.

The event that had brought Bodkin Adams to the attention of the press – and the police – was the apparent suicide of one of his patients, Mrs 'Bobbie' Hullett. Bobbie Hullett had been shattered by the death of her second husband Jack, a rich, retired businessman, who was suffering from a cancer of the bowel. This was the second husband that she had lost in five years, and the death of the first had also brought her close to suicide.

In July 1956 Bodkin Adams spent an evening with her, and she gave him a cheque for £1,000 – money that she said her husband had intended to give the doctor for a new car. Two days after this, she retired to bed suffering from dizziness and headache. Bodkin Adams called to see her. The next afternoon she went into a coma, and died in hospital a few days later. It looked to the doctors very much like suicide. Bodkin Adams wrote a letter to the coroner, mentioning that he had been prescribing small doses of sodium barbiturate as a sleeping tablet, and added the odd phrase: 'She could not possibly have secreted any of this.' He added that he had examined her room for empty bottles or cartons, and found nothing to suggest she had any poison.

When the coroner, Dr A. C. Sommerville, read this letter his suspicions were immediately aroused, and he called for a second post-mortem. When that proved inconclusive, he asked for a third post-mortem to be performed by the famous 'crime doctor', Francis Camps. Camps took some of Mrs Hullett's organs back to London with him. The coroner made an unusual decision to hold the inquest in private and without informing the press. That in itself suggested that he suspected there was 'dirty work afoot'. When the inquest was adjourned awaiting further information, a journalist on the local newspaper, the *Brighton Argus*, was informed about the secret investigation. He hurried to the police station for more details but the Chief Constable shook his head saying, 'I cannot go into it further.' As he was leaving the police station, a police officer remarked casually, 'You on this Hullett job? Well it's about time somebody caught up with that bloody doctor.'

What had 'that bloody doctor' done to incur suspicion? He had, to begin with, been phenomenally successful. Adams was an Ulster Protestant, who had arrived in Eastbourne in 1923 in answer to an advertisement for 'a Christian young doctor-assistant'. He started his rounds on a motorbike. Two years later he was driving a two-seater car. And within three years of joining the practice, he was being driven by a chauffeur. Eastbourne was full of rich, retired businessmen, and Bodkin Adams was always a popular guest at their social gatherings.

There were also many lonely but wealthy old ladies in Eastbourne and Dr Adams seemed to have a natural gift for bringing them comfort. In 1935 one of these old ladies, Mrs Matilda Whitton, left him £3,000, a very substantial sum for those days, and equivalent to about £30,000 in the devalued currency of today. He was also the executor of her will, which caused many raised eyebrows. The will was challenged in court by the family, but it was upheld. That was the beginning of the whispering campaign against Bodkin Adams. Then, over the years, the doctor received many more bequests: £1,000 from a spinster, Irene Herbert, £4,000 in shares from Mrs Emily Mortimer, £1,000 from Mrs Amy Ware, a Rolls-Royce from Mrs Edith Morrell, £200 from Mrs Annabella Kilgour, £100 from Mrs Mary Prince, £100 from Mrs Theodora Hullett – the previous wife of Jack Hullett, £800 from Mrs Julia Bradnum, £500 from Mrs Annie Dowding, £5,200 from Mrs Clara Miller, £750 from Miss Florence Cavill, £100 from Sidney Prince, £250 from George Blunt, and £1,000 from James Downs. These bequests amounted to a total of nearly £22,000, most of it from elderly widows and spinsters, some of whom had left Dr Adams a substantial part of their fortune. (Clare Miller, for example, left Adams £5,200 out of a total estate worth £7,000.) Not to mention the Rolls-Royce, silver cutlery and other such items . . .

It can be seen that Bodkin Adams was both a very charming and a very lucky man. It would not be surprising if overworked police officers felt a certain envy as they saw his name figure again and again in reports of legacies in the *Brighton Argus*. Yet a dozen or so legacies do not constitute proof that the man who received them is guilty of murder. In late August 1956 most of the British press chose to ignore this simple piece of logic. The Bodkin Adams case was discussed as if there could be no doubt that he would shortly be charged with mass poisoning. One of the few sane voices was that of Percy Hoskins, the *Daily Express*

11

crime reporter. He wrote an article in which he pointed out that, so far, it was a case of smoke without fire. It was not true that 400 wealthy widows had been murdered; it was not true that the murderer had been at work for 20 years; it was not true that more that £1 million was involved. But this was not the kind of story that the great British public wanted to read. It was not even the kind of story that Hoskins's boss, Lord Beaverbrook, wanted to read; he told Hoskins that he had better be right, or his head would be on the chopping-block.

Bodkin Adams seemed to have a gift for putting his own head on the chopping-block. Just before the continuation of the inquest of Bobbie Hullett he wrote the coroner another letter, admitting that two months before her death he had been on a trip to Dublin with Mrs Hullett and two other ladies. Mrs Hullett had forgotten her sleeping tablets so he had given her eight barbiturate tablets. Looking back on it now, he realized that she was in possession of more barbiturates than might be good for her – enough to kill herself, for example. The coroner felt that this was highly suspicious. At the inquest, he went out of his way to ask a police superintendent, 'Has the Chief Constable of Eastbourne invoked the aid of Scotland Yard to investigate certain deaths in this neighbourhood?' The superintendent replied that he had done so. The question was totally irrelevant but the coroner seemed to be telling the press to expect further spectacular developments. However, the verdict of the inquest was that Bobbie Hullett had committed suicide.

Two days later, Hoskins travelled up to London on the same train as Bodkin Adams and was startled that the doctor seemed unaware of the seriousness of the situation. He warned him that his whole future, perhaps his life itself, was in danger. Yet Bodkin Adams seemed wholly unconcerned. He was either innocent or supremely confident.

Whether he liked it or not, Bodkin Adams had become a celebrity. Newspaper men from all over the world flooded into Eastbourne. One French newspaper ran a headline: IS THE BLUEBEARD OF EASTBOURNE ABOUT TO BE UNMASKED? The British press had to be slightly more cautious, but the implication was as plain as a banner headline.

Superintendent Herbert Hannam, who was in charge of the Scotland Yard investigation, had a difficult task ahead of him: studying the records of over 100 deaths. But on 2 November 1956 he was ready to present his case against Bodkin Adams. There were 13 charges, nine of them fairly minor accusations about 'feloniously' giving drugs to patients who were not supposed to receive them. These were mainly to prepare the ground for the major accusations: that Bodkin Adams had concealed the fact that he had a pecuniary interest in the deaths of Amy Ware, Edith Morrell, James Downs and Jack Hullett, and had 'procured their burial' or cremation. In other words, that Bodkin Adams was anxious to conceal that he was a beneficiary in the wills of these patients until he had their bodies safely buried or burned.

Bodkin Adams may have been unaware that his life was in danger but his solicitor had no illusions about it. He asked the doctor if he had any detailed records about the various cases, particularly the Morrell case. Adams shook his head vaguely. Probably not. All he could remember was that he did receive a parcel of nurses' records after her illness, but he could no longer remember what had happened to it. His solicitor made him search the house. At 3 a.m. they unearthed the missing parcel containing eight small notebooks. It was these that would provide the most dramatic moment of the trial.

On 18 December 1956 Superintendent Hannam arrested Bodkin Adams, and charged him with the murder of Mrs Morrell. The solicitor's instinct about her case had been correct. The next morning, Bodkin Adams faced a long list of charges, the last of which was that in November 1950 he did 'feloniously, wilfully and of malice aforethought . . . kill and murder Edith Alice Morrell'. Adams was then taken to Brixton prison.

Why was Adams in the dock when there was no real proof against him? Superintendent Hannam's inquiries had led him to believe that he was dealing with a cunning swindler and an infinitely subtle killer. He came to believe that Adams had altered wills on several occasions and the bodies of his patients were cremated instead of being buried. He believed that in the last few days of one woman's life, Adams had forged cheques to the value of £18,000. He uncovered one suspicious deal in which

13

Adams had influenced two women to leave their house and live in a flat. He then sold the house, and kept the money for three years until he was forced to reimburse it after a writ was served on him. Whether or not Adams was a murderer, he was certainly a greedy and rather dishonest man. On one occasion, he had been struck by a gold-headed cane and chased out of the house by an indignant husband after saying, 'Leave your estate to me and I'll look after your wife' – the man's wife was lying seriously ill in bed at the time.

Then there was the case of Mrs Annabella Kilgour, not mentioned in the indictments. In 1950, Adams called on Mrs Kilgour, and her nurse reported that she was restless. 'I'll give her an injection to give her a good night's sleep', said Adams; and, to the nurse's astonishment, gave the old lady an injection with a dose that seemed far too high. Mrs Kilgour fell into a coma immediately and died the next morning. When Adams called that morning the nurse told him, 'Mrs Kilgour is dead. You realize, doctor, that you've killed her?' She recalled later, 'I have never seen a man look so frightened in my life.' Mrs Kilgour left Adams £2,000.

It would appear, therefore, that Hannam had every reason to suspect Bodkin Adams of being a mercenary and greedy man who had no hesitation in administering overdoses to his patients.

The trial opened at the Old Bailey on 18 March 1957. The case against Bodkin Adams was presented by the Attorney General, Sir Reginald Manningham-Buller, and it sounded damning. Mrs Morrell was 81 years old when she died. She was suffering from hardening of the arteries of the brain and from the effects of a stroke, which had left her paralyzed in the left side. She was rarely in any pain – such a condition is seldom attended with pain. Yet Bodkin Adams prescribed huge doses of pain-killing drugs – morphia, heroin, barbiturates and sedormid. Why should he do that unless it was his aim to make his patient a drug addict, who would be grateful to him for keeping her supplied?

Adams had called on Mrs Morrell's solicitor, and told him that Mrs Morrell had promised to leave him a Rolls-Royce and a case of silver cutlery. He also said Mrs Morrell had recollected that she had forgotten to do this, so she wanted her solicitor to prepare a codicil. If it did not meet with her approval it could be destroyed later. The solicitor called on Mrs Morrell and she executed the codicil. It was then that Adams made a tremendous increase in the quantity of drugs he was prescribing her, and she spent much of the time in a coma. It would seem that Adams killed her by giving her these massive overdoses. On the last evening of her life he had prescribed an injection in a 5cc syringe, instead of the usual 2cc syringe. Three hours later he had repeated the dose. One hour after that Mrs Morrell died.

But for those who, like the reporter Percy Hoskins, felt that Adams, was 'a dead duck', there was a great surprise to come.

Four of the chief prosecution witnesses were undoubtedly the nurses who had attended Mrs Morrell at the end of her life, and who had provided the prosecution with the evidence about massive overdoses. On the second morning of the trial, the prosecution questioned Nurse Stronach, a stocky woman with a firm jaw. She testified that the patient had been 'rambling and semi-conscious'. She admitted that the patient had told her she was suffering pain, 'but I considered it neurotic'.

Then the defence, Mr Geoffrey Lawrence, took over. He asked her what injections she had given the old lady and whether it had been a quarter grain of morphia? The nurse agreed. Had not Dr Adams then arrived and given Mrs Morrell a further injection, without telling her what it was? The nurse agreed. Lawrence asked her if it was not the practice that all injections were noted down in a book. She agreed.

The defence now exploded its bombshell. Mr Lawrence produced an exercise book. He asked, 'Is that the night report for June 1950? Is that your handwriting?' The nurse had to agree that it was. Lawrence then read aloud a long passage, which demonstrated that Nurse Stronach had, indeed, recorded exactly what she had given the patient – milk and brandy, a sedormid tablet, more milk and brandy. She had also recorded that the patient had called her a nasty, common woman. Then Lawrence read out another entry – a description of the old lady's lunch consisting of partridge, celery and pudding, followed by brandy and soda. Hardly the lunch of a semi-conscious woman. . .

Lawrence pressed home the attack. Nurse Stronach had declared earlier that Mrs Morrell had been dopey and half asleep when Dr Adams had given her an injection; this was because she had already given Mrs Morrell an injection. But the record showed that Nurse Stronach had not given her an injection . . . Nurse Stronach had to agree that her memory had been at fault.

This was, in fact, the turning point of the trial. The defence had established that the nurses were not as reliable as the prosecution believed. The same point was reinforced when the other three nurses were cross-examined. Nurse Randall was asked about the normal dose of paraldehyde, the drug that was supposed to have killed the old lady. She answered, 'Two cc would be a normal dose.' Lawrence pointed out that the British Pharmacopoeia gave the full dose as 8cc, and the embarrassed nurse admitted that she had not known that.

The crucial point, of course, was that last injection of 5cc, which Dr Adams was alleged to have prepared, and which had been given by Nurse Randall. The record showed that no such injection had been given. The trial was to continue for 13 days more; but in effect, it was now over. It was almost a formality for the judge to find Bodkin Adams not guilty. When Percy Hoskins returned to his office, Lord Beaverbrook rang him and told him, 'Percy, two men have been acquitted today – Adams and Hoskins.' After that, Adams and Hoskins left for a secret hideaway, perhaps where Hoskins could write up the story of Dr John Bodkin Adams at his leisure.

But were two men acquitted? Was Hoskins right to believe that Bodkin Adams was innocent? He was possibly right to believe Adams was no sinister Bluebeard who carefully planned the murders of his patients. Yet we must remember that Adams was tried only for one murder. Would the verdict have been the same if the jury had known as much about him as Superintendent Hannam knew? He was found innocent because it was proved that the nurses had been mistaken on so many minor points. But were they lying when they alleged that Bodkin Adams had turned Mrs Morrell into a drug addict?

We know that Bodkin Adams was almost childishly greedy and avaricious. We know he was capable of putting pressure on his patients to make them leave him money in their wills. We know he was capable of giving at least one old lady an overdose that killed her – whether deliberately or out of carelessness. Is it not conceivable that he did the same to others when it suited his purposes? It is difficult to believe that Bodkin Adams was the wronged innocent that Percy Hoskins makes him out to be. In fact, it is hard not to feel that if the jury had found him guilty, no great injustice would have been committed.

JANICE WESTON

A lay-by on the northbound carriageway of the A1 is one of the most unlikely spots for a murder. Not only is the A1 one of the busiest roads in Britain but the lay-by in question is extremely narrow and completely exposed to view. But one has to remember that the murder took place at night, and that it was raining hard.

Nevertheless, the man who struck down Janice Weston, a wealthy solicitor, on the night of Saturday, 10 September 1983, must count himself remarkably lucky that he was not seen committing the deed in the headlights of a vehicle flashing past.

The body was discovered the following morning by a cyclist who had stopped to answer a call of nature. The body had been thrown into the ditch alongside the lay-by. It was badly battered – particularly the back of the head – but the murderer had made no attempt to cover it before hurriedly driving off in the victim's car.

Within 48 hours the police knew that the dead woman was 36-year-old Janice Weston, a brilliant company-law specialist and a partner in the Lincoln Inn's firm of Charles Russell & Company.

Janice Weston came from a comfortable background. After doing well at her convent school she had gone on to read law at Manchester University. When she qualified as a solicitor she was offered a post with the well-known London firm of Herbert Oppenheimer, Nathan & Vandyk. She was a career girl and dedicated to her work.

It was during her time at Oppenheimer's that she met the two men who were to play an important part in her life. The first was Tony Weston, a property developer, one year older than herself. He was married with two children. The other was Heinz Isner, 40 years older than she, and chairman of the Mettoy Company which made children's Corgi cars. He was a wealthy merchant banker and a Jew who had fled to Britain from Nazi Germany. Janice was Mettoy's legal adviser.

In 1975 Isner's wife died. Soon he began to invite the firm's

18

petite and well-turned out legal adviser to dinner at his Chelsea flat and to take her out to the theatre and ballet. The relationship developed until one day Isner revealed to his step-granddaughter that he had proposed marriage to Janice but that she had turned him down. Nevertheless, the couple continued to see each other until Heinz Isner died in July 1977. Janice was a major beneficiary in his will and she received paintings, furniture, shares and money totalling some £140,000.

Her career continued to prosper, and five years later at the age of 35 she married Tony Weston, who was by now divorced. The couple together bought an old country mansion, Clopton Manor in Northamptonshire, which they began to modernize and convert into flats, using one of the flats themselves. They both continued their separate careers – Janice, by now, a partner at Charles Russell. She also began researching for a book on computer law. Meanwhile, Tony Weston was negotiating the purchase of a château in France. As a successful professional young couple they had a lifestyle many would envy.

Janice had made her will 39 days after her wedding. Of her £300,000 estate, nearly £100,000 was to go to her sister and £10,000 to her widowed mother. The income from the rest of the estate was left for life to her husband, with the capital after her death being shared between his two children and her nephews and nieces.

During the weekend of 10–11 September 1983, Tony Weston was away in France on a business trip concerning the château. Janice, being the perfectionist and hard-worker that she was, took the opportunity of going to her office to work. At about 5 p.m. that Saturday afternoon one of the other partners called into Russell's and found her there. He thought she had been expecting someone, but she was still alone when he left a short time later. It appears she returned home to the couple's flat in Holland Park where she had a light snack. The police subsequently found that nothing had been cleared away afterwards – uncharacteristic of the fastidious Janice. It seems she left the flat in a hurry for she did not take her handbag with her. She did, however, take her purse which was eventually discovered, with £37 in it, tucked under the driving seat of her silver Alfa Romeo.

19

It was a filthy night and one wonders why she had gone out. Was she driving somebody somewhere? Had she received a telephone call summoning her to a meeting place? Or was she going to Clopton Manor – only 15 miles from the lay-by on the A1? It hardly seems likely as their flat was unfinished and sparsely furnished; there were not even sheets on the beds, only sleeping-bags.

After the discovery of Janice's body at 9 a.m. on the Sunday morning, the police, under the supervision of Detective Chief Superintendent Leonard Bradley, were soon at the scene together with Dr Ian Hill, a Home Office pathologist. After examining the body his verdict was that she had been killed with the car jack found by the police in the nearby field. She had probably died between 9 p.m. on the Saturday night and 2 a.m. on Sunday morning.

On Monday morning colleagues at Charles Russell became concerned when Janice did not appear for her appointments. They had telephoned her home and then, knowing that her husband was away, they telephoned her sister. News of the body of an unidentified woman found beside a lay-by on the A1 had already been reported in the press that morning. Her sister became worried and her husband contacted the police. Later that morning they identified Janice's body.

Tony Weston returned from France that Monday and told a reporter that he called 'on any member of the public with knowledge or reasonable suspicion of the person who committed this crime to come forward to the police'. Within a further 24 hours a keen-eyed policeman found Janice's Alfa Romeo. It was parked in Camden Square, London NW1, not three miles from her flat. The interior was smeared with blood but there were no fingerprints.

The police investigation intensified but, if anything, the mystery deepened. The owner of a car-spares shop in Royston, Hertfordshire, telephoned the police to say that at about 11 a.m. on the Sunday a man between 25 and 35 years of age had bought a couple of spare car plates from him. Their number was that of Janice's car. Two other witnesses corroborated his story. Neither the man nor the number plates have been seen since.

It also transpired that on the Saturday morning, Janice had collected a spare tyre that had been repaired. Before leaving for France Tony Weston had had a puncture while visiting Clopton Manor. A workman on the site had changed it for him and one of his staff in London had taken it to be repaired. A mechanic had put the spare tyre, with Tony Weston's name and telephone number still chalked on the inside, into the boot of the Alfa for Janice. The old spare remained on her rear nearside wheel. When the car was discovered, the newly repaired tyre was back on the Alfa and the spare was missing. Later police inquiries revealed that Janice might have stopped at the lay-by because a tyre needed changing. Six witnesses said they had seen a man changing her tyre.

In December 1983 Tony Weston was held for 55 hours by the police. His solicitor appealed to a High Court judge that he should either be charged or released. Later Tony Weston said, 'I walked into a London police station for a progress meeting. Nine hours later TV News showed me leaving St Neot's Police Station, 60 miles away, handcuffed and with a blanket over my head. To most people that blanket means only one thing. No smoke without fire . . . Guilty.'

He does, indeed, seem to have been a leading suspect for a while, although he could prove his movements in Paris that weekend, and a hotel clerk remembered him collecting his room key on the Saturday evening. He was later completely eliminated from police inquiries.

Police investigations continued. Isner's step-granddaughter was questioned about his will and the relationship between Janice Weston and her step-grandfather. She was asked where she had been on the night of the murder – her alibi was checked and her fingerprints taken. Janice's legacy had been slightly reduced after Isner's stepdaughter appealed to a High Court over his will. But clearly no member of the Isner family was involved in the murder.

At the inquest in April 1984 the jury returned a verdict of unlawful killing. What really happened that night in September 1983 may never be known, but there are several possibilities. Janice may have given a lift to a hitch-hiker who then killed her.

21

But why then did her car not turn up further north on the A1 rather than in London? Or a passing motorist may have stopped to change her tyre – and killed her. It is baffling.

Detective Chief Superintendent Bradley says, 'We're still pursuing active lines of inquiry and interviewing people, such as persons detained in other parts of the country who might have had an opportunity to commit the crime. We are still hopeful of bringing our efforts to a successful conclusion.'

THE LINDBERGH BABY KIDNAPPING

On 21 May 1927 Charles Lindbergh became the most famous young man in the world. For 33 hours, the whole of Europe and America had held its breath as his tiny plane, *Spirit of St Louis*, made the first solo flight across the Atlantic. As one biographer remarked, he had single-handedly christened and launched the air age.

Less than five years later, however, Lindbergh had become one of the most deeply pitied men in the world. On the evening of 1 March 1932, his 19-month-old son, Charles junior, was kidnapped from his cot. It was the beginning of a ten-week ordeal that left Lindbergh an embittered man whose only desire was to escape from America.

The Lindberghs were all suffering from colds on that rainy and windy day in March, which is why they had decided to delay their departure to the home of Lindbergh's in-laws at Englewood, New Jersey, by 24 hours. At 7.30 that Tuesday evening, Anne Lindbergh and the nurse Betty Gow put the baby to bed in his cot, and closed and bolted all the shutters, except one which was warped and refused to close. Fifty minutes later, Charles Lindbergh arrived back from New York – only half an hour's drive away from their new home in Hopewell, South Jersey. Supper was waiting, and they ate in front of a blazing fire. At about 9.10 Lindbergh looked up sharply. 'What was that?' He had heard a sound, he said, like an orange crate smashing. But there was no further noise, and he forgot about it.

Just after 10 o'clock, Betty Gow knocked on the door of the Lindberghs' bedroom and asked, 'Mrs Lindbergh, do you have the baby?'

'Why, no.'

They went down to the library to see if Lindbergh had taken the child – he was fond of practical jokes. Then all three rushed back to the baby's bedroom. They could see the imprint of young Charles's head on the pillow, and it would obviously have been impossible for him to have climbed out on his own. Lindbergh said, 'Anne, they've stolen our baby.'

23

Then he saw the envelope on the radiator under the window. He told them not to touch it. When the police opened it an hour later, it was found to contain a ransom demand for $50,000.

There were few clues. Under the window, the police found some smudged footprints; nearby there was a ladder in three sections and a chisel. The ladder – a crude home-made one – was broken where the top section joined the middle one; this was almost certainly the noise Lindbergh had heard earlier. There were no fingerprints; the kidnapper must have worn gloves.

The kidnapping caused a nationwide sensation. But at this stage the Lindberghs were not too worried. Anne wrote to her mother-in-law: '. . . the detectives are very optimistic though they think it will take time and patience. In fact, they think the kidnappers have gotten themselves into a terrible jam – so much pressure, such a close net over the country . . .' And the pressure was indeed tremendous; crooks all over the east coast had reason to curse the kidnappers as the police turned on the heat. Sympathetic letters arrived literally in sackloads – 200,000 of them in a few days. Carloads of police, F.B.I. agents and secret servicemen arrived in Hopewell; so did many reporters and photographers. The Lindberghs were given no privacy. The great American public continued to love 'Lindy', but Lindy's love affair with the American way of life was at an end.

The note offered few clues. It had various spelling mistakes; 'anyding' for anything, and 'gut' for good; a handwriting expert said it had been written by a German with low educational qualifications. It was signed with two interlocking circles, one red and one blue.

But the kidnapper was obviously scared off by the hullabaloo; he made no attempt to contact the Lindberghs. From his prison cell, Al Capone, America's most famous gangster, offered to recover the baby if he was allowed out; the authorities declined. Mrs Lindbergh broadcast an appeal, and newspapers printed a diet sheet of the baby's meals. This drew a letter from the kidnapper – signed with the two coloured circles – explaining: 'We can note [sic] make any appointments just now', and promising to adhere to the diet. It had the typical German

24

spelling errors: as before 'gut' for good, and 'aus' for 'out'.

A week after the kidnapping, a well-wisher named Dr John F. Condon sent a letter to his local newspaper in the Bronx, offering $1,000 of his own money for the return of the child. The result was a letter addressed to Condon signed with the two circles. It began: 'Dear Sir, If you are willing to act as go-between in the Lindbergh cace pleace [sic] follow stricly instruction.' It asked him to collect the money from Lindbergh and then place an advertisement in the *New York American* reading: Mony is Redy. Then further 'instruction' would be forthcoming.

When Condon succeeded in speaking to Lindbergh, the famous flyer sounded exhausted and indifferent – until Condon mentioned the signature of interlocking circles. Then his voice became excited, and he offered to see Condon immediately. The advertisement duly appeared in the *New York American*: 'Money is ready, Jafsie.' That same evening, a man's deep voice spoke to Condon on the telephone – Condon could also hear another man in the room speaking in Italian – and told him that the gang would shortly be in touch. The next day he was handed a letter that instructed him where to find yet another message.

The second message told Condon to meet the writer at a cemetery at 233rd Street. At the cemetery gates, a young man wearing a handkerchief over his face asked Condon if he had brought the money – the demand had now been increased to $70,000. Condon explained that the notice had been too short. Suddenly the man took fright. 'Have you brought the police?' Condon replied, 'No! You can trust me.' But the man ran away. Condon chased after him, and caught up with him in a nearby park. Here the young man, who identified himself as 'John', asked a peculiar thing, 'Would I burn if the baby is dead?' Appalled, Condon asked, 'Is the baby dead?' But 'John' assured him it was alive. It was on a boat, about six hours away (he pronounced it 'boad'). Finally, 'John' offered a token of his good faith – he would send Condon the baby's sleeping suit. And, in fact, it arrived by post; the Lindberghs identified it as that of their son.

On 2 April a second rendezvous at a cemetery was made.

This time, Lindbergh himself accompanied Condon; he was carrying $70,000 in a cardboard box. Unknown to Lindbergh, the Treasury had listed the number of every bill. Condon spoke to the kidnapper, and managed to persuade him to accept only $50,000. As he returned to Lindbergh's car, the kidnapper shouted after him, 'Hey, doctor'. Lindbergh heard the voice clearly. A moment later Condon handed over the money, and 'John' promised to send details of the whereabouts of the missing baby by the next morning's post.

The letter, when it arrived, claimed that the child was on a boat called the *Nelly*, near Elizabeth Island. Condon accompanied Lindbergh on the flight to look for the boat at the specified location. It was not there. Bitterly, they realized they had been tricked.

Five weeks later, on 12 May 1932, the last hope vanished when a Negro teamster, walking in the woods near the Lindbergh home, found a shallow, leaf-covered grave. It contained the decomposing body of a child. The shirt in which the body was dressed had been made by Betty Gow from a flannel petticoat. Charles Lindbergh Junior – 'Buster' – had been dead since the night on which he was taken from his cot; he had died of a blow on the head.

The trail seemed to be cold, yet the hunt for the kidnapper and killer was intensified. A member of the Lindbergh household was for a time widely suspected by the public, but the Lindberghs were convinced she was innocent. Another person suspected of complicity – Violet Sharpe, a maid at the home of Lindbergh's in-laws – committed suicide with poison.

Meanwhile, a wood technologist named Arthur Koehler was continuing his own investigations and examining the ladder used by the kidnapper. He had written to Lindbergh offering to try to trace its wood, using the laboratory of the Forest Service. It took him 18 months, and dozens of visits to lumber yards but eventually he found the place where the wood had been bought: The National Lumber and Millwork Company in the Bronx. It confirmed what the police had already come to accept: that the kidnapper of the Lindbergh baby lived somewhere in the Bronx – the reason he had seen Condon's original advertisement so quickly . . .

In May 1934, President Roosevelt abandoned the gold standard. This was unfortunate for the kidnappers, for $35,000 of the ransom money had been in gold certificates. These were now called in as they had ceased to be legal tender.

A break finally came on 15 September 1934. A dark-blue Dodge sedan drove into a garage in upper Manhattan; the man who drove asked for fuel with a German accent, and paid with a $10 gold certificate. The gas attendant hesitated but the man said, 'They're all right – any bank will take them.' So the attendant gave him his change. But not before he made a note of the number of the car. Other gold certificates had been exchanged in New York and they had proved to be part of the Lindbergh ransom money, but no one had ever noticed the person who had changed them. The certificate was taken to the local bank.

Four days later, a bank teller realized that this was another gold certificate from the Lindbergh ransom money. On the back of the note was a car registration number: 4U-13-41-N.Y. He tracked the gold certificate back to the service station in Manhattan. The police now checked with the New York State Motor License vehicle bureau as to who owned a car of that number. The answer soon came back: Richard Hauptmann, 1279 East 222nd Street, the Bronx.

Police surrounded the small frame house all that night, and when a man finally stepped out of the front door, they still waited, watching him climb into the blue Dodge sedan and drive off. A few minutes later, they forced him over to the kerb – perhaps working on the theory that a man with a steering wheel in both hands would not be able to pull out a gun and start shooting. But Hauptmann was unarmed. In his wallet, they found a $20 bill that was also from the Lindbergh ransom. Back at Hauptmann's home, in the garage a further $14,600 in ransom bills was found, carefully concealed. On a strip of wood in a dark closet they found Condon's telephone number. When asked to write down a passage containing words used by the kidnapper, Hauptmann misspelled them exactly as they appeared in the notes.

When asked how he came to be in possession of the money,

Hauptmann said it had been left in his care by a friend, Isidor Fisch, who had since died.

Hauptmann was a carpenter by trade, and he was 35 years old. He also had a criminal record in Germany – burglary and highway robbery – and had been sentenced to five years' imprisonment. He had been released on parole but had been arrested for more burglaries. He escaped and fled the country. He had entered the United States illegally, married a waitress, and set up in business as a carpenter. He was extremely successful, earning $50 a week. He had not worked for the past two years, and his account books, which he kept meticulously, showed that his fortunes had improved considerably since 1932.

Hauptmann's own story was that he and Fisch had gone into business in 1932, and that Fisch owed him $7,500. In 1933 Fisch had gone to Germany, but had died in Leipzig in 1934. Later that year, heavy rain had seeped into a closet in which he had left a shoe box that Fisch had consigned to his care, and only then had Hauptmann discovered it was full of money, which he dried out. But he failed to tell his wife, or Fisch's family, about his find. He had started using occasional bills from the shoe box because, after all, Fisch owed him money.

But perhaps the most damning piece of evidence at Hauptmann's trial, which opened in Flemington, New Jersey, on 2 January 1935, was the ladder. In Hauptmann's attic, claimed the prosecution, the police had discovered that a floorboard was missing. Sawdust showed that it had been sawn off. And the left-hand board of the kidnap ladder – known as 'Rail 16' – was of the same type of wood as the missing board. When placed in position in the attic floor four nail holes in Rail 16 matched exactly the four nail holes in the joist below. That seemed to prove emphatically that Hauptmann had made the ladder. Hauptmann replied scornfully that he was a skilful carpenter and that the ladder had been made by an incompetent amateur, not a man who took pride in his work. But the jury discounted his protest.

On 13 February 1935 the jury found Hauptmann guilty of murder. By October, the Court of Appeals had denied Hauptmann's appeal. The prison governor Harold Hoffmann interviewed Hauptmann in his cell in December, and emerged a puzzled man. Hauptmann again pointed out that he would never have made such a ladder, and begged to be given a truth drug or lie detector test. Hoffmann felt that his pleas rang true and began an investigation into the case. A few days after Hauptmann's arrest, Mrs Hauptmann had left home, unable to stand the continual commotion. A short time afterwards, the police had 'found' the missing board. Could they have removed it themselves? They could certainly have planted Condon's phone number in the dark closet. Condon had at first been uncertain that Hauptmann was 'John'. It was only later that he changed his mind. The prosecution had insisted that Hauptmann was alone in planning and carrying out the kidnapping, but what about the Italian voice Condon had heard on the telephone?

Governor Hoffman's intervention was interpreted by most of the American press as an attempt to get publicity, and others felt he was politically motivated – he was attempting to sack the Attorney General, David Wilentz, who had prosecuted Hauptmann. For Lindbergh this was the last straw. Totally convinced that Hauptmann was the man who had killed his son – and that American justice could be influenced by politicians – he sailed for England. He would remain in Europe for nearly five years, and was to become an admirer and frequent guest of the Nazis. During World War II he would try hard to prevent America entering the war on the side of the Allies.

Hauptmann was finally electrocuted, on 3 April 1936. For many years, there were no doubts that justice had been done. Everyone felt that the villain had finally got his 'come-uppance'. Only Hauptmann's wife Anna continued to plead that her husband was innocent.

But as the years went by, an increasing number of people began to agree with her – or at least, to agree that Hauptmann had not been proved guilty. Anthony Scaduto's book *Scapegoat* is an extremely powerful presentation of the evidence in favour of Hauptmann. But another book, *In Search of the Lindbergh Baby*, by Theon Wright, a reporter at the trial, raises a startling possibility: that 'Buster' Lindbergh was not murdered at all. A Connecticut businessman named Harold Olson had been told as a child that he belonged to a family of gangsters, who had placed him with Roy and Sarah Olson when he was a baby. His real father, he was told, may have been Al Capone. But when he was an adult, his mother's cousins had told him that he might be the son of Charles Lindbergh. Furthermore, a woman who had been his nurse as a baby told him authoritatively that he was the Lindbergh child. Olson was certainly the right age for the Lindbergh baby, and photographs of him as a child show similar eyes to 'Buster' Lindbergh's, and the same scar on the chin. Olson spent years trying to track down his origins, and finally came to believe that the Lindbergh kidnapping was a plot organized by Capone lieutenants to get their boss out of jail – it may be recalled that Capone offered to locate the Lindbergh baby in exchange for his freedom.

But what about the child's body? A photograph in Wright's book shows that it was little more than a skeleton. The shirt in which it was wrapped was rotten, so little faith can be placed in Betty Gow's identification of it as the one she made. In *The Trial of Richart Hauptmann* there is one rather odd piece of evidence, given by William J. Allen, the truck driver who found the body; he said that the land on the other side of the road belonged to 'a Catholic home – a kind of hospital for children that ain't got no home'. Could the skeleton – which even Lindbergh was doubtful about identifying – have come from there?

This may seem a far-fetched theory. Yet one thing is certain: Bruno Richard Hauptmann should never have been found guilty on the evidence offered by the prosecution.

WILLIAM HERBERT WALLACE

The Wallace murder case might have been devised by Agatha Christie. In spite of recent evidence that seems to point towards a solution, it retains that tantalizing quality of a classic unsolved mystery.

William Herbert Wallace gave the appearance of being a completely ordinary little man. The critic James Agate once said of him: 'That man was born middle-aged.' But this undistinguished appearance concealed a certain sadness and unfulfilment. Wallace was born in Keswick, in England's Lake District, in 1878, the child of lower-middle-class parents. But he had an intellectual turn of mind, and when he discovered the *Meditations* of the Roman emperor Marcus Aurelius, decided that he was by nature a stoic – that is, one who doesn't expect much out of life, but who thinks it can be improved by hard work and discipline.

Like H. G. Wells's Kipps or Mr Polly – of whom he constantly reminds us – he became a draper's assistant, and found the life just as boring as they had. His quest for adventure took him to India – but still as a draper's assistant – then to Shanghai; he found both places a great disappointment, and caught a bad dose of dysentery which further undermined his already delicate constitution. So with his Marcus Aurelius in his pocket, he returned to England.

He became a Liberal election agent in Yorkshire, and while on a holiday in Harrogate met a mild-looking, dark-haired young lady named Julia Thorp. She was undoubtedly more intelligent than Wallace; she was well read, spoke French, played the piano and made excellent sketches. They talked about Marcus Aurelius and other intellectual matters and, in a rather leisurely manner, decided they liked one another enough to get married. They married in 1913 and lived in Harrogate. In the following year the outbreak of World War I cost Wallace his job – political agents were not needed during a war. Fortunately, it also caused many job vacancies and he soon found employment as an insurance agent in Liverpool, working for the Prudential.

The couple moved into a rather dreary little terrace house in a cul-de-sac called Wolverton Crescent, in the Anfield district, and for the next 17 years lived a life of peaceful and rather penurious dullness.

Wallace pottered about in a chemical laboratory in his home, and even gave occasional lectures at the technical college. He also joined a chess club that met regularly in the City Café in North John Street. Julia read library books and sang at the piano. They had no children and, apparently, no real friends. And although life on less than £4 a week was hardly idyllic, they seemed happy enough.

The evening of 19 January 1931 was chilly and damp, but by 7 o'clock a few members had already arrived at the chess club in the City Café. Shortly after 7.15, the telephone rang. Samuel Beattie, captain of the club, answered it. A man's voice asked for Wallace. Beattie said that Wallace would be in later to play a match and suggested he ring back. 'No, I'm too busy – I have my girl's 21st birthday on.' The man said his name was Qualtrough, and asked if Beattie could give him a message. Beattie wrote it down – it asked Wallace to go to Qualtrough's home at 25 Menlove Gardens East the following evening at 7.30. It was, said Qualtrough, a matter of business.

Wallace slipped quietly into the club some time before 8 o'clock. Beattie gave him the message and Wallace made a note of the address in his diary.

The following evening, Wallace arrived home shortly after six, had 'high tea' – a substantial meal – and left the house at a quarter to seven. He instructed his wife to bolt the back door after him – that was their usual practice. Julia Wallace, who was suffering from a heavy cold, nevertheless went with him to the back gate and watched him leave. Wallace walked to a tramcar, asked the conductor if it went to Menlove Gardens East, and climbed aboard. The conductor advised him to change trams at Penny Lane, and told Wallace where to get off. The conductor of the second tram advised him to get off at Menlove Gardens West.

Wallace now spent a frustrating half-hour or so trying to find Menlove Gardens East. Apparently it did not exist; although there was a Menlove Gardens North and Menlove Gardens West. Wallace decided to call at 25 Menlove Gardens West, just in case Beattie had taken down the address wrongly; but the householder there said he had never heard of a Mr Qualtrough. Wallace tried calling at the house of his superintendent at the Prudential, a Mr Joseph Crew, who lived in nearby Green Lane, but found no one at home. He asked a policeman the way, and remarked on the time, 'It's not 8 o'clock yet.' The policeman said, 'It's a quarter to.' He called in a general shop, then in a newsagent's, where he borrowed a city directory, which seemed to prove beyond all doubt that Menlove Gardens East did not exist. He even asked the proprietress to look in her account book to make sure that there was no such place as Menlove Gardens East. People were to remark later that Wallace seemed determined to make people remember him. Finally, even the pertinacious Wallace gave up, and returned home.

He arrived back at 8.45 p.m., and inserted his key into the front door. To his surprise, it seemed to be locked on the inside. He tried the back door; that was also locked. Receiving no reply to his knock, he called on his next-door neighbours the Johnstons, looking deeply concerned, and asked them if they had heard anything unusual – only a thin partition wall separated them from the Wallaces. They said no. John Johnston suggested that perhaps Wallace should try the back door again. And this time, to Wallace's apparent surprise, it opened. He entered the house, and the Johnstons waited outside politely. A few moments later, Wallace rushed out, looking shocked. 'Come and see – she's been killed.' They followed him through to the sitting room, which was at the back of the house. Julia Wallace was lying on the floor, face downward, and the gash in the back of her head made it clear that she had been the victim of an attack. The floor was spattered with blood.

Wallace seemed curiously calm as he lit a gas-mantle, walking around the body to do so, then suggested that they should look in the kitchen to see if anything had been taken. There was a lid on the kitchen floor, which Wallace said had been wrenched from a cabinet. He took down the cash-box from a shelf, looked inside and told the Johnstons that he thought about £4 had been taken. Then, at Johnston's suggestion, Wallace went upstairs to see if anything was missing, and came down almost immediately saying, 'There's £5 in a jar they haven't taken.'

At this point, Johnston left to fetch the police. Wallace had a momentary breakdown, putting his hands to his head and sobbing, but quickly recovered himself. Mrs Johnston and Wallace then returned to the sitting room, where Wallace commented, 'They've finished her – look at the brains.' And indeed, Julia Wallace's brains were oozing on to the floor. Then Wallace exclaimed with surprise, 'Why, whatever was she doing with her mackintosh and my mackintosh?' There was a mackintosh under her body, which Wallace identified as his own.

Shortly afterwards, a policeman arrived. Wallace told him about his fruitless search for Qualtrough, then accompanied him upstairs. Constable Williams felt that Wallace seemed 'extraordinarily cool and calm'. The bedroom appeared to have been disturbed, with pillows lying near the fireplace.

Another policeman arrived, then, just before 10 o'clock, Professor J.E.W. MacFall, the professor of forensic medicine at Liverpool University. MacFall concluded that Mrs Wallace died of a violent blow or blows to the back left-hand side of the skull – and deduced that she had been sitting in an armchair, leaning forward as if talking to somebody, when the blow had been struck. She had fallen to the floor, and the attacker had rained about 11 more blows on her. He also reached the interesting conclusion that Mrs Wallace had died about four hours earlier – that is, at 6 o'clock . . .

This, it later proved, was impossible, for the 14-year-old milk boy, Alan Close, was to testify that he had delivered a can of milk at 6.25 p.m., and that Mrs Wallace advised him to hurry home because he had a cough.

But MacFall had planted suspicion on Wallace in the minds of the police. Two weeks later, on 2 February 1931, Wallace was charged with his wife's murder. He became very pale and replied, 'What can I say to this charge, of which I am absolutely innocent?'

His trial began on 22 April, before Mr Justice Wright. The prosecution case was that Wallace had concocted an elaborate plan to murder his wife, and had phoned the café to make the appointment with Qualtrough on the evening before the murder. The endless and elaborate inquiries about Menlove Gardens East were intended to provide him with a perfect alibi; but Mrs Wallace was already lying dead in her sitting-room when William Herbert Wallace left the house. In the closing speech for the Crown, Mr E. G. Hemmerde made much of the 'inherent improbabilities' in Wallace's story: that surely an insurance agent would not spend his evening on such a wild goose chase – that he would have hurried back home the moment he knew that a Menlove Gardens East did not exist. He also made much of Wallace's apparent calmness immediately after the discovery of the body, and mentioned in passing the possibility that Wallace had stripped naked and then put on his mackintosh, and battered his wife to death, before leaving the house to look for Qualtrough.

The judge's summing up was favourable to Wallace, and there was some surprise when, after only an hour, the jury returned a verdict of guilty. Wallace was shattered; he had been confident of acquittal. But he appealed against the verdict, and indeed the following month, the Court of Criminal Appeal quashed it, and Wallace was freed.

He was taken back at his old job. But most of his colleagues had doubts about his innocence. He was given a job in the office. He moved house, to Meadowside Road in Bromsborough, a Liverpool suburb. And on 26 February 1933 – less than two years after his ordeal – he died in hospital of cancer of the liver. Ever since that date, writers on crime have disputed his guilt or innocence.

The main problem, of course, is that of motive. Wallace was a lifelong keeper of diaries, and his diaries make it clear that his married life was peaceful and serene. There was no suggestion of another woman, or that he was tired of his wife. His diaries after his trial continue to protest his innocence, with entries like: 'Julia, Julia my dear, why were you taken from me?' The crime writer Nigel Morland, who examined the case at length in

Background to Murder and who was convinced of Wallace's guilt, has to fall back on generalizations like: 'The human heart is always a vast mystery . . .'

Yseult Bridges, who also wrote about the case, became convinced of Wallace's guilt when she read a series of 'ghosted' articles about his life which appeared in *John Bull* in 1932. There Wallace remarks that he had matched his brains against some of the greatest chess players in the world. Yseult Bridges comments that 'he was never more than a third-rate player in an obscure little club', and concludes that Wallace was a pathological liar. But another writer, Jonathan Goodman, looked more closely into the matter, and concludes (in *The Killing of Julia Wallace*) that Wallace was telling the truth after all; in the 1920s he had played in 'simultaneous exhibition matches' against world-famous players like Capablanca – and been thoroughly beaten.

Kenneth Gunnell, a parliamentary candidate from Redruth, Cornwall, independently discovered that Wallace was telling the truth about his chess opponents, and so began to study the case in detail. He made one odd discovery. Amy Wallace, the wife of Wallace's elder brother Joseph, was a tough and dominant lady, and Gunnell found out that in Malaya – where she had lived in the 1920s – Amy had been a member of a flagellation sect, and indulged in beating black boys. He noted that after his acquittal, Wallace sometimes acted like a man with something on his mind – not murder, perhaps, but some guilty secret. Could it be that Amy Wallace was Herbert Wallace's mistress, and that she murdered Julia? Mr Gunnell even speculated that the murder weapon was the metal handle of a riding whip. Unfortunately, Mr Gunnell's stimulating theory remained unpublished. Yet when I read the typescript of his book, I found myself ultimately unconvinced. Although my view of Wallace was rather negative – he seemed to me a cold-hearted egoist who had married Julia for her money (which he used to pay his debts), then treated her purely as a piece of domestic furniture – it seemed clear that he was simply not the type to engage in affairs with highly dominant women. Amy Wallace probably terrified him.

In 1960, I collaborated with Patricia Pitman on *An Encyclopedia of Murder*. Mrs Pitman was convinced of Wallace's guilt; I, in spite of misgivings about his character, of his innocence. He simply had no reason to kill Julia. Two or three years later, she surprised me by telling me that she was now convinced of Wallace's innocence. It seemed that she had been talking to one of Britain's leading crime experts, J. H. H. Gaute, a director of the publishers Harrap, and he had told her the real identity of the murderer. I hastened to contact Joe Gaute, with whom I had had much friendly correspondence about murder. It was from him that I first heard the name of the man he was certain was the killer of Julia Wallace: Gordon Parry. Wallace himself, it seemed, had believed that Parry murdered his wife, and after his retirement he had made a public statement to the effect that he had had an alarm button installed inside his front door as a safety precaution.

After the murder, Wallace had been asked by the police what callers might have been admitted to the house by his wife; he named 15 people (including his sister-in-law Amy). Asked if he suspected any of them Wallace hesitated, then admitted that he was suspicious of a young man named Gordon Parry. This man had called at his house on business, and was trusted by Julia. But he had a criminal record. And he knew where Wallace kept his collection money. At the time of the murder, Parry was heavily in debt. Questioned by the police, he alleged that he had been with 'friends' on the evening of the murder, and his friends corroborated this. However, two years later, Parry admitted that this had been 'a mistake'.

Joe Gaute had been curious about Parry's present where-abouts, and had casually looked him up in the London Telephone Directory. It was a long shot, but it paid off. Parry was listed at an address in south London. The author Jonathan Goodman, who was writing his book on the Wallace case, and another crime expert, Richard Whittington-Egan, went to call on him. Parry, a powerfully built, little man with sleeked-back grey hair and a military moustache, received them with the 'bogus bonhomie of a car salesman', and talked to them on his doorstep. They decided that 'his manner masks . . . considerable firmness, even ruthlessness. He would be a nasty man to cross.' Parry hinted that he could reveal much about Wallace, and described him as 'a very strange man' and 'sexually odd'. He seemed to know what had become of everybody involved in the case, as if he had been carefully following its aftermath over the years. And when he finally dismissed Goodman and Whittington-Egan, they both had the feeling that he was thinking that he had fooled better people than they were. In his book *The Killing of Julia Wallace*, Goodman refers to Parry as 'Mr X', and it is fairly clear that he regarded him as the chief suspect.

In 1980, a news editor in Liverpool's Radio City, Roger Wilkes, became interested in the Wallace case, and started researching it for a programme. He contacted Jonathan Goodman, who at first was understandably cagey about revealing Parry's identity, in case he found himself involved in a libel suit. But through Wallace's solicitor, Hector Munro, Wilkes tracked down Parry's identity. At the time of the murder, Parry was 22, the son of well-to-do parents. He had worked for the Prudential for a while, but had failed to pay in various premiums he had received; his parents had paid the money. Parry had been charged at various times with theft, embezzlement and indecent assault – at his trial for the latter a medical expert called him 'a sexual pervert'.

Wilkes persisted; but when he finally tracked down Parry to North Wales he discovered that he had died a few weeks before, in April 1980. Nevertheless, he continued with his investigation. Who were the 'friends' who had given Parry his alibi for the night of the murder? It emerged that there was only one – a Miss Lily Lloyd, to whom Parry was engaged. And from Jonathan Goodman he learned that when Parry had jilted her two years later, Miss Lloyd had gone to Wallace's solicitor and offered to swear an affidavit saying that the alibi she had given for Parry for the night of the crime was false. Wilkes then managed to track down Miss Lloyd. She had played a piano in a cinema in the 1930s and if the police had taken the trouble to check her alibi they would have discovered that she could not have been with Parry at the time of the murder as she was working in the cinema.

Finally, Wilkes uncovered the clinching piece of evidence. At the time of the murder, a young garage mechanic named John Parkes had been working near Parry's home. He knew Parry as a 'wide boy' – he had been to school with him. On the night of the murder, Parry had called at the garage in an agitated state, and washed down his car with a high-pressure hose. Parkes saw a glove in the car, and pulled it out to prevent it getting wet. It was soaked with wet blood . . .

Wilkes had finally tracked down the murderer of Julia Wallace – but half a century too late.

ADELAIDE BARTLETT

The Adelaide Barlett poisoning case does not qualify as one of the great murder mysteries; yet most students of Victorian crime will agree that it is one of the most peculiar cases of all time.

Theodore Edwin Bartlett was a hard-working and highly ambitious grocer; by the time he was 29, he and his business partner owned a chain of small shops in south London. Although he was a good-looking man, fond of the open air, he had never married – life was too busy for romance. Then, one day in the early 1870s, he went to call on his brother Charles, who lived in Kingston, and was introduced to a dazzlingly attractive 18-year-old girl named Adelaide Blanche de la Tremoile. She had dark curly hair, large and appealing eyes, and a sensual mouth. Edwin found her fascinating. But it seems likely that, at this stage, marriage did not enter his head.

Adelaide was definitely a lady, and therefore far above him socially. Then he learned that there was an odd secret in her background. Adelaide's mother had borne her out of wedlock. Her father was a wealthy Englishman who preferred to keep his identity secret – it has been suggested that he was a member of Queen Victoria's entourage when she visited France in 1855, and was therefore probably titled. Now Adelaide lived with a guardian in a house in Richmond – she was staying in Kingston as a guest of Charles's 16-year-old daughter. So it seemed that, although she was a lady, her chances of being accepted into English society were minimal. Edwin saw his opportunity, and pursued it with single-minded vigour.

He called on her when she returned to Richmond, and seems to have persuaded her guardian – or her father – that a virtuous and successful grocer would make a desirable husband. He explained to Adelaide solemnly that his intentions were more than pure; there was no element of carnal desire in his feeling for her, and when they were married, their relationship would be wholly platonic. By way of proving his good faith, Edwin Bartlett packed off his newly wedded bride to a ladies' finishing school in Stoke Newington. She came to stay with her husband during the school holidays but – according to Adelaide – their relationship was like that of father and daughter. And when she had finished at the Stoke Newington school, Edwin sent her off to a convent in Brussels. She stayed there until 1877 – two years after their marriage – when she returned home to a newly furnished flat above Edwin's largest shop in Herne Hill. For just one month, life was pleasant and peaceful, and Adelaide no doubt enjoyed being a young married woman in charge of her first home. Then Edwin's mother died, and the dutiful son invited his father to come and live with them.

It was a mistake. The old man was a bad-tempered old sponger and he had never liked Adelaide. He made himself so unpleasant that Adelaide ran away from home – possibly to the house in Kingston where Edwin had first met her. This seems to have led to further trouble. Edwin's younger brother, Frederick, also lived in the house, and the old man suspected a love affair. One writer on the case states that Adelaide became Frederick's mistress, but there is no evidence whatsoever for this assertion. All we know is that the old man accused Adelaide of having an affair with Frederick, and that Edwin was so incensed he made his father sign an apology drawn up by a solicitor. Then an uneasy peace reigned in the household.

Four years later, in 1881, two things broke the monotony of their lives: Edwin had a nervous breakdown (brought on, according to his father, by laying a floor), and Adelaide had a stillborn baby. The latter incident was Edwin's fault; the nurse he engaged to look after his wife had sensed that this might be a difficult birth, and begged Edwin to call in a doctor. But the Victorian Edwin was rather shocked at the idea of another man 'interfering with her', and refused. By the time a doctor was finally called in, the baby was dead.

Soon after this, perhaps to distract her, they moved to the village of Merton, near Wimbledon. Edwin's motive may also have been to get rid of his father. He selected a house that had no spare bedroom, so the old man was forced to find a home elsewhere.

Early in 1885 – the Bartletts had now been married ten years

– the couple decided to try another place of worship one Sunday morning. They attended the Wesleyan Chapel in Merton. The preacher that day was a young man named George Dyson; he had a black moustache, a receding hairline, and was of slight build. Dyson made a pastoral call on the Barletts soon after that. And when he told Edwin Bartlett that he was about to go to Trinity College Dublin, to take his degree, Bartlett was deeply impressed. He had an almost pathetic admiration for anyone with education – he himself was an avid but disorganized reader. He cross-examined Dyson about his studies and pressed the young man to come and visit them again as soon as he returned from Dublin. Slightly overwhelmed – for he was modest and not very clever – Dyson agreed. And a warm, if peculiar, friendship began between these three rather lonely people.

Dyson found Edwin Bartlett 'exceedingly odd'. He seemed to have eccentric ideas on all kinds of subjects. For example, he was a devotee of a work called *Esoteric Anthropology* by Thomas Low Nichols, whose long sub-title declared it to be a 'confidential' treatise on the passionate attractions and perversions of the most intimate relations between men and women. It was not, as the judge later assumed, disguised pornography, but an early 'women's lib' discourse on the unfairness of using women as sexual objects. It recommended birth control and suggested that sexual intercourse should only be practised for the purpose of begetting children. Another of Edwin's rather peculiar beliefs was that men should have two wives, one for 'use' and one for intellectual companionship. He was also, like many Victorians, interested in hypnotism, and in the doctrines of Anton Mesmer, according to which human beings possess a 'vital magnetic fluid' that can be passed from one to another.

Soon, Edwin Bartlett was professing the warmest affection for the Reverend Dyson. In fact, he proposed that Dyson should continue Adelaide's education, teaching her geography, history, Latin and mathematics. Dyson, who was making a mere £100 a year, agreed. He would arrive in the morning, while Edwin was out at business, and often stay all day. During most of this time, he was alone with Adelaide. Whether she became his mistress

42

depends on one's final view of her guilt or innocence; but certainly she often sat at his feet, with her head on his knee, and he often kissed her – alone and in her husband's presence. And, oddly enough, Edwin seemed delighted with the whole arrangement. His wife was lonely – she had only one close female friend, a Mrs Alice Matthews – and now he had found her a male friend and teacher who could be trusted implicitly. Edwin had unlimited faith in clergymen. If he found Dyson still in the house when he came in for supper, he warmly pressed him to stay for the evening.

When the Bartletts went to Dover for a month, Edwin tried to persuade Dyson to accompany them too, and offered him a first-class season ticket so that he could rush down from London whenever he was free. Dyson refused, but Edwin still found time to travel to Putney and whisk him off to Dover as an overnight guest. He also asked Dyson to be an executor of his will, in which, naturally, he left everything to Adelaide.

In the September of 1885 the Bartletts moved into a new lodging in Victoria – it was to be their last. Edwin told their landlady, Mrs Doggett, that they would be having a regular visitor, a clergyman, as a dinner guest. George Dyson continued to call as regularly as ever, travelling from Putney, where he was now in charge of his own church, on a season ticket given him by Edwin Bartlett. They even kept a special jacket and slippers for him to change into. Dyson was finding this close friendship with a young married woman disturbing, and he confessed openly to Edwin that he was growing attracted to Adelaide and that it was upsetting his work. He felt he ought to stop seeing them. Edwin dismissed the idea, assuring Dyson that Adelaide had become a better and nobler woman since she had known him. He seemed to be trying to throw them into one another's arms. Mrs Doggett noticed one day, after Dyson had left, that the window curtains were not merely drawn, but pinned together. It is hard to imagine why they should do this unless they were having an affair.

Suddenly Edwin became ill. One day he felt so exhausted at work that he hurried home. The next morning, he and Adelaide and Dyson went to a dog show – dogs were one of Edwin's main

43

interests – but he felt so ill that they had to return home. Adelaide went out to fetch a doctor. She found a young man called Alfred Leach, whom she had never met before, but who immediately accompanied her to her home. Edwin was suffering from sickness, diarrhoea and bleeding of the bowels; he had also had toothache. When Dr Leach looked into his mouth, he observed a blue line round the gums – a symptom of mercury poisoning. When he asked Edwin if he had taken mercury, Edwin denied it, but admitted that he had swallowed a pill he had found in a drawer – he had no idea what it was for. Leach arrived at another explanation. Edwin's teeth were in an appalling condition, and his breath smelt foul. Apparently the dentist who made his false teeth had failed to draw the stumps; for some reason, he had sawn off the teeth at the gums. When these had rotted, the dentist merely made more false teeth, and the condition of his mouth made it impossible for Edwin to clean his remaining teeth. Leach's theory was that Edwin had, at some time, got a dose of mercury into his system, and that the sulphides produced by his rotting teeth had combined with it to form mercuric sulphide – hence the blue line.

A dentist who was called in verified that Edwin was suffering from mercury posioning, and extracted 15 roots and stumps. So throughout December the patient remained in bed. On Christmas Day 1885, he received an unpleasant shock when he went to the lavatory and passed a round worm. He was naturally something of a hypochondriac, and this gave him 'the horrors'. He swore that he could feel worms wriggling in his throat and became deeply depressed.

On the last day of December – and the last day of Edwin's life – he went to the dentist for yet another tooth extraction. Young Dr Leach, who had become a devotee of Adelaide, went with them. On the way Adelaide remarked that they had just been saying that they sometimes wished they were unmarried, so they could have the pleasure of getting married again. Later, when Edwin got home, his appetite had improved, and he ate a large meal of oysters, jugged hare and cake, with a helping of chutney. He told Mrs Doggett that he would have a haddock for his breakfast. It seemed he was at last on the road to recovery.

Just before 4 a.m. on New Year's Day, Adelaide knocked on the Doggett's bedroom door. 'Go and fetch Dr Leach. I think Mr Bartlett is dead.' She explained that she had fallen asleep, holding Edwin's foot – which apparently soothed him – as she sat beside his bed. She had awakened and felt that he was cold. She had tried to revive him with brandy but without success. Dr Leach observed a glass of brandy on the shelf, with a smell of chloroform.

The moment old Mr Bartlett heard of his son's death, he concluded he had been murdered. He sniffed his son's lips, then turned to Dr Leach and said, 'We must have a post mortem.'

The post mortem revealed a baffling and astonishing fact: that Edwin Bartlett had died of chloroform poisoning. This was so astonishing because chloroform is an unpleasant-tasting substance that would be almost impossible to swallow; moreover, it causes vomiting. If chloroform was poured down someone's throat when he was unconscious it would get into the lungs – which seemed to point to the completely mystifying conclusion that Edwin Bartlett had drunk the chloroform voluntarily. Yet his cheerfulness before he went to sleep, and the fact that he had even ordered his breakfast, made it unlikely that he intended suicide.

Where had the chloroform come from? This was soon revealed. The Reverend Dyson had bought it, at Adelaide's request. He had even gone to three separate chemists to get a fairly large quantity, claiming that he wanted to use it as cleaning fluid. Adelaide had told him she wanted it to make her husband sleep. And now, when he heard that chloroform had been found in Edwin's stomach, Dyson was panic stricken. He saw it as the end of his career. He rushed along to see Adelaide, and when Mrs Matthews came unexpectedly into the room, she heard Dyson saying, 'You did tell me Edwin was going to die soon.' When Adelaide denied it, he bowed his head on the piano and groaned, 'Oh, my God!' Later that day, he saw Adelaide alone, and she asked him to say nothing about the chloroform. Dyson refused and said he was going to make a clean breast of it.

And so he did. The result was that Adelaide Bartlett found herself on trial for murder. When, in the spring of 1886, it became known that he was to be tried for poisoning her husband, and that the Reverend George Dyson would probably stand in the dock beside her, public excitement was intense. It had all the signs of being a thoroughly scandalous murder case, complete with revelations of secret adultery and a plot by the lovers to kill the husband. When it was known that the great advocate Edward Clarke would defend Adelaide, people nodded significantly. Clarke was not one of those barristers who depended on verbal fireworks and bullying to win his cases; he was known for a certain quiet sincerity. Yet for all that, he had a formidable reputation. It was obvious that no suburban grocer's wife could afford his services, which could only mean that her mysterious father had intervened.

In the event, Adelaide finally stood alone in the dock; Dyson had managed to clear his own name by shamelessly doing his best to hand her over to the hangman. Edward Clarke had an apparently impossible task – to convince a Victorian jury that this pretty Frenchwoman, quite probably an adulteress, was innocent of her husband's murder. He had only one thing on his side: the total mystery of how even the most cunning murderess could have got the chloroform into Edwin Bartlett's stomach.

Clarke's defence was brilliant. His line of argument was that Edwin was a highly eccentric man who had almost thrown his wife into the arms of the clergyman, and who had told them that he expected them to marry when he was dead. He had insisted that his marriage to Adelaide should be purely platonic, and they had only had sexual intercourse once, as a result of which a baby had been born. But in the last days of his illness, Edwin had suddenly shown a desire for sexual intercourse. Adelaide felt this was wrong, since she now regarded herself as affianced to Dyson. So she asked Dyson to get her chloroform, so she might wave it in his face if he made sexual demands. However, she had been unable to go through with it. She had never been able to keep a secret from Edwin, and on that last evening of his life, had confessed her intention and showed him the bottle of chloroform. Edwin had been rather upset about it, and had placed the bottle on the mantelpiece. Somehow, while Adelaide dozed by her husband, holding his foot to comfort him, some of that chloroform had got into Edwin's stomach. (She admitted she had disposed of the rest by throwing it from the window of a train.) The main point of the defence was that Edwin was eccentric to the point of insanity, and that such an unpredictable man might easily have swallowed chloroform – perhaps simply to upset his wife and gain attention.

Amazingly enough, the jury believed this unlikely story of a wife too virtuous to permit her own husband sexual intercourse, even when it was revealed that Edwin had rubber contraceptives in his pocket and undoubtedly used them in making love to Adelaide. But the central point of the defence, of course, was that baffling mystery of the chloroform; if Adelaide poisoned her husband, how did she get it into his stomach? To that question the prosecution had no answer. After that, there could only be one verdict. 'Although we think there is the gravest suspicion attaching to the prisoner, we do not think there is sufficient evidence to show how or by whom the chloroform was administered.' So the verdict had to be not guilty.

The question of Adelaide's guilt or innocence has been argued by criminologists ever since. Some, like Nigel Morland, have no doubt that she was innocent, and that Edwin took the chloroform himself in a spirit of resentment or mischief. The majority is inclined to believe that Adelaide was poisoning Edwin from the beginning with some mercury compound, and only decided on the dangerous expedient of ether when he looked like recovering. Yseult Bridges believes that Adelaide somehow used hypnosis to induce Edwin to swallow the chloroform. None, as far as I know, has hit upon what seems to be the simplest and most obvious solution.

Let us try to reconstruct a hypothetical scenario. When Edwin Bartlett meets the beautiful Adelaide, he is too shy to hope that she will become his mistress as well as his wife, and so he assures her that their relationship will be a purely platonic one. But after two years of marriage, he is less humble and self-effacing, and insists on his marital rights. Adelaide becomes pregnant but, due to her husband's peculiar ideas about doctors, she loses the baby.

Edwin's curious attitude – his feeling that a doctor who

examined his wife would be 'interfering with her' – indicates a powerful physical jealousy. It is surely the attitude of a man who has the utmost difficulty in persuading his wife to let him make love to her, so the idea of another man examining her intimately arouses intense jealousy. Adelaide, for her part, finds sex with her husband rather unpleasant, perhaps because his rotten teeth cause permanent halitosis, and she does her best to persuade him to abide by their 'platonic' contract by petting him, fussing over him, showing him a great deal of affection – in fact, everything but allowing him into her bed. (At the trial, it was emphasized that they seemed to be an extremely happily married couple.) She makes use of the standard excuse, that she is afraid of becoming pregnant again, but Edwin counters that by buying contraceptives.

For Edwin, life becomes a permanent siege on his wife's virtue, with very infrequent successes. In his efforts to soften her, he deliberately introduces the Reverend George Dyson into their household and encourages a flirtation. In effect, he is asking the clergyman – whom he trusts implicitly – to 'warm her up'. While she is feeling kindly and grateful to her husband, she can hardly refuse him the occasional embrace.

Edwin falls ill. We do not know whether – as Yseult Bridges believes – she has been administering small doses of lead acetate or some mercuric poison. But it gives her a flash of hope; she sees the end of her martyrdom in sight. Then he begins to recover, and to indicate that his sexual appetites are returning to normal. Perhaps she finds the contraceptives in his pocket.

It is at this point that she asks Dyson to buy the chloroform. Presumably the idea of killing Edwin is at the back of her mind – it is hard to believe that she intends to soak a handkerchief in the drug and try and press it over his nose whenever he becomes amorous. But she also knows Edwin well enough to know that, as a hypochondriacal invalid, he quite enjoys taking 'medicines'. He is in a state of neurotic depression about his 'worms'. Dr Leach has given him all kinds of medicines for them, without effect; Edwin is convinced he is still swarming with worms. All Adelaide needs to do is to produce the chloroform and tell Edwin that Dr Leach has recommended this to get rid of worms.

Perhaps only the lightest of hints is needed. Perhaps she offers him a little chloroform mixed with brandy, but he finds it unpleasant. Then, as she sits beside him, he decides that he will win her approval by taking his medicine, and he cautiously reaches out for the bottle . . .

Sir James Paget, a well-known doctor, made the famous comment, 'Now the case is over, she should tell us in the interests of science how she did it.' The answer is surely that she did not do it; Edwin did. Whether it was at Adelaide's suggestion we shall never know.

LIZZIE BORDEN

The crime of Lizzie Borden has entered the realm of folklore; there is even a ballet about it called 'The Fall River Legend'. But was it Lizzie's crime? And if so, what was her motive in committing it? This is the problem that has intrigued students of crime for almost a century.

Fall River is a small mill town in Massachusetts, and in 1892, one of its most respected residents was Andrew Jackson Borden, a man who made a fortune in property and banking. He lived at 92 Second Street with his second wife Abby and his two daughters, Lizzie and Emma. Oddly enough, the house in which this wealthy family lived was thoroughly uncomfortable; the lavatory was in the basement and the only running water in a sink room off the kitchen. But Andrew Borden was of Puritan stock, and regarded these discomforts as minor inconveniences.

The day dawned hot and bright on 4 August 1892; by 7 in the morning the temperature was already in the eighties. Andrew and Abby Borden and John Vinnicum Morse, Andrew's brother-in-law by his first marriage, ate a breakfast of mutton and mutton soup. This may sound surprising in such hot weather but Mrs Borden had cooked a large joint of mutton on the previous Sunday, and now they were eating mutton for every meal – Andrew Borden was a notoriously tight man. Fall River had been struck by a heat wave that week and the repeated appearance of the mutton may explain why the family was suffering from stomach pains and vomiting; Mrs Borden even suspected that someone was poisoning them. The Irish maid Bridget Sullivan, who had been ordered to clean all the windows, had to break off to be sick in the garden.

Lizzie rose rather late. Her sister Emma – nine years her senior – was away staying with friends. Lizzie was feeling tired and depressed. She was plain, overweight and 32 years old, and no man ever looked at her twice. She adored her father – although she disliked his rudeness and meanness – and detested her stepmother, who was even more overweight and unattractive than Lizzie herself. To add to her problems, it was the wrong

50

time of the month, so she felt physically miserable. Listlessly, she began to do some ironing. Her stepmother was upstairs, cleaning the guest room. Poor Bridget was still cleaning the windows and struggling with nausea.

At 10.45 a.m. Andrew Borden came back from his office and was surprised to find the screen door latched and the front door locked. Bridget let him in and discovered that the patent lock had been released, and that both bolts had been drawn. She exclaimed out loud, and at that moment heard Lizzie laugh. Then Lizzie came forward and asked her father how he felt now – he had been as ill as the rest of them. He was still feeling weak. Lizzie told him that her stepmother had gone out to visit someone who was sick -- a note had been delivered to the house. Andrew Borden then went into the sitting-room, which was a little cooler than the rest of the house, and lay down on the horsehair sofa. Bridget decided to sneak upstairs and have a rest; as she lay on her bed, she heard the town hall clock chime 11.

Ten minutes later, Lizzie shouted upstairs, 'Come down quick. Father's dead. Somebody came in and killed him.'

Andrew Borden was lying on the sofa, his face a mass of blood. His skull had been cleft open, and an eye hung out on its socket. Bridget was hastily dispatched for the doctor, who lived across the road. He arrived together with several neighbours. When Dr Bowen had cleaned the blood from Andrew Borden's face, and ascertained that he had been killed by blows from a hatchet, he asked Bridget to find a sheet to cover the body. Bridget said she was afraid to go upstairs alone – after all, the burglar might still be in the house, perhaps hiding under a bed. A neighbour named Mrs Churchill accompanied her upstairs. And when she returned, she asked Lizzie what had become of Mrs Borden. Lizzie's reply was, 'I don't know but she is killed too, for I thought I heard her come in.' Again Bridget and Mrs Churchill went upstairs. They found Abby Borden lying, face downward, in the guest room. Her skull had been even more savagely battered than that of Andrew Borden.

For about 24 hours the inhabitants of Fall River were in a state of nervous tension; there was a maniac at large who crept into houses and killed with a chopper. News of the murders flew by means of Mr Edison's telegraph all over America. Then suspicion settled on a member of the family: Uncle John Vinnicum Morse, Andrew Borden's brother-in-law, who had stayed in the house the previous night. Morse was running one of Borden's farms and was in effect his business manager. Rumour had it that his arrest was expected hourly. When he walked out of the Borden home, a menacing crowd, estimated at 2,000, followed him along the street. But a policeman, Special Officer Harrington, had already fixed on Lizzie as his chief suspect. It was not a matter of evidence: merely that her demeanour seemed too calm for one who had just suffered a bereavement.

Bridget, by comparison, was in a state of terrified hysteria. And it was Harrington who made another important discovery: on the day before the murders, a woman answering Lizzie's description had tried to buy prussic acid in a local pharmacy – she said she needed it to kill moths in a fur coat. The pharmacist declined to sell her the poison, but it later emerged that the woman had tried two other pharmacists, with the same result. Later that day, it also emerged, Lizzie had visited a friend named Miss Russell, and had mentioned her suspicion that their food had been poisoned. She had also talked about a mysterious burglary that had occurred in the previous June; over $100 had been taken from Mr Borden's desk. Lizzie thought the thief had probably entered through the cellar door. (Oddly enough, Andrew Borden had told the police to drop their investigation because the 'real' culprit would probably never be found.) And finally, before leaving Miss Russell, Lizzie had made a curious prediction: 'I'm afraid somebody will do something . . .'

Now suspicion began to focus on Lizzie. Another uncle, Hiram Harrington, a blacksmith, told the press that there had been constant disputes in the house about money – the girls were jealous of the money that Mr Borden made over to his wife, and insisted on being treated identically. Lizzie often quarrelled with her father and would refuse to speak to him for days. His refusal to allow her to spend money on entertaining her church friends angered her, and she was resentful of his meanness.

Harrington added significantly that the motive for the crime was unquestionably money and pointed out that Andrew Borden would probably leave half a million . . .

One week after the murders, as everyone now expected, Lizzie was arrested. The following morning she was arraigned and a date was set for the preliminary hearing. The town split into two factions: those who were convinced of her guilt, and those who were sure she was a persecuted innocent. After all, there was no real evidence against Lizzie. The murder weapon had not been found – although the police had located in the cellar the head of a hatchet covered in ashes, with a short piece of broken handle attached. If Lizzie had killed her parents – her stepmother with 17 blows and her father with nine – surely she would have been covered with blood? Yet no bloodstained dress had been found. It is true that Lizzie had burned one of her dresses the Sunday after the murder, saying that it seemed to have some blood spots on it, but that itself was unsuspicious. If she had been wearing this dress to kill her family, it would have been soaked in blood. Besides, she would have had two blood-stained dresses, for Mrs Borden had been killed at least an hour before her husband. In short, there was no real evidence against Lizzie, who had been, as she claimed, out in the barn when the murders had taken place.

The anti-Lizzie faction pointed out that only Lizzie could have killed the Bordens. Nothing was less likely than that some homicidal maniac had sneaked into the house around 9.30 a.m. and killed Mrs Borden, then waited, concealed, for an hour or so until he could creep down and kill Andrew Borden as he lay asleep. And why had she been trying to buy poison on the day before the murders, if not to kill her stepmother?

The trial opened on 5 June 1892. The prosecution pointed out that Lizzie had tried to buy poison, and suggested that she had tried to lure Bridget out of the house by mentioning a sale of cheap cotton goods. She claimed that Mrs Borden had left the house after she received a note saying that someone was sick; but no such note had been found. She claimed that she had been in the barn at the time, but there were no footprints in the dust.

When Uncle John Morse was called to the stand, he proved to

Lizzie Borden with her sister and friends in court

have a cast-iron alibi – he had been to visit a nephew and niece in the town, and had not arrived back until 20 minutes after the bodies were discovered. There was not the remotest possibility that Uncle John was the murderer.

When finally asked if she had anything to say to the jury in her own defence, Lizzie replied, 'I am innocent. I leave it for my counsel to speak for me.' The jury believed her; after retiring for an hour, the foreman announced the verdict of not guilty. There were wild cheers and Lizzie found herself something of a popular heroine.

There were those who expected her to move to some other place; but she did nothing so obvious. She and her sister stayed in Fall River – they only moved to a larger house. They could afford to: Andrew Borden had left them $175,000 each. Five years later, Lizzie once more appeared on the front pages of the newspapers. Two paintings that had been stolen from a big store had been traced back to her, and a warrant had been issued for her arrest. But nothing more was heard of this matter as it was settled out of court. In later life, she became an ardent theatregoer, and caused some scandal by throwing a lavish party for an actress, Nance O'Neil. This seems to have caused a separation between Lizzie and her sister Emma. When Lizzie died in 1927, at the age of 67, she left an estate of $265,000, much of it to the animal rescue league.

When the American crime expert and bibliophile Edmund

Pearson came to edit *The Trial of Lizzie Borden* in 1937 he left no doubt that he regarded Lizzie as guilty; he said the same thing in two essays on the case. He was convinced that the murders had been planned several days before. But if that was so, why had Lizzie tried to buy poison on the day before she killed her parents with a hatchet?

In 1961, a crime writer named Edward Radin challenged Pearson's verdict. In *Lizzie Borden, The Untold Story,* Radin admitted that he had always considered Lizzie guilty – on the strength of Pearson's books – until he came upon one small anomaly. Pearson had always emphasized that Lizzie had given the police a silk dress to examine, claiming it was the dress she had been wearing on the morning of the murders. Who, asked Pearson, would wear a silk dress to do the housework? Radin discovered that the dress was made of a material known as bengaline silk – a cotton or wool fabric with a few threads of silk interwoven. Disturbed by this and some other minor errors, Radin went to Fall River to look at the minutes of the trial. They revealed that Pearson had been highly selective. 'To put it bluntly, Pearson presented such a biased version of the case that it might be considered a literary hoax.' Pearson had deliberately omitted evidence that revealed that, far from being heartlessly calm, Lizzie had been in tears just after the bodies had been discovered, while another witness said she was so pale she thought she was going to faint. Radin found evidence that suggested Lizzie had indeed been up in the barn, as she claimed. And he listed many other points on which he felt that Pearson had shown deliberate bias. He shows beyond all doubt that Pearson was inclined to omit evidence that pointed to Lizzie's innocence.

All this, says Radin, leaves only three possible suspects: Uncle John Morse, Emma Borden and Bridget Sullivan. He soon eliminates the first two. That, inevitably, leaves Bridget. He points out that there is a basic discrepancy between Bridget's evidence and Lizzie's. Lizzie said Bridget began washing the windows at 9 o'clock. Bridget said it was 9.30 a.m. That half-hour would have sufficed for Bridget to kill Abby Borden. But why should Bridget have killed Mrs Borden? Perhaps because she was angry at having been ordered to wash the windows when she was feeling sick. Radin speculates that she may have asked Mrs Borden if she could leave the windows until later, and Mrs Borden refused. So she went to get an axe, sneaked up behind her employer, and battered her to death with 17 blows. Why then should she kill Andrew Borden? Perhaps because he had overheard Mrs Borden's refusal, and therefore knew Bridget had a motive.

Three years after Radin's book appeared, a selection of Pearson's crime essays was published under the title *Masterpieces of Murder*, and its editor, Gerald Gross, takes the opportunity to defend Pearson. He points out that if Pearson omitted evidence of Lizzie's innocence, Radin omits evidence of her guilt – he plays down Lizzie's hatred of her stepmother. Yet Gross admits that Radin has made some telling points. He ends up believing that Bridget was Lizzie's accomplice in the murder. There is a legend – repeated by some writers on that case – that Bridget went back to Ireland with a large bank balance. Gross believes Lizzie paid Bridget to help her with the murders. His final comment is that, until someone finds a signed confession, we shall never be sure who killed the Bordens.

In fact, such a signed confession had been published, in a book called *Mutiny and Murder* by Edgar Snow (1959). Snow tells how he received a letter from an elderly gentleman named Thomas Owens, who claimed that he had Lizzie's confession. He harked back to the story that a warrant had been issued for Lizzie's arrest for the theft of two pictures; the store in question was called Tilden-Thurber, and it was in Providence, Rhode Island. After Lizzie visited the shop, the assistant found that two expensive portraits on porcelain were missing. Some time later, another lady took one of the portraits into the shop asking if a crack could be repaired; asked where she obtained it, she said from Lizzie Borden. According to Owens, the manager of the store had then offered Lizzie a deal: confess to the murders, or be prosecuted. Lizzie refused, and the story appeared in a Providence newspaper. This led Lizzie to change her mind, and she typed the confession which read: 'Unfair means force my signature here admitting the act on August 4, 1892, as mine alone, Lisbeth A. Borden.' Owens, who was a photographer, had been asked to make a photograph of the confession, and had made an extra one for himself. He tried to sell it to Snow for $100; Snow persuaded him to take $50.

But Radin decided to look into this piece of evidence. He soon established that the signature was a forgery, lifted straight from Lizzie's will. So the 'confession' story was a hoax, although the story about the theft of the paintings is true enough, and, indeed, indicates a peculiar and dishonest side to Lizzie's character.

In 1967, there appeared yet another book on the Borden murder but this time by someone who had known Lizzie when they had lived on the same block in Fall River. *A Private Disgrace, Lizzie Borden by Daylight* finally supplies some of the missing pieces that enable us to understand the Borden murder case. Its author, Victoria Lincoln, knew one family secret: that Lizzie often suffered from fits of dizziness. She argues carefully, from medical evidence, that Lizzie suffered from psychomotor epilepsy of the brain, which afflicted her about four times a year, usually during menstrual periods.

The book is not an attempt to prove that Lizzie committed the murders in some kind of trance. Miss Lincoln is convinced that Lizzie did intend to murder her stepmother – but by poison. Furthermore, Victoria Lincoln was able to unearth the motive. The Borden sisters and their stepmother had been involved in a quarrel about a house that Andrew Borden intended to give to his wife. A similar quarrel five years before, again about a house, had led to immense bitterness, and Lizzie had then ceased to call Abby 'mother', and called her 'Mrs Borden'. On the morning of the murder, the transfer was due to be signed. That was why Andrew Borden came back home, bringing the transfer deed with him. The deed vanished, but a half-burned roll of paper was found in the stove by a policeman. Lizzie knew about the transfer – that may have been why she had forced her way into her father's desk in June, taking money to pretend it was a burglary. Having failed to buy poison, she took the hatchet from the cellar and killed Abby Borden. Miss Lincoln believes she then killed her father to spare him the horror of realizing she was a killer, as he inevitably would have guessed. Yet, knowing of Lizzie's increasing resentment about her father's meanness and rudeness, it seems more likely that killing him was the only logical way of obtaining some kind of freedom for herself and her sister – and, no doubt, a diet of something less uninspiring than boiled mutton.

In *Blood in the Parlour*, Dorothy Dunbar provides an amusing footnote to the case. Before Lizzie's arrest, children in the streets of Fall River were chanting:

Mr Borden he is dead
Lizzie hit him on the head!

Obviously this was the original crude form of the far more celebrated quatrain:

Lizzie Borden took an axe
And gave her mother forty whacks.
And when she saw what she had done,
She gave her father forty-one.

TONY MANCINI

Brighton has the unusual distinction of having been associated with two trunk murders. And, as if to stretch the coincidence to its limit, both occurred at the same time and the bodies were discovered within 200 yards of one another. One murder was easily solved, although the full story did not emerge for another four decades; the other remains unsolved to this day.

Mancini was a small-time crook, but an exceptionally unpleasant one. His real name was Cecil Lois England, and while still a teenager he deserted from the RAF. Almost immediately, he became a member of London's underworld, working for a gangster named 'Harry Boy' Sabini as a strong-arm man. He admitted later that he began to get 'kicks' out of violence: 'It was like a drug addiction.' He was once ordered to mark a man for life as a punishment for 'informing'; he walked into the pub where the man was leaning on the bar, pulled an axe from under his coat, and chopped off his left hand; leaving the axe embedded in the bar, he walked out of the pub. Everyone knew he was responsible, but his associates had arranged for him to have a cast-iron alibi, and witnesses were afraid to talk. On another occasion, he turned the handle of a meat grinder while a gangster had his hand forced into it – this was a punishment for dipping his hand into the till.

On his 'collecting rounds', Mancini met a pretty, slim ex-showgirl, a blue-eyed blonde named Violet Saunders, who preferred to be known as Violette Kaye. She was 42 years old, 17 years Mancini's senior. Her work as a dancer became more difficult to obtain so she had turned to prostitution. Mancini became her pimp. In September 1933, just after Mancini had emerged from a six-month spell in jail for theft, they decided to move down to Brighton, 'the place where it was all happening in those days'. Many of Violette's wealthier clients still called to see her, travelling from London in their Rolls-Royces. It may have been that her landlords objected when they discovered the source of her income; perhaps, too, her increasing alcoholism and addiction to morphine made her an impossible tenant; at all events, the couple moved, on average, once a fortnight. Their thirteenth home, at 44 Park Crescent, proved to be unlucky for both of them.

It was an unfurnished basement flat. They picked up bits and pieces of furniture in second-hand shops and markets. Mancini did the cooking and housework, and their day was punctuated by the arrival of clientele who tramped down the narrow, worn steps, and left after half an hour or so. Violette seems to have been genuinely dependent on Mancini; when he considered taking a job, she dissuaded him on the grounds that he would be away from her all day. But on 5 May 1934 he took a job as a cook, waiter and general handyman at the Skylark Café, facing the sea.

Violette seems to have missed him, or perhaps she was jealous of the waitresses and female customers. She had met Mancini when he was working in a restaurant near Leicester Square. On Thursday 10 May she arrived unexpectedly at mid-afternoon, obviously a little the worse for drink. Mancini cooked her a meal then sat and talked to her while she ate – it was a slack period. Then he went away to get the staff their tea. Among these was a young waitress named Florence Attrell, who had started to work at the same time as Mancini. When Mancini handed the girl her tea with the comment, 'Here you are, mate', it seems to have aroused Violette Kaye's worst suspicions. She said in a loud voice, 'I won't have it. Don't call her mate.' The café fell silent and Mancini told her to pull herself together. What looked like turning into an ugly scene was terminated when she walked out of the café. She sat outside for a while, then went away. Mancini later claimed he got the sack as a result of the quarrel. His memory on this point seems to have been defective, for he arrived for work as usual the following morning, and told his fellow workers that Violette had left him and gone away to Paris. Violette's sister-in-law, who was due to come to Brighton for a holiday the following Monday, received a telgram: 'Good job sail Sunday will write – Vi.'

In fact, by that time, Violette Kaye's body was lying in a cupboard in the basement flat, wrapped in bedclothes. The cause of her death was a number of blows to the head.

That weekend, Mancini took Florence Attrell dancing twice; he also took her back to the flat and gave her some of Violette's clothes, explaining that he had promised to send them on but didn't think he would bother. In fact, he had already taken lodgings elsewhere, in Kemp Street, a mere 200 yards from Brighton station. He told his former landlord, Mr Snuggs, that Vi had walked out on him and that he could not afford to keep the flat on. Mr Snuggs was sympathetic. As they were talking, a large strapped trunk was waiting in the middle of the room; Mancini had bought it in the market for 7s. 6d., and the dealer had delivered it. When Mancini departed, with the trunk on a handcart, he left behind the tray out of the trunk, for which he had no use. His landlord noticed a stain in the bottom of the cupboard, although it was clear that someone had tried to wash it away. Mancini moved into 52 Kemp Street with the corpse of Violette Kaye – and for two months, as the smell increased (his friends asked him, 'Do you keep rabbits?'), he seems to have wondered what to do with it.

Another killer had shown rather more imagination. On 6 June, Derby Day, a trunk was deposited in the left-luggage at Brighton station; 11 days later, an attendant noticed an unpleasant smell coming from it. The police were asked to force the locks and inside they found the torso of a woman, wrapped in brown paper, on which the letters 'ford' were written – obviously half a word. The head and limbs were missing. The legs were found in a suitcase at the left-luggage office in Kings Cross Station, London, the following day. The killer was obviously a man capable of foresight and planning; he had deposited the trunk at Brighton during the rush hour on Derby Day, when it was unlikely that he would be noticed. In spite of a massive police investigation that extended to four countries, the body was never even identified.

But the Brighton trunk caused Mancini some inconvenience, for the police began door-to-door investigations in the area of the station. They also heard about the disappearance of Violette Kaye, and asked Mancini to come to the station to make a statement. He was allowed to leave afterwards. On Sunday, 15 July he left Brighton for London by an early train, and a few hours later, the police called at Kemp Street, entered the basement flat, and forced open the trunk, whose smell now left little doubt what it contained.

It took the police 48 hours to catch up with Mancini. He had spent the two days eating in cheap East End cafés and sleeping in the Salvation Army hostel. He had fled on Sunday; on Monday morning the newspapers were headlining the discovery of the second body in a trunk in Brighton. At one point Mancini had picked up a 17-year-old waif, taken her for a walk and asked her to provide him with an alibi for the murder. She had agreed – because he looked so formidable a character with his scarred face. Then Mancini's fear got the better of him, and he decided to leave London. The police picked him up as he trudged towards Maidstone in Kent. When they told him he fitted the description of a man who was wanted for the murder of Violette Kaye, Mancini wearily agreed, 'I'm the man. But I didn't murder her . . .'

The case caused a sensation. The notion of keeping a woman's body in a trunk for two months touched a strain of morbidity in the national character, and Mancini – one of the most incompetent crooks of all time – was regarded as a monster. A brutal-looking, scar-faced photograph did nothing to improve his image. Fashionably dressed girls booed him and threw things as he was taken to court in Lewes.

Mancini, however, had had one supreme stroke of luck. The task of defending him had been undertaken by one of the most brilliant advocates of the period, Norman Birkett. Birkett was not, like so many advocates, an actor *manqué*; he seldom descended to court-room fireworks or the bullying of witnesses. He was quiet, courteous and kindly – and as a consequence, he impressed juries as a man of complete integrity.

Birkett's task was not easy. Yet in this case, there was one basic fact in favour of the accused: no one could prove that it was his hand that had killed Violette Kaye. She was a prostitute and the killer could have been one of her customers. This was Mancini's story – that he had returned to the flat after his day's work in the Skylark to find her already lying dead. This was a plausible defence. The afternoon they had quarrelled, a man

62

named Kerslake had called at their flat to tell Violette that one of her regular customers had just been certified insane. Violette had come to the door; she looked upset and shaken, and seemed to be drunk. Kerslake could hear voices in the back room. So Violette had had visitors after her quarrel with Mancini; one of these could have been her killer. Mancini's story was that he had panicked; a man with his record could not expect a fair trial.

Birkett built up his case carefully, like a great novelist setting a scene. Each witness was questioned until he had established one single point in Mancini's favour. A police inspector was made to admit that the stairs down to the basement were narrow and worn; and later, pathologist Sir Bernard Spilsbury was made to concede that the injury to the dead woman's forehead could have been caused by a fall down these steps. Another pathologist, Dr Roche Lynch, was made to admit that he was not sure whether Violette Kaye had died from morphine. Birkett even took the amazing step of insisting that Mancini's previous convictions should be read in court – two for stealing and one for loitering with intent. Birkett wanted to establish that Mancini had never been convicted for violence. If the jury had known about the episode with the hatchet or meat grinder, they might have been less impressed. The main point of the brilliant defence speech was to insist that the prosecution had not proved that Mancini had killed Violette Kaye.

Mancini was called, and he impressed the jury favourably; he seemed chastened and unsure of himself. He told Birkett that he loved Violette, and perjured himself to the extent of declaring that they had never quarrelled. At one point, he even shed a few tears. Asked why he had not fetched the police when he found Violette's body he asked incredulously, 'With my record?'. It sounded spontaneous and convincing. And in his final speech, Birkett shrewdly pointed out that the 'voices' Kerslake had heard in Violette Kaye's flat on the day of her murder had never come forward. He concluded, 'People are not tried by news-papers, not tried by rumour, not tried by statements born of a love of notoriety, but tried by British juries, called to do justice and decide upon the evidence.'

On 14 December 1934, after one of the most brilliant defences ever heard in a British court of law, the jury brought in a verdict of not guilty, and Mancini walked out of court a free man.

For a year after his trial, Tony Mancini worked in a travelling fair. He was billed as 'The Infamous Brighton Trunk Murder Man', and his stunt involved cutting off the head of a pretty girl with a trick guillotine. In later years there were two broken marriages. In 1976, he suddenly decided to tell the truth about the death of Violette Kaye. The *News of the World* for 28 November appeared with a headline I'VE GOT AWAY WITH MURDER. The story, as reported by Alan Hart, begins:

A man acquitted of killing his mistress, after one of the most famous murder trials in British history, has now confessed to me that he was guilty. Ex-gangster Tony Mancini has lived 42 years with the secret that he was responsible for what became known as the Brighton Trunk Murder.

Mancini told Hart:

When I gave evidence I had carefully rehearsed my lines like an actor. I had practised how I should hold my hands and when I should let tears run down my cheeks. It might sound cold and calculating now, but you have to remember that my life was at stake. I was charged with murder, and in those days the penalty was death.

There are a few respects in which Mancini's story does not tally with the version given at the trial. He says that when Violette found out he had taken a job at the Skylark, 'she started a blazing row'. In fact, he had been there for five days, with Violette calling in daily, before the row. Mancini claims that he was sacked, and that he called a taxi and took Violette home. If that is true, then he himself may have one of the two voices heard by Kerslake – the other probably being a client.

Mancini's story was that Violette was cold and asked him to make a fire. As he was bending over, blowing on the burning paper, he felt a crack on his head; Violette had hit him with a hammer. He took it away from her and started to walk towards the cellar. When she shouted, 'Give me that hammer', he yelled,

'I'll give you the hammer all right', and threw it at her with all his strength. It caught her on the left temple, 'and she spun around twice like something on a fairground'. She fell on to the brass fender surrounding the fire. Mancini claims he shouted, 'You stupid bitch, look what you've made me do,' and began banging her head up and down, gripping her shoulders. He thought he was banging it on the floor; in fact, he was banging it on the fender. 'Suddenly blood started to trickle from her mouth and I froze. I realized what I'd done. I honestly didn't mean to kill her – I had just lost control of myself in the heat of the moment.'

In an interview he gave to the journalist Stephen Knight (shortly before the latter's death), Mancini gives a considerably different account of the quarrel and what led up to it. He says he had been working in the Skylark Café 'about three or four months' and Violette had no idea of where to find him. One day she came into the café very drunk and under the influence of drugs, and caused a scene. He picked her up by the shoulders and carried her outside, and she finally went home. When he got home at about 7 o'clock that evening, there was a violent quarrel and 'she came at me with her hands and scratched my face'. Then she picked up the hammer and tried to hit him with it. 'So I hit her.' Violette fell against the brass fender, and when he tried to pick her up, she spat in his face. Mancini insisted, 'I'd never hit her before . . . I don't hit women.' But on this occasion, 'I just got hold of her, of her shoulders, and was banging her head on the floor like that. I said, "Don't you spit at me!" And I don't know how long I was like that. And when I came to out of my rage, she was lying like that . . . quite still you see.'

'So what killed her was not the accidental fall . . . it was you banging her head on the fender?', asked Knight.

'Yes . . . I don't remember really, but that's what I must have done . . .'

A jury who heard that story in court would probably have concluded that this was Mancini's attempt to exculpate himself – the equivalent of the schoolboy's excuse: 'It came apart in my hands.' A modern jury would undoubtedly have brought in a verdict of manslaughter. If the jury Mancini faced at Lewes had known the full truth, there seems little doubt that he would have gone to the gallows.

I can add an amusing footnote to this story. In my book, *Order of Assassins*, I mentioned Mancini's name in a list of twentieth-century killers. It was a careless slip, of the sort easily made – I was confusing Mancini with John Robinson, a trunk murderer who was found guilty. A friend who has an encyclopedic knowledge of crime wrote to me subsequently reminding me that Mancini had been acquitted . . . For the next six months or so, I kept my fingers tightly crossed that no one pointed out my slip to Mancini. Then, in 1976, the *News of the World* came out with its headline: I'VE GOT AWAY WITH MURDER. I heaved a sigh of relief.

A year later, I received a letter from a lawyer. It pointed out that I had included his client, Mr Mancini, in a list of murderers, and that Mr Mancini had been acquitted. Would I, the letter inquired blandly, prefer to settle the libel out of court?

I searched my press-cutting file frantically for the *News of the World* story, and was unable to find it. Then I rang my encyclopedic friend. By the next morning's post, a photocopy of the story arrived. I slipped it into a large envelope, and posted it off to the lawyer, without bothering to enclose a covering letter. That was the last I heard of it.

THE AXEMAN OF NEW ORLEANS

It was 5 o'clock in the morning of 24 May 1918 when Jake Maggio, an Italian cobbler, was awakened by a groaning sound. It seemed to be coming from the other side of the thin partition wall that separated Jake's bedroom from that of his brother Joe. When the groan was repeated, Jake got out of bed, and shook his brother Andrew, who slept in the same room. Andrew was snoring and smelt of alcohol, but Jake finally succeeded in making him open his eyes. As he did so, the groan was repeated, followed by a choking noise. Jake told Andrew, 'There's something wrong in there. Come on with me.'

The first thing they saw as they entered the bedroom was Joe's wife; she was lying on the floor in a pool of blood with her head almost severed from her body. Joe Maggio was lying half in and half out of the bed. As they stood there, too shocked to move, he gave another groan. Then his eyes opened and he saw his brothers. He made a convulsive effort to move, and fell on to the floor. In that position, they could see that his throat had also been cut, and that his face was a mass of blood. They lifted him back on to the bed, then rushed out to call the police.

By the time the police arrived, the brothers had discovered how the intruder had entered the house. A panel in the back door had been neatly chiselled out. And on the steps leading down into the backyard lay a bloodstained axe and a cut-throat razor.

The detective looked at the razor and asked, 'Is this yours?' Andrew was a barber. He shook his head and said 'I don't know.'

'Where were you last night?' asked the detective. A neighbour who had followed the police into the house said, 'I can tell you that. He came home drunk around 3 o'clock this morning.'

The detective turned to Andrew saying, 'I'm placing you under arrest.'

Jake protested. 'Andrew didn't do it. He sleeps in the same room I do.'

The detective said, 'All right, you're under arrest too.'

The news was on the streets shortly after midday. The New Orleans newspaper, *The Times-Picayune*, prided itself on being the first with the story. It had a photograph of the bedroom of the murdered couple, and even a photograph of their wedding 15 years before. The account mentioned that a safe in the bedroom had been found open and empty. Yet $100 had been found below Joe Maggio's pillow and Mrs Maggio's jewellery, including diamond rings, lay untouched on the dressing table. The police were inclined to believe that robbery was not the motive – the safe had been left open only to mislead them. That was obviously why they suspected Jake and his brother Andrew, who had just been drafted into the army. But they were soon forced to release both for lack of evidence.

Detective Theodore Obitz, in charge of the case, was pondering another curious clue. Two streets away from the Maggio's grocery store, someone had chalked on the pavement the words: 'Mrs Maggio is going to sit up tonight, just like Mrs Toney.' Who was Mrs Toney? Then someone recollected that seven years earlier, in 1911, there had been three axe murders of Italian grocers: a Mr Cruti, a Mr Rosetti, and a certain Tony Schiambra and his wife. Could she be the 'Mrs Toney' referred to? The murders had been attributed to the 'Black Hand', a criminal secret society (and predecessor of the Mafia) that demanded 'protection' money from many successful Italian businessmen. New Orleans, city of the Mississippi gamblers, was one of the most crime-ridden spots in the United States.

Before Detective Obitz had a chance to investigate the possible connection of the earlier murders with the latest double killing, he was shot through the heart by a Negro he had arrested for burglary.

The sinister trademark of the murderer continued to worry the Italian community of New Orleans – the panel chiseled out of the back door. Most of those wooden frame houses of New Orleans had open backyards, so anyone could wander in and out. Most people kept chickens and had an axe in the woodshed. The police had identified the axe that struck the Maggios as their own. The Italians of New Orleans felt themselves frighteningly vulnerable.

On 28 June, five weeks after the murders, a baker named John Zanca called to deliver bread at the grocery store of Louis Besumer. As he was about to knock on the back door he froze in horror; one of its panels had been chiseled out. Nervously, he knocked on the door, and sighed with relief as he heard someone unlocking it. Then he almost screamed as the door was opened by a man with blood streaming down his face. Louis Besumer was groaning, 'My God, my God!' Mr Zanca went into the house, and saw that a woman was lying on the bed, her head bleeding from a gaping wound. Zanca called the hospital, then the police.

In this case, both the victims were still alive. *The Times-Picayune* was able to reveal that the woman, known as Mrs Besumer, was not Besumer's wife. Her real name was Harriet Lowe, and she was many years Besumer's junior, being still in her twenties. Besumer himself was apparently regarded by neighbours as a suspicious character. He declared that he was a Pole, but was generally regarded as a German. During World War I all Germans were suspected of being spies. Besumer's story was that he had been knocked unconscious while asleep, and had awakened to find Harriet Lowe outside the bedroom door, bleeding badly. He had carried her back to bed, then had heard Zanca knocking on the door.

Rumours immediately began to spread that Besumer had attacked his 'wife' because she had found out too much about his espionage activities, then had given himself a blow on the head to make it look like an axeman attack. This theory was confirmed when Harriet Lowe regained consciousness, and was asked whether Besumer was a spy. Her reply was that she had long suspected it. He was immediately arrested. But when she was questioned again, she withdrew her accusation, saying it was ridiculous. She had a curious story to tell. She had been walking into the kitchen when she was struck on the head. When she opened her eyes again, she saw a white man standing over her, making threatening motions with a hatchet but not striking her. Then she lost consciousness again.

Mrs Lowe died after an operation, but just before her death she seemed to mumble that Besumer had struck her with an axe.

Besumer was charged with murder.

That same night, however, the 'mad axeman' attacked again. Edward Schneider, a young married man, returned home shortly after midnight on 5 August 1918 to find his heavily pregnant wife lying in bed and covered with blood. She was rushed to hospital, where she was able to describe waking up and seeing a man holding an axe above her. One week later, she gave birth to a baby girl. No axe was found on the premises, and no panel had been chiseled out of the back door, and it was presumed that the attacker had entered by an open window.

Five days later, there was another attack. This time the victim was a barber, Joseph Romano. His nieces, Pauline, 18, and her sister Mary, 13, woke up soon after 3 o'clock in the morning; noises were coming from the next room where their uncle slept. Pauline had been nervous for weeks about the 'axeman', and now she crept fearfully to her uncle's room, turning on her own light as she opened the connecting door. What she saw made her scream. A man she later described as 'dark, tall, heavy-set, wearing a black slouch hat' was standing by her uncle's bed, holding an axe. Mary also screamed, at which the man 'vanished as if he had wings'. Their uncle had staggered into the parlour; when they propped him in a chair they could see that he had two large cuts on his head. He groaned, 'Call the Charity Hospital,' then fainted. Two days later, he died in hospital. A panel of a rear door had been chiseled out and the bloody axe was found outside in the yard. Nothing had been stolen, although Romano's room had been ransacked.

Now, at last, there could be no doubt that there was an axeman in New Orleans. The panic was not unlike that which had swept London 30 years before, when Jack the Ripper had killed 'fallen women' in Whitechapel. One grocer reported finding an axe and a chisel outside his back door in the morning; another found that a panel had been chiseled out of his door when he was absent for the day. Yet another grocer, who lived close to Romano, told of finding a panel chiseled out of his door in the previous June, and an axe lying nearby. No one felt safe in their beds. When someone reported seeing a man with an axe jumping over a fence one evening, the neighbourhood was suddenly alive with angry people armed with home-made weapons. A shot was fired, and a young man claimed he had fired his shotgun at the axeman. Police arrived and advised everyone to go to bed.

On 30 August a man named Nick Asunto heard a noise in his house and went to the head of the stairs; near the front door he saw a heavily built man holding an axe. When Asunto yelled, the man fled by the front door. Such reports became a regular item in the newspapers. As people began taking extra precautions, the number of sightings of the axeman seemed to diminish. Perhaps he had decided it was too dangerous to show himself.

On 11 November 1918 World War I ended; there had been no attacks for three months. When Christmas and the New Year passed without incident, people began to hope they had heard the last of the axeman. But on 10 March 1919 Iorlando Jordano, a grocer who lived in Gretna, just across the river from New Orleans, heard screams from a house on the other side of the street, where another grocer called Cortimiglia had his business. He went into the house and found Mrs Cortimiglia sitting on the floor, blood gushing from her head, and a dead baby in her arms. Her husband Charles lay nearby. The Cortimiglias were rushed to the Charity Hospital. When the police arrived they found the now-familiar axeman signatures: the panel chiseled out of the back door and the abandoned axe. Nothing had been stolen.

Rosie Cortimiglia told of waking up to see her husband being attacked by a white man wielding an axe with which he gave Cortimiglia a violent blow. Mrs Cortimiglia picked up two-year-old Mary from her cot screaming, 'Not my baby,' The axeman's blow killed the child instantly, and another blow struck Mrs Cortimiglia to the floor.

Yet when Mrs Cortimiglia was able to speak, two days later, she accused the man who had found her – Iorlando Jordano. She also accused his son, Frank. Although Charles Cortimiglia insisted his attacker was nothing like Iorlando Jordano, both Jordanos were arrested. The police had their doubts – for one thing Frank Jordano was too big to be able to squeeze through the door panel – but they had to take account of Mrs Cortimiglia's positive identification.

The citizens of New Orleans now no longer seemed so terrified of the axeman. Somebody wrote a song called 'The Mysterious Axeman's Jazz, or Don't Scare Me Papa', and there were reports of axeman parties. Three days after the Cortimiglia attack, *The Times-Picayune* received a letter signed 'The Axeman'. It was datelined: 'Hell, 14 March 1919', and began: 'They have never caught me and they never will.' He claimed to be invisible, 'a fell demon from the hottest hell'. He continued: 'When I see fit I shall come and claim other victims . . . I shall leave no clue except my bloody axe, besmeared with blood and brains of him whom I have sent below to keep me company.' In his infinite mercy, he said, he was going to make a proposition to the people of New Orleans. 'At 12.15 (earthly time) on next Tuesday night, I am going to visit New Orleans again . . . I am very fond of jazz music, and I swear by all the devils in the nether regions that every person shall be spared in whose home a jazz band is in full swing . . .' The following Tuesday was St Joseph's Day, which was usually celebrated as a welcome break in Lent. That St Joseph's Night, according to New Orleans chronicler Robert Tallant, was the loudest and most hilarious on record. Some students even inserted an advertisement in *The Times-Picayune* inviting the axeman to come and join their party; they said they would leave a window open so that he need not ruin their back door. But the axeman ignored their invitations. In fact, there was no sign that he made any appearance in New Orleans that night.

At the end of April, the 'spy' Louis Besumer went on trial, but was acquitted. Everyone expected an acquittal when the Jordanos went on trial in the following month. Charles Cortimiglia flatly denied that the Jordanos had been the attackers, and a stream of character witnesses vouched for their good reputation and honesty. Yet, to everyone's astonishment Mrs Cortimiglia's evidence prevailed, and they were found guilty: Frank was sentenced to be hanged, his father to life imprisonment. There was universal indignation; no one in New Orleans believed they were guilty.

The attacks continued. On 10 August 1919 a grocer named Steve Boca woke up and saw a dark shape above his bed, and an uplifted axe. When he woke up again, he was bleeding from a skull wound. He managed to stagger down the street to the home of a friend, Frank Genusa, who called an ambulance. Boca's back door had been chiseled and the axe was in the kitchen; nothing had been taken. Frank Genusa was arrested but released when Boca insisted that he was not the attacker.

On 2 September a druggist named William Carlson was reading late at night when he heard an ominous scratching sound at his back door. He shouted, then fired through the panel with his revolver. Police found what appeared to be chisel marks on the panel of the door.

On 3 September neighbours became alarmed for the safety of 19-year-old Sarah Lauman, who lived alone, and broke into her house. She was unconscious in bed; several teeth were knocked out and her head was injured. A hatchet was found beneath an open window. She recovered from brain concussion, but could remember nothing.

What was to be the last attack occurred on 27 October. Mike Pepitone, a grocer, slept in a separate room from his wife. She woke up to hear sounds of a struggle, and reached his bedroom door in time to see a man disappearing through another door to the room. Her husband lay dead in bed; the axe blow that had killed him had been so violent that it had spattered blood up the wall. Her six children were awakened by her screams. When the police arrived, they found the chiseled door panel and the bloody axe on the porch.

Then the murders stopped. More than a year passed with no fresh attacks. The Jordanos remained in jail, while their lawyer lodged unsuccessful appeals. But on 7 December 1920 Rosie Cortimiglia, their accuser, burst into the office of *The Times-Picayune*, and fell on her knees. She had become thin and ill – in the previous year she had been an attractive woman – and she was now covered in smallpox scars. 'I lied, I lied. It was not the Jordanos who killed my baby.' She confessed that she had lied because she hated the Jordanos. 'I have suffered for my lie. My baby is dead, my husband has left me, I have had smallpox. St

Joseph told me I must confess.' The Jordanos were quickly released.

Then the New Orleans police learned of something that had happened five days before in Los Angeles. A heavily veiled woman, dressed in black, stepped from a doorway and emptied a revolver into a man who had been walking along the pavement. He was from New Orleans, and his name was Joseph Mumfre. When taken to the police station, the woman at first refused to speak. Some days later, however, she revealed that she was the widow of Mike Pepitone, the axeman's last victim. She had seen the murderer escape from her home and she asserted that Mumfre was the axeman.

Mumfre had a criminal record, and when the New Orleans police checked his history they realized that he could, indeed, have been the axeman. He had been released from prison just before the murders in 1911 but he was then returned to jail, where he spent most of World War I. He had been released just before the first attack of 1918, on the Maggios. In the lull after the attacks of August 1918 Mumfre had been back in prison, being released in March 1919, just before the attack on the Cortimiglias. Soon after the killing of Mike Pepitone, he had left New Orleans.

Mrs Pepitone was tried in Los Angeles; she pleaded justifiable homicide. But there was no evidence that Mumfre was the axeman, and she was sentenced to ten years. She was released after three.

If Mumfre was the axeman, what was his motive? In retrospect, this seems fairly clear. He was in the grip of some kind of sadistic obsession involving axes. We note that in the Maggio case, Joe Maggio was left alive, while his wife's head was almost severed. And someone, probably the axeman, wrote on the pavement: 'Mrs Maggio is going to sit up tonight, just like Mrs Toney.' It was women he enjoyed attacking – their husbands had to be knocked unconscious so that he could carry out the attack. Louis Besumer, aged 59, was only knocked unconscious, but his attractive 29-year-old 'wife' died from her injuries. Mrs Edward Schneider was in the house alone when she was attacked. When the axeman attacked Joseph Romano, he was probably looking for his 18-year-old niece Pauline, but her screams and those of her sister frightened him away. He was evidently a coward for it took very little resistance to make him flee. In the Cortimiglia and Pepitone cases, it again seems likely that he encountered the husband when in search of the wife. Harriet Lowe's evidence is of particular interest – that she woke up after the first blow to see the axeman standing over her, making threatening motions with the axe, yet not attacking her again. It was part of his aim to frighten his female victims.

In *A Glastonbury Romance*, John Cowper Powys, himself a self-confessed sadist, writes of a character called Evans, who is obsessed by fantasies of a 'killing blow with an iron bar'. The axeman's fantasies were of splitting female skulls with a hatchet.

Why Italian grocers? In fact, several victims were not Italian, but most kept shops. A small shop is a place where an attractive wife often serves behind the counter and so can be observed at leisure by a mentally unstable pervert who has fantasies of attacking women with an axe . . .

THE ORDEAL OF JEREMY CARTLAND

It was typical March weather in the Provence area of southern France, with a mistral wind blowing. It was in this beautiful setting that the Impressionist painters created some of their masterpieces, and the area around Pelissanne remains a favourite camping site for holidaymakers.

The two Englishmen who drove a Hillman car towing a caravan looked strangely alike – as well they might. They were father and son. John Basil Cartland, aged 60, ran a language school in Brighton, and his 29-year-old son, Jeremy, was a schoolmaster in the same town. They had enjoyed a holiday mixed with business in Spain, before driving into France. They intended to visit friends in Marseilles, but had decided to park for the night near the village of Salon-de-Provence, where they had filled up with fuel. It was getting late and neither liked the idea of driving in the dark.

They had chosen a quiet, isolated spot to camp for the night, and after supper settled down to sleep. At just after 1 o'clock in the early hours of Sunday, 18 March 1973, Jeremy was awakened by strange noises. He sat upright and saw that his father was not in the caravan – and neither were the noises. They were coming from outside, from the darkness, savage sounds which alarmed Jeremy. Still groggy from sleep, he stepped out of the caravan and stared blankly at the back of a strange man who was trying to open one of the doors of the Hillman car. At that moment, before he could even open his mouth to call out, he was struck over the head from behind, losing consciousness immediately.

Shortly afterwards, a passing motorist, commercial traveller Frederick Delaune, spotted the caravan on fire, the mistral wind causing the flames to leap from the roof. He immediately stopped to render what assistance he could. He ran over to the scene of the blaze, and by the light of the reddish-glare of the flames he saw a sight out of a nightmare. A young man lay slumped near the caravan, blood oozing from stab wounds. Some distance further, about 15 feet from the caraven, lay a much older man, his grey hair matted with blood. He was very obviously dead, with many wounds to his head and stab wounds to the body. Beside him lay the murder weapon: a bloodstained axe.

The Frenchman managed to drag the young man to his car, and on the way to the nearest hospital the man recovered sufficiently to tell him that his name was Jeremy Cartland, and that he and his father had been attacked by mystery assailants. Then he lapsed back into unconsciousness, and it was left to M. Delaune to furnish these scanty details to the local police. By dawn they had examined the caravan, and finding no money or valuables either in the car or the caravan concluded that robbery had probably been the motive for the assault. They set to work with tracker-dogs to scour the immediate area. Meanwhile, the son who had survived the savage night attack lay recovering in hospital.

As soon as his wounds had been treated, and the doctors certified him fit to talk, waiting detectives at his bedside began questioning him. Could he describe the attackers? How many had there been? Jeremy had no answers. It had been dark, he was struck unconscious almost as soon as he saw the back of the strange man. When he was told that his father was dead, he wept quietly. By the simple exercise of deductive logic the French police were able to establish that there must have been at least two attackers – the one Jeremy had seen in front of him, trying the car door, and the one who struck him over the back of the head. Examination of the dead man revealed that he had put up a fierce fight for his life, the degree of resistance measured by the many wounds he had received. He had been struck repeatedly on the head with the axe, and stabbed in the body.

With no immediate leads to follow up, the detectives ordered fingerprints to be taken, and also blood samples. While they waited for the forensic evidence to become available, they concentrated on finding out more about the victim. It was quickly apparent that John Cartland was quite a distinguished victim, one likely to receive demands for a speedy solution to the crime from both the British Consul and the English press. He was Professor Cartland, a well-known scholar, and he had been a secret agent during World War II. Parachuted into Occupied

France as an SOE operative, he had worked with the Resistance, the Maquis, organizing and supplying them in their silent and deadly war with the enemy. It was likely that John Cartland had maintained some kind of link with British Intelligence, for it was an old axiom that once in the 'Firm', you never really left. You might retire, but you would always be available for that 'special job'. Had John Cartland been on a mission for SIS in France? Might that perhaps explain his mystery death – not a common robbery, but an assassination by foreign agents hostile to the British?

Examination of the records revealed some strange patterns, too closely linked to be mere coincidence. For a start, the murder had taken place in the same isolated Provence countryside where, almost 21 years previously, Sir Jack Drummond, aged 52, his wife and daughter, were murdered while on a caravan holiday. Drummond too had been a wartime agent . . . Another coincidence was that a film about those murders had just been released in Paris cinemas. An old peasant farmer, Gaston Dominici, had been convicted of the Drummond murders and sentenced to death. But he was later freed on a Presidential pardon and died aged 87 in 1964. Jean Gabin played the role of the peasant in the film, *L'Affaire Dominici*, which had been released for public showing only weeks before the murder of John Cartland. Could it be that this was an imitative murder?

Other British people murdered in France over the previous 20 years included Miss June Marshall, secretary to Sir Jack Drummond, murdered in Dieppe in 1956. Another wartime agent in the link was Sir Oliver Duncan, murdered in Rome in 1964. More strangely still, just a couple of months previously, on 29 January 1973, a retired British army major died at Cannes, victim of an attack outside his home. Major Michael Lassetter, aged 71, had lived alone since the death of his wife three years previously. Had the Major been involved in Intelligence work? Was it all coincidence – or was there indeed some sinister link? Lacking a swift resolution to these questions, and to the murder of John Cartland, French police were only too aware that with English people being murdered in their area, there would be strong criticism from Britain, and political pressure to find solutions that would satisfy national pride.

It was perhaps as a result of this pressure that Jeremy Cartland, himself the victim of a brutal attack and having lost his father, became dimly aware that he was now the chief suspect in police eyes. His ordeal was not over, but had only just begun. He had stepped into a nightmare scripted by Simenon and directed by the bungling Clouseau. And there would be more than a touch of Kafka about the months which followed . . .

The English press, meanwhile, had published the bare account of the murder of a national in France. They had researched the background of the victim by speaking to his housekeeper, Miss Janet Gibson. She said that John Cartland and his son had been to Benidorm, and were in France to visit friends. John Cartland was a quiet, scholarly man who rarely spoke to neighbours. He had run his language school, catering mainly to foreign students, for several years. The son, Jeremy, was a poet as well as a teacher, having had various poems published. The secretary of the English Poetry Association described him as being 'a very good poet indeed'. At this point it would have seemed inconceivable that French police would label the poet a parricide.

Sir Denis Wright wrote the obituary of his old friend John Cartland, which was published in *The Times*. describing him as a good scholar, soldier and excellent hunter, he summed him up with the phrase: 'He was brilliant and unconventional to the point of eccentricity.' He revealed that Cartland had served with the Political Warfare Executive in London during World War II.

By 22 March, just four days after the murder, the press reported that Jeremy Cartland was 'helping police with their inquiries'. He had, in fact, been questioned for six hours by Grigoire Krikorian of the Aix-en-Provence criminal investigation department. Afterwards, the commissioner emphasized that Jeremy was 'simply a witness, although naturally an essential one'. Police had not revealed the results of the fingerprint and blood tests ordered on the Monday. Jeremy was told he could leave hospital – and France – but the police wished him to remain in order to assist them.

The French legal system – the *Code Napoleon* – is unlike the British process. The examining magistrate has complete power in how he conducts an investigation, and can interrogate witnesses and suspects at will. Essentially, he becomes a policeman investigating a crime – with more powers and less restraints than the policeman. By now Jeremy had become thoroughly alarmed at the line of questioning, and had engaged a French lawyer, Maitre Lombard. On his advice Jeremy lodged an action with the investigating magistrate as *partie civile* against 'X'. This legal procedure was a device whereby Jeremy would become a plaintiff in the case – regardless of any criminal proceedings – and as such he could not be questioned except by the magistrate in the presence of his lawyer. The police could not spring surprise questions on him. He had been questioned the previous evening for nine hours. In a statement issued by his counsel, Jeremy reaffirmed his innocence and emphasized that as a son he was naturally anxious to do everything 'to help the hunt for the murderers'.

Shocked by police suspicions, he gave a press conference at the Marseilles offices of his lawyer, saying 'I am innocent. I am at the disposal of the French police to discover the murderers of my father.' His sister, Elizabeth, aged 24, herself a lawyer, stood by his side, stating firmly that both she and her mother were convinced that he was deeply shocked to learn that police suspected him. The tabloids in both France and England were having a field day with gossip, speculation and innuendo. It was in this climate that Jeremy, depressed by police questioning, announced he would be returning to England.

Jeremy landed at Heathrow Airport to be met by reporters with quick-fire questions. After a few days' rest he flew back to France, again accompanied by his sister. Asked why he had gone to England, he replied, 'I was very tired. I had to see my friends and family.' By the end of March the wartime Resistance background of the case was being publicly linked to the Cartland murder, with Jeremy's lawyers expressing 'great interest' in this angle. The BBC had received two letters signed 'A Friend of Britain' alleging that members of the Maquis had been settling old scores, and had killed John Cartland in revenge because he had deliberately destroyed a list of Frenchmen who had collaborated with the Germans. Jeremy was quoted as saying, 'There could be some truth in it.'

However, the French police remained deeply suspicious of Jeremy, for no apparent reason other than the fact that he had received only minor stabwounds in the attack, and the post-mortem on his father revealed that he had been killed with a single blow of the axe. The other wounds with the axe, and the stabbings, had all been gratuitous, inflicted on an already dead man. By now Jeremy was sufficiently alarmed by police suspicions to attend court before the examining magistrate armed with three French lawyers, and an English barrister, Christopher Heggs. The French press was already critical of the whole affair and its potential effect on Anglo-French relations. Reporters scornfully derided the police for not having sealed off the murder-site immediately after the crime; as it was, many valuable forensic clues had been irretrievably lost. The French police remained sceptical about the alleged Maquis link to the murder, especially when they identified the anonymous letter-writer as one Henrico Polydeskis, a stateless person of Greek origin. He was a notorious 'espionage freak', who showered prominent people with his letters. President Pompidou had been a recipient.

Jeremy shuttled back and forth between England and France, returning on 4 April for further questioning by the examining magistrate, André Delmas. He was questioned for two hours. On 26 April, after a further six hours of interrogation, Jeremy emerged from the court to tell waiting pressmen, 'I am out of the wood. I think it impossible that I will be charged now.' But he complained bitterly about the French police, accusing them of 'falsification of evidence and perversion of justice'. He hinted that the police had acted on a report leaked to them by Scotland Yard, which virtually accused him of being a liar.

The following day Scotland Yard's Interpol office denied that it had ever sent the French police any doctor's report on Jeremy Cartland, which he alleged had been used to 'frame' him. Professor James Cameron, the distinguished pathologist who had examined Jeremy after the attack, said he knew nothing of any report. He said that his notes on the case were still in his desk and had never been shown to any policeman. He denied that his notes stated that the son's words 'could not be relied upon'.

Once again Jeremy flew to England, complaining of police irregularities and saying that the case had cost him some £10,000 in legal fees and expenses. On 5 May Detective Inspector Krikorian flew into London to follow up the British aspect of the case. 'His mission is essentially to find out who might have wanted to kill Cartland,' said the examining magistrate. Scotland Yard assigned a senior Murder Squad detective – Detective Chief Superintendent Ron Page – to assist him. Krikorian said he had no plans to interview Jeremy in England, but his visit served only to fan the flames of rumour once again. The French Ministry of Justice issued a statement 'deeply regretting' the controversy over the investigation into the Cartland murder. Krikorian interviewed the Cartland housekeeper, Janet Gibson, at Brighton police station, before finally returning to France.

On 19 May the French authorities announced that they had virtually found Jeremy guilty of murder, by issuing an inter-national warrant for his arrest. They said they did not intend to apply for extradition, but expected Jeremy to stand trial for murder in England. Jeremy's sister, Elizabeth, tried to halt the proceedings by citing 20 points critical of the evidence, and suggesting that the magistrate had issued the warrant out of a fit of pique when Jeremy failed to attend his court for yet more questioning. On 21 May Jeremy's French lawyers demanded a re-examination of the entire case, after producing two new witnesses. Raymond Blasco and his wife said they were at the scene of the murder at the right time, and saw two men, one blonde, the other dark, near the caravan. Blasco refuted police suggestions that he had confused them with firemen at the scene, saying 'My eyes did not deceive me.' The magistrate refused to hear any new witnesses; in his view the case was over, the culprit identified . . .

When John Cartland's will was published, it was revealed that he had left his entire estate, valued at £30,000, to Janet Gibson, his 57-year-old housekeeper. Thus one possible motive for murder was firmly ruled out.

On 5 July the French sent the 2,000-page transcript of their investigation to the Foreign Office, for forwarding to the Director of Public Prosecutions with a view to putting Jeremy on trial in England. Jeremy's lawyer said, 'Mr Cartland is delighted with this latest move and cannot wait to clear his name. He is willing to meet with a member of the Yard's Murder Squad at any time . . .' Detective Chief Superintendent Ron Page was asked by Sir Robert Mark to start an investigation into the Cartland murder, right from the beginning. The detective flew to France to examine for himself the scene of the crime, and had five more detectives sent out to help him. A satisfied French Ministry of Justice said, 'The situation now is as if the murder had been committed in Britain.' They had washed their hands of an embarrassing affair.

In early August new witnesses were found, a couple who had been driving behind a large black Citroen which appeared to be 'shadowing' the Hillman and its caravan. The Citroen would not let them pass, and when the Hillman parked for the night, the Citroen parked too.

In September, French magistrates refused to grant Jeremy an injunction for the seizure of a book about the case which had been on sale in Paris bookshops for several weeks. The book, *The Enigma of Pelissanne. Jeremy Cartland: Innocent or Guilty?* by Paul Glaude Innocenzi, simply reviewed the evidence and came to no conclusion.

It was at this point, with English detectives busy in France, that Jeremy said bitterly, 'I wish they would charge me! At least I could fight . . . ' On 21 December Jeremy was questioned for 7½ hours at Scotland Yard, and on 4 January 1974 the Director of Public Prosecutions announced his decision not to prosecute Jeremy Cartland for the murder of his father. The evidence, he said, was 'insufficient to prosecute'. Jeremy said he was 'relieved to hear the news' but complained that it had cost him £20,000 to establish his innocence, and he wanted to sue the French police to recover some of that money, if that was possible.

Scotland Yard refused to comment on the end of its six-month investigation, and the French announced that Jeremy could visit France without fear of arrest. On 28 February *The Times* printed an apology for a piece published on 21 March 1973 which may have implied that Jeremy might have been guilty or could reasonably have been suspected of being guilty of the murder of his father. 'We offer our sincere apologies.'

The annals of crime usually lead to definite conclusions of either guilt or innocence. Jeremy Cartland is left in a curious state of limbo, being denied any legal process to clear his name. The stigma of being a named suspect will stay with him for ever. The French effectively condemned him; the British equivocated and said 'the evidence is insufficient'. Thus the ordinary citizen cannot hope to have his name cleared – unlike the madman released from an asylum who can at least claim proof of his sanity.

This case exposed a legal anomaly, but it also left in its wake the essential unsolved mystery. Destined to remain unanswered are the crucial questions: Who killed John Cartland – and why? Who was driving that black Citroen? And who were the two men seen near the Cartland's caravan?

JACK THE RIPPER

The August morning was still dark when a carter named George Cross walked along Bucks Row, Whitechapel, on his way to work. It was a narrow cobbled street with the blank wall of a warehouse on one side, and a row of terraced houses on the other. In the dim light, Cross saw what he thought was a bundle of tarpaulin, and he went to investigate. It proved to be a woman lying on her back, her skirt above her waist. Cross decided she was drunk, and when another man approached, said, 'Give me a hand getting this woman on her feet.' The other man, a market porter, looked down dubiously; his first impression was that she had been raped and left for dead. He bent down and touched her cheek, which was cold, then her hand. 'She's dead. We'd better find a policeman.' He pulled down her skirt to make her decent.

In fact, the beat of Police Constable John Neil took him through Bucks Row, and a few minutes after the men had left, the light of his bull's-eye lantern showed him the woman's body, which lay close to a stable door. It also showed him something the men had been unable to see: that the woman's throat had been cut so deeply that the vertebrae were exposed.

An hour later, the body – which was that of a middle-aged woman – lay in the yard of the local mortuary, and two paupers from the workhouse next door were given the job of stripping it, while a police inspector took notes. It was when they pulled off the two petticoats that the inspector saw that the woman's abdomen had been slashed open with a jagged incision that ran from the bottom of the ribs to the pelvis.

The woman was identified through a Lambeth workhouse mark stencilled on her petticoat. She was Mary Ann Nicholls, a prostitute who had been living at a common lodging house in Thrawl Stret – one of the worst slums even in that proverty-stricken area. A few hours before her death she had staggered back to the lodging house, her speech slurred with drink, and admitted that she lacked the four pence necessary for a bed. The keeper had turned her away. 'I'll soon get the money,' she shouted as she went off down the street, 'See what a jolly bonnet I've got.' She went looking for a man who would give her the price of a bed in exchange for an uncomfortable act of intercourse on the pavement in a back alley. What had happened, the police surgeon inferred, was that her customer had placed his hands round her throat as she lay on the ground, and strangled her into unconsciousness – there were bruises on her throat. Then he had cut her throat with two powerful slashes which had almost severed the head, raised her skirt, and stabbed at the stomach in a kind of frenzy.

Oddly enough, the murder caused little sensation. Prostitutes were often killed in the slums of London, sometimes by gangs who demanded protection money. In the previous April, a prostitute named Emma Smith had dragged herself into the London Hospital, reporting that she had been attacked by four men in Osborn Street. They had rammed some object, possibly an iron bar, into her vagina with such force that it had penetrated the womb; she had died of peritonitis. In July, dismembered portions of a woman's body had been recovered from the Thames. On 7 August 1888 a prostitute named Martha Tabram had been found dead on a landing in George Yard Buildings, Whitechapel; she had been stabbed 29 times with a knife or bayonet. Two soldiers were questioned about her murder, but proved to have an excellent alibi. Evidently some sadistic brute had a grudge against prostitutes. It was hardly the kind of story to appeal to respectable newspaper readers.

This attitude was to change dramatically eight days after the murder of Mary Nicholls, when another disembowelled body was found in the backyard of a barber's shop in Hanbury Street, Whitechapel. It was a place where prostitutes often took their customers, and this is evidently what Annie Chapman had done at about 5.30 on the morning of Saturday, 8 September 1888. A neighbour had seen her talking to a dark-looking man 'of foreign appearance', dressed in shabby, genteel clothes and wearing a deerstalker hat. Half an hour later, a lodger named John Davis went downstairs and into the yard, where the lavatory was situated. He saw the body of a woman lying against the fence, her skirt drawn up above her waist and her legs bent at the knees. The stomach had been cut open, and some of the intestines pulled out. The murderer had placed the woman's rings and some pennies at her feet, and a torn envelope near her head. Medical examination revealed that the killer had also removed the uterus and upper part of the vagina.

Now, suddenly, the press awoke to the fact that the unknown killer was a sadistic maniac. *The Star* that afternoon carried a headline: 'Latest Horrible Murder in Whitechapel'. When Mrs Mary Burridge, of Blackfriars Road, South London, read the story, she collapsed and died 'of a fit'. Sir Melville Macnaghten, head of the CID, would write later in his memoirs: 'No one who was living in London that autumn will forget the terror created by these murders. Even now I can recall the foggy evenings, and hear again the raucous cries of the newspaper boys: "Another horrible murder, murder, mutilation, Whitechapel . . . ".'

In our own age of mass violence, we find it impossible to imagine the shock created by the murders. A journalist who reported the crimes later began his account of them in a popular booklet:

In the long catalogue of crimes which has been compiled in our modern days there is nothing to be found, perhaps, which has so darkened the horizon of humanity and shadowed the vista of man's better nature as the series of mysterious murders committed in Whitechapel during the latter part of 1888.

'Shadowed the vista of man's better nature . . .' – this is what so frightened Londoners. It was as if an inhuman monster, a kind of demon, had started to hound the streets. Hysteria swept over the whole of Britain. There had been nothing like it since the Ratcliffe Highway murders of 1811, when two families were slaughtered in East London, and householders all over England barricaded their doors at night.

On 29 September 1888, the Central News Agency received a letter that began: 'Dear Boss, I keep on hearing the police have caught me but they won't fix me just yet.' It included the sentence: 'I am down on whores and I shan't quit ripping them till I do get buckled,' and promised: 'You will soon hear of me with my funny little games. It was signed 'Jack the Ripper' – the first time the name had been used. The writer requested: 'Keep this letter back till I do a bit more work, then give it out straight.' The Central News Agency decided to follow his advice.

That night, a Saturday, the Ripper killed again – this time not one, but two prostitutes. At 1 a.m. on Sunday morning, a hawker named Louis Diemschutz drove his pony and cart into the backyard of a working man's club in Berner Street. The pony shied and Diemschutz saw something lying in front of its feet; a closer look showed him that it was a woman's body. The Ripper was either in the yard at that moment, or had only just left it as he heard the approach of the horse and cart. When Diemschutz returned a few moments later with a lighted candle, he was able to see that the woman's throat had been cut. There had also been an attempt to cut off her ear. She was later identified as Elizabeth Stride, an alcoholic Swedish prostitute.

The killer had been interrupted, but his nerve was unshaken. He hastened up Berner Street and along Commercial Road – this murder had been further afield than the others – and reached the Houndsditch area just in time to meet a prostitute who had been released from Bishopsgate police station ten minutes earlier. Her name was Catherine Eddowes, and she had been held for being drunk and disorderly. He seems to have had no difficulty persuading the woman to accompany him into Mitre Square, a small square surrounded by warehouses, only a few hundred yards away. A policeman patrolled the square every 15 minutes or so, and when he passed through at 1.30 a.m. he saw nothing unusual. At 1.45, he found the body of a woman lying in the corner of the square. She was lying on her back, her dress pushed up round her waist, and her face had been slashed. Her body had been gashed open from the base of the ribs to the pubic region, and the throat had been cut. Later examination revealed that a kidney was missing, and that half the ear had been cut off.

The murderer had evidently heard the approach of the policeman and hurriedly left the square by a small passage that runs from its northern side. In this passage there was a communal

A graphic depiction in *Police News* of the fate of the Ripper's fifth victim

sink, and he had paused long enough to wash the blood from his hands, and probably from his knife. In Goulston Street, a ten-minute walk away, he discarded a bloodstained piece of his victim's apron. The policeman who found it also found a chalked message scrawled on a nearby wall: 'The Juwes are not the men that will be blamed for nothing.' The Police Commissioner, Sir Charles Warren, ordered the words to be rubbed out, in spite of a plea from the CID that they should be photographed first. Sir Charles thought they might cause trouble for the many Jews in Whitechapel.

Macnaghten admitted later, 'When the double murder of 30 September took place, the exasperation of the public at that non-discovery of the perpetrator knew no bounds.' The 'Jack the Ripper' letter was released, and the murderer immediately acquired a nickname. And early on Monday morning, the Central News Agency received another missive, this time a postcard, from Jack the Ripper. It said: 'I was not codding [joking] dear old boss when I gave you the tip. You'll hear about Saucy Jack's work tomorrow. Double event this time. Number one squealed a bit. Couldn't finish straight off. Had not time to get ears for police. Thanks for keeping last letter back till I got to work again.'

The public exploded in fury. Meetings were held in the streets, criticizing the police. Sir Charles Warren's resignation was demanded. The murderer was suspected of being a doctor and men carrying black bags found it dangerous to walk through the streets. The police decided to try using bloodhounds, but to no avail for the dogs promptly lost themselves on Tooting Common.

Yet as October passed with no further murders, the panic began to die down. Then, in the early hours of 9 November the Ripper staged his most spectacular crime of all. Mary Jeanette Kelly was a young Irishwoman, only 24 years old, and she lived in a cheap room in Miller's Court, off Dorset Street. At about 2 o'clock that morning, she was seen talking to a swarthy man with a heavy moustache; he seemed well dressed and had a gold watch chain. They entered the narrow alleyway that led to her lodging: Room 13.

At 10.45 the next morning, a rent collector knocked on her door but received no reply. So he put his hand through a broken pane of glass in the window and pulled aside the curtain. What he saw sent him rushing for a policeman.

Jack the Ripper had surpassed himself. The body lay on the

bed, and the mutilations must have taken a long time – an hour or more. One of the hands lay in the open stomach. The head had been virtually removed, hanging on only a piece of skin; so had the left arm. The breast and nose had been removed, and the skin from the legs stripped off. The heart lay on the pillow, and some of the intestines were draped round a picture. The remains of a fire burned in the grate, as if the Ripper had used it to provide himself with light. But this time, medical examination revealed that the Ripper had taken away none of the internal organs; his lengthy exercise in mutilation had apparently satisfied his peculiar sadistic fever.

This murder caused the greatest sensation of all. The police chief, Sir Charles Warren, finally resigned. Public clamour became louder than ever; even Queen Victoria made suggestions on how to catch the murderer. Yet the slaughter of Mary Kelly proved to be the last of the crimes of Jack the Ripper. The police, hardly able to believe their luck as weeks and months went by without further atrocities, reached the conclusion that the Ripper had either committed suicide or been confined in a mental home. A body taken from the river early the following January was identified as that of a lawyer who had committed suicide, and Scotland Yard detectives told themselves that this was almost certainly Jack the Ripper. But their claims have never been confirmed.

There have, of course, been many fascinating theories. Forty years after the murders, an Australian journalist named Leonard Matters wrote the first full-length book on Jack the Ripper. He ended by telling an extraordinary story: how a surgeon in Buenos Aires was called to the bedside of a dying Englishman, whom he recognized as the brilliant surgeon Dr Stanley, under whom he had studied. Dr Stanley told him a horrifying story. In 1888, his son Herbert had died of syphilis contracted from a prostitute two years before; her name had been Mary Jeanette Kelly. Dr Stanley swore to avenge Herbert's death, and prowled the East End of London looking for the woman. He would pick up prostitutes, question them about Mary Kelly, then kill them to make sure they made no attempt to warn her. Finally, he found the woman he was seeking, and took his revenge. Then he left for Argentina.

Matters admitted that his own search of the records of the British Medical Association had revealed no Dr Stanley, and no one who even resembled him. But there are other reasons for regarding the Stanley story as fiction. If Dr Stanley was only trying to silence his first four victims, why did he disembowel them? In any case, syphilis is unlikely to kill a man in two years – ten is a more likely period. But the most conclusive piece of evidence against the Dr Stanley theory is that Mary Kelly was not suffering from syphilis.

Ten years later, an artist named William Stewart published *Jack the Ripper: A New Theory*. Stewart had studied the inquest report on Mary Kelly and discovered that she was pregnant at the time of her death. He produced the remarkable theory that Jack the Ripper was a woman – a midwife who had gone to the room in Miller's Court to perform an abortion. After killing Mary Kelly in a sadistic frenzy, she had dressed up in her spare clothes and left, after burning her own bloody garments in the grate. The immediate objection to this theory is that Mary Kelly had no spare clothes – she was too poverty-stricken. But the major objection is that there has never yet been a case of sadistic mutilation murder in which the killer was a woman. Stewart's 'Jill the Ripper' is a psychological improbability.

In 1959, the journalist Donald McCormick revived a theory that dated back to the 1920s. A journalist named William LeQueux described in a book called *Things I Know* how, after the Russian Revolution, the Kerensky government had allowed him to see a manuscript written in French by the 'mad monk' Rasputin, and found in a safe in the basement of Rasputin's house. It was called *Great Russian Criminals*, and declared that Jack the Ripper was a sadistic maniac called Alexander Pedachenko, who was sent to England by the Russian secret police to embarrass the British police force. Pedachenko, said LeQueux, was later arrested after he tried to kill a woman in Tver in the U.S.S.R. In fact, LeQueux wrote three books about Rasputin, all full of cynical invention. Although they were written before *Things I Know*, they all fail to mention this extraordinary theory. But the strongest objection to the Rasputin-Pedachenko theory is that Rasputin did not speak a word of French, and that he lived in a flat on the third floor in a house with no cellar.

In the same year as McCormick's book, Daniel Farson investigated the Ripper murders for a television programme, and succeeded in securing an extraordinary scoop. Sir Melville Macnaghten had hinted strongly in his memoirs that he knew the identity of Jack the Ripper, and spoke of three suspects, although he finally dismissed two of these. Farson succeeded in obtaining Macnaghten's original notes, and learned the name of this chief suspect: an unsuccessful barrister named Montague John Druitt – the man whose body was found in the Thames in early January 1889. Farson did some remarkable detective work, and learned a great deal about Druitt's life and death.

Alas, when Macnaghten's comments are examined closely it becomes very clear that he knew little or nothing about Druitt. He calls him a doctor when he was a barrister. He says he believes Druitt lived with his family, when in fact he lived in chambers, like most lawyers. He says he believes Druitt's mind snapped after his 'glut' in Miller's Court, and that he committed suicide the following day. We know that Druitt killed himself three weeks later, and that he did so because he was depressed after going to see his mother, who had become insane – he was afraid that the same thing was happening to him. In fact, Macnaghten joined the police force six months after the Ripper murders came to an end, and it is obvious that his Druitt theory was pure wishful thinking, without a shred of supporting evidence.

When, in 1960, I published a series of articles entitled 'My Search for Jack the Ripper' in the London *Evening Standard*, I was asked to lunch by an elderly surgeon, Thomas Stowell, who told me his own astonishing theory about the Ripper's identity: that it was Queen Victoria's grandson, the Duke of Clarence, who died in the 'flu epidemic of 1892. Stowell told me that he had seen the private papers of Sir William Gull, Queen Victoria's physician, and that Gull had dropped mysterious hints about Clarence and Jack the Ripper, as well as mentioning that Clarence had syphilis, from which he died. When, subsequently, I asked Stowell if I could write about his theory, he said no. 'It might upset Her Majesty.' But in 1970, he decided to publish it himself in the magazine *The Criminologist*. Admittedly, he did not name his suspect – he called him 'S' – but he dropped many hints that it was Clarence. Journalists took up the story and it caused a worldwide sensation. Stowell was so shaken by all the publicity that he died a week later, trying to repair the damage by claiming that his suspect was not the Duke of Clarence.

Michael Harrison, a writer engaged on a biography of Clarence, carefully re-read Stowell's article, and realized that there were many discrepancies between the career of 'S' and that of the Duke of Clarence. He concluded that Sir William Gull had indeed referred to a suspect as 'S', but that it was not the Duke of Clarence; it was, however, someone who was closely acquainted with him. Studying Clarence's acquaintances, he discovered the ideal suspect – James Kenneth Stephen, a poet, lawyer and man-about-town who had become distinctly odd after being struck on the head by the vane of a windmill, and who, like Clarence, had died – in a mental home – in 1892. Harrison had no trouble in disposing of Clarence as a suspect, pointing out that at the time of the Miller's Court murder, Clarence was celebrating his father's birthday at Sandringham. But he was far less successful in finding even a grain of positive evidence to connect Stephen with the crimes. It is almost impossible to imagine the intellectual young aesthete, author of a great deal of published verse, stalking prostitutes with a knife.

The next major book on the Ripper was optimistically entitled *Jack the Ripper: The Final Solution*, and was by a young journalist, Stephen Knight. Knight's candidate for Jack the Ripper was incredibly Sir William Gull himself. But the story behind the murders involved the Duke of Clarence. According to this story, Clarence had met an artist's model at the studio of the painter Walter Sickert. She had become pregnant, and he had married her. The baby's nurse was a young Irishwoman named Mary Jeanette Kelly. When the royal family found out, Clarence was placed under lock and key in the palace, and his wife was confined in a mental home. But Mary Kelly told the secret to some of her prostitute friends in Whitechapel, and they made the mistake of trying to blackmail the government. The Prime Minister, Lord Salisbury, gave orders that they were to be silenced, and the man chosen to do the job was Sir William Gull, who was driven to whitechapel in his private coach . . . Knight admitted that Gull had had a stroke in the year before the murders, but insisted that he was spry enough to disembowel a few prostitutes in the privacy of his coach.

The source of this incredible farrago was Walter Sickert's son, Joseph Sickert, who claimed that his father had married the Duke of Clarence's child, and that he, therefore, was really Clarence's grandson. Unfortunately, a few days after Knight's book appeared in paperback, Joseph Sickert admitted in a newspaper that his whole Jack the Ripper story was a hoax – although still insisting that he was the Duke of Clarence's grandson. And so the most absurd of all the Ripper theories exploded like a bubble.

Does all this mean that we shall never know the identity of Jack the Ripper? Possibly. Yet the investigations undertaken by the various authors underline one fascinating point: that there is still an incredible amount of information lying in various archives, waiting to be unearthed. The identity of Jack the Ripper may yet be revealed to some casual browser in the Public Records Office or the archives of the Lunacy Commission.

'ZODIAC'

America in the 1980s has seen the emergence of a new and terrifying social phenomenon – the serial killer: the man who, for no apparent reason, kills again and again. Of course, there have always been mass murderers, from Caligula to Jack the Ripper. Yet the modern phenomenon is still frighteningly different. Charles Casey, head of the Criminal Intelligence Bureau in California, says, 'These are people who love to kill. We like to tack some deep psychological meaning to it, but really they're just killing for fun – just plain fun.'

In this sense, criminologists of the future will probably regard the unknown maniac known as 'Zodiac' as the first 'serial killer'.

On 20 December 1968, two teenagers – David Farraday and Bettilou Jenson – were out on their first date near Vallejo, California. They had parked near a pump-house up above Lake Hermon Reservoir, and were listening to pop music on the radio. Suddenly, there was a tap on the driver's window, and as the 17-year-old boy wiped away the mist, he found himself looking down the barrel of a gun. A podgy, bespectacled man ordered him to lower the window, then told him to get out of the car. As he started to obey, a bullet entered his head, and he fell dead. Bettilou screamed, flung open her own door and began to run. In the moonlight, five shots struck her, and she collapsed.

Only a few minutes later, a passing woman driver saw the bodies in her headlights; she drove on, and waved frantically at an oncoming police car. When the police arrived at the pump-house minutes later, both teenagers were dead. There was no obvious motive. David Farraday's wallet was untouched, and Bettilou lay where she had fallen, her clothing undisturbed.

The police investigation soon ground to a halt. There were no jealous lovers hovering in the background; no one seemed to have the slightest motive for killing the teenagers. Whoever did it was obviously 'psychologically disturbed'. And the frozen earth had not left tyre marks.

By July 1969 the teenagers were merely statistics in California's alarming list of unsolved murders. Two miles from the pump-house above the reservoir, another young couple sat in their car in Blue Rock Springs Park: they were a 22-year-old waitress, Darlene Elizabeth Ferrin, and 19-year-old Michael Renault Mageau, whose father ran a pest-control agency. Neither was much disturbed when another car drove in beside them in the parking lot. When a blinding light shone in through the window, the couple assumed it was a police patrol car. Then a man stepped out of the 'patrol car' and came towards them. There was an explosion of gunfire; two shots struck Darlene, who was sitting at the wheel, and another entered Michael Mageau's neck. The assailant walked back to his own car and drove off, his tyres screaming. Another nearby car with several people in it also drove away – they were, apparently, determined not to get involved. Michael Mageau, who was trying to crawl towards them, lost consciousness.

At four minutes past midnight, a phone call to Vallejo police headquarters reported a double murder. A man's voice told the operator the precise location of the car park. He added, 'They are both shot with a 9-millimetre Luger. I also killed those kids last year. Goodbye.'

When police arrived, Darlene Ferrin, the mother of an 18-month-old baby, was dead. Michael Mageau, although alive, was unable to speak. But as he recovered in hospital he was able to describe his assailant: a stocky, round-faced man about 5 feet 8 inches tall, with light brown hair that was wavy or curly. His age would be about 30.

Although the gun was not the same one that had killed the teenagers in December, the police knew the man was telling the truth when he said he was also their murderer. Now Detective-Sergeant Leslie Lundblad, who investigated the previous case, knew he had been correct in his assessment: this was a 'nut', a homicidal maniac who killed out of some odd resentment.

Lundblad reasoned that the killer was probably an inhabitant of Vallejo, a small town 20 miles or so from San Francisco. At least, he seemed familiar with the area and in that case, someone might recognize Michael Mageau's description. But no one, apparently, did.

One thing was obvious – the killer had a curious craving to be known as a multiple murderer. Otherwise, why volunteer the information about the previous double murder? This argued that he was a man who in his personal life felt ineffectual and insufficiently appreciated. He was trying to make society 'pay attention'. This was the conclusion formed by the police psychologists.

Four weeks after the Darlene Ferrin murder, this was confirmed when the *Vallejo Times-Herald* received a crudely scrawled letter from a man who claimed to be the killer – he added details that had not been made public, so the police had no doubt that he was telling the truth. It was signed with a circle containing a cross, a little like the telescopic sight of a rifle. There was also an enclosure – a torn sheet of paper containing a strange cipher. More of the cipher was sent to two other newspapers, the San Francisco *Chronicle* and *Examiner*. The killer was evidently determined to obtain maximum coverage. The letters were identical to the one sent to the Vallejo newspaper. They also contained a threat that if they were not published that day – 1 August 1969 – the murderer would 'cruse around' [*sic*] and kill a dozen people. The letters also explained that the fragments of cipher would reveal his identity.

All three newspapers published the complete text of the cryptogram, but they withheld the murder threat – there would be no point in causing a panic. They also asked that the writer should provide more proof of his identity. He promptly obliged with a letter that began: 'This is Zodiac speaking', and giving more details of the crimes.

Naval experts attempted to crack the code. But the man who succeeded was an amateur cryptoanalyst, a schoolmaster named Donald Harden, who lived in Salinas. He looked for groups of signs that might fit the word 'kill', and ended with a 'translation' which read:

I like killing people because it is so much fun it is more fun than killing wild game in the forest because man is the most dangerous animal of all to kill something gives me the most thrilling experience it is even better than getting your rock off with a girl the best part of it is when I die I

98

cipher on your front page by Fry. Afternoon Aug 1-69, If you do not do this I will go on a kill rampage Fry night that will last the whole week end. I will cruse around and pick of all stray people or couppeles that are alone then move on to kill some more untill I have killed over a dozen people.

Zodiac's threat published by the *Vallejo Times–Herald* on 1 August 1969

will be reborn in paradise and all I have killed will become my slaves I will not give you my name because you will try to slow down or stop my collecting slaves for my afterlife . . .

It ended in an incomprehensible jumble: 'ebeori et eme thh piti'.

The public offered more than a thousand tips. Every one was checked but none led to new discoveries.

The next murder happened on the afternoon of Saturday, 27 September, on the shores of Lake Berryessa in Napa Valley. Two students from Pacific Union College, 20-year-old Bryan Hartnell, and a dazzlingly pretty blonde, Cecilia Shepard, who

99

was 22, had gone for a picnic. They had just finished eating when a hooded figure advanced on them from the trees; on the part of the hood covering his chest was a circle containing a cross drawn in white – the sign of the zodiac. He had a gun in one hand and a knife in the other. In a gruff voice he asked Hartnell for money; Hartnell said he was welcome to what he had on him. The man then volunteered the information that he was an escapee from Deer Lodge State Prison in Montana and needed their white car. He then produced some plastic clothes line and proceeded to tie them up. As he bent over, Hartnell saw that he was wearing glasses behind the hood. Then he said, 'I'm going to have to stab you people.' The man plunged the knife repeatedly into Hartnell's back. Then he attacked Cecilia. This was what he had been looking forward to; after the first stab he went into a frenzy. Eventually he turned her over and stabbed her in the stomach. Finally, he went over to their car, wrote something on the door, and left.

A fisherman on the lake heard their screams and rowed over

The cipher that accompanied the letter to the *Vallejo Times–Herald*

Student Bryan Hartnell recovered from his brutal attack but his girlfriend died shortly afterwards. Zodiac wrote this inscription in black felt-tip pen on Hartnell's car after the stabbings.

to the headquarters of the park ranger. Within half an hour, ranger William White was kneeling by both victims, who were still alive. Soon after, the Napa police arrived; they had been alerted by a gruff voice on the telephone that told them he wanted to report a double murder, and described the location.

Cecilia died two days later in hospital; Bryan Hartnell recovered slowly. By then, the police knew they were dealing with Zodiac – he had written his sign on the passenger door with a black marker pen, adding also the dates of the previous two attacks. The police also located the telephone from which the killer had rung them; it was only six blocks from police head-quarters, and it was still swinging loose. But it had no fingerprints on it.

A check with Deer Lodge Prison revealed, as the police expected, that there had been no escape. Zodiac had told this story to give his victims the impression that they were in no danger while he tied them up.

What was to be Zodiac's last recorded murder took place two weeks later, on 11 October 1969. A San Francisco taxi-driver named Paul Stine picked up a fare near the Fairmont Hotel on Nob Hill – a stocky, brown-haired man with horn-rimmed glasses. A quarter of an hour later, the taxi pulled into the kerb at the intersection of Washington and Cherry Streets, and two youths standing nearby heard a gunshot. A man climbed out of the back seat, and leaned in through the driver's window. There was a tearing sound, and the man began wiping the cab with a piece of cloth, evidently to remove fingerprints. Then he saw the youths, and began to trot away towards the open space called the Presidio.

Paul Stine, a 29-year-old student who was a part-time taxi-driver, was slumped over the wheel, shot in the back of the head. His wallet was missing, so was a piece of his shirt, which had been used to wipe the taxi-cab.

Four days later, the San Francisco *Chronicle* received a letter that began: 'This is Zodiac speaking. I am the murderer of the taxi-driver . . .'. It enclosed a bloodstained piece of Paul Stine's shirt. The letter went on to jeer at the police: 'They could have caught me last night if they had tried . . .' Then he went on: 'School children will make nice targets. I think I shall wipe out a school bus some morning . . .'

From then on, armed deputies began to ride on all school buses. But the precaution was unnecessary, for Zodiac would never try and kill where he might be caught – he preferred stealth. And now the heat was on. The police had a good description and were able to issue photofit pictures of a crew-cut man with horn-rimmed glasses. There was a notable drop in courting couples in lovers' lanes. Moreover, the police had one clue that seemed to guarantee that the killer would eventually be brought to justice – they had his fingerprints, taken from a telephone.

But if Zodiac had decided it was too risky to go on killing, his craving for publicity was still unsated. Ten days after the murder of Paul Stine, a gruff voice spoke on the telephone to the Oakland Police Department, and made a number of remarks that left no doubt he knew unpublished details about the five murders. But the caller's most astonishing message was that he had decided he wanted to give himself up. His condition, he said, was that he should be represented by some famous lawyer like Melvin Belli of F. Lee Bailey. He would also like to speak on a famous television talk show – the Jim Dunbar programme.

It sounded absurd, but the 'Zodiac Squad' decided it was worth a try. They asked Melvin Belli, who had an office in San

Francisco, if he was willing to try and help them capture Zodiac; he agreed immediately. Next, they asked Jim Dunbar if he would reserve space for a telephone call on his breakfast chat show. They then contacted the three people who had heard Zodiac speak – victim Bryan Hartnell, and the two switchboard operators.

When the show went on the air, at 6.45 a.m., it had a good audience. At 7.41, a soft, boyish voice came on the line; he rang off, but called back five minutes later. This time he identified himself as Zodiac but said he preferred to be called Sam. In the studio, Bryan Hartnell and the switchboard operators shook their heads. Unless Zodiac had been lowering his voice when they heard him, this man was a fake.

'Sam' rang back in all 15 times. He explained that he had been suffering from headaches since 'I killed that kid last December', and he punctuated his remarks with groans of pain, which he explained 'were the headache speaking'. Belli tried hard to persuade the caller to give himself up but 'Sam' refused. Finally, when the conversation was taken off the air, Belli persuaded 'Sam' to meet him in front of a store in Daly City, south of San Francisco. Predictably, the caller failed to arrive. But the policemen who were hidden around corners told themselves that they did not believe the caller was Zodiac anyway.

Yet they could have been wrong. Just before Christmas, Belli received a letter signed 'Zodiac'. It began 'Dear Melvin', and asked for help. And, to prove his identity, the sender enclosed another piece of Stine's bloodstained shirt. If the television caller had been a hoaxer, surely the real Zodiac – assuming he was the letter writer – would have denounced him?

The letter seemed to indicate that Zodiac's mental state was deteriorating; the spelling was worse than usual, and the note of desperation sounded genuine. 'I cannot reach out for help because of this thing in me won't let me. I am finding it extremely difficult to hold myself in check and I am afraid I will lose control and take my ninth and possibly tenth victim. Please help me I am drownding . . .'

The implied claim that he had killed eight people led to frenzied activity in the San Francisco Police Department. They could find only one likely case: of a girl named Cheri Jo Bates, who had been found dead in her car in the college car park. But the killer had cut her throat and that was a departure from Zodiac's known methods.

Police now began to receive many 'Zodiac' letters, most undoubtedly from hoazers. One letter taunted them for being unable to catch him, and added the figure '17 plus' implying that there had been a dozen more victims. In fact, a 'Zodiac' letter of 1974 – four years later – claimed that the total had now reached 37. Internal evidence suggests that this letter was genuine. As far as is known, this was the last authentic communication from the killer.

Many psychologists studied the Zodiac material, and produced interesting commentaries. One of these, Dr Laurence Freedman, wrote: 'He kills senselessly because he is deeply frustrated. And he hates himself because he is an anonymous nonentity. When he is caught, he will turn out to be a mouse, a murderous mouse . . .'

Freedman's remarks sound like an anticipation of another mass killer, New York's 'Son of Sam', David Berkowitz, who terrorized the city in the mid-1970s, strolling up to courting couples and shooting at random. He killed six and wounded many more before he was caught, by accident, through a parking ticket. Berkowitz also proved to be a 'mouse of a man' who was mentally retarded.

What is perfectly clear about the Zodiac case is that the killer was, as Freedman said, a nonentity who hated himself for being a nobody. Like the bad behaviour of a naughty child his crimes were a cry of 'Look at me!'. And also, as absurd as it sounds, 'Love me!'. What he would now like is to be publicly chastised, then forgiven and taken to everyone's heart.

With the murders, he had achieved what he always craved: public recognition, a kind of fame. Yet the fame is self-defeating. He can walk along the street and think, as he sees the newspaper headlines, 'Yes, I am famous' – yet no one knows him. He can address the famous lawyer as Melvin, yet he does not dare to give his own name. All he dares to do is try to stay in the centre of the stage by writing more letters threatening violence. And even so, there comes a time when the public is bored with him; he has cried wolf too often. He is finally forced to face up to the irony of the situation. If he had gained notoriety in a hundred ways that were publicly acceptable – from betraying government secrets to streaking at a football match – he could enjoy his fame; as it is, he is condemned to the same obscurity that drove him to the crimes in the beginning. He does not even dare to do anything that might draw too much attention, for now the police have his fingerprints and he may be captured at any time. The Zodiac case is the classic demonstration of the ultimately self-defeating nature of murders of this type.

WHAT HAPPENED TO THEM?

FREDDIE MILLS: A PUZZLE

Any visitor to London's West End can easily find Goslett Yard. All you have to do is walk along Charing Cross Road towards Oxford Street and there, just at the top on the left-hand side, is the small L-shaped cul-de-sac.

You turn into the long part of the L and, neatly tucked away round the corner is the exact spot close to a solitary street lamp where, early in the morning of Sunday, 25 July 1965, Freddie Mills, perhaps the most famous boxer Britain has ever known, was found dead in the back of his own car.

Twenty-one years later, his widow, Mrs Christine Mills, still remembers the scene vividly, 'Freddie was on the rear seat, behind the front passenger seat. His head was down and his hands were on his knees, as if he was asleep. I opened the off-side back door, got in and sat next to him. I had a white suit on. I put my arms around him. They had told me he was sleeping and they couldn't wake him up. "Come on Fred, what's the matter?" And then I realized that I couldn't get close enough. There was something between us, and I thought it was a starting handle. I lifted this thing across the front of my knees and laid it beside me; as I did so I saw blood on my white jacket. I turned round and the penny dropped.

I said to my son, standing outside, "Donny, it's a gun! Get the police!" I went berserk.'

The ex-light-heavyweight champion of the world, television star, night-club owner and popular entertainer had been shot through the eye by the .22 fairground rifle that his wife had found propped on the seat beside him. He had died almost instantly. But why? Who would want to kill Freddie, whom everybody loved, and what possible reason could there be for this tough, hungry fighter ever to have killed himself?

Even the scene of his death adds to the mystery to this day. Tucked away from the main road, it is an ideal setting for a man to choose to kill himself – *or* for a murderer to hunt down his victim.

Frederick Percival Mills was born in Bournemouth in 1919. His father gave him a pair of boxing gloves on his eleventh birthday. Later as he grew into a stocky, good-looking youngster, he began to throw punches for 'nobbins' – the coins spectators threw into the ring after a good scrap – in the smokey, fairground boxing-booths of the West Country. It was a tough, blood-spattered, poorly paid training ground. As he once told my colleague, Alan Hoby, 'It was a good night if you made £3.'

He was a rampaging bull of a fighter with just one basic idea – to batter his opponent into submission. There was never any doubt that boxing was going to be his career. On August Bank Holiday weekend 1941, Ted Broadribb, the famous boxing manager, went to Leicester to see this new contender fight. Broadribb took his wife and daughter Chrissie with him. Chrissie was to become the future Mrs Mills.

Some years later, after her marriage had failed, she and Freddie got married. Chrissie's son from her first marriage, Donny McCorkindale, lived with them and they had two daughters of their own. At the time of their marriage, Freddie was world light-heavyweight champion.

He won the title in 1948, but lost it – and five teeth – two years later when he was knocked out in ten rounds by American Joey Maxim. Still only 31, the career that had made him clamber into the ring more than 100 times was over. He announced his retirement. He had wanted to continue but his wife had persuaded him to the contrary.

Unlike some professional boxers, the ex-champion had no financial worries. In the latter days, Freddie had earned good money in the ring. Besides, in 1946, with three partners, he had opened Freddie Mills's Chinese Restaurant in London's Charing Cross Road.

The business was a success and so was Freddie's new career, as a television entertainer. People today still remember his weekly appearances in '6.5 Special' with Pete Murray and Jo Douglas. Freddie's cheery, extrovert nature bubbled away with the sheer enjoyment of living, and he and his family enjoyed the material fruits of success as well. Their large comfortable house in Denmark Hill in south London had a swimming pool. As the 1950s gave way to the 1960s, life continued to be good.

Then, in 1962 when Chinese restaurants had become two-a-penny, Freddie's restaurant became a night club called Freddie Mills's Nite Spot. Freddie now had only one of his original partners, a man named Andy Ho. To the outside world, he was still the same old Celebrity Freddie, but Mrs Mills now tells me: 'Turning the restaurant into a night club was the worst thing we could ever have done. We were not night-club people, and instead of being a working pleasure, the club became a nightly routine.'

Freddie was not really a late-night sort of person. He got into the habit of going for a sleep in his car parked at the back of the club, in Goslett Yard, for half an hour or so every night, before he was called on to give a performance and be the cheerful host, shaking hands and chatting. 'He would go to the club at about 10 o'clock,' remembers Mrs Mills, 'and then at about 12.00 or so he'd say, "I'm going for my little egg and dip" – his kip. He would go out to the car, and then they'd call him down to introduce the floorshow or talk to the customers.'

That was exactly the routine on the night of Saturday, 24 July 1965. It had been a perfectly normal day, and shortly after 10 p.m. Freddie left for the club saying to his wife, 'I'll see you at midnight.' They had arranged that when her son, Donny, had returned home that evening after borrowing her car, she would drive up to town and have a late-night supper with Freddie at the club. Donny and his wife, Kate, were delayed in getting back to Denmark Hill with Chrissie's car. Nevertheless, she invited them to join her at the club.

It was sometime after midnight when they arrived, to find an anxious Andy Ho waiting for them. He told them that Freddie was sleeping in his car round the back as usual, but they could not wake him. Mrs Mills and her son went to investigate – and found that scene of silent horror in the stationary Citroen.

What had happened after Freddie had arrived at the club that evening?

The senior police officers who investigated the ex-champion's mysterious death have long since retired or left the force. I am told that the papers at New Scotland Yard are no longer available. However, I have been fortunate enough to obtain copies of the witnesses' statements made to the detectives operating out of London's West End Central Police Station.

This then is their account of Freddie Mills's last hours. At about 10.30 p.m. a man, whom the doorman had never seen before, came up to him and said that Freddie was in his car at the back of the club and would he go and see him. The doorman went round and saw Freddie sitting in the driving seat. Freddie told him he did not want to go into the club, that he was going to have a sleep, and the doorman should wake him up in half an hour.

At about 11.10 p.m., the young doorman went back to the car where Freddie was still in the driving seat. He said, 'You told me to wake you up.' But Freddie replied, 'No, come back in half an hour.' At 11.45 the doorman again went back into Goslett Yard. The car was still in the same position, but Freddie was now in the nearside rear seat. He was sitting upright with his head slumped forward. The offside rear window was wound down. So the young man went to it and called, 'Mr Mills', several times and banged on the car door.

Freddie did not respond. So the doorman opened the door, leant in and pushed Freddie's right shoulder and patted his right cheek. He still did not respond. There was what appeared to be saliva round his mouth and nostrils. The young man felt uneasy but did not think that anything was really wrong. He shut the car door, went back into the club and told the head waiter what he had seen. At about 1 a.m. the head waiter went to wake up Freddie, and concluded he was ill. He informed Mr Ho, who telephoned Mrs Mills at her home. But she, of course, had already left for the club.

Was it suicide or murder? The police later discovered that

Freddie had obtained the .22 fairground rifle that killed him and which was found lying beside his body from an old lady who owned a fairground rifle-range at the Battersea Fun Fair. He had known her for years, and within the past few days had asked her to lend him the rifle. He was attending a charity fête at Esher and would be dressed as a cowboy. It was only after he had left that she realized he had also taken some ammunition from a box on her mantelpiece. It transpired that there was no charity fête at Esher.

Even so, Jack Solomons, who knew Freddie well, told Chrissie Mills the very next day, 'If Freddie stood here and said to me, "Jack, I shot myself", I wouldn't believe it. But I'm warning you, be prepared. They may try to bring this in as suicide.'

Indeed, that was the official verdict at the inquest, held without a jury, at Westminster Coroner's Court on 2 August 1965. From that day to this, Mrs Mills and her son, Donny, have not believed it for one munute. 'If I live for a million years I will never accept that Freddie killed himself,' Mrs Mills told me. She and Donny McCorkindale are convinced that Freddie was murdered by one of the gangs that in the mid-1960s were extorting a fortune in protection money from restaurateurs and night-club owners in the West End – allegedly under the benign eye of certain policemen.

'If he had been threatened, Freddie would have refused to pay for protection,' says Donny. 'He would have told them exactly what they could do with themselves!' Freddie never mentioned any threats to Chrissie, but she says, 'He would not have told me. He knew what a worrier I was.'

Mother and son know of an ex-wrestler (now dead) whose club was destroyed only two weeks before Freddie died because he refused to pay protection money. They are sure that Freddie was killed as an example to deter any others similarly minded to defy the villains. Sitting asleep in his car at the back of his club, as was his habit, he would have been an easy prey for any killer. But ex-Commander Leonard 'Nipper' Read, who, three years later, led the team that put the Kray brothers and their confederates behind bars, is adamant that, if this were true, he would have heard something about it.

A major obstacle in the murder theory is the evidence of the elderly rifle-range owner at the Battersea Fun Fair who said that Freddie borrowed the weapon that killed him from her, and that he also stole three rounds of ammunition. Surely that must knock on the head any murder theory?

Not necessarily. For, as a good friend has told Chrissie Mills, the fairground people at Battersea Fun Fair were having their own problems with the protection gangs. It is not impossible that the evidence supplied to the police was false, given under duress by an elderly woman who feared that 'the boys' would come in and 'rough up' her place. She is now dead so I cannot ask her myself.

Certainly, Mrs Mills insists that she never saw the rifle until she found it in Freddie's car that night.

The insistent question remains: what possible motive could have been strong enough for a man like Freddie Mills who never quit in the ring to end his own life?

In a book published in 1977, Jack Birtley revealed that Freddie had fallen in love with a girl nearly 20 years younger than himself. Mrs Mills tells me, 'Yes, he did have an affair with a girl, but that was all finished the year before. It had nothing to do with his death.'

Undoubtedly, Freddie was having serious money troubles. He grossed over £100,000 from boxing, yet died with only £387. Before his death he had, unknown to Chrissie, sold off all his properties to meet pressing debts, and at the end some £12,000 could not be accounted for. No one to this day has any idea where the money went – or why. Yet surely financial worries, however onerous, were not enough to make a man like Freddie kill himself?

The police investigation into his death seems to have been remarkably apathetic. It is amazing, to my mind, that the ambulance summoned to the scene took Freddie's body away before the police arrived. I have never known of such an event in a firearm fatality. Mr Read says, 'I agree that it was unfortunate that the ambulancemen removed the body before the arrival of the police. This precluded the taking of photographs, which in the event would have been most helpful in determining precisely what happened. I cannot account for this.'

What makes this all the more intriguing is the persistent, nagging worry in the minds of the family, and in my own mind, about the position of the rifle. Mrs Mills and her son find it difficult to believe that Freddie could have killed himself with the rifle and than have placed it neatly beside himself in the back of the car. They think it far more likely that he was shot with the rifle from outside the open window and that the weapon was placed beside him by the killer.

What really happened, and why, remains a baffling mystery.

THE PRIME MINISTER DISAPPEARS

Shortly before midday on 17 December 1967, two cars arrived at Cheviot Beach, about 60 miles south of Melbourne in Australia. The beach was forbidden to the general public, since it was part of an Officer Cadet Training School; but the driver of one of the cars was the Australian Prime Minister, Harold Holt, and he could go anywhere he liked.

The sea was rough, and Cheviot Beach is known to be one of the most dangerous in the state of Victoria. Holt showed no hesitation as he changed into swimming trunks and walked straight into the surf. Most of the others in the party – a neighbour of Holt's and her house guests – were disinclined to follow him. However, a young businessman named Alan Stewart remarked, 'If Mr Holt can take it, I'd better go in too,' and followed the Prime Minister.

Holt seemed to be swimming dangerously far out. Alan Stewart stopped swimming when he felt an undertow dragging at his legs but the Prime Minister seemed to be swimming, as calmly as a seal, in the general direction of Tasmania. His neighbour, Mrs Marjorie Gillespie, stared after him with anxiety, wondering why he was going so far. Suddenly, the water around the Prime Minister seemed to boil and bubble, and his head disappeared. That was the last time he was seen.

Within hours, dozens of skin divers were searching the sea, while helicopters flew as low as they dared. The search continued for six days, but no body was ever found. Many distinguished statesmen attended Holt's memorial service, including Lyndon Johnson, Harold Wilson, Edward Heath and Prince Charles.

Inevitably, there was speculation that Holt may have committed suicide. He had been Prime Minister for two years, and had been in trouble from the beginning. Young Australians demonstrated vigorously against his commitment to the war in Vietnam – Holt had trebled the Australian contingent to 8,500 troops. He had been accused in parliament of using airforce planes as a personal taxi service for himself and his family. His party lost two by-elections under his leadership, and also suffered in elections for the Senate. There were persistent rumours that his own Liberal Party wanted to get rid of him, and nothing would have humiliated Holt more deeply – he was a man who was very sensitive to snubs and setbacks. When he left Canberra that weekend to travel to his seaside home in Portsea, Holt looked tired and depressed. His opponents in parliament felt he showed signs of cracking under the strain.

However, those who had seen him that weekend scoffed at the idea of suicide. Harold Holt had a remarkable capacity for relaxing and forgetting his worries, and to his housekeeper, his stepson and his various friends, he had seemed to be a man without any serious problems. At 59, after more than 30 years in politics, Holt had become accustomed to the ups and downs of the life of a statesman.

Fifteen years after his disappearance Harold Holt became the centre of a scandal that eclipsed anything that had happened during his lifetime. A book by a highly respected journalist, Anthony Grey, accused him of leading an extraordinary double life. The title tells its own story: *The Prime Minister Was a Spy*. Grey claimed to have reliable information from Chinese sources which revealed that Holt was not drowned on that December afternoon. He had swum out to a Chinese submarine and been taken to the People's Republic of China.

The story sounds incredible, and most reviewers of the book were scathing. The story told by Anthony Grey with its wealth of detail needs to be absorbed slowly. Anyone who does this will agree that Grey has made a strong case for the notion that Australia's Prime Minister was a Chinese spy.

Harold Holt was the type of politician more often found in America than England: the charming, flamboyant spellbinder. He once stated that if he had not been a politician, he would have been an actor – an admission that no doubt led many of his opponents to retort, 'You are.' He was certainly born under the right astrological sign for an actor, that of Leo, in the year 1908. Holt's background was theatrical: his father was a self-made impressario, while his mother was a member of a well-known family in the theatre. When he was still a child, his parents moved to England, where his father had become the representative of J. C. Williamson, Australia's biggest theatre group. Holt and his brother were educated at a private school, Wesley College, with a minimum of parental affection or interference. When he was only ten his parents divorced.

At Queen's College, Melbourne, Holt studied law. It was not that he found the subject particularly attractive but it seemed to offer opportunities to exercise his considerable theatrical talent – at college he proved to be a brilliant orator and debater. He also played in the cricket team, acquired fashionable left-wing opinions, and showed himself to be an ardent enthusiast of the opposite sex. He lacked money to entertain his girlfriends, but at least his theatrical contacts provided him with endless complimentary tickets to the theatres and cinemas of Melbourne.

It was in July 1929, when he was 20 years old, that Holt delivered, at the college debating society, a paper advocating a closer relationship between Australia and China. China was at that time in turmoil, with Communists and Nationalists, under Chiang Kai-shek, struggling for supremacy. Young Australian Liberals had mounted a 'Hands off China' campaign. Holt went to see the Chinese Consul to request information for his paper. The Consul asked if he could see a copy of his paper when it was finished. Holt obliged. And, according to Anthony Grey, Holt was later asked to tea by the Consul, who told him that a small publishing firm wanted to print his paper on China, and gave him £50 for it. He was urged to write more articles on China and was delighted to oblige. He needed the money and the payments of £50, rising soon to £100, were extremely generous.

In 1931, Grey (who claims to be quoting official Chinese sources) reveals that Holt was asked by his Chinese contact if he would become a member of the Chinese Intelligence Service. His brief seems to have been vague, simply 'to help China's cause'. Holt promptly agreed. After all, there was no hostility between China and Australia, and he was working for Chiang Kai-shek's Nationalists, not for the Communists who might well have been regarded as enemies.

In the following year, Holt set up in a law partnership that quickly prospered, largely due to his old theatrical contacts. His father, now back in Melbourne, also did his best to push

115

business his son's way, in spite of the fact that Harold was refusing to speak to him. The reason for this behaviour sheds an interesting light on Harold's character. When his father returned to Melbourne, he invited Harold to a dinner party, where he found himself sitting next to a beautiful young actress named Lola. Being a fast worker, the young man was soon making advances only to be rebuffed and told that she was in love with his father. The humiliation was like a slap in the face; he walked out of the party and never spoke to his father again. When invited to the wedding of his father and Lola, he ignored the invitation. Later he went so far as to tell new acquaintances that his father was dead.

In December 1931 Harold Holt met Robert Menzies, the distinguished right-wing politician who had attended the same school. They liked one another, and the result was that in 1934 Holt was invited to contest a by-election in Melbourne. His chances seemed minimal for his opponent was an ex-Labour Prime Minister. Holt's charm and spellbinding oratory came close to gaining him the seat. In the following year, at the age of 27, he again stood for the United Australian Party (Liberals) at Fawkner, and gained the seat. On Monday, 23 September 1935, he swore the oath of allegiance.

Holt's socialist sympathies were widely known, but his party was liberal in spirit as well as name. A month after entering parliament, he received a dressing-down from the Prime Minister, Menzies, for attacking the Italian invasion of Abyssinia in terms that sounded distinctly Communist. The young politician learned his lesson and subsequent speeches showed tact and restraint, as well as a thorough grasp of his subject.

Grey states that Holt's activities as a 'spy' did not involve the kind of betrayal of his country that we associate with the names of Kim Philby or Alger Hiss in the U.S.A. He was merely a kind of glorified information officer. His position meant that he had access to information from all over the world. In the 1930s, when the world was seething with political turmoil, such information was worth having. Holt could openly ask questions in parliament on matters that might affect China – such as whether Britain would sell Australia old airforce planes which China urgently wanted to purchase. The answers could play an important, if indirect, part in the complicated chess game of world politics.

A few weeks after the outbreak of World War II, Holt acquired a position that made him even more valuable to the Chinese – he became Minister without Portfolio to the Ministry of Supply and Development. He was still only 31 and known to his friends as something of a playboy – a keen race-goer, a friend of theatre and film personalities, and a frequenter of night clubs (where his preference for wearing a top hat earned him the nickname 'Topper' Holt). His political success made him one of the most desirable bachelors in Australia. Moreover, he was appointed Minister of Air and Civil Aviation in 1940.

Then came an episode that disturbed his Chinese friends. After a snap election, the Liberal Party was returned with a majority of only one. Menzies had to form a coalition and Holt (as the youngest Minister) lost his post and was returned to the back benches. Most politicians would take such a demotion in their stride, but it seemed to shatter Holt. He announced that he was leaving the government to join the army as a private. His Chinese contact, who called himself Mr Wong, tried hard to dissuade him but when Holt insisted he told him to regard himself as temporarily 'deactivated' as an agent. To report on military matters as a soldier would be far more dangerous than as a minister.

In fact, Holt was soon back in government: three ministers were killed in a plane crash and he was subsequently offered the post of Minister of Labour and National Service. He accepted with delight and relief. But the Chinese must have felt that his fit of pique revealed a certain weakness of character.

In 1948, Holt was again 'deactivated' as a result of the new political turmoil in China – with Mao Tse-tung now making an all-out effort to overthrow Chiang Kai-shek. He remained deactivated for three and a half years. At the end of that time, in 1952, his old friend Wong contacted him again and asked him to provide more information. Anthony Grey tells us that Holt did not know that Wong had now defected to the Communists (who had been in power since 1949). So although unaware of it, Holt was working for Mao.

If Grey is correct, the rewards for spying were considerable – around £30,000. Holt's value as a spy increased during the Korean War, and even more so when it became clear that Menzies was grooming him to be the next Prime Minister. When he came to England in 1953 to attend the coronation of Queen Elizabeth II he was made a Privy Councillor.

In the following year, Holt told 'Mr Wong' that he had ceased to sympathize with the Chinese Nationalists, and had decided not to spy for them any more. Three years later Wong was told to admit to Holt that he was working for the Communists, and ask for his help again. Holt had, by this time, discovered that 'Wong' was really a Vice-Consul named Y. M. Liu, and summoned him to a meeting to explain himself. 'Wong' took the opportunity to confess the deception. However, when he left the meeting Holt had agreed to become once more an information gatherer for the Chinese. After all, he was a socialist and the Chinese were preparing to break with Soviet Russia.

According to Grey, the Chinese first became seriously worried about Holt in 1964, when a series of political and personal setbacks seemed to have shaken him as deeply as his loss of the ministerial post in 1940. Not for the first time, the Chinese prepared a contingency plan to 'evacuate' Holt by submarine. But the situation stablized, and an evacuation proved to be unnecessary.

Then, in 1966, Sir Robert Menzies unexpectedly announced his resignation, after 17 years; Holt was appointed Prime Minister. For the first month or so, he was immensely popular. Menzies had been a remote, rather aristocratic figure; Holt was a 'populist' who could set the crowds cheering. He had taken to skin-diving and when he was photographed on a beach with his three beautiful daughters-in-law, the press made remarks about James Bond, and showed a disposition to treat him like a film star.

The honeymoon period was soon over, and things began to turn against him. He was accused of lying to parliament about the use of airforce planes as 'taxis'; he interrupted the maiden speech of a new MP, and was booed and jeered by the whole

Above left: Dr John Bodkin Adams, the prosperous Eastbourne doctor suspected of murdering many of his patients. He was however charged only with the murder of Mrs Edith Morrell, and the trial opened at the Old Bailey on 18 March 1957.

Above right: Mrs Edith Morrell. She had promised to leave Adams a Rolls Royce and a case of silver cutlery.

Below right: Janice Weston, at 36 already a wealthy and outstanding company law specialist, was brutally murdered on 10 September 1983.

Left: A police reconstruction at the scene of the murder on the A1.

Below left: Janice Weston's silver-coloured Alfa Romeo was found in north-west London, but yielded no incriminating evidence.

Above left: Charles Lindbergh became the idol of America after his flight across the Atlantic in *Spirit of St Louis* in May 1927.
Above right: Bruno Richard Hauptmann, the 35-year-old carpenter charged with the Lindbergh baby murder, seen here in court on 10 January 1935.

Left: Charles Junior, the adored child of the Lindberghs, aged 19 months.
These pictures were taken shortly before his abduction in March 1932.
Right: Hauptmann, convicted in February 1935 of the kidnapping and murder of the Lindbergh baby, in the death cell at Flemington, New Jersey. Hauptmann vehemently denied his guilt to the end, and his case has continued to attract controversy to the present day.

Above: A wooden plank concealing a gun and $860 of the Lindberghs' ransom was found in Hauptmann's garage – a damning piece of evidence. Suspicion remains however that some of the evidence may have been planted.

Above: William Herbert Wallace was arrested on 2 February 1931 for the murder of his wife. Could this mild-mannered man have committed a bloody murder inside 20 minutes and immediately thereafter have been travelling unconcernedly around the Liverpool suburbs unstained and self-possessed?

Left: Mrs Julia Wallace, whose body was found by her husband in their home. William Wallace became the prime suspect, was tried and found guilty. The conviction, however, was quashed by the Court of Criminal Appeal. Many students of crime have considered the Wallace case to be the perfect murder; but more recent evidence has pointed to the identity of the true murderer.

Below: Wallace leaving court after his acquittal. He was however to die of cancer within two years.

Above: The cross-examination of Mr Bartlett by Edward Clarke. The *left* inset shows Adelaide Bartlett, and the *right* the Reverend Dyson, her best friend who turned prosecution witness.

Below left: Lizzie Borden, accused of murdering her father and step-mother at Falls River Massachusetts, on 4 August 1892. The Brutality of the murders, committed with an axe has made them legendary in the annals of crime.

Below right: A contemporary drawing of the Lizzie Borden trial shows the defendant with her counsel, ex-Governor Robinson. Robinson proved an excellent defender. Shrewd and worldly, he was nevertheless able to address a jury of his own state in the homespun terms that won their confidence. A verdict of Not Guilty was returned.

Above: Professor John Cartland, murdered while on holiday in France.
Right: Jeremy Cartland and his sister fly to Marseilles for further questioning.

Above: A graphic description in *Police News* of the fate of the Ripper's fifth victim. The Whitechapel murders in the autumn of 1888 caused unprecedented panic and formed the basis of a continuing legend.

Above: Harold Holt (left) with Harold Wilson, and their wives, at No. 10 Downing Street during the new Prime Minister's visit to Britain in July 1966.

Right: Holt soon became a personality, taking up skin diving and other pursuits. He was a powerful swimmer, yet he disappeared suddenly on 17 December 1967 while swimming in the sea off Cheviot Beach near Melbourne. The astounding yet well authenticated claim is now made that he was picked up by a Chinese submarine.

Left: Lindy Chamberlain heavily pregnant, was found guilty of murdering her daughter, Azaria. She was subsequently pardoned however, and is now seeking complete exoneration.

Left: Rudolf Hess, prisoner no. 6 in Spandau Jail in 1982. There had been doubts about whether the prisoner was in fact Hitler's deputy, and further mystery now surrounds him as a result of the circumstances of his death.

bove: Hess's Me 110 after it crashed in Scotland in May 1941. The pilot had bailed out
0 miles from his target – the Duke of Hamilton's estate.

Above: To Robert Maxwell the external trappings of being a very rich and powerful man meant a great deal, and in his often tasteless posturings he was perhaps compensating for the poverty of his youth. One of his prized possessions was the <u>Lady Ghislaine</u>, a 155-ft yacht named after his youngest daughter, which he had bought from the Khashoggi brothers for £15 million. True to his precept that possessions only become status symbols after they are seen, he poses in this picture with his 'toy' in the background.

house. When he rose to his feet and stalked out, his Labour opponent, Gough Whitlam, felt that he had begun to 'dig his own grave'. In May 1967, he was shown a secret file on various Soviet spies in Australia, and was shocked to discover his own code name 'H. K. Bors' among them. For a while, he was terrified that the intelligence services knew all about him. It was then, says Anthony Grey, that he decided the time had come to make a getaway to China. The Chinese, observing the signs of nervous tension and exhaustion, were glad he had made the suggestion before it became necessary for them to step in. So, on that December day in 1967, Holt swam out to a prearranged point off Cheviot Beach, where two Chinese skin divers were waiting. Their inverted 'air bubble' almost escaped them, causing the water to boil and bubble (as Alan Stewart and Mrs Gillespie had observed) but Holt was successfully steered into the air pocket, and propelled by a small undersea vehicle to the escape hatch of the waiting submarine.

Anthony Grey believes this is the incredible story of the escape of Harold Holt. It raises the obvious question: where did he get his information and how much of it can be cross-checked? Grey claims that in May 1983, he was approached by an Australian businessman who wanted his help to publish a book on the true story of Harold Holt. The man had been in the navy when Holt disappeared, and had noted inconsistencies in 'confidential reports' that had crossed his desk. In Baghdad in 1973, a comment by an aide to the Iraqi Oil Minister about a 'high Australian government official' who had sought asylum abroad led him to institute inquiries among business associates in Peking.

The most baffling and unbelievable part of the story is that Peking was apparently willing to tell him the story, albeit in fragments and tantalizing hints. What is more, his own researches seemed to vouch for its truth. In the archives of Melbourne University, he found that original debating paper urging closer friendship between Australia and China. He saw the secret file that terrified Holt so much when he found his own code name in it – and was able to check that Holt had initiated an inquiry about the real name of Mr Wong. The businessman also claimed that the Chinese had showed him photostats of the receipts Holt signed for various sums of money in those early days.

Altogether, it must be admitted that it all sounds very convincing. So many parts of the story can be easily checked that it is hard to see why either the businessman or Mr Grey should lie about them. So it seems that the story of how Harold Holt slipped gradually into the role of a Chinese 'spy' (or information gatherer) is highly plausible.

The question remains, however, as to why the Chinese should want to tell the story. Grey suggests that it may be out of a desire to emphasize that, unlike the Russians, they are not given to 'dirty tricks' and underhand activities. That is, indeed, in keeping with the Chinese character and could well be a part of the answer.

Grey's book itself suggests a rather more likely explanation. According to Grey, some of Holt's government colleagues had their doubts about him. Sooner or later, the story of Holt's spying activities was bound to leak out in Australia. If the Chinese themselves 'leaked' the information and declined to supply the precise corroborative details then their story would be only half-believed. In fact, the reception of Grey's book proved the point: very few reviewers took it seriously. If this was, indeed, the Chinese motive, then they have showed a psychological subtlety worthy of Machiavelli. They have allowed the truth to be told, in the certainty that no one will believe it . . . If Harold Holt was alive to read the book – a point on which the Chinese informant declined to comment – he must have felt totally justified in placing implicit reliance in his old allies and co-conspirators.

THE 'DINGO' BABY

It was 8 o'clock on a warm August evening, and most of the occupants of the camping site below Ayers Rock, the mammoth red-stone landmark that rises out of the desert of central Australia, were engaged in preparing supper. This included 32-year-old Alice Lynne ('Lindy') Chamberlain and her 36-year-old husband Michael, a minister in the Seventh Day Adventist Church. Their elder son, seven-year-old Aidan, was still awake; the other two children, Reagan, four, and Azaria ('Blessed of God'), nine weeks old, were already asleep in the tent.

It was Michael Chamberlain who asked, 'Is that Bubby crying?', and Lindy Chamberlain returned to the tent. A moment later she shouted, 'My God, the dingo's got my baby!' Michael rushed to the tent. The baby's blankets were scattered round the empty carrycot.

Within minutes most of the campers on the site were rushing into the darkness with torches. Lindy explained that, as she approached the tent, she had seen a dingo – a wild dog – walking away from it, with its rear towards her. It had been moving its head from side to side, although she had been unable to see whether it was carrying anything. The night was pitch black, without a breath of wind; although 300 searchers scoured through the scrub, they found nothing. Back in the camp, some women were praying. Lindy Chamberlain was trying to quieten Aidan, who was crying, 'Don't let the dingo eat our baby.' Frank Morris, the local police officer, arrived to organize the search. But he suspected that Azaria Chamberlain was already dead.

By dawn, it was obvious that he was right. Lindy Chamberlain had also come to accept it. Over the radio telephone she told her parents, 'Our baby was killed by a dingo last night.' Then she sobbed.

By mid-morning, the Chamberlains had another problem: their story had caused a nationwide sensation – Baby Stolen by Dingo at Ayers Rock – and press and television reporters were beginning to arrive. Michael Chamberlain agreed to talk to them – a decision that was later to arouse some criticism. Meanwhile, Lindy told her story to the police: how her elder son had been in bed when he said he was still hungry. Instead of fetching him some food as he lay in bed, she made the fatal mistake of telling him to come with her; and, since he would be returning in a few minutes, she left the tent flap unzipped. Before the day was out, Michael Chamberlain had already noticed that some people were asking questions in an oddly suspicious way, as if they felt that the idea of a baby being stolen by a dingo was preposterous.

This was not the view of the police. The day after Azaria's disappearance, they began shooting dingos and wild dogs in the area of Ayers Rock, hoping to find the child's remains in the stomach of one of them. They shot several dingos but their search was unsuccessful. On Tuesday, the Chamberlains returned to their home in Mount Isa, Queensland. Their religious faith had given them the strength to accept the tragedy. But there were many people who felt they had accepted it a little too stoically.

In fact, they might have received far more sympathy if they had been less religious. As Seventh Day Adventists, they were regarded as a little 'odd'. Seventh Day Adventists have been described as 'Fundamentalists of Fundamentalists'. Like the Jehovah's Witnesses, they believe in the literal truth of every word of the Bible, and in an imminent return of Christ to earth. Their movement was founded in the first half of the nineteenth century by an American, William Miller, who announced that the end of the world would occur in 1843 or 1844. On 22 October 1844, 20 families sat out all night in Phoenixville, Pennsylvania, waiting for the end, and two children froze to death. That night was known as the Great Disappointment. But the Adventists declared that the Second Coming had been delayed by their failure to recognize Saturday as the Sabbath, and that it could be expected fairly soon. In spite of the Great Disappointment, the sect continued to prosper.

Modern Seventh Day Adventists disapprove of alcohol, gambling, jewellery, cosmetics, cinema and television, with the inevitable consequence that there is a tendency among the worldly to regard them as cranks and 'killjoys'. This helps explain why, instead of receiving universal sympathy and commiseration, the Chamberlains found themselves confronted by a curious hostility after the loss of their baby.

Eight days after Azaria's disappearance, a tourist on the west side of Ayers Rock noticed some clothing; it proved to be a bloodstained stretchsuit, napkin, singlet and booties. Yet there was not the slightest trace of flesh. It looked as if the dingo had removed the baby from the stretchsuit and taken it to its lair. Oddly enough, the singlet was inside out. How could a dingo do that? One local theory was that the dingo had dropped the baby, which had then been taken home by a camp dog, and that the owner of the camp dog, worried about being implicated, had removed the clothes and buried the body. But that still failed to explain why such a person had not simply buried the baby with her clothes on.

The Chamberlains were questioned several times by the police. A rumour began to circulate that she had fallen from a supermarket trolley and become spastic, and that her parents had decided to kill her for this reason. Another rumour was that Azaria meant 'the sacrifice', and that she had been sacrificed on top of Ayers Rock in some gruesome ceremony.

Forensic evidence seemed to throw some doubt on the story about the dingo. A stuffed stretchsuit was dragged across the ground from the camp site to the base of Ayers Rock, then examined by botanists. There were fragments of charcoal in the experimental stretchsuit, as might have been expected, since there had been bush fires in the area. Yet there was no charcoal on Azaria's suit. Forensic tests seemed to indicate that Azaria's clothes had been rubbed in the dust at the base of the rock. A dead goat was put into the baby clothes and thrown into the dingo pen at Adelaide Zoo. The dingo buried the carcass and clothes in various parts of the pen. Forensic experts concluded that the damage caused to the clothing – particularly the teeth-marks – was quite unlike the damage to Azaria's stretchsuit. Moreover, the blood that soaked the stretchsuit seemed to suggest that the baby had been in an upright position during the bleeding. Michael Chamberlain, pursued by journalists who wanted to know what he thought about this suggestion that his baby had not been taken by a dingo, admitted that it was possible that a human being had carried Azaria off, 'but he or she would have been a maniac'. But where was the baby? It seemed unlikely that a dingo had eaten every morsel of a 9lb baby.

The inquest opened in Alice Springs in December, and moved to Ayers Rock. By that time, the Chamberlains were living in an atmosphere of continual hostility – there were even death threats. Many people simply doubted that a small wild dog would steal a nine-week-old baby. And when the police forensic laboratory announced that the holes in the garment had been made with an instrument like a pair of scissors, the Australian public began to feel that there was more in this case than met the eye. On Wednesday, 18 February 1981 Coroner Barritt startled everyone by announcing that because of the widespread interest in the case, he had granted permission for television to film the findings of the inquest. But Australians who hoped for some sensational revelation, or accusation, were disappointed when the coroner found that Azaria Chamberlain had met her death through a wild dingo. He added that it was untrue that Azaria meant 'sacrifice in the wilderness'.

The debate continued. In September that year the police were ordered to reopen their investigations. In November, a supreme court judge ordered a new inquest. It opened on 14 December 1981. Just before the inquest, the police received a letter from an anonymous couple who claimed that they had seen a dingo carrying what they thought was a doll, and that when one of them threw a stone at the dog, it dropped its burden, which they found to be a badly mutilated child. The couple decided to bury the baby, so the parents would not see it in this condition; they undressed it, and later got rid of the clothes at Ayers Rock. But the writers could not be located.

At the inquest, Michael Chamberlain was asked whether he had cleaned blood out of the car. He agreed that he may have cleaned 'some blood', but insisted that it was not much. Lindy was asked why she had sent a bloodstained tracksuit – which she had worn on the night of the baby's disappearance – to the cleaners. When a policeman told how he had unbolted the front seats of the car and found bloodstains on the cross section, the court sensed that this inquest was, in fact, a trial of the Chamberlains. This became even clearer when Joy Kuhl, a forensic biologist, told how she had discovered fetal bloodstains on a pair of nail scissors, and on the inside of a yellow container found in the car. But the most sensational evidence came from a British expert in legal medicine, Professor James Cameron. He had been sent the baby's clothing at the London Hospital Medical College, and his examination had led him to conclude that the blood on the stretchsuit suggested that it had flowed down from above. He also commented that the holes in the stretchsuit had been made with scissors, and that he had been surprised at the absence of teeth-marks or of animal saliva around the neck of the suit. And when he added that ultra violet light had revealed a bloodstained handprint on the stretchsuit – a print too large to be a child's but too small for a man – it was obvious that the finger of guilt was now pointing at Lindy Chamberlain.

When the inquest resumed after Christmas 1981, Mr Desmond Sturgess, the barrister appointed to help the coroner, finally made the accusation that everyone was expecting. He believed that Azaria had been killed in the family car, and her body concealed in a camera bag. The coroner then committed Lindy Chamberlain for trial on a murder charge, and Michael Chamberlain was charged as an accessory after the fact.

The trial of Lindy Chamberlain began on 13 September 1982, and the prosecuting counsel, Ian Barker QC, announced that he would attempt to prove that Azaria Chamberlain died of a cut throat while Lindy Chamberlain was in the front passenger seat of the car. The prosecution case was that Lindy Chamberlain had taken the baby from the tent and into the front seat of the car, where she had cut Azaria's throat. The case depended largely on forensic evidence. It lacked one vitally important element – a reason why Lindy Chamberlain, mother of a happy family, should have murdered her own baby.

The defence called experts who disagreed that the stains found in the car were fetal haemoglobin, and a dental expert argued that the holes found in the stretchsuit were caused by an animal's teeth. Lindy Chamberlain's doctor testified that she was not suffering from post-natal depression after the birth of Azaria. A mother testified that a dingo had tried to grab her 12-year-old child by the elbow at Ayers Rock on the evening before Azaria disappeared. A Geelong pathologist flatly denied that the bloodstains on the tracksuit could have been caused by a head injury or a cut to the throat. And he denied that there was a bloodstained handprint on the suit.

The one point that emerged very clearly from the trial was that the evidence of the various experts could not be accepted as scientifically unshakeable. The defence made the telling point that if Lindy Chamberlain had murdered her baby, surely she would have claimed that the child had been carried off in the dingo's mouth? From the beginning she had stuck to her story of only seeing the dingo moving away into the darkness.

The trial lasted for seven weeks. When the jury returned from six and a half hours of deliberation, the foreman announced that their verdict was unanimous: the Chamberlains were guilty as charged. Thereupon the judge, Mr Justice Muirhead, told Lindy Chamberlain, 'There is only one sentence I can pass upon you – hard labour for life.' She was taken away to Berrimah Jail where, within a few days, she would give birth to another daughter. Michael Chamberlain was sentenced to an 18-month suspended sentence.

When, in April 1983, the Federal Court rejected Lindy Chamberlain's appeal, it seemed that the Dingo Baby Case was finally over. But soon Lindy Chamberlain support groups were formed all over the country. In February 1984 the High Court of Australia rejected Lindy Chamberlain's appeal. But soon after that a family described how, eight weeks before the disappearance of Azaria, a dingo at Ayers Rock had dragged their child from the car. The chief ranger from the Ayers Rock district, Derek Roff, wrote to the *National Times* saying he was convinced the dingoes might well attack a child. Thirty-one scientists signed an open letter protesting about the conclusions drawn from Joy Kuhl's evidence. A psychologist who had examined Lindy Chamberlain in prison stated on television that he was unable to account for criminal behaviour on her part, and affirmed his conviction that she was totally innocent.

Although these pleas had no effect on the authorities, Lindy Chamberlain was released from prison on 7 February 1986 on the grounds that she had paid her debt to society. She had served just over two years of her life sentence. After her release, she announced that she and her husband would continue the fight to establish their innocence. Part of that campaign was a long television interview with reporter Ray Martin, in which she spoke frankly about the charges against her, and of the reasons why so many had felt her to be guilty – her apparently cool demeanour during the inquests and in television appearances. She pointed out the obvious – that if a mother who has lost her baby is then faced with a campaign of rumour and innuendo, her reaction is bound to be one of anger, and she is not likely to look bereaved and miserable. During the course of the programme, one of the jurors who had been responsible for the guilty verdict announced that she had since become convinced that Lindy Chamberlain was innocent. She went on to admit that many of the other jurors had felt doubts but said that the forensic evidence had seemed conclusive.

In retrospect, it is difficult to see why Lindy Chamberlain was ever suspected of murder. No one disputed that the Chamberlains were a happy and affectionate family unit, and no one was ever able to allege any kind of motive. It seems fairly certain that the Lindy Chamberlain case will be regarded as Australia's most tragic miscarriage of justice.

It was later announced that Lindy Chamberlain had been pardoned. This followed the tabling in Darwin of the Inquiry conducted by Mr Justice Morling in which he found that the evidence was such that he could not rule out the child having been taken by a wild dog.

Mrs Chamberlain said she would now seek complete exoneration by the quashing of the conviction.

DONALD CROWHURST

Donald Crowhurst was 15 when he and his parents returned to England from India in 1947. He was bright, mathematically inclined, and 'on the pushy side' according to a school chum at Tilehurst, on the fringe of Reading, where his family settled.

His favourite people seem to have been those who refused to accept defeat. Men like Hillary and Tensing were his heroes, and when Everest was conquered on Coronation Day 1953 he said he felt frustrated because he believed there was nothing left of comparable achievement to be tackled. He was in the RAF then and accepted a challenge of dubious merit from fellow officers – to ride a motorcycle at speed through a Nissen hut full of sleeping aircraftmen in the middle of the night. Dangerous havoc naturally resulted and he resigned his commission as a consequence of the escapade and transferred to the army. Again he took up a foolish challenge and tried to steal a car after a long pub crawl. He was caught and once more resigned the service – this time for married life in a 'semi' in the river port of Bridgwater, Somerset, where he got a job as an electronics engineer.

'We all thought marriage would take that aggressive look off his face,' said his Tilehurst chum. Indeed in 1957 he soberly settled down and concentrated on the invention of a new navigational aid to shipping – the Navicator – which his mother, now a widow, helped to finance. Another apparent sign of his abandonment of youthful indiscretions was his adoption of the tranquil leisure pursuit of 'messing about in boats', for which he'd acquired a 20-foot dinghy named *Pot of Gold*.

The New Elizabethan Age had begun with the conquest of Everest. As the 1950s reached into the 1960s the challenges and triumphs came thick and fast, giving the lie to Crowhurst's gloomy prognostication. Olympic Games produced new records; a new 'fastest crossing' of the Atlantic by the liner *United States* was achieved; the International Geophysical Year promised the launch of satellites into space and Yuri Gagarin became the first man to orbit the earth in a spacecraft; and on terra firma Jack Brabham captured the driving championship of the world in a car of his own construction. On the oceans tremendous enthusiasm was raised by the yachtsmen Francis Chichester and Alec Rose, both of whom circumnavigated the globe in tiny craft and were rewarded with knighthoods – Chichester's at Greenwich, whither the Queen made her way specially for the dubbing, as her namesake had made her way to Deptford in 1581 for the knighting of Francis Drake after his circumnavigation in *Golden Hind*. Long-distance sailing made a special appeal to a wide public because radio linkage and aerial sightings could keep track of the sailors, keeping them in touch with the world at large.

In 1968, *The Sunday Times* promoted a contest that was at once a circulation spinner and a tribute to the spirit of the age. Citing Chichester and Rose as exemplars, the newspaper agreed that there was little left of the world to explore, but pointed out that there were still increasingly daring ways to encircle it. They offered a prize of £5,000 for the fastest circumnavigation of the globe by a singlehanded yachtsman, and a Golden Globe trophy for the first sailor to return regardless of speed. There were, of course, conditions – among them that there should be no help accepted from other vessels and that there should be no putting in to any port for repairs. It was to be a loner's race.

Donald Crowhurst had been fortunate in finding a market for his Navicator device through Pye Radio, which bought up the Crowhurst firm and gave him some capital for the new enterprise that now seized his imagination. Novice though he was at sailing he got it into his head that he could win the *Sunday Times* contest. Not, of course, in *Pot of Gold*, which was scarcely bigger than a rowing boat, but in a craft that he would have designed and built specially, leaving nothing to chance in either the design or the construction.

He did not realize until he started to cost the venture that he would need a great deal more capital than he had available, bearing in mind that he had the domestic problem of providing for his wife and four children and the mortgage during his absence (which he optimistically estimated at eight months) as well as fitting himself out for the voyage. Somewhat deflated, he tried to save the cost of the boat by borrowing Chichester's yacht *Gipsy Moth IV*, but without success. Meanwhile, time was running out.

The start had to be made in British waters between the beginning of June and the end of October 1968. Compromise and a philanthropic businessman, Stanley Best, came to the rescue. Best and the BBC led the sponsors who had been sold on the idea of backing a cheeky challenger competing with experienced yachtsmen such as Chay Blyth, Robin Knox-Johnston, and Nigel Tetley. Rodney Hallworth, who handled PR for Teignmouth in Devon, saw a great deal of publicity coming the town's way if he acted as Crowhurst's agent. He chipped in with the sort of news stories and gossip paragraphs that built up the image of the tough little fighter against formidable odds.

The nationals picked up the press releases and headlines like WHACK 'EM, DON! proliferated. For weeks there were 'work in progress' photographs of the building of the boat in the Norfolk yards, and features about comparable heroes who had overcome all to achieve fame and glory. It was the stuff dreams were made of for Donald Crowhurst.

He had decided that in the matter of design he would go all out for speed, since that would give him two chances – to be either first home or fastest; or, with an inordinate amount of luck, both. 'Nothing daunts Donald' was the headline message.

Expert sailors were invited to give their views on the trimaran ketch that gradually took shape. The consensus was that a triple-hulled boat was a daring venture for an inexperienced sailor. There could well be problems caused by the lack of a keel to give the boat stability. Also, there was much head shaking over the completion date to ensure meeting the deadline for the start of the race. Boat building is not an activity that should be hurried. But hurried it had to be – and with alarming consequences: some of the hatches leaked, and on the trial runs excessive vibration necessitated several returns to the boatyard for trimming and adjustments.

The three days Crowhurst had budgeted for the maiden voyage to Teignmouth stretched into a fortnight. He arrived there putting on a show of debonair calm for the press that must have belied his inner state of tension, for he had only a day to make final preparations, load his stores, and check his radio, tape recorder, camera, and Navicator.

The press, of course, loved it, and built up the drama of the preliminary race against time. The hero was pictured in nautical rig, a book called *The Great Yacht Race* on the chart table (it was the story of millionaires racing their yachts across the Atlantic in 1866), and confidence brimming in his eyes as he pointed proprietorially to the name painted on the prow: *Teignmouth Electron*. They were the last pictures he posed for. He was towed across the bar and set sail with only nine hours to go before the deadline of midnight on 31 October. He was now alone with the world before him.

Radio transmissions gave cheering reports of his progress. In early December he announced that he had sailed 243 miles in a single day, and Rodney Hallworth's publicity began to whisper of the possibility of Crowhurst being a winner, five of the original nine entrants having withdrawn for one reason or another. Only Robin Knox-Johnston, the French yachtsman Bernard Moitessier, and Commander Nigel Tetley (also in a trimaran) remained as competitors. Hopes of possible success seemed to be reinforced in January, when the news was that Crowhurst was southeast of Gough Island in the south Atlantic and had logged 1,086 miles in the previous week. Radio stations in the vicinity of Cape Horn, he said, should prepare to listen for his transmissions – though for the moment he was closing down his transmitter to effect some repairs to the generator.

There followed a prolonged silence.

Tetley rounded the Horn on 20 March and Robin Knox-Johnston was sighted on the homeward leg of the voyage on 6 April. Moitessier had abandoned his attempt, so there were only the three entrants left. Of Crowhurst nothing more was heard until the end of April, when he reported being in the area of the Falkland Islands.

The long silence had caused much anxiety, and some suspicion. Chichester, who was chairman of the judges, said publicly that a lot of explaining had to be done to account for it. Nevertheless, Teignmouth was preparing for a hero's welcome even before it was learned that Tetley had been forced to abandon ship on 21

May and that, it was presumed, Crowhurst and Knox-Johnston were racing for a neck-and-neck finish. This was the stuff of real drama. 'May the best man win' was the 'in' cliché of the day.

But drama of a more tragic kind was to be the payoff.

On 10 July the mailboat *Picardy*, heading for Florida, found *Teignmouth Electron* abandoned in mid-Atlantic. No sign of Crowhurst, but nothing else untoward. The life raft was intact, the radio in working order; there was no shortage of food or water, the logbooks were displayed – with the last entry date nine days earlier.

'It was like the *Mary Celeste* over again,' said Captain Box of *Picardy*.

What clues there were to Crowhurst's disappearance had to be pieced together from the logbooks, the tape recorder, the camera, and the damning evidence that was submitted by the coastguard station at Montevideo, where Crowhurst had been logged on 19 March as heading for Buenos Aires for repairs – an act that alone would have disqualified him.

It was a depressing picture that resulted – a picture of a man beset by vainglory who had entered a contest in the preparation for which care had been sacrificed to haste, and which was right out of his league so far as seamanship was concerned. As the log revealed, cursory attention had been given to the most important matters, and he had found himself lacking essential spares and without even a working pump to rid the boat of the water that constantly leaked into the 'watertight' compartments. (The boxes containing spares had been forgotten; they were found later in the boathouse at Teignmouth.) 'With so much wrong with the boat,' he had written, 'it would perhaps be foolish to continue. I will . . . think about the alternatives open to me.' And that was only two weeks after leaving Teignmouth.

The logs, which had to be accurate to ensure proper navigation, also told a very different story of the miles sailed from that of the boastful broadcasts. For weeks his average had been no more than 50 miles a day. This revelation was followed by another indication of mind-wracking indecision: 'Racked by the growing awareness that I must soon decide whether I can go on in the face of the actual situation . . .'

The honourable alternative would, of course, have been for him to quit. There would have been no disgrace in throwing in his hand; but Donald Crowhurst could not bear to be a loser – not even a gallant one. He continued to cook up the glowing reports of his progress in the hope that some miracle would aid him. Indeed the hint of such a miracle came when he detected nothing in the worldwide broadcasts of the contestants' progress to indicate that it was known that he had put in to Buenos Aires for repairs. Evidently the coastguards had failed to notify their inland headquarters. Perhaps some gods were on his side after all . . . Lie low, keep radio silence, and log weather reports as if he had received them from radio stations on his homeward-bound course while he was really lying becalmed with numerous technical troubles to contend with: that was the cheating tale the logs seemed to tell. But it was a desperate move, one that he must have known would be discovered as false on inspection of the logs by the judges. So, it was conjectured, in his approaching mental breakdown he started keeping a false log as well as the true one, perhaps to conceal his failure even from himself, and in the confusion of his mind could not distinguish between truth and falsehood.

He evidently sailed on as best he could, in his lucid moments encouraging his own and the public's belief in a neck-and-neck finish when he was still 1,000 miles from home in mid-Atlantic. It remains a mystery to this day why he did not radio for help. His fraud would have been discovered, but the race was lost anyway. It seems uncharacteristic of his audacious nature that he should not have tried to turn his deception into a sort of victory with stories of hazards risked and perils triumphantly overcome.

It was assumed that, burdened with guilt and failure to satisfy his ego, he abandoned ship and life too. His body was never recovered, and theories were advanced suggesting that he might have been picked up and taken perhaps to South America to begin a new life. Whatever his fate, a charitable view of his attempted cheat was taken, and an appeal fund was launched for his family. The unrivalled winner, Robin Knox-Johnston, contributed his £5,000 prize money.

IDENTITIES: TRUE OR FALSE?

THE RIDDLE OF RUDOLF HESS

The mystery surrounding Rudolf Hess is not just a question of whether the old man who lingered for so long in Spandau Prison, last of the Nazi war criminals, was or was not the real one-time Deputy-Führer of the Third Reich. It goes much deeper than that, to the problem of what may have happened to Rudolf Hess, which in itself leads to many other questions.

Hess was born in 1894 in Alexandria, where his father was a businessman. He spent the first 14 years of his life in Egypt and went to a local German school. When the family returned to Germany he was sent to a boarding school at Bad Godesberg on the Rhine, and as soon as World War I began he volunteered for service in a Bavarian infantry regiment. He became a lieutenant and was wounded three times: by shrapnel in his left hand and upper arm in June 1916, in the left upper arm in July 1917, and finally, in October 1917, he was seriously wounded by a bullet through his left lung. Although this put an end to his active infantry service, after four months in hospital he recovered sufficiently to join the Flying Corps and complete his training as an officer pilot just before being demobilized in December 1918. The bullet through his lung left entrance and exit scars and thereafter he suffered from shortness of breath and attacks of bronchitis.

In the general confusion after the war, Hess became deeply involved in politics. In May 1919 he was wounded yet again, this time in the leg, during the street rioting that drove the Communists out of power in Bavaria. In 1920 he became an undergraduate at Munich University, and in April of that year

134

joined the National Socialist German Workers' Party (NSDAP) – the Nazis – as one of its founder members under the leadership of an Austrian named Adolf Hitler.

Hess fell completely under Hitler's spell and became his loyal and devoted lieutenant. On one occasion in a Munich beer cellar, someone threw a beer mug at Hitler. Hess deliberately stood in its path and received a permanent scar on his head. He marched beside Hitler in the abortive Munich Rising in November 1923, when the Bavarian State Police opened fire and killed a number of National Socialists. Hitler was arrested and imprisoned in the fortress of Landsberg. Hess escaped, but returned and gave himself up when he heard what had happened to Hitler. He joined Hitler in Landsberg, and being well educated gave the future Dictator of Germany invaluable assistance in the writing of *Mein Kampf*, which became the Nazi bible.

These historical details have their place in the riddle because the scars left by war wounds and differences of political opinion provide positive identification, and it is important to establish the elationship between Hess and Hitler. Hess was a gifted administrator and organizer, the true architect of the Nazi Party, a skilled negotiator and one of the few men in whom Hitler confided.

In 1927 Hess married Ilse Pröhl, and their son, Wolf-Rüdiger, was born ten years later. By making Hess the head of the Central Party Commission in 1932, Hitler put him in charge of all political activities, and when Hitler became Chancellor in 1933 he appointed Hess as his Deputy. Hess now had enormous power in every field of State affairs, yet he lived frugally and without ostentation. He neither smoked nor drank, was a vegetarian and very careful about what he ate. Although he took homoeopathic drugs there is no doubt that in May 1941, the critical month in the story, he was in excellent physical and mental health. He had various obsessions: a hatred of Jews and Communists, but to him, Soviet Russia was the real enemy.

He came to the conclusion that if peace could be made with England, Germany would be free to deal properly with the Russians. His close friend Albrecht Haushofer knew various prominent people in England, and Hess began to investigate the possibility of meeting one or more of them on neutral ground. One of Haushofer's acquaintances was the Duke of Hamilton who, though distinguished in many ways, did not possess any political influence at that time. In September 1940 Hess wrote to the Duke of Hamilton, through an intermediary in Portugal, suggesting a meeting in Lisbon, but the letter was intercepted by the British Security Service and was not seen by the intended recipient until March 1941. In the meantime, other negotiations were in train with Dr Carl Burckhardt, President of the Swiss Red Cross, to bring about a meeting with the British in a neutral country. There was, therefore, no apparent need for Hess to do what he did on 10 May 1941.

On that day, accompanied by one of his adjutants, Karlheinz Pintsch, he drove the 35 miles from his house in Munich to the airfield at Augsburg, beside one of the Messerschmitt factories, wearing Luftwaffe (airforce) uniform. During the previous six months he had flown a considerable number of training sorties from this airfield, and was well known to everyone there as a skilful and experienced pilot. He found that someone had removed his leather flying suit from its hook in the changing room, so he borrowed one clearly marked with the name of its owner, Helmut Kaden. He climbed into a Messerschmitt 110D which was not fitted with additional long-range fuel tanks, and took off.

A fighter aircraft of that type had a range of about 850 miles in optimum conditions; the distance from Augsburg to Glasgow in a straight line is about 850 miles. But a direct flight would mean crossing the east coast of England in the area of Hull and risking attack by fighters for the next 200 miles. If it was Hess's intention to fly to Scotland to see the Duke of Hamilton, he would have to make a detour over the North Sea – and probably run out of fuel.

He left Augsburg at 5.45 p.m. and was tracked by German radar all the way to the coast northeast of Amsterdam, which he crossed at 7.30 p.m. Two hours and 40 minutes later, at 10.10 p.m., radars on the Northumberland coast picked up a single aircraft approaching from the east. Flying due west and identified as a Messerschmitt 110, it was tracked on a somewhat strange course over Scotland until it crashed about an hour later near the village of Eaglesham, south of Glasgow. The pilot came down by parachute, was arrested by a local farmer to whom he gave his name as Hauptmann (Captain) Alfred Horn, and then later said he was Hitler's Deputy, Rudolf Hess, and wished to see the Duke of Hamilton. He had intended to parachute into the grounds of Dungavel House, the Duke's seat, but had missed his target by 30 miles.

After deep research and meticulous checking, the story of Hess and the pilot who landed in Scotland has been set down by Mr Hugh Thomas, a consultant surgeon, in his fascinating book *The Murder of Rudolph Hess*. In 1973, when serving in the British Military Hospital, Berlin, as an officer in the Royal Army Medical Corps, he was required to make two examinations of the man known as Rudolf Hess, Prisoner No. 7 in Spandau. His painstaking, five-year investigation and his book were the direct result of those two examinations.

As a surgeon with considerable experience of gunshot wounds – gained in Northern Ireland – Mr Thomas makes the point that the scars of wounds such as those suffered by Hess, and confirmed by his army record of service, do not disappear, and there was no trace of them on the body of Prisoner No.7. His careful comparison of what was known of Hess before 10 May 1941, and the physical and mental characteristics of the man in Spandau, revealed discrepancies so obvious as to leave him in no doubt that the man who took off from Augsburg was not the man who landed in Scotland.

Hess was a fussy vegetarian: Prisoner No.7, code-named Jonathan while a prisoner of war in England, ate anything and everything voraciously. Hess was a neat, fastidious man, one of the few so-called 'gentlemen' (implying reasonable manners and education) in the Nazi hierarchy: Jonathan ate like an animal. Hess was fit and mentally stable: Jonathan was excessively thin and had to remain in the care of psychiatrists. Hess had a gap between his two front teeth: Jonathan had no gap. Hess's lung wound caused him respiratory problems: Jonathan, when allowed to go on escorted country walks, could out-distance his companions up steep hills and never suffered from bronchitis.

Admittedly, Frau Ilse Hess said that the handwriting of the man in Spandau was that of her husband, but added later she had no specimens dated before May 1941 because Rudolf always telephoned during any period of separation. It is significant that Jonathan refused to see her or her son for 28 years after his landing in Scotland, that he suffered from attacks of amnesia when questioned about the past, and when he finally agreed to see his wife she commented at once on the change in his voice – it was so much deeper. Increasing age has exactly the opposite effect on vocal chords.

The man who parachuted into Scotland had no identification papers of any kind. He produced some photographs which he said were of himself as a child; he also had two visiting cards in the names of Albrecht Haushofer and his father Karl Haushofer; and he had an envelope, postmarked Munich, and addressed to Alfred Horn. He also had a Leica camera later identified as belonging to Frau Hess. There was no name inside his leather flying suit.

As a result of Mr Thomas's research, it would seem that the real Rudolf Hess vanished into the North Sea and that Jonathan, his physical but by no means his mental double, in a different aircraft, possibly from Norway, took his place. He had no identity papers because they had gone down into the sea with Hess.

But how and why did Hess disappear, and why did his double, assumed at his death to be about 93, continue to play the part of Hess and endure more than 40 years of imprisonment? Why didn't he say who he was? The lack of scars on Jonathan's body would appear to be conclusive. Why did Hess try to fly to Scotland in the first place? Why did Göring, known to have been a bitter enemy of the real Hess, appear to be so friendly when sitting beside 'Hess' during the long Nuremberg Trial? Why didn't the British ever take advantage of the arrival of Hess for propaganda that could have been immensely damaging to the Third Reich?

There are many questions left unanswered, although Mr Thomas has tried to tackle most of them. To take the last question first: if the impostor was subjected to the standard interrogation by MI5 experts, his cover would have been blown in about five minutes. It may be that MI5 and the Government knew he was not Hess – certain relevant files have been carefully 'weeded', others are not available and, significantly, precautions were taken to ensure Hess was never photographed while he was in England.

The only clue to the disappearance of the real Hess is in a book called *The First and the Last*, the memoirs of Adolf Galland who commanded fighter squadrons in Holland at the time. He says Göring rang him up 'early in the evening' of 10 May 1941, told him the Deputy Führer had gone mad, was flying to England and must be brought down. According to Galland, he scrambled a few aircraft without giving them a mission; they failed to find anything and returned. Galland took steps to avoid seeing Mr Thomas when he tried to check this. The inference – and it is no more than that – is that Hess was seen and shot down. The substitution of a double presupposes the existence of a carefully prepared plot, because the double had to be briefed, learn Hess's background, practise his handwriting, and so on. So what lay behind this plot?

Mr Thomas suggests it was all inspired by Himmler, author of numerous plots against Hitler. The removal of Hess would in effect be the removal of the brains behind the Nazi Party – and anyone who reads the memoirs of Walter Schellenberg, the man responsible for Nazi Intelligence, will know that nothing was too fantastic for a Nazi plotter. But why go to such lengths in dealing with Hess? It was so easy to arrange fatal accidents in the Third Reich; why go to all the bother of sending Hess's double to Scotland? Presumably because Himmler had some good reason for prolonging the belief that Hess was still alive.

But the theory of Himmler's plot raises all sorts of other questions: how could Himmler have had the foreknowledge of Hess's intentions in time to find, brief and train a double, and transport him to another country so that he could take Hess's place at such short notice? Furthermore, in 1941 Hitler's standing in the German nation was higher than it had ever been, so why should Himmler, whose general appearance was so mild and inoffensive, plot against him, especially when there were rivals like Heydrich and Göring to compete with?

There is a possible answer to the first question in the part that may have been played by Karlheinz Pintsch, the adjutant Hess trusted. He could have been one of Himmler's many agents. Pintsch could have obtained the photographs, the visiting cards and the camera belonging to Frau Hess that were in the possession of the double when he arrived in Scotland. He could also have taken Hess's flying suit from the changing room in Augsburg. In the foreword to Mr Thomas's book, Rebecca West makes the point that the Nazis kept a stable of doubles, for use when the need arose. A man closely resembling Hess physically could well have been spotted before the war began and it would have been a matter of routine for him to acquire the skills and attributes of the man he might have to impersonate at very short notice. Amnesia provided the excuse when he could not answer questions.

Himmler was responsible for the security of high-ranking Nazis. He moved in a mysterious way, and it is more than likely Hess never knew he had a double. But did Himmler plot against Hitler before the tide had turned? After the defeat of the Afrika Korps and the disaster at Stalingrad in 1942 the tide flowed strongly against Hitler, and there was more than one attempt to assassinate him. But were there any plots before that? We do not know for certain, but we do know that for all his apparent mildness, Himmler was a ruthlessly ambitious man as well as a mass-murderer on an unprecedented scale. He had very little time for Hitler and thought he was mad. Himmler controlled the Schutzstaffeln, the SS, which made him the most powerful man in Germany. Walter Schellenberg implies in his memoirs that he was a compulsive plotter.

Sir Winston Churchill in *The Grand Alliance* devotes half a dozen pages to the story of Hess in which there is no suggestion of doubt about his identity. Churchill had made up his mind on the subject and would not be persuaded otherwise.

Why didn't the double speak up, say who he really was and reveal the plot? Himmler had killed himself before the Nuremberg Trial began, and at any time during imprisonment in England, or during the trial, this *doppel-gänger* could have told the truth to the British or Americans, saying he was the victim of a Himmler plot, and asked for asylum. This, perhaps, is the real riddle of Rudolf Hess – the enigma of his double. Mr Thomas explains it by referring to *Sippschaft* – meaning literally 'kin' or 'kindred' – Himmler's system of exterminating a whole family when one member of it was disloyal to the Party. He feels this threat hung over Hess's double and ensured his silence.

Perhaps he is right. Perhaps the old man in Spandau was not Hess, but if he wasn't, surely there must have been some more powerful reason for his silence. Surely, by the time of his death he had outlived his would-be executioners – or had he? We shall probably never know.

Even in death Hess has managed to add to the riddle; did he hang himself or was he helped out of this world: and what has happened to his body?

To say he hanged, or was helped to hang, himself is not strictly accurate since hanging implies suspension from a rope, cord or wire round the neck – the Nazis hanged Admiral Canaris, wartime head of the German Intelligence Service (*Abwehr*), with piano wire in Flossenberg Prison. Hess was garotted with a length of flex, and his death was announced officially on 17 August 1987. His body had been found in the garden pavilion of Spandau Prison, in Berlin, where he had been the sole inmate for the past 21 years. A length of flex had been looped round his neck and tied to the handle of a window. He had been sitting in an armchair and the flex had strangled him when the chair was tilted to one side. Two autopsies failed to establish whether he actually killed himself or was helped to do so, and there were stories, at the time, that Hess at the age of 93 was incapable, physically, of killing himself.

There is, however, the evidence of Pastor Charles Gabel, the French military chaplain at Spandau, who had known Hess for 9 years and had talked to him privately for three hours every week, to the effect that Hess had a deep-rooted fear of lapsing into senility. It is also known that when Pastor Roehrig succeeded Gabel as prison chaplain it used to take Hess several minutes to realize who the new pastor was when he came to visit. Perhaps

Hess regarded this as an indication of the symptoms he dreaded. Thus it is neither unlikely nor impossible that Hess did in fact kill himself, but we don't know for certain.

But what has happened to Hess's body?

Some years before his death, during one of Gabel's visits, Hess gave him a handwritten note which constituted his will. In it, Hess nominated his son, Wolf-Rüdiger, his solicitor Alfred Seidl and Gabel himself as his executors, and stated that he wanted to be buried beside his parents and his brother in the churchyard at Wunsiedel in Bavaria, and the service was to be a simple one, conducted by Gabel.

The time and date of Hess's funeral was fixed for 2 p.m. on Wednesday 26 August, 9 days after his death on the 17th. Pastor Gabel arranged with Hess's family to go to Munich on Monday, spend the night in a hotel, go to Wunsiedel on Tuesday to make the final arrangements, spend the night there and take the funeral service on the following day.

Matters were somewhat complicated by the fact that Wolf-Rüdiger had just had a stroke, had been taken to hospital and was in no state to attend the funeral of his father. Gabel waited in his room for a message from Hess's widow or sister, but the telephone did not ring; and then, while watching the 7 p.m. news on television he learned that the funeral of Hess had already taken place. No details were given.

Next day, the family told him he could return home because there was nothing for him to do at Wunsiedel, and the mystery deepened a few weeks later, in October, when Wolf-Rüdiger asked him if he would come back one day to conduct a proper burial service for his father.

It is obvious that the funeral of Rudolf Hess, the Prisoner of Spandau, would have been an event swamped by journalists, cameramen and television crews, as well as acting as a focal point for neo-Nazis. It is equally obvious that this would have been extremely distasteful to the family and to the West German authorities in Bonn. In the light of Wolf-Rüdiger's remark to him in October, Pastor Gabel believes that Hess's body is in cold storage in some place known only to the family and the West German authorities, awaiting a suitable time for quiet burial in Wunsiedel.

This, too, is neither unlikely nor impossible.

THE TICHBORNE CLAIMANT

The dignified, aristocratic old lady crossed the floor of the room in a Paris hotel, and approached the bed. The man lying on it was vastly more bulky than the slim one she had expected – but so many years had passed . . .

His face was turned to the wall. She bent to look at him: he was not only gross, but coarse-featured, yet there was something about the ears, the way the eyelids under the heavy brows twitched recurrently.

It was enough. 'Like his father!' she declared, and stooped further to kiss him. One of the onlookers, a lawyer, turned to another, a servant, and demanded that she bear witness that, in her sight and hearing, the Dowager Lady Tichborne had acknowledged her long-lost son, Roger.

Had the old lady's gesture and statement been enough to satisfy the rest of the family, the saga of 'the Tichborne Claimant' would have ended then and there. The gross man would have accompanied his mother back to England to take up his inheritance of the fine house, park, lands, ancient church, and exquisite village in the Itchen valley of Hampshire.

For a dozen years, since hearing of the loss of the ship bearing him from South America to the West Indies, Lady Tichborne had kept a candle burning in Roger's room, convinced that he had survived and would come home. Against the advice of her family, she had kept more or less open house at Tichborne House for merchant seamen who might bring a clue or rumour to keep that belief alive. She had advertised extensively in English and Colonial newspapers, offering a handsome reward for information.

He sailed from the port of Rio de Janeiro on the 20th of April 1854, in the ship *La Bella*, and has never been heard of since, but a report reached England that a portion of the crew and passengers of a vessel of that name was picked up by a vessel bound to Australia – Melbourne, it is believed. It is not known whether the said Roger Charles Tichborne was amongst the drowned or the saved. He would at the present time be thirty-two years of age, is of a delicate constitution, rather tall, with very light brown hair and blue eyes. Mr Tichborne is the son of Sir James Tichborne, baronet, now deceased, and is heir to all his estates . . .

That advertisement was printed in Australian newspapers in 1865, and among those who read it was a New South Wales solicitor, Mr Gibbes, of Wagga Wagga. Gibbes had recently acquired a new client, a butcher named Tom Castro, who was seeking his advice on the delicate procedure of bankruptcy. Castro had mentioned that he had some property in England, and wondered whether it might have to be taken into account.

Gibbes called his client again. In casual conversation, he remarked that he would sooner be sailing his boat on Sydney Harbour than sitting in his office on so fine a day. Castro responded that if Gibbes had ever known what it was like to be shipwrecked, he might prefer to stay ashore. As he spoke, he produced his pipe to accept a fill of the lawyer's tobacco. Mr Gibbes's sharp eyes widened when they saw the initials carved on the pipe's stem – RCT.

He determined not to beat about the bush, and, with further leading questions, persuaded Castro to admit that the initials stood for Roger Charles Tichborne, and that he was indeed the missing heir, who had chosen to stay on in Australia and make a new life after being saved from the shipwreck.

On Gibbes's prompting, Castro answered the advertisement. The Dowager's joy on receiving his letter was in no way diminished by its spelling mistakes – her son's Stonyhurst education had not made much impression on him. She recalled his letter:

My dear Mother,
The delay which has taken place since my last letter dated April 22nd, 1854, makes it very difficult to commence this letter. I deeply regret the truble and anxiety I must have cause you by not writing before . . .

There inevitably followed a request for money, but the Dowager remained cautious. Sir Roger had better come home and show himself.

Mr Gibbes was hedging his bets, too. If all went well, he could expect a worthwhile reward in return for lending his client a few hundred pounds. But the fat, uncouth-looking butcher far from resembled the advertised description. Against that, two genuine former servants of the Tichborne family, now living in Sydney, had come forward as a result of press stories that the missing heir had been found. They were a gardener and a West Indian valet, named Bogle, and each said he recognized Tom Castro as Roger Tichborne, though changed by time and hardship.

Gibbes lent some £700, and the claimant, as he had become known in both Australia and England, moved to Sydney, to be in the limelight and raise more funds to enable himself and his wife and child to travel home in style. He had no difficulty in achieving this, throwing money about as fast as it was pressed on him, engaging a secretary, nursemaid, and valet – the old family retainer, Bogle. When there was some difficulty over paying their hotel bill, he bought the hotel with a cheque of a London bank, signed 'Roger Tichborne'.

It turned out later that the missing Tichborne had never banked at that London bank. By this time he had sailed with his entourage for England, where an excited reception awaited him from press and public, if not the Tichbornes. The Dowager herself was away in Paris, where he duly went, accompanied by a man he had met in a billiard parlour, and a lawyer whom the man happened to know. They and the servant were present when Lady Tichborne accepted Castro as her son.

The news provoked a sensation, especially when artists' impressions of the claimant appeared. The Tichbornes, remembering Roger as frail and slight, with sloping shoulders and a little beaked nose, were derisory.

Meanwhile, agents acting for the interested parties were hard at work in England, Australia and South America. The claimant, advised by his knowing valet and lawyers, sought out anyone and everyone who had known Roger Tichborne at Stonyhurst College and during two years as an officer in the 6th Dragoon Guards. Of their own accord, or with prompting, they signed affidavits identifying him. In due course, he had over a hundred men and women prepared to testify in his favour.

It was, however, expensive being a claimant. His supporters' donations dwindled before the onslaught of bills and writs from hoteliers and tradesmen, and the bankruptcy which had started the whole train of events became reality, making his situation a win-or-lose, all-or-nothing affair. All of 18 months passed before a formal hearing was convened, to prepare the way for a full trial of the claim.

Nothing overtly sensational emerged – apart from the claimant himself, who had been keeping out of public sight, and who could now be wondered at in the fullness of his 24 stones. A casual piece of evidence came up which was to have considerable consequences: when questioned about his assumed name of Castro, he was asked if he had known a man called Tomas Castro in South America. He answered, 'Yes, he was a man I knew at Melipilla.' It was observed that no reference to Melipilla had been made in the submissions but the claimant retorted, in his brusque manner, that he had not mentioned every town or village he had travelled through on the journey that was in question, from Valparaiso to Santiago. Nevertheless, his lawyer, spotting the possibility of further useful affidavits, quickly made inquiries in Melipilla about a visiting English milord who had passed that way, and might be remembered. He did not get what he hoped for. The only English visitor at the relevant time, remembered by many, was a poor boy in his 'teens, whom they had called Arturo, but thought was named Arthur Horton or Orton.

The Tichborne family lawyers had also not been slow to follow up this line of inquiry, with the same result. In their case, it caused excitement. They had the claimant watched from the moment of his arrival in London. That very first day in England had been Christmas Day 1866, and he had gone to Wapping, in the London's East End dockland area, and visited a house there. It belonged to a butcher and his family, and their name was Orton. The Tichbornes lost no time in hiring a private detective to visit Wapping again to find out more about the Ortons, in particular a son named Arthur, who had gone abroad a good few years before.

In March 1868 the claimant lost the one witness on whom

above all he depended – the Dowager Lady Tichborne, who died suddenly. Her affidavits, however, were already safely sworn, and there remained all the other witnesses too. He was going to need them more than ever by the time the case came to trial on 11 May 1871.

The trial was bound to be long and costly: as a measure of its importance, it was to be heard before a special jury of men of property. Should the claimant come out loser of such a marathon, it was bound to cost him dearly.

The judge was Sir William Bovill, Chief Justice of the Common Pleas. Mr Serjeant Ballantine, one of the leading counsels of the day, appeared for the claimant, while the Tichborne family was represented by the Solicitor-General, Sir John Coleridge, later Lord Chief Justice. The whole of England hung upon the proceedings and split into factions favouring either side.

The claimant's counsel paraded that long assemblage of generals and colonels, J.P.s, Deputy-Lieutenants of counties, clergymen, ladies, servants and others, all of whom had known Roger Tichborne at various ages and in differing capacities, and were certain that the man claiming to be he was genuine, though admittedly much changed. Having questioned him in their own way, at their initial interviews, and received answers which, on the whole, it seemed to them that only the real Sir Roger could have given, they were satisfied. His eyes were the most memorable feature for most of them.

The eagerness of some of them to be believed led to some exchanges which produced laughter in court. Roger Tichborne had been bad at English and spelling. Judging by the claimant's virtual illiteracy, he had lapsed further with the years. But the late Lady Tichborne had been French, and had brought up her son to speak it fluently, so that even his English had a French accent. When, at last, to everyone's eager anticipation, the claimant himself was put into the witness-box, and was asked about his knowledge of French, he claimed to have forgotten it completely. The subject of Roger Tichborne's three years at Stonyhurst College was debated as follows:

SOLICITOR-GENERAL: Is there more than one quadrangle?

CLAIMANT: What do you mean by quadrangle? You may have a different meaning.

SOLICITOR-GENERAL: What did *you* mean by it?

CLAIMANT: I meant the staircase at the side of the house.

SOLICITOR-GENERAL: Do you really mean to say you do not know the meaning of 'quadrangle'?

CLAIMANT: I mean to say I am explaining to you where it is, and you will not understand.

SOLICITOR-GENERAL: Did you ever go to the Seminary at Stonyhurst?

CLAIMANT: To what?

SOLICITOR-GENERAL: To the Seminary.

CLAIMANT: Do you mean the cemetery?

The claimant said he had studied Hebrew, Latin and Greek.

SOLICITOR-GENERAL: Did your studies in Greek go as far as the alphabet?

CLAIMANT: I don't remember how far they went.

SOLICITOR-GENERAL: Could you read a line of Latin now?

CLAIMANT: No, I'm certain I could not.

SOLICITOR-GENERAL: Is Caesar a Latin writer, or a Greek?

CLAIMANT: I don't remember, but I should think he was Greek.

SOLICITOR-GENERAL: That was the Stonyhurst edition, I suppose.

Sir John, having shown up the claimant's ignorance of his childhood in France, his schooldays, French and any other language, his experience in the army, and other areas where memory could not possibly have been totally expunged by time and travel, then asked him about Wapping, and Arthur Orton. The claimant admitted he had often met him in Australia, and that his agents had been unable to find him to produce him as a witness. Sir John continued:

SOLICITOR-GENERAL: Are you not yourself Arthur Orton?

CLAIMANT: I am not.

SOLICITOR-GENERAL: Are you the son of George Orton, of 69 High Street, Wapping, a butcher?

CLAIMANT: I am not.

SOLICITOR-GENERAL: Were you born in June 1834?
CLAIMANT: I don't think a man can know when he was born.

The trial dragged on for over three months. Serjeant Ballantine had had enough and asked to be allowed to withdraw the suit. The jury agreed, and the judge heartily endorsed its view, adding that the claimant had been shown to be deserving of trial for perjury. He ordered his arrest for trial at the Central Criminal Court. The charges were based on forgery.

The subsequent trial lasted 188 days. When it ended, the Lord Chief Justice, Lord Cockburn, addressing the claimant as 'Thomas Castro, otherwise called Arthur Orton, otherwise called Roger Charles Doughty Tichborne, Baronet', sentenced him to two consecutive terms of seven years each. It was a long sentence, but so had been the trials in the face of much conflicting evidence.

The culprit was released after ten years, returning to Australia, where he published a signed confession of his imposture in the Melbourne *People*. He subsequently retracted this confession before dying in poverty.

The claimant had caused a lot of people much trouble and expense. There are several mysteries which still attend this much-debated case. How could so many people, mostly of impeccable character, have been truly convinced that he was the missing heir? How had he managed to answer correctly many questions about Tichborne's life, yet display appalling ignorance of the most elementary matters?

It has been suggested that the Dowager Lady Tichborne must have known at once that he was not her son, but pretended he was out of spite for the family, with whom she was at loggerheads. Did she die in the happy belief that she had regained the son whom she had always believed would come home – or triumphing at having, so to speak, set a Castro among the Tichbornes?

If he was not Tichborne, was he Castro, or Orton, or neither? A great jurist of more recent years, the late Lord Birkett, wrote: 'The jury in the civil case decided that the Claimant was not Roger Tichborne, and that was undoubtedly the right decision.

The jury in the criminal case . . . said the Claimant was not Roger Tichborne, but a man named Arthur Orton, and in this last finding they were almost certainly wrong.'

Birkett's view was that a 'coarse and unlettered butcher' would not, and could not, have embarked on an imposture of such magnitude, and been able to keep up 'an attitude that for a time staggered the faith of thousands, baffled the force of argument, and seemed to hold in temporary abeyance the very laws of evidence themselves'. It is a view which many lawyers – who may not care to think of their profession having been hoodwinked – are still inclined to share.

WAS CHESSMAN THE RED LIGHT BANDIT?

On the evening of 19 January 1948, a man and a woman were sitting in a Chevrolet, enjoying the view of the lights of West Pasadena, California, which stretched below them. A car pulled up behind them and, since it had a red spotlight beside the driver's door, both assumed it to be a police car. A man with a flashlight approached them and asked to see their identification. Naval veteran Jarnigan Lea fumbled for his wallet, and suddenly found himself looking down the barrel of an automatic pistol as the man pronounced, 'This is a hold-up.'

The man grabbed Lea's wallet, and asked his companion, Mrs Regina Johnson, for her handbag. In the dark, Mrs Johnson quietly dropped a diamond watch and some rings on to the floor. As she reached out to hand him the bag, the man snapped, 'All right, keep your faces turned the other way.' They heard a click as the gun was cocked, and, for a moment, both suspected he was about to shoot. Instead the man said to Mrs Johnson, 'Keep your purse. I'm taking you with me.' He pointed his gun at Lea's head. 'Stay where you are and don't make a move, or I'll let you both have it.' Then at gunpoint, he forced Mrs Johnson to get into his car. His face was hidden by a handkerchief mask.

Once in his car, he ordered her to remove her panties; he threatened her with death until she complied. As she struggled out of her underwear, he unzipped his fly. In tears, the woman told him she was menstruating, and begged him not to rape her. 'All right', said the bandit, 'you can do it this way', and forced her face down into his lap.

Although paralyzed with fear and disgust, Mrs Johnson was also infuriated by the way this brute had humiliated her. When the headlights of a car came up behind them, she said, 'Better drop your mask – it might be the cops.' The man did as she suggested, and she was able to see his face. The passing car proved to be full of teenagers. When its tail-lights had receded, the bandit made her give him $5 from her purse; then, with more threats, allowed her to go back to the other car. The robbery and sexual assault had taken about ten minutes.

When the couple reported the incident at the sheriff's office, the police had no doubt that the robber was the man who had become known as the Red Light Bandit. In the past 24 hours, there had been two other hold-ups committed by a man driving a car with a red spotlight; in both cases he had demanded to see the driver's identification, then taken his wallet. A countrywide bulletin on the Red Light Bandit had gone to police stations. When Jarnigan Lea and Mrs Johnson had been robbed, the newspapers had not yet picked up the story, so they had no reason to be suspicious of the car with the red spotlight.

Less than three hours after the assault, the bandit struck again, in the Hollywood Hills, driving up in front of a car containing a young couple and taking a few dollars. The girl was a pretty airline hostess. Fortunately, the bandit did not seem interested in further attempts at rape. During this robbery, his handkerchief mask slipped, and the young man, a truck salesman named Gerald Stone, was able to see his face. He was convinced that he would recognize him again if he saw him.

Three days later a young man, Frank Hurlburt, was sitting in his car with a pretty 17-year-old girl whom he was escorting home from a dance in a church hall. A car with a red spotlight pulled up in front, and a man wearing a mask ordered him to hand over his money. When Hurlburt said that he had none, the bandit said, 'All right, I'll take the girl.' Mary Alice Meza was forced into the gunman's car. Then the man ordered Hurlburt to pull down the road, on to the hard shoulder, and drove away fast.

Dozens of police cars combed the area. But when they arrived at Mary Alice's home she was already back. She was in tears and badly shaken, but was able to give an account of her ordeal to a policewoman.

The bandit had driven around for several hours, until he found a quiet place. Then he ordered the girl to strip and to climb into the back seat; he removed all his own clothes, except his shoes and socks. Like Mrs Johnson, Mary Alice was menstruating, but this did not deter the bandit. He ordered her to lie, face down, on the seat and tried to enter her; an obstruction convinced him that she was a virgin. This seemed to cause him to change his mind; instead, he ordered the girl to commit fellatio. She pleaded, 'I never did anything to you – why should you do this to me?' The bandit ignored her pleas, and pointed the gun at her head. The girl did as he asked. After this, the man asked her where she lived, drove her to within a short distance of her home, and allowed her to go.

At 6.30 the following evening, on 23 January 1948, two men walked into a clothing store at Redondo Beach, 20 miles away from Hollywood, and pulled out guns. The owner, Melvin Waisler, and his clerk, Joe Lescher, were forced into the back of the store and made to hand over their money. Then the robbers took over $200 from the till, helped themselves to a quantity of clothes, and left in a hurry. Although Waisler was suffering from a head wound, where one of the robbers had struck him with his gun, he hailed a cab and chased the bandits' car, but he soon lost it in the traffic.

This time, however, the bandits were not to escape. An hour and a half later, two policemen in a patrol car saw a vehicle that fitted the description of the robbers' car. When they tried to stop it, the car drove off at top speed. They radioed for help, and other police cars joined the chase. Finally, the vehicle was rammed as it tried to make a wide turn; two men jumped out, and one of them immediately raised his hands; he had a moustache, and sounded like the man who had struck Waisler on the head. The other man made a run for it, and police officer Robert May chased him, firing shots after him. The man turned into a back yard, and found he was trapped; May closed with him, hit him on the head with his gun, and handcuffed him.

There could be no possible doubt that these two men were the robbers of the clothes store for their car contained the stolen money and clothes. At the police station, they identified themselves as David Knowles, aged 32 – he was the man with the moustache – and Caryl Chessman, aged 26. The police looked at Chessman with considerable interest. He was a 'tough-looking egg' – a description given by one of the victims of the Red Light Bandit. He had a long face with a pointed chin and a bump in the middle of his nose, characteristics of the Red Light Bandit observed by his victims, including Regina Johnson and Gerald Stone.

Both the bandits were, according to Chessman's later account, severely beaten by the police. Chessman agreed that it was a 'fair cop', and that he had been one of the robbers of the clothes store. But when the police told him that his description fitted that of the Red Light Bandit, he looked astonished and said, 'I wasn't on the sex jobs, and I don't work late at night.' Pressed about other robberies, Chessman admitted to one near the Rose Bowl in Pasadena. This was the second stick-up of the Red Light Bandit. The victims had been a man called Floyd Ballew and his girlfriend, Elaine Bushaw. Ballew had described the bandit as having a pointed chin.

According to the police, the most damaging admission of all came when Chessman was asked about the red spotlight he had used. He replied that he converted an ordinary spotlight with the use of red cellophane. Chessman was then taken to the house of Mary Alice Meza. As a result of her ordeal three days earlier, her face had swollen so that her eyes were narrow slits. Chessman stood on the sidewalk, while Detective-Sergeant Colin Forbes went into the house and brought the girl to the window. She pointed at Chessman, 'That's the man . . . The one with the crooked nose.'

Forbes had decided that the best way to get a confession out of Chessman was to treat him with sympathy. (This is a well-known interrogation method – a brutal beating, followed by warmth and sympathy from a fellow officer, which induces such relief in the prisoner that he breaks down.) They took Chessman for a T-bone steak in a nearby diner.

'I tell you I'm not a sex maniac,' Chessman insisted.

'Then who committed the assaults?' asked Forbes.

'A guy called Terranova,' Chessman is alleged to have answered. But he declined to say more. The relentless questioning continued at the police station. Finally, Forbes asked him, 'How long did you have the Meza girl in your car?'

Chessman answered, 'About two hours.' He went on to admit the assault on Mary Alice Meza, and to robbing Jarnigan Lea –

although he denied assaulting Mrs Johnson. These were the admissions that would finally bring Chessman to the gas-chamber under the 'Little Lindbergh' law that makes kidnapping a capital offence.

Carol Whittier Chessman – he later changed the spelling to Caryl because he felt Carol looked 'cissy-ish' – had been in trouble since he was in his mid-teens. His childhood had been plagued with illnesses, the most serious of which was brain fever – encephalitis – which left him tone deaf and subject to temper tantrums and moods of violence.

His mother was a quiet, withdrawn woman, a dreamer; his father, a carpenter, was weak and inadequate, a born failure. And at the age of ten, fate struck another blow that must have left Caryl shattered. A neighbour invited him and his mother for a drive, but as the vehicle turned into a traffic stream it was struck by a heavy touring car. Chessman's nose was flattened, giving him the 'tough egg' look, and his mother was paralyzed from the waist down. She was a religious woman and told Caryl it was the will of God; Caryl's reaction was rage, frustration and, later, atheism. At 15 he almost died of diptheria. His father tried twice to commit suicide and the family had to live on poor relief. One day, a schoolfriend saw Chessman's father walk into the house with a poor-relief package, and commented, 'Gee, you must be poor to eat that stuff. I feel sorry for you.' One week later, Chessman committed his first crime – stealing milk and fruit from someone's doorstep.

At school, he was unpopular, being small, puny and bookish, and his schoolfellows called him 'hooknose'. But then he began to acquire a reputation as a criminal, and suddenly, he found people seemed to regard him with a sneaking admiration. He stole cars for 'joy rides', provoked police cars into wild pursuit and committed burglaries. After his first arrest, for auto-theft, he escaped. The next morning he was arrested in a drug store, caught in the act of emptying whisky over a pile of cigars.

After each term in reformatory, he went back to crime, graduating to hold-ups. In 1940, at the age of 19, he married and promised his bride to reform. But after a week or so, he decided that robbery was easier than work, and held up a fuel station. He saw himself as a romantic rebel and liked to imagine that he was the French robber-poet François Villon. Again and again these fantasies landed him in jail; he was in custody almost continuously until a month before the Red Light crimes. He was paroled in December 1947, and immediately joined a criminal gang who extorted money from bookmakers. Then, in January 1948, the Red Light crimes ended his freedom for ever.

His trial began on 4 May 1948, and from the beginning Chessman did not stand a chance. His prospects were not improved by his decision to conduct his own defence. The first witness was Mrs Regina Johnson, who described how she was forced to undress, then perform fellatio. She confirmed that Chessman was her assailant. When Chessman cross-questioned her, he asked, 'How long were you in the bandit's car?' she asked demurely, 'In the car with you?'. Chessman became angry, so much so that the judge had to caution him. No one was surprised when, on 21 May Chessman was found guilty of 17 out of 18 charges, and sentenced to death.

However, for the first time in his life, luck was now with him. Two days before the end of the trial, the court shorthand reporter dropped dead. By law Chessman was supposed to be supplied with a complete daily transcript of his trial, but the hostile judge, Charles Fricke, had denied him this right. Now Chessman seized on this legal loophole and demanded a retrial. He demanded law books and set out to overturn the verdict.

At first, the fight seemed hopeless. After a three-year struggle, the Supreme Court of California confirmed Chessman's sentence, so an execution date could be set. It was to be 28 March 1952. An appeal succeeded and the date was postponed to late June 1952. At this point, Chessman decided to write a book about his struggle. With advance money from the publisher, he hired a private detective to find proof of his innocence. When *Cell 2455 Death Row* came out in May 1952, it became an immmediate bestseller, and turned Chessman into a *cause célèbre*. Surely he could never be executed now? His appeal was turned down the day after publication.

Yet he continued to fight. He made more appeals, which delayed his execution, and wrote two more books. On 2 May

1960, as he was being escorted to the San Quentin gas-chamber, yet another stay of execution was granted. The secretary of the judge who granted it dialled the wrong number when she rang the prison, and by the time she got the right number, the cyanide pellets had been dropped, and Chessman was dying.

It seems almost superfluous to ask: was he guilty? Surely he had to be guilty? He admitted to being the robber of Floyd Ballew, using a red spotlight. It follows, therefore, that he was the man who held up Mrs Johnson 24 hours later. This logic is hard to deny.

However, Milton Machlin and William Woodfield, the authors of *Ninth Life*, the major study of the Chessman case, raise one very serious doubt. They succeeded in examining an early report on the case which included depositions by Mrs Johnson, Gerald Stone and Mary Alice Meza. Oddly enough, Mrs Johnson said that two bandits might have both been present in the car – the second, presumably, in the back. Stone stated positively that there were two bandits, one of whom remained in their 'red light' car. Mary Meza gave the interesting information that she had asked the bandit if he was Italian, to which he replied that he was.

Moreover, the authors tracked down police documents showing that 'red light' crimes were committed before Chessman left prison in December 1947, and after his arrest in January 1948. In one of these, the bandit made a girl get out of the car and forced her to undress.

Witnesses also spoke of the Red Light Bandit as being of slight stature and having a scar on his face. Neither of these descriptions fitted Chessman.

Then who did they fit? The answer is an Italian criminal named Charles Terranova. We may recall that, soon after his arrest, Chessman said that the Red Light Bandit was a man named Terranova. In court, the prosecutor announced that Terranova was a figment of Chessman's imagination. He was not. He was, in fact, a close acquaintance of Chessman's and probably a member of the same criminal gang that he joined on leaving prison in 1947.

When Chessman was first in prison, his father visited him,

and told him that he had received a threat from one of Chessman's friends. His father continued, 'He told your mother to send you word to keep your mouth shut. He said that if you didn't, he'd blow your mother and me sky high some night . . .' This friend could not have been David Knowles, the man who was arrested with Chessman and imprisoned at the same time. It was almost certainly another member of the gang. And *what* was he so anxious that Chessman should not divulge? Almost certainly the identity of the 'other man' in the car.

If Machlin and Woodfield are correct, Chessman himself was that other man, and the man who committed the sexual assaults was Charles Terranova. The two men were so much alike that when Terranova's wife saw a 'mug shot' of Chessman, she asked, 'Where did you get that picture of Charley?' They told her that it was not Terranova, but Caryl Chessman. 'That's funny – he looks just like Charley.'

So in the event it seems that the state of California may have executed an innocent man. They certainly executed a man who possessed remarkable intelligence, pertinacity and courage.

OSCAR SLATER

In most famous miscarriages of justice, the blame can be laid on the imperfections of the legal system. There are, however, a few instances in which fate itself seems to conspire against an innocent victim. Such was the case of the unfortunate Oscar Slater.

It should have been impossible for a thief to get into the home of Miss Marion Gilchrist. The door of her first-floor flat in West Princes Street, Glasgow, had not only an ordinary lock, but two spring locks and a bolt and chain. The back windows were kept fastened. The downstairs street door could be opened by pulling a handle inside the apartment. Inside that flat, Miss Gilchrist should have been as safe as in a fortress.

Moreover, she was seldom alone. Her maid and companion, 21-year-old Helen Lambie, was with her most of the time. Helen had been working for Marion Gilchrist for three years. She found her rather mean – 'She made one kipper do for two' – but they got along well enough.

Why had the 83-year-old woman turned her flat into a fortress? Her main concern was for her remarkable collection of jewellery, which she kept in the flat. Her rings and brooches were in all kinds of hiding places – in clothes in the wardrobe, in secret pockets, in drawers in the spare rooms. Malicious neighbours said she trafficked in stolen goods; in fact, her considerable fortune was the result of shrewd management and frugal habits.

On 21 December 1908, the rain fell steadily on the streets of Glasgow, but the shops were still crowded with late Christmas shoppers. At 7 o'clock, Helen Lambie went out for an evening paper, and locked the door behind her. When she returned, ten minutes later, she was surprised to see a man waiting outside the door of the flat. It was Arthur Adams, the ground-floor neighbour. He seemed astonished to see her. 'There must be something wrong if you've been out.' He explained that there was undoubtedly someone in the flat making loud noises. A few minutes earlier, he had heard a heavy crash from the flat overhead, followed by three knocks. It was a code that he had arranged with Miss Gilchrist – if anything was wrong, she would knock three times on the floor. Adams had hurried upstairs and rung the doorbell, noticing, as he did so, that the street door was open. There was no reply. Then he heard a crashing sound 'as if the servant was breaking sticks in the kitchen'. This was why he was so surprised to see Helen Lambie.

Helen took out her keys and opened the door. And as the two of them stood there, a man came walking towards them from the direction of the spare bedroom. He was well dressed, and looked quite calm and self-assured, as if he had every right to be there. He walked past them, and on down the stairs, then he suddenly accelerated and rushed out, slamming the street door.

Helen Lambie had gone to the kitchen to see if the clothes pulley had fallen down – she was convinced that this was the noise Adams had heard. But the pulley was still in place. Then the girl went into the dining room, calling, 'Are you there, ma'am?' She screamed loudly. Arthur Adams, standing behind her, saw Miss Gilchrist lying on her back, her head towards the fireplace. Her face was partly covered with a rug. When this was removed, they could see that her head was a mass of blood. Now Adams could understand the banging noises, 'like someone chopping wood'. She had been attacked so violently that blood was dripping from the coal scuttle and covered the fireplace. The weapon, apparently, had been a chair. One eye had been driven into the brain. She was still breathing faintly, but was dead before the arrival of a doctor summoned by Arthur Adams who also fetched a policeman. The flat was soon swarming with detectives.

Meanwhile, Helen Lambie had rushed a few blocks to Blythswood Drive, where Miss Gilchrist's niece lived. Helen is reported to have said, 'Miss Birrell, Miss Gilchrist has been murdered, and I saw the man who did it.' When asked by Miss Birrell, 'Who?', she replied, 'I'm sure it was . . .'. Helen Lambie went on to name the man she thought she had recognized. We do not know the name of this man, who was almost certainly the murderer. We only know that Margaret Birrell was shocked and told Helen Lambie she must be mistaken. She also advised her not to mention this to the police, for fear of 'smearing the man's reputation'.

Back at the flat, the police had discovered that the murderer's apparent objective was a wooden box of private papers in the spare room. This had been smashed open, and its contents strewn around, as if someone had been looking for something. Whether he found it is not known. It was quite obvious that robbery was not the motive, for Miss Gilchrist's jewellery lay exposed on various tables – a diamond, two rings and some gold objects. When the various items of jewellery had been assembled from around the flat, Helen Lambie maintained that only one thing was missing: a diamond brooch shaped like a crescent.

There were not many clues. The murderer had lit the gas in the spare bedroom and left his matches behind. On the back of the chair that had probably been used to kill Marion Gilchrist, there was a bloody handprint. That alone should have brought the murderer to justice, for fingerprinting techniques had been in use at Scotland Yard since the beginning of the twentieth century. The first murder to be solved by them – that of two old people in Deptford by the Stratton brothers – had occurred in 1905. But the Scottish police were inclined to stick to old and tried methods.

The murder caused a sensation in Glasgow for Miss Gilchrist had been well known. But although the police expended a great deal of energy and manpower, their results were not fruitful. They issued a description of the suspect, based on the glimpse that Helen Lambie and Arthur Adams had caught, as well as on a sighting of a fleeing man reported by a 14-year-old girl named Mary Barrowman. She had described him as tall and slim, about 28 or 30 years of age, with no beard or moustache. But although a number of men of this description were arrested, none was held.

Four days later, on Christmas night, a man asked to talk to a detective dealing with the Gilchrist murder. He identified himself as Allan M'Lean, a cycle dealer. He was a member of a small club in India Street, and had met there a new member named Oscar Slater, a German Jew. This man, he said, had been offering for sale a pawn ticket for a diamond crescent brooch.

The club in question turned out to be a gambling club, and there the police talked with Slater's best friend, and presumably his proposer, a man called Cameron. Cameron was able to tell them that the man they were looking for had probably now left the country. Early in December he had mentioned that he would be sailing for San Francisco and had tried to sell the pawn ticket for a diamond brooch. But that was long before Miss Gilchrist had been murdered, so the brooch could not be the one they were looking for. Nevertheless, Slater sounded a possible suspect. He was obviously a suspicious character, making money from gambling and, according to Cameron, women. He lived just around the corner from Miss Gilchrist and had only been in Glasgow for 18 months. A plate on his door claimed that he was a dentist but he had no dental equipment.

The police rushed to Slater's flat, and found that they had missed him by only a few hours. He had left for London with a lady friend known as Madame Junio. There was still a 17-month tenancy to run on the flat. Why should he leave unless he had some guilty secret?

The brooch itself proved to be a false lead. It had been pawned on 18 November, more than a month before Miss Gilchrist's death. That meant that there was nothing to connect Slater with the murder of Marion Gilchrist. But the Glasgow police were desperate. Slater was their only suspect and they were determined not to let him go. A man who gambled and lived off women must be some sort of a crook . . .

It was not difficult to discover that Slater had sailed on the *Lusitania* under a false name – Otto Sands. In fact, the suspect's real name was not Slater but Leschziner, and he also called himself Mr Anderson, Mr Sando and Mr George. He was born at Oppeln, in Germany, in 1870, so he was about ten years older than the suspect the police were looking for. Nevertheless, Oscar Slater was arrested when the ship arrived in New York. Helen Lambie and Mary Barrowman were taken across the Atlantic to identify him before the Americans would grant an extradition order. Arthur Adams was also taken to New York, although he protested that he was so short sighted he would not have been able to identify the man he saw leaving Miss Gilchrist's flat. By coincidence, the three Scottish witnesses were standing by the court room door when Slater was brought in. Detective-Inspector Pyper of the Glasgow police later claimed that Helen and Mary exclaimed simultaneously, 'There is the man.' But a marshal named Pinckley, who was escorting Slater, declared it was Charles Fox, the attorney appearing against Slater, who said to the girls, 'That's the man.'

Helen Lambie's evidence seems to have contradicted some of the things she had said earlier. In Glasgow she had said the man was wearing a dark cloth cap and a light grey overcoat; now this was changed to a Donegal tweed hat and a fawn-coloured waterproof. She also claimed that she was able to recognize Slater by his walk, because she had not seen his face. Later, at the trial, she changed this, and claimed to have seen his face.

Slater seemed perfectly calm. And when his attorney argued his case, he insisted that there was no sound legal reason why Slater should be extradited. However, since he had nothing to hide, he was willing to return to Glasgow of his own free will. He was apparently convinced that British justice would soon establish his innocence.

When the s.s. *Columbia* sailed up the Clyde, crowds were waiting to see the famous suspect, and as Oscar Slater disembarked, one sailor was seen to kick him. A light hammer and a fawn-coloured waterproof were found in his luggage, and the police took possession of these. Slater was put into an identity parade, and witnesses who had seen a man hanging around outside Miss Gilchrist's flat on the night of the murder were taken into the room. Since they had all by now seen pictures of Slater, and the rest of the men in the line-up were policemen, they had no difficulty in picking out the chief suspect.

The trial of Oscar Slater opened on 3 May 1909 in the High Court of Judiciary in Edinburgh. The man who stood in the dock had dark hair and a dark moustache, and a Roman nose with a slight twist at the end. He was rather heavily built. The case against him opened with 12 witnesses who had seen a man standing outside Miss Gilchrist's flat on the evening of the murder. One lady said she identified Slater by his profile and said he had worn a heavy tweed coat and had a delicate build. She was surprised to see that Slater was undoubtedly a well-fed man. Mary Barrowman identified a soft black hat as the Donegal tweed hat the running man had been wearing on the night of the murder. She was one of the witnesses who said that the man had been clean shaven; Slater's barber was to testify that at the time of the murder, Slater wore the same black moustache that he now wore.

Perhaps more important than the witnesses who were called were the witnesses who were not called. The doctor who had first seen Miss Gilchrist's corpse, Dr Adams, believed that she had been killed by blows from a chair. The crown case was that she had been killed by the hammer found in Slater's baggage. Dr Adams was not called. A Liverpool policeman, Chief Inspector Duckworth, had been asked to check on Slater's movements in Liverpool before he sailed for America, and report if he behaved like a man in flight from justice. He had discovered that Slater had behaved with complete openness, signing his own name in the hotel register and talked openly about sailing on the *Lusitania*. Inspector Duckworth was not called. A man named Duncan MacBrayne, who had seen Slater standing outside his flat at 8.15 on the evening of the murder, when any reasonable person would suppose he would be in hiding or washing off bloodstains, was also not called.

But the witness who undoubtedly convinced the jury that Slater was guilty was Helen Lambie. She declared dogmatically that the fawn raincoat found in Slater's luggage was the coat worn by the man she saw. She now claimed that she had seen the face of the man, and when asked why she had denied this in New York, replied snappishly, 'I'm saying so now.' At the end of four days, the jury found Oscar Slater guilty by a small majority. As he cried passionately, 'I am innocent,' the judge donned the black cap and sentenced him to death.

Oddly enough public opinion, which had so far been against Slater, now began to turn around. If Slater had broken into Miss Gilchrist's flat to steal her jewellery, why did he not do so? And if Miss Gilchrist went to so much trouble to fortify herself behind locked doors, what was she doing to admit a stranger with a strong German accent? The Lord Advocate at the trial had promised to tell the jury how Slater had come to know that Miss Gilchrist possessed jewellery, but he had not done so. These and similar inconsistencies began to trouble the conscience of the British public, and doubts began to be voiced in the press. The result was that two days before the date set for his execution, the death sentence was commuted to imprisonment 'during His Majesty's pleasure'.

If Slater had been tried in England, he could have turned to the recently constituted Court of Criminal Appeal; but this did not yet exist in Scotland. The man who was most responsible for its establishment in England was the novelist Arthur Conan Doyle, creator of Sherlock Holmes. Three years earlier, Doyle had done his best to right a case of flagrant injustice. A short-sighted Parsee barrister named George Edalji had been found guilty of some horrible cattle mutilations at Great Wyrley in Staffordshire. It was obvious to Doyle that this frail, half-blind little man could never have prowled around at night with a razor. Doyle's efforts failed to force officialdom to admit its error, but raised so much public sympathy for Edalji (who had now been released) that the Court of Criminal Appeal was founded.

Slater had been in jail for five years when Doyle received a letter from David Cook, Slater's solicitor, and its contents shocked him. It seemed that a Glasgow police officer named John Trench had searched his conscience and decided that he had to speak out. It was he who told the story of how Helen Lambie had recognized the intruder in the flat, and he insisted that the police themselves had refused to accept her identification, and bullied or cajoled her into identifying Slater. He also believed that Mary Barrowman had been forced to lie when she identified Slater as the man she saw rushing out of the house. Doyle studied the case, realized that there was not the slightest thread of evidence to connect Slater to Miss Gilchrist, and wrote a pamphlet called *The Case of Oscar Slater*. This led to an official inquiry; but the police merely repeated their actions in 1909 and persuaded Helen Lambie and Mary Barrowman to repeat their identifications of Slater. The police denied that Helen Lambie had disclosed the identity of the intruder to them. Slater was once more found guilty; and the courageous police officer Trench was disgraced.

However, the story was not yet over. In October 1927 *The Empire News* printed an interview with Helen Lambie, now living in America, in which she admitted that she had recognized the intruder, and that the police had refused to accept her identification. She also admitted that the police had forced her to identify Slater as the man she saw. After this, Mary Barrowman also stated that she had also been forced to identify Slater as the man. She now said he was definitely not the man.

The Prime Minister, Ramsay MacDonald, ordered Slater's release pending an inquiry. After 18 years in prison, he was freed. Slater broke down in tears when he saw a bed with fresh sheets and a hot-water bottle. Conan Doyle rewrote his pamphlet and sent it to every member of parliament. Relations between Doyle and Slater cooled when Slater wanted to withdraw his appeal because he would not be allowed to give evidence personally. He was persuaded to drop his objection. Helen Lambie refused to come from America, afraid of a perjury charge; the *Empire News* reporter, however, gave evidence. The result was that Slater's sentence was quashed, and he received compensation of £6,000 from the Scottish Office. Ironically, Slater and Doyle now had a bitter disagreement because Slater declined to reimburse people who had spent money getting him out of prison. Doyle probably wished he had been left in jail.

Who did murder Marion Gilchrist? Almost certainly some close relative – in fact, Doyle was certain that it was her nephew. Only Helen Lambie could have named the killer, and she was never heard of again after Slater's release.

ACCIDENTS

THE GREAT BOMBAY EXPLOSION

Sabotage? A lucky hit by a bomb from an undetected Japanese aircraft? Or a mishap in unloading one of the cargo vessels crowding Bombay's docks that hot wartime afternoon of 14 April 1944? These were only some of the rumours which ran through the teeming Indian city as distraught people wondered what had caused one of the most devastating explosions the world had ever known. Even today, though most of the events leading up to it can be identified, an element of doubt remains.

It all began on a chill February day in Birkenhead, when a convoy of 20 ships left port. One was the s.s. *Fort Stikine*, built two years earlier in Canada from Lend-Lease funds and presented to Britain by the U.S. government. She was a single-screw, coal-burning vessel, one of 26 identical cargo ships whose names were all prefixed *Fort*. This one owed her name to the Stikine River in British Columbia.

Her place lay in an outside lane of the convoy, well away from the other ships; closer proximity would have been a danger to all. As well as crated gliders and Spitfires bound for Karachi for the RAF, her cargo was largely explosives – 1,395 tons of assorted shells, torpedoes, mines and incendiary bombs, all destined for Bombay. One direct hit by a torpedo or bomb, and *Fort Stikine* would be blown to kingdom come.

Leaving the convoy in the Mediterranean, she made her way alone through the Suez Canal and round Arabia, to arrive safely at Karachi on 30 March. Three days later, when all the gliders and Spitfires had been off-loaded, there were plenty of empty spaces left in her five holds. A wartime rule was that no cargo ship should sail with anything less than a full load, and soon stevedores were filling up every available gap with goods for Bombay.

Alexander Naismith, captain of *Fort Stikine*, viewed his additional cargo with disgust and anxiety. Rice, timber and scrap iron were all very well, but the fish manure stank. More seriously worrying were the sulphur, resin, hundreds of drums of lubricating oil, and thousands of bales of cotton. It would have been hard to concoct a more inflammable cargo. His protests at the folly of loading it all on to a ship carrying explosives fell on deaf ears. It was vital for the Indian economy that the raw cotton be rushed to the cloth mills in Bombay. The captain could only grit his teeth and obey orders.

He was not alone in his fears. His chief officer, William Henderson, was sure he had read about the danger of mixing cotton and explosives; but he could not lay his hands on any book which would verify it. His and his skipper's worries were not enough to have the cotton taken off the ship, but they were justified. *Modern Ship Stowage*, a standard reference work published two years earlier in America, identified the fire hazard of cotton, which the merest cigarette end could set alight. Also, 'cotton bales which are, or have been, in contact with oil or grease are very liable to spontaneous combustion'. A similar warning was in the regulations of the Board of Underwriters of New York about explosives: 'These should never be stowed in the same hatch with cotton, but must be stowed in a properly constructed magazine erected in the opposite end of the ship from that in which cotton is stowed.'

Both explosives and cotton were together in three of *Fort Stikine*'s holds. In No. 2 hold, 4,100 bales of cotton weighing 769 tons were packed beneath layers of timber and scrap iron, old dynamos and wireless sets. Above them, stacked on tarpaulins which barely covered the deck between upper and lower compartments, stood 1,089 small drums of lubricating oil. (The maximum number of oil drums allowed above cotton by the New York underwriters was 250.) Right on top, level with a steel tank which contained 124 bars of gold worth £1 million, lay

168 tons of category 'A' explosives, the most highly sensitive kind.

When *Fort Stikine* left Karachi on 9 April she was virtually a floating bomb. 'We are carrying just about everything that will burn or blow up,' the captain told his officers. 'The least we can do is to have extra fire drills.' The whole crew responded with extra zeal, familiarizing themselves diligently with the location and use of the fire-fighting apparatus.

The voyage down the west coast of India to Bombay took three days, made extra uncomfortable for all aboard by their anxiety about the cargo, not to mention the foul reek of fish manure. Everyone was relieved when the *Fort Stikine* anchored early on 12 April in the roadstead between Bombay Island and the mainland. An official came aboard and gave the captain a copy of the Port Rules and Dock By-laws. In return, Captain Naismith signed a declaration that his ship was carrying explosives. International Code required all ships with a dangerous cargo to fly a red flag when entering port, but the practice had been abandoned in wartime since the flag would attract the notice of enemy aircraft and saboteurs. The general formalities completed, *Fort Stikine* steamed to a quayside berth in Victoria Dock with no more indication of her contents than the great wooden horse had given when the Trojans welcomed it inside their city walls. All the same, she was granted a certificate of urgency for offloading to begin at once, and the stevedores' foreman was told that the explosives made up much of the cargo.

Ideally, first priority should have been given to the removal of the category 'A' explosives. But regulations stated that, whereas the safer categories, 'B' and 'C', could be unloaded direct on to the quay, category 'A' must be transferred only into lighters coming alongside the ship. No lighters turned up until almost the following afternoon, so the most dangerous explosives had to be left where they were. The stevedores concentrated instead on the drums of oil. Some of these were found to be leaking. Although it was noticed that the tarpaulines on which they had stood, above the cotton in No. 2 hold, were quite damp with oil it seemed hardly worth bringing to the attention of anyone in

170

authority.

The ship's officers had a more urgent concern: they wished the stevedores would hurry up and take off all that abominable fish manure, lying heaped in No. 1 hold. The Indian dockers jovially agreed. An extra gang was set to helping them clear it, working through the night. What happened that night may have had a crucial bearing on subsequent events. Did one of the stevedores slip away for a few minutes' relief from the disgusting atmosphere, to puff a forbidden cigarette in No. 2 hold? Did the smouldering butt fall among the cotton? It was one of the theories advanced for the start of the nightmare that was about to break over Bombay.

All next day, 13 April, the stevedores worked on. The lighters finally arrived at midday, but only a few of the workers were set to unloading the category 'A' explosives.

The following day's progress in No. 2 hold was good. By lunchtime everything had been cleared from it except a huge piece of scrap iron which weighed three tons, about 11,000 pieces of timber, the 4,100 bales of cotton – and the 168 tons of category 'A' explosives above them.

While the stevedores were away eating and resting in the shade, eight watchmen were supposed to be on guard against sabotage and enforcing the no-smoking rule. Two were sailors, the rest civilians – and on this occasion there was a misunderstanding. The sailors thought the civilians were supposed to be on duty during the lunch hour, while the civilians believed the lunch hour was for their benefit as well. No one was keeping watch.

Could a saboteur have seized this opportunity to slip aboard and into No. 2 hold? It is not beyond the bounds of possibility, and it was during the next hour that the first signs of impending disaster showed. Independently of one another, several men on ships berthed nearby noticed wispy smoke curling up from one of *Fort Stikine*'s ventilators. Convinced that if anything had been wrong someone aboard would have raised the alarm, none of them thought any more about it. In fact, no one in *Fort Stikine* had seen the smoke at all.

The stevedores came back at 1.30 p.m., descended into No. 2

hold – and then clambered up again, talking excitedly. One of the seamen looked for the cause of the commotion, saw the smoke, and raised the alarm at least.

It was over an hour since the smoke had been seen by others. Even so, there should have been plenty of time to put out the fire before it reached the explosives. What followed instead was a series of mishaps, mistakes and misunderstandings which reacted together to bring cataclysmic disaster. If the original cause of it all was never explained fully, no less hard to credit is the way in which events conspired to thwart man's puny efforts.

The first problem was that the fire hoses, rapidly uncoiled and coupled to standpipes, were not long enough to reach into the hold for their jets to be aimed at the seat of the fire. The case was the same with the hoses brought by firemen who manned the dockside emergency trailer pump. Reinforcements were needed quickly, and the fire crew's section leader sent a man to put through an emergency message to the Bombay Fire Brigade. In his confusion, he failed to make the call, only breaking the glass in an ordinary fire alarm. That brought just two engines to the dockside, instead of the required fleet.

The next person on the scene was Captain Brinley Oberst, the ordnance officer in charge of explosives in the docks, who needed only to look at *Fort Stikine*'s stowage plan to realize the gravity of the situation. Warning Naismith that the whole of the docks would be destroyed if the fire reached the explosives, he recommended that the ship be scuttled. It was an impossibility; the sea-cocks in all *Fort* ships had non-return valves, to let water out but not in.

Naismith was still confident that the fire could be put out. The emergency message was at last telephoned to the Fire Brigade. Eight more appliances rushed to the scene, with Bombay's chief fire officer, Norman Coombs, to take charge of operations. Soon 32 hoses were pouring water into No. 2 hold – yet the smoke and heat grew mysteriously. The reason, only discovered with hindsight, was that the water, while still missing the seat of the fire, was flooding the hold. The burning cotton bales were starting to float, rising ever nearer to the explosives above. Far from putting out the fire, the millions of gallons of water were bringing catastrophe closer.

At 2.50 p.m. the general manager of the docks, Colonel Sadler, arrived. His solution to the crisis was to tow the ship out into the harbour and sink her. The idea horrified Coombs, the fire chief. He pointed out that it would mean withdrawing the hoses, which were fixed to dockside pumps. Without their jets to keep the fire in check the ship would blow up before she could reach deep water.

Things might have been better if one person had been in undisputed authority over the rest, and able to issue decisive orders. No one had this power. No one even acted to clear the docks of all other people. Sailors, stevedores, carpenters, engineers and lightermen all went about their usual business. Those who had to pass the hubbub around *Fort Stikine* paused at the spectacle of other people's problems.

There was one last chance to avert disaster. Just before 3 o'clock the trailerpump's driver felt heat on his face. Looking up, he saw the grey paint bubbling over a small patch on the ship's side. The paint suddenly began to fly off in hardened flakes. The man gave a shout – he had found the seat of the fire.

Coombs sent at once for a gas-cutting appliance from the Fire Brigade's emergency tender. If a hole could be cut in the ship's side, a hose could be fed through at last to direct water at the fire's heart. The gas-cutter was brought so promptly that someone else, who had also sent for a gas-cutter from another course, saw it and cancelled his request.

It was the last tragic mistake; the gas-cutter which had been brought was faulty. No searing flame came when a match was put to its jet, only black smoke. Coombs sent for another gas-cutter – but too late.

As 4 o'clock approached, thick black smoke billowed out of the hold, lit by tongues of flame. The firemen on deck staggered back, choking. Recovering for a last heroic effort, they ran forward again and aimed their hoses at the ammunition cases in the hold. It was hopeless. Five minutes later a huge flame shot up, rising higher than the top of the ship's mast. Coombs ordered his men to get clear. They scattered, as Naismith gave the command to abandon ship. The crew, who had stayed on board to a man, were quick to obey. Captain Naismith made a last tour of his ship; then, satisfied that no one remained aboard, he walked down the gangway to join his chief officer on the quayside.

Seconds later, *Fort Stikine* exploded. No trace of Naismith or his chief officer, Henderson, was ever found.

It was like an earthquake and a volcanic eruption combined. Searing metal fragments, bursting drums of oil and blazing cotton bales hurtled through the air, starting new fires wherever they fell. A tidal wave lifted the stern of the *Jalapadma*, a steamer berthed close by *Fort Stikine*, 60 feet into the air and dropped it on the roof of a dockside shed. Hundreds of people were killed or maimed instantaneously; others with them did not suffer a scratch, though some had their clothes blown completely off.

The worst was still to come. *Fort Stikine* had stayed obstinately afloat, and the fire in her raged on. Just over half an hour after the first explosion it reached the 790 tons of explosives in the after hold. A second and far more devastating explosion occurred. Debris was flung up as high as 3,000 feet, to rain down in a lethal shower over a largely residential area inflicting terrible injuries.

Rescue work in the docks was hampered by continued lack of organization. Though some officers set themselves up as a general staff to deal with the situation, they had no guidelines for coping with so widespread a calamity on such a scale. Thousands of volunteers rushed to help, but the acts of individual heroism were offset by many costly mistakes. As the Bombay *Free Press Journal* summed up later: 'Symbolic of the way the city met the disaster is the solitary figure plying his hose without knowing exactly how.'

Army officers requisitioned spare pumps from fire stations for soldiers who had little idea how they worked. When the water pressure soon fell the men decided the pumps were faulty and abandoned them. Any one of the experienced firemen who had been deprived of the pumps would have known that floating cotton had got into the suction hoses and blocked the water flow from the pumps. With the hoses uncleared, the unlimited water supply, only yards from the raging fires, was useless.

Immediately after the first explosion a port offical had sent home all the Alexandra Dock shed supervisors and most of the stevedores. They had gone before it was found that nearly 40,000 heavy boxes of ammunition were in the sheds. Soldiers were sent to shift them urgently, only to be refused entry by docks police because they had no passes. They had to force their way in.

The worst blunder was the decision to abandon both Victoria Dock and the adjacent Prince's Dock to their fate, after several Army and Navy officers agreed that rescue workers could not hope to reach them. Later evidence showed that this was simply not correct; a concerted effort could have saved many ships from destruction.

The volunteers worked on all through the night and into the following day. By now, a shattered Bombay public was clamouring for explanations. Hundreds were dead and injured, thousands were destitute. The explosions had rocked every building in the city. Something terrible had happened; but what? All that the government of Bombay would say was that an accidental fire had broken out on a ship in the docks, resulting in two violent explosions. The military and fire services had soon got the situation under control.

Everyone in Bombay could see that the government was covering something up. Rumours of sabotage spread rapidly, with others claiming that a Japanese aircraft had bombed the docks. Offical denials, coming too late, only added to the rumours, which were believed in Bombay up to years afterwards. The true cause of the fire which set off the explosions was never to be explained to everyone's satisfaction.

The final estimate of those known to have died was 1,376, but the real figure must have been much higher. Thousands were severely injured. Huge stocks of grain were destroyed, and thousands of tons of seeds, spices, butter and oil. Fifty thousand people lost their jobs. Three thousand lost everything they owned. The Allied shipping loss added up to 34,639 tons.

If the disaster itself was exacerbated by incompetence and disorganization, the reverse was true of the rebuilding of the docks. Under Army control, 8,000 men achieved wonders. Incredibly, the docks were restored and working again only seven months later.

THE MOORGATE CRASH

At 8.45 on the morning of Friday, 28 February 1975 passengers waiting on Platform 9 at Moorgate Underground Station in London could not believe their eyes and ears as the incoming train approached.

Platform 9 serves an end-of-the-line tunnel blocked off with buffers and a wall of sand. There were not many passengers awaiting the arrival of the train. The dozen or so who heard its crescendo approach and readied themselves in anticipation of boarding it were casuals rather than regular commuters; they were waiting for this shuttle service to stop, reverse, and take them south to Bank Station where they would get the City Line line, the 'drain', to Waterloo. But though the waiting passengers were few the approaching train was packed, its six coaches carrying probably rather more than 600 commuters, most of them straphanging or crushed into the vestibule ends of the coaches. These were the regulars arriving for the day's work in this, the banking and insurance heart of the City.

What was unbelievable was that the train, instead of slowing down as it entered the station, gathered speed and hurtled towards the blind end of the tunnel. The three or four seconds that elapsed before the front coach hit the buffers were, in the words of one platform passenger, 'Like that moment in a nightmare when you're on the edge of screaming and then you wake up. But this time there was no waking up.'

The cacophony of impact, of ripped steel, shattered glass and falling debris from the roof of the tunnel could have been that of a high-explosive bomb exploding in the middle of the city. The second coach had telescoped into the first, and the top half of the third, split asunder lengthwise, rode over the top of the second.

The first emergency call for help was logged at 8.53 a.m., and ambulances and fire-brigade rescue tenders with heavy lifting gear filled the streets round the station – Moorgate, Finsbury Circus, London Wall – for the rest of the day, and indeed for the rest of the nightmare weekend. The nearest hospital, St

Bartholomew's, seems to have been misinformed as to the extent of the disaster, but it prepared for casualties – the first of which were those passengers who could be extricated through the windows and buckled doors of the rear three coaches. Most of these had broken limbs or were suffering from multiple cuts and bruises and, of course, shock.

The subterranean location caused many additional difficulties, not least for the firemen, whose heavy rescue gear had to be taken down escalators and along tunnel passages that were in many cases too small to admit it without its being stripped down. Oxy-acetylene cutting equipment was the first priority; in the low-powered emergency lighting (the track current was off) firemen started to cut away at the indescribably twisted mass of wreckage of the first three coaches.

By mid-morning a railway-breakdown gang had managed to get within winching distance of the wreck and the rear coaches were being winched back at the rate of 1 inch every ten minutes. Apertures little more than 3 feet square were cut in the wreckage and through these torn and broken bodies were squeezed, those beyond help being set aside with cursory deference to be transported to the mortuary for identification. Of these the number mounted rapidly as the hours passed. The known death toll was to be 23 before the day's end, and nearly twice that number by the time the rescue work was completed. On the platform an emergency operating theatre was set up in the glare of portable arc lights, and the heat of these and the lack of oxygen doubled the difficulties for the rescue teams. The one press man who was allowed on the scene to represent the whole of Fleet Street (he was from *The Daily Telegraph*) reported:

Platform 9 was like something out of a wartime film. The platform was choked with helmeted firemen, police, ambulance men, doctors, nurses, and welfare workers. The *up* escalator was working, bringing up blackfaced and tired rescuers. Everybody was sweaty, ghastly haggard, and filthy; and amidst the sounds of rescue I could hear the sound of people laughing hysterically. The heat was intense – it must have been 120 degrees.

Relays of doctors arrived as and when they could be spared from the nearest hospitals, and supplies of blood for transfusions were rushed from the blood banks. Volunteers donors queued for hours and the midday editions of the papers pictured them and the grim burdens that were being carried on stretchers to the surface. Hurriedly written leaders demanded immediate full-scale public inquiries.

Rumours were rife as to the cause of the crash – the most heavily subscribed being that the driver had had a heart attack. This was contradicted by the semi-knowledgeable, who spoke of the Dead Man's Handle and the fact that this device had been contrived for the very purpose of ensuring safety in the case of the sudden collapse of the driver. Others flourished the opinion that there should always be a second man in the driver's cab in case of emergency. Others again laid the blame fully at London Transport's door for keeping rolling stock far beyond its reliable life. The fact was, of course, that no one knew; and the inspecting engineers who were soon on the scene had very little chance of making their examination while the rescue work was going on.

The evening editions of the newspapers, though also edging toward the censorious, balanced their muted criticism with stories of courage and endurance gathered by reporters waiting above ground in the drizzling rain. Typical was the story of the 19-year-old policewoman who was trapped in the wreckage for many hours and had had to have a foot (and subsequently a leg) amputated and had been asked if she would like one or two of her WPC colleagues to be with her and had spiritedly replied that she'd 'rather have a few men'.

It was not until late Saturday morning that inspecting officers could begin to piece together the grim evidence in the driver's cab. The recovery of the body was of vital importance. It had sustained terrible injuries; but as the pathologist who conducted the first examination said, 'we can deduce a lot from a little'. (The macabre edge to the remark earned him a newspaper comment as 'unfeeling'.) The mutilated corpse had his on-the-spot report attached to it and was taken to the pathology laboratory while the engineers took measurements, made calculations, and cut away the control mechanism for examination by metallurgists and other forensic experts. Perhaps because the impact had been at buffer level it was the undercarriage and bogies that had sustained the greatest damage. What remained of the upper part of the cab would surely reveal, the newspapers insisted, 'vital clues'.

The first vital clue established by the inspectors was that the brakes had not been applied. So, since no man in his right mind would deliberately hurl himself and the hundreds of people in his care toward injury and death, mental aberration or physical incapacity on the part of the driver must have figured; and 'the establishment of one or both of these states', one leader said, 'is the crux of the matter.'

But there were other cruxes, some of them bound up in complex mechanical technicalities that had to be explained by expert witnesses. These were called to give evidence, together with pathologists, analysts, and others at the inquest which opened on Tuesday, 15 April before the Coroner, Mr David Paul, sitting with a jury. The business of the court, he said, was to establish the cause of the tragic deaths of 42 people, and to decide whether the driver himself, or some defect in the train or in the signalling system, had caused the crash.

The signalling system was immediately exonerated. All the signals commanding the approach and entrance to the station had been at clear, and there were in any case safety devices that would have halted the train if a red light had been passed. As for the brakes, there were two systems on every train – the normal one and the Westinghouse emergency non-fail system which the driver could bring into immediate operation if the normal system failed. How? By turning the control beyond its normal stopping point. And the so-called Dead Man's Handle? That was a device to stop the train if for any reason such as physical collapse the driver released his pressure on the main control handle. And had such pressure been released? The indentation of the palm of the hand suggested that it had not.

What about the guard? He had power to apply emergency brakes if he noticed anything unusual, but he admitted to reading a newspaper and failing to notice that the train was entering the station at abnormal speed. 'A feckless young man,' the Coroner remarked.

The questioning went on for two days dealing with technical questions and at the end no positive proof of any fault in the train had been found.

What, then, of the driver?

His name was Leslie Newson, he was 55 years old, a quiet family man with no known emotional or financial difficulties to bother him. He had passed as a fully qualified driver nearly a year previously and his instructor-examiner, Ronald Deedman, confirmed that he was over- rather than under-cautious. Apart from a single occasion when he had slightly overrun a platform his record was unsullied.

Were conditions conducive to safety?

The shuttle run was short and dull and to avoid inattention due to monotony drivers were permitted to do only two hours without a break. On the morning of 28 February, Newson had completed only one hour of his shift at the time of the accident. His wife said he had given her the usual 'peck on the cheek' before leaving home for work, and his colleagues at the depot had noticed nothing unusual in his behaviour.

The Home Office pathologist said that his examination had revealed no sort of disease that would have caused a sudden attack or any hint that Driver Newson was under the influence 'of any substance'. But then came a bombshell. Dr Ann Robinson, a senior analyst, said that Newson's blood had contained 80 mg of alcohol for each 100 ml of blood – an amount equivalent to five single whiskies.

At this Mrs Newson bridled. Through her solicitor she asked for Dr Robinson's evidence to be re-examined. Her husband, she said, was not a pub *habitué* and was most modest in his drinking habits. He liked a glass of brown ale sometimes after his evening meal, but he had not had one on the night before the tragedy. 'There were certainly spirits in the house – Bacardi and things like that for festive occasions like Christmas, but he never touched them. He didn't like spirits.'

'Never a spot to keep out the cold on such a morning as the 28th of February?' she was asked.

'Never,' she replied.

One of Newson's colleagues at the depot confirmed that he had had a cup from Newson's flask of tea and that there had been no taste of alcohol in it. Then another expert witness took the stand and told the court that alcohol levels in the blood can rise considerably through fermentation after death if the blood is not stored in a refrigerator. This way and that, the medical arguments went on for another two days. *The Times* Science Correspondent summed it up:

Though the tiniest traces of alcohol can be detected in the blood and body tissues by new methods of analysis known as liquid-gas chromolography, the conditions of the Moorgate crash make the job of interpreting the results nightmarish. Six experts in forensic science, pathology, and public analysis could see no clear way yesterday of guaranteeing how much alcohol was in the body and how much had formed after death.

Dr Paul dealt with the impasse in his summing up to the jury:

If on the evidence you form the view that the level of alcohol, whatever it is, was the result of swallowing drink, and the level contributed or caused Driver Newson to overrun in this tragic manner, you are entitled to look at his conduct in drinking [and] to say if it measures up to the degree of negligence defined as wicked, careless behaviour, deliberately putting at risk the safety of others. This would entitle you to consider returning a verdict of manslaughter.

The jury was out for one hour and 15 minutes. Their verdict was accidental death.

Through her solicitor Mrs Newson thanked the court for the consideration shown her throughout the inquest and wished Dr Robinson to know that she had never borne her any ill will for bringing forward the matter of alcohol content. 'She was only doing her job.'

So there the matter rests. Was Leslie Newson a secret drinker? Or did he suffer some unaccountable mental brainstorm that caused him to drive blindly towards certain death, thus blackening the pages of London Transport's history with the worst disaster ever? The question marks remain.

ENIGMAS OF AIR AND SEA

KOREAN AIRLINES FLIGHT 007

One day in the late summer of 1985, a Japan Airlines (JAL) Boeing 747 took off from Tokyo for Paris via Moscow. Not long after departure, the aircraft was pushed off its track (known as Romeo 11) by strong westerly winds. There was a good deal of turbulence. In an attempt to make life more comfortable for his passengers, the captain altered course to fly around a large cloud mass. With his attention distracted, and the first officer not sufficiently monitoring his actions, he put his Inertial Navigation System on to the wrong setting. What it amounted to was that he gave it instructions without empowering it to carry them out. The result became apparent some while later, when a couple of Soviet MIG fighters sped into view.

The 747 was 60 miles off course and fast approaching Sakhalin Island – a piece of Russian territory that commands the eastern approaches to Vladivostok. Sakhalin is understandably sensitive from a security point of view. The fighters waggled their wings and went through the rest of the 'get away from here' routine. The pilot realized his mistake, apologized profusely, and sharply altered course. No one was hurt, there was no diplomatic crisis: the only victim was the captain – who was subsequently reduced to the rank of first officer as payment for his error.

Shortly afterwards, Captain Hidermaro Nagano, special assistant to JAL's president, published a paper entitled *Mental Fitness for Duty and Control of Arousal State*. The gist of his findings was that, on a long flight, pilots are apt to be lulled into a state of false security. As the automation in cockpits becomes more and more sophisticated, their dependence upon it is liable to increase.

Their minds may wander; they could become less responsive; and mistakes are possible. The message was emphatic: let the pilot beware.

If we accept Captain Nagano's hypothesis, we may find the solution (or some of it) to a mystery that had occurred about two years earlier – on 1 September 1983. The aircraft concerned was also a Boeing 747, in this case the property of Korean Airlines (KAL). It was shot from the sky by a Russian Sukhoi SU15 interceptor when on a flight from Anchorage, Alaska, to Seoul in South Korea. All 269 people on board died. The place of its destruction was, again, in the region of Sakhalin Island. The pilot of the KAL jumbo, Captain Byung-in, had also made an error of navigation: in this case, he was 365 miles to the north of where he believed himself to be. But, unlike the JAL captain, he either ignored, or else was completely unaware of, the Russians' considerable attempts to attract his attention.

KAL Flight 007 left John F. Kennedy International Airport, New York, on the night of 31 August. It was scheduled to land at Anchorage, after which it would proceed non-stop to Seoul. The weather in New York was appalling. High winds and heavy rain had caused part of the aerodrome to be flooded, and some incoming flights had to be diverted to Baltimore. Among them was one from Georgia carrying Congressman Larry McDonald. Mr McDonald was also chairman of the John Birch Society, an extreme right-wing organization. He was travelling to Seoul to attend the 30th anniversary of the United States-South Korean Mutual Security Treaty. The diversion made him late. He missed the aircraft he had intended to take, and was allocated a seat on Flight 007. Among the other passengers were 81 Americans and 28 Japanese. The rest were mainly Koreans.

The flight to Anchorage was uneventful. Here Captain Byung-in and his crew took over. A flight plan, prepared for him by the Continental Airlines computer at Los Angeles, was sent to Anchorage by telex. There was nothing remarkable about this: it was frequently done. Among its contents was a list of all the waypoints over which the 747 would have to pass on its way to the South Korean capital.

Somebody defined the shortest distance between two points

as a straight line. He was obviously not thinking about navigation. The world, after all, is a sphere. To get from A to B by the most direct course you take the Great Circle route. The section from Anchorage to Seoul is known as Romeo 20. If you have to depend upon a magnetic compass (the 747 in question had two of them, but they were only for emergencies), it involves continually changing course and adds considerably to the workload. But Captain Byung-in, like most other airline captains, had a much better means at his disposal. It is known as INS – inertial navigation system.

Basically, it works by dead reckoning with a very advanced computer at its heart. It can fix the aircraft's position with amazing accuracy; it can reveal the altitude; and it can instruct the automatic pilot. Along the route, there are radio beacons known as waypoints. One minute before a waypoint is reached an amber light comes on in the cockpit. It remains lit until two minutes after the beacon has been passed. By this time, the captain should have radioed his position and his estimated time of arrival at the next. If he fails to do this, an emergency is declared.

The problem about waypoints is their tolerance. If an aircraft is anything up to 200 miles off course as it flies overhead, the reassuring amber light will still light up. It is only when this limit is exceeded that it fails to function. Thus it is possible to make mistakes without being aware of them. Captain Byung-in certainly did.

INS asks only two things of those who use it. The first, and paramount, necessity is that the correct coordinates (the latitude and longitude) shall be punched into its system at the point of departure – it must, after all, be given some clue of its whereabouts. The other is that, when one waypoint has been passed, it should be told the coordinates of the next. It is, of course, also a good idea to inform the automatic pilot that it is to obey these orders. To do this, a so-called mode selector is used. It is easy enough to carry this out, but care is counselled. One click in the wrong direction will put the magnetic compass in control – which is all very well if you wish to use it, but fatal if you believe yourself to be flying by INS.

As this may suggest, the risk of selection of mistakes is small but it exists nevertheless.

Captain Byung-in was an experienced aviator. He had begun his career by serving in the air force as a fighter pilot. Now he was 45 years old. Since joining KAL in 1972, he had put in 6,619 hours at the controls of the 747s and this was to be his 88th crossing of the Pacific. Back on his home ground, he belonged to a small élite of pilots selected to fly the South Korean president about his business. The aircraft he was flying that night had been completed in 1972 for Lufthansa. Seven years later, it was sold to KAL. It had now flown for 36,718 hours and made 9,237 landings.

When Flight 007 took off from Anchorage, the radio beacon was not functioning. It had been closed down 12 hours earlier for routine maintenance. But this was thought to be a matter of no importance. The local radar had a range of 175 miles, and, anyway, there was a waypoint at Bethel, 400 miles away.

Beyond any reasonable doubt, Captain Byung-in made his greatest mistake when the aircraft was still on the ground. When the 747 flew out of radar range, it was seen to be 6 miles to the north of track Romeo 20. This was considered to be a small error – doubtless the captain would correct it. There was nothing to worry about. At Bethel, however, it was seen to be 40 miles off track and this might, indeed, have been an occasion for anxiety. The gap was becoming larger: unless somebody told Byung-in, it might very well continue to increase until it became more than 200 miles – and the lack of an amber light would signal the mistake. But nothing was said. Flight 007 continued on its unfortunate way, its flight crew still under the illusion that it would reach Seoul at 5.33 a.m. local time.

So what had Byung-in done wrong? There are two possibilities. Either he fed the wrong coordinates to the INS before taking off (such mistakes are by no means unknown), or else he put the mode selector to the wrong setting. A trace of the distance flown by the 747 shows that it was flying continuously on a bearing of 246 degrees. This is exactly what might have been expected had the autopilot been keyed in to the magnetic compass – and certainly not what a correctly informed INS would have produced. Obviously there was some carelessness. Nor is it to the credit of First Officer Son, whose duty it was to monitor whatever his captain did – to act, as it were, as his guardian angel.

On a less-sensitive route, the errors would probably not have produced a disaster. When he reached a waypoint and no amber light came on, the pilot would have checked his position, found that he was in the wrong place, and done something about it. The flight would have been late on arrival, but it would have arrived. Romeo 20 passed close to some of the more sensitive parts of the U.S.S.R. On the Kamchatka Peninsula, there is a Soviet nuclear-submarine base and an arsenal of ballistic missiles. Visitors are not welcome. Farther on at Sakhalin Island, there is the naval base that is the key to Vladivostok's supply route. This, too, is remarkable for the number of notices bidding strangers to keep out. By an unhappy coincidence, Red Army units at Petropavlovsk on Sakhalin were due to test a new weapon early that morning. Quite often, the authorities at Tokyo are tipped off about these operations. The air-traffic controllers at Anchorage are informed, and a NOTAM (notice to airmen) is put up. But, on this occasion, the Russians said nothing.

Nevertheless, it seems possible that the Pentagon may have had suspicions that something was scheduled to take place. Among the informative devices at the disposal of the U.S. airforce is a Boeing 707 that has been modified almost out of recognition. It is designated an RC135 and is used for operations classified as ELINT (electronic intelligence gathering). It does not need to trespass into Soviet air space – indeed, at night, it flies with its navigation lights turned on – but this is not to underrate its ability to intercept military radio signals. As it happened, an RC135 was in the vicinity as the 747 blundered towards Soviet territory. The two aircraft were flying at the same height (31,000 feet), the same speed (540 knots), and they came so close to each other that, for 10 minutes, their blips on the Russian radar screens merged (despite President Reagan's insistence that they were always at least 75 miles apart).

Consequently, there may have been some confusion down

The planned, and reported, route of Flight KAL 007, and the path of the reconnaissance aircraft

below. The Soviet authorities knew perfectly well about these ELINT missions, and they almost certainly knew that one was taking place that night. The trouble seems to have been that they did not realize that two aircraft were involved, and that one of them was a civilian plane.

The RC135, its mission completed, quietly turned away and flew back to its base. The 747, now far to the north of its track, pursued its erroneous course.

Down on the ground at Petropavlovsk, the Russians decided that the game had gone on for long enough. The missile test was cancelled, and a flight of interceptors was ordered to become airborne. With the assistance of radar, it was easy enough to locate the target. Oddly, the pilots reported that it was not showing any navigation lights. As subsequent events showed, this was untrue. The 747, albeit misplaced, was flying quite normally.

There was nothing trigger-happy about the exercise. The Sukhoi SU15 pilots wiggled their aircrafts' wings, flashed their lights on and off, even called up Flight 007 on the distress frequency. For some reason that cannot be explained, the flight deck crew of the 747 appeared blind and deaf to all these demonstrations. The giant aircraft just flew doggedly onwards. Eventually, the fighters reached the limit of their range, and had to turn back for fear of running out of fuel.

As Flight 007 cleared the coastline of the Kamchatka Peninsula, the waypoint NIPPI lay 180 miles to the south – just within the 200-mile limit. The amber light came on in the cockpit.

Sakhalin Island is separated from the northernmost island of Japan by a mere 80 miles. The fighters at Petropavlovsk had been scrambled on the spur of the moment. Consequently, they did not get off the ground sufficiently quickly: the 747 was some way ahead of them, and it took time to catch up. On Sakhalin Island, there are four bomber bases and four interceptor airfields. Presumably, the latter had been warned to expect a visitor: at all events, their reaction was very much more immediate. We know what the pilots said once they were in the air, but there was no way of listening to the instructions from ground control.

One of the fighters certainly fired a burst of tracer cannon shells, presumably to attract attention. We can also be reasonably sure that Captain Byung-in never saw them. In any case, he had other things on his mind. He had decided to ascend from 31,000 feet to 35,000 feet, where the thinner air would reduce his engines' fuel consumption. He was busy telling First Officer Son to inform Tokyo air-traffic control of his intentions, and to obtain permission to carry them out. Tokyo gave the necessary assent, but here is a small mystery. Flight 007 must have shown up on the ATC radar scopes by now, but it does not seem to have occurred to anyone to question its position. Not only was it in the wrong place; it was also, as Byung-in would have realized had he paid more attention to what was going on outside, in a very dangerous place.

One possible answer is that a long night was coming towards its end. The controllers were tired and they did not pay sufficient attention to the situation. Another hypothesis is that civil aircraft were in the habit of overflying this corner of the Soviet realm. It probably clipped a few miles off the route and, once one had got away with it, others followed. If this were the case, the ATC men would have found it unremarkable. It might also follow that Russian patience had at last run out. It was necessary to make an example.

To be fair to the Soviet fighter pilots, they had done everything within their power to attract attention and they had failed. Unlike their comrades at Petropavlovsk, they noticed that the 747 was showing navigation lights. But this did not save Captain Byung-in, his flight crew of three, seven stewards, his 13 stewardesses, and his 246 passengers. At the Dolinsk-Sokol air base on the southern tip of the island, somebody pretty high up in the hierarchy reached a decision. Since it had been impossible to get the message across, the intruder must be destroyed. At this point, the nearest Sukhoi SU15 was 2 kilometres away from the jumbo jet. The pilot noticed that it now seemed to be reducing speed – occasioned, one must suppose, by the start of its 4,000-foot climb. He was given the order to attack: an order that, perhaps, surprised him. At all events, he asked, 'Say again.'

Two heat-seeking missiles tore apart Flight 007 – one of them controlled by radar, the other by infra-red. Both found their targets. From First Officer Son: 'Korean zero zero seven . . . rapid decompression . . . descending to one thousand.' That was rather too optimistic. The 747's descent came to an end in the Soya Strait, just outside Russian territorial waters. There were no survivors; and, when the Japanese authorities attempted to retrieve the flight recorder, a Soviet naval vessel turned them away. Ironically the position was 350 miles to the north of waypoint NOKKA. On this occasion there would have been no amber light.

President Reagan was angered by the loss of American lives – especially that of Congressman Larry McDonald. His invective against the Russians reached new heights of acerbity, and the hands of the 'Doomsday Clock' moved another minute or two towards midnight. But the Russian leaders themselves did not appear to have been pleased with the performance of their men on the spot. Heads fell afterwards: possibly because of the unwanted international incident produced by the tragic episode; or possibly because they would have preferred the trespasser to have been taken alive. They were certainly shedding no tears for Congressman McDonald.

There had, indeed, been a previous incident of a civil aircraft that had strayed into forbidden air space being brought down in the U.S.S.R. Nobody was hurt: the aircraft was impounded – but, after interrogation, the crew and passengers were released.

The question in the case of Flight 007, of course, arose as to what, precisely, did the Russians think they were dealing with. Was the 747 seen to be an airliner, or was it mistaken for the RC135 that had gone back to its base? But if the latter were the case, surely an alert military pilot might have been expected to change course and make a run for it – instead of plodding on and getting ever deeper into trouble. Furthermore, greater effort might have been made, not only to attract attention, but also to force it down. The capture of a spy-plane would have served a useful propaganda purpose: the inspection of such an aeronautical oddity would have been richly rewarding. And, then again, its crew would have been useful currency for swopping secret agents. When, in 1960, Lieutenant Francis Gary Powers was shot down over Sverdlovsk flying his high-altitude photo-reconnaissance U-2, he was eventually exchanged for one Rudolph Abel. Before he made one or two fatal mistakes, and was sentenced to 30 years' imprisonment, Abel had been Russia's top spy in the United States. The U.S.S.R. was glad to have him back.

It is not too difficult to deduce the nature of the error that took Captain Byung-in so far off track. It is fairly easy to assume that, down below on Russian territory, someone may have blundered. The real mystery about Flight 007 is why the flight crew allowed so many warnings to go unheeded. Even guesswork contributes little to its solution.

ROYAL TRAGEDY AT EAGLE'S ROCK

On 26 August 1942, the King and Queen were at Balmoral in Scotland. During dinner that evening, His Majesty was called to the telephone. It seemed that Sir Archibald Sinclair, Secretary of State for Air, wished to speak to him. When he returned to the dining room, the monarch looked drawn and sad. He had just learned that, on the previous afternoon, his youngest brother had been killed in an air crash. The RAF Sunderland flying boat, which should have taken the 39-year-old Duke of Kent to Iceland, had smashed into the side of a hill shortly after take-off. He was the first son of a British sovereign to die on active service for 500 years.

Prince George Edward Alexander, second Duke of Kent, was intelligent, well informed, had a good sense of humour, and his easy charm suggested that he was unscathed by the oppressive upbringing his father, George V, inflicted on his sons. His marriage to Princess Marina of Greece was, by all accounts, extremely happy. When in 1936, Edward VIII gave up the throne in favour of Mrs Simpson, there were some who suggested that he should succeed him. The reason was that, unlike the next in line (the Duke of York – later King George VI), he had a son. Kings, it seems, were preferred to queens – at any rate in this corner of the realm.

The first ten years of the Duke's career were spent in the Royal Navy. Afterwards, he held the rank of Rear-Admiral and that of Air Vice-Marshal in the Royal Air Force. When World War II broke out in 1939, he was preparing to set off for Australia to take over the duties of Governor General.

He immediately changed his plans and asked to be excused from the appointment. With Britian pledged to destroy Nazi Germany, he had no intention of departing to the other side of the world. The place for him, he decided, was in the Royal Air Force.

The rank of Air Vice-Marshal was an honorary one: something that involved no executive tasks, a mark of respect that pleased the RAF as much as it did the Duke. It would, he believed, be ridiculous to assume the rank as a working officer. He would, after all, be associating with very much more experienced colleagues. He was, he knew, an amateur; they were professionals. With a nice sense of fitness, he virtually demoted himself to Group Captain. He was appointed to the staff of the RAF's Inspectorate General with particular responsibility for welfare services.

By 1941, he had been promoted to Air Commodore. In the autumn of that year, he embarked in a Liberator bomber for Canada. His mission was to tour airforce establishments set up under the Commonwealth Training Plan. On his way home, he visited New York, where he was a guest at Hyde Park – the home of President Franklin D. Roosevelt. The two men got on famously.

On his return to the U.K., the Duke treated himself to three weeks' leave. His next assignment was to take him to RAF units in Iceland. Departure was scheduled for 25 August. An RAF Sunderland flying boat from 228 Squadron based at Oban would fly him from Invergordon (on the east coast of Scotland) to Reykjavik. On the face of it, Oban might seem to have been a more suitable starting point for the journey. Invergordon was chosen for its proximity to Inverness. It was easier to reach by rail from London.

The commanding officer of 228 Squadron, Wing Commander T.L. Moseley, was an Australian who had graduated at the RAF College, Cranwell. His previous appointment had been at the Air Ministry as Deputy Director of Training (Navigation). His association with flying boats dated back to 1934 – which suggests, rightly, that he was well experienced in their ways. He proposed to accompany the Duke on his trip.

The flying boat in question was W4026 captained by another Australian, Flight-Lieutenant Frank Goyen – 25 years old and with four years in the RAF to his credit. He, too, had considerable experience in the handling of this type of aircraft. Over 1,000 flying hours of his total had been spent in Sunderlands on patrol over the Mediterranean and the South Atlantic. On one occasion in 1940, while keeping a discreet watch on the Italian fleet, his supply of petrol ran low. Nothing daunted, he waited until dark and then came down on to the sea. He and his crew spent the rest of the night watching the distant Italian ships. Then, at dawn and with a flourish, the Sunderland took off and headed homeward.

All told, the crew for the Duke of Kent's trip amounted to ten: two pilots (the co-pilot was also an Australian), two radio operators, a navigator, an engineer, a fitter, and three gunners manning the .303-inch Browning machine-guns. Such, indeed, was the armament, that *Luftwaffe* aircrews used to refer to the flying boats as 'Flying Porcupines'.

The trip to Reykjavik was 900 miles and was expected to last seven hours. However, nothing could be taken for granted. The possibility of bad weather over Iceland had to be accepted: a state of affairs that might make it necessary to abort the landing and to return to Invergordon. With this in mind, it was considered essential that W4026 should set off with her fuel tanks loaded to capacity. The Duke would be accompanied by two aides and his batman. Wing Commander Moseley would be present – making, with the crew, a total of 15 men. The aircraft would be carrying its normal load of depth-charges in case any U-boats were sighted on the flight. What with one thing and another, it would be uncommonly heavy. Once it had settled down at its cruising altitude (5,000 feet for the coming flight), this would pose few problems. The speed would be somewhat reduced, admittedly. The Sunderland is billed as having a maximum of 213 mph. A simple sum makes clear that it would be flying at an average of 128 mph. This, however, was a matter of no concern. W4026 was well able to look after itself – once it had been established in the air. The problem, if such there was, was to get there. Or, to put it another way, the rate of climb would be slow and the distance taken longer than usual.

The most direct route to Reykjavik would have been to follow a northwesterly course after take-off, passing over Sutherland and so over the Atlantic by way of Cape Wrath. The RAF briefing authorities considered and quickly rejected it. As they knew very well, the country is on the hilly side – mountainous, indeed. Two of the peaks exceed 3,000 feet; several more are very nearly that height. With the Sutherland made sluggish by so much weight, such a route would have been foolhardy. Better by far, they decided, to strike off on a northeasterly bearing: to fly over the sea as far as John o'Groats. From there, the pilot would overfly the Pentland Firth and then head directly for Iceland.

Even discounting the possibility of enemy attack, flying in those days was still something of an adventure. The Duchess of Kent was known to worry when her husband took to the sky, but so did many other wives. On this particular occasion, she seems to have experienced no presentiment when, in the late afternoon of 24 August, her husband drove away from Coppins – their country house at Iver, Buckinghamshire – for Euston. She would be seeing him in a week's time, or so she thought: it was something to look forward to.

At the railway terminus, the Duke was met by his private secretary (Lieutenant J.A. Lowther RNVR), an equerry (Pilot-Officer The Hon. Michael Strutt), and his batman (Leading-Aircraftsman John Hales). Strutt was deputizing for the Duke's normal air equerry, who had been taken ill. The train journey to Inverness was uneventful. A car was waiting at the station: at just after 1 p.m. on the 25th, the party walked along the jetty at Invergordon, where a tender was waiting to take them to the aircraft.

Goyen and his crew had flown over from Oban on the previous day. The weather at Invergordon confirmed the good sense of the planners in deciding to resist the tempation of the more direct route. It was pouring with rain and the cloud base was down to 800 feet. On the other hand, the surface of the Cromarty Firth was placid, unruffled by wind. This was not altogether an advantage. A brisk northeasterly and some waves would have assisted W4026's take-off.

Under such conditions, was there a case to be made for delaying the flight: for waiting until the sky cleared and the Sunderland's crew could see what lay beneath them? The authorities decided that there was not. Many flying boats had departed in such circumstances before: there was nothing to suggest that this trip would be jinxed. In any case, W4026 would be passing over the Faroes about midway on its journey.

Up there, or so the meteorological reports suggested, the weather would be likely to improve.

If Goyen and his companions were impressed by the identity of their illustrious passenger, they showed no signs of it. This was just another job of work – probably safer than many of their assignments. The aim, after all, was to deliver the Duke to Iceland and to bring him back again. If a U-boat were sighted, they would certainly engage it, but this was of secondary importance. Transportation, not combat, was the name of this particular game. Nevertheless, their skill at navigation would be tested to the full in such unkind conditions. The Sunderland was fitted with radar, but this was the centrimetric version specifically designed for anti-submarine operations. As an aid to discovering their whereabouts – or for any other purpose, come to that – it was useless.

A few minutes after 1 o'clock, the giant flying boat set off down Cromarty Firth, laboriously trying to get off the water and into the sky. With such a heavy load, it took time and distance, but this was no cause for anxiety. There was plenty of both. And, sure enough, W4026 did eventually heave itself into the air; it climbed slowly and pointed its nose in a northeasterly direction.

We know a little about what happened during the next 30 minutes, but nothing like enough. There was one survivor from the crash, but he was the rear-gunner, snug in his turret at the tail end and some way removed from the cockpit. Almost certainly, Dunrobin Castle, home of the Dukes and Earls of Sutherland, was glimpsed over to port on its remote cliff-top perch. But then the mist closed in and Goyen was flying blind. There is some evidence to suggest that, searching for a hole in the cloud mass through which to catch a reassuring sight of the sea, he brought the Sunderland down to 1,200 feet, but this is mostly conjecture. If it is true, then Goyen cannot have been on top form. Assuming that he was sticking to his planned route, and assuming that he was making the right allowance for drift, no such reassurance should have been necessary. The object, surely, was to gain altitude rather than to lose it.

But strange things were happening on the flight deck of

W4026. A glimpse of the sea, the land, anything, would have been helpful. The Sunderland had indeed strayed from its intended path. At some point after that brief view of Dunrobin Castle, the aircraft must have crossed the coastline and wandered into the air space of Sutherland and then Caithness. Goyen had, by accident, done the very thing his flight plan had been designed to avoid. He was now, unknowingly, in a region full of potential hazards. Not only was he in danger of falling prey to what is described as the 'Rocks in the Sky syndrome' (that is, collision with a mountain), there was also the matter of turbulence.

The action of wind on mountains has been compared to that of waves breaking on rocks. It accelerates, becoming ever more powerful, as it drives upwards towards the peaks. This up-draught can continue until it has reached a point well above the summits. Once over the top, however, it breaks downwards, throwing any aircraft unfortunate enough to be in its thrall into a state of utter confusion. The airspeed can increase or diminish by as much as 50 knots. It can pitch; it can yaw; it can slip. It can also be hurled downwards until it makes a disastrous impact with the ground. Given sufficient altitude, of course, it is not difficult for the pilot to regain control. But, in this instance, altitude was a commodity of which the Sunderland was gravely deficient.

Not very far from the Duke of Portland's Langwell House near Berriedale on the coast, there is a 2,313-foot peak named Morven; and, adjacent to Morven, stands a rather less imposing hill, about 800 feet high, the Eagle's Rock. Its lower slopes were grazed by sheep belonging to a farmer, David Morrison. On that Tuesday afternoon, Mr Morrison was going about his business with his son, Hugh, when the two men heard the sound of an obviously low-flying aircraft. Seconds later, or so it seemed, there was the din of a crash: after that, silence.

The younger Mr Morrison hurried down to the foot of Eagle's Rock, where his motorbike was parked. Calling at crofts and farms on the way, he reached Berriedale in admirably short time. He alerted the police and also informed the local doctor – 71-year-old Dr Kennedy.

Before very long, a search had been organized, but the weather remained obdurate. Groping through the thick mist, the seekers could find nothing. At nightfall, the operation was called off until first light on the following morning. And, even then and with greatly improved visibility, it was not until the early afternoon that the remains of Sunderland W4026 were discovered. Its path to disaster was marked by a swathe scorched in the heather, about 600 feet long by 300 feet wide. There were no signs of any survivors; the aircraft was considerably fragmented. It was Dr Kennedy who came across a figure, half hidden by the heather, wearing the uniform of an Air Commodore and with a platinum watch on its wrist. It seemed to be strangely peaceful, almost as if the man were asleep. The watch had stopped at 1.20. For a minute or two, Dr Kennedy was perplexed. The man's face made him think of somebody – and then he remembered. It was one that he had often seen in the newspapers: the Duke of Kent.

It seems probable that the Sunderland just about cleared the summit of Eagle's Rock and was then flung by a downdraught on to a shoulder jutting out on the far side. The impact caused the tail to break off, hurling the occupant of the rear turret, Sergeant Andrew Jack, clear of the remainder of the wreck. Sergeant Jack was knocked unconscious, received severe burns to his face and hands, but he survived. He managed to extricate himself and to search the wreckage to make sure that nobody else had come through the disaster alive. Again he passed out. When he came to, his overwhelming ambition was to get off the hill: to find some sort of sanctuary. There was, he noticed, a path that led downwards and he decided to follow it.

A colossal effort of will was needed. All the time, as he stumbled over the rough ground, he was tormented by the desire for sleep. After a while, he could endure it no longer. He curled up in the shelter of a clump of bracken and closed his eyes. When he awoke, it was late the next morning. The mist and the overcast had been replaced by a clear, bright summer's sky. He resumed his trek until, at last, he came upon a cottage. The lady of the house gave him a drink of milk and did her best to dress his injuries.

The King was informed that evening. Some days afterwards, he attended his brother's funeral at Windsor and, later, paid a visit to the place where the Sunderland had crashed. 'I felt I had to do this pilgrimage,' he said. Inevitably, there was a Court of Inquiry into the accident. It was, its members concluded, 'due to the aircraft being on wrong track . . . captain changed flight plan for reasons unknown and descended through cloud without making sure he was over water and crashed . . . weather conditions should have presented no difficulties to crew of such experience.'

But did Flight-Lieutenant Goyen change the flight plan – and, if he did, why? Did, for instance, the Duke find fault with it and insist that the more direct route should be taken? To accept such an hypothesis, one has to rethink the characters of both men. As his conduct at the outbreak of war demonstrated, the Duke of Kent respected the professionals. He would certainly have agreed with the recommendations of Goyen – and, come to that, of Wing Commander Moseley. As for Goyen, he was well aware that when he was at the controls of his flying boat he was outranked only by God. He was, indeed, a stubborn man who, when in disagreement, would sometimes say, 'I wouldn't do that if the King told me!' He may not have intended this as more than a figure of speech. Nevertheless, he was unlikely to have been influenced by the prince on a subject in which, he reckoned, he had more than sufficient expertise.

All manner of reasons have been hazarded for the disaster's cause – even the possibility that the crew was drunk. But this, too, seems out of the question. In wartime, aviators are under a lot of stress and they may, on occasion, become excessively thirsty. But this assignment was not an exacting one: it should have been, as they say, 'a doddle'. Furthermore, although Goyen and his crew did not know until shortly before take-off whom they would be taking to Iceland, Moseley did. Without a doubt, his authoritative eye would have been on his subordinates to make sure nobody overstepped the mark. And, finally, they had been carefully selected as men who were stable, skilled and experienced.

The Court of Inquiry attributed the disaster to pilot error, and there seems no reason to doubt this. If you look at a map, you will see that the Sunderland's final resting place is roughly to the northeast of Invergordon. And if, as seems likely from Sergeant Jack's evidence, the crew had glimpsed Dunrobin Castle, this would suggest that the flying boat was not sufficiently far offshore. Wind drift may have nudged it farther to the west, and the turbulence over the hills would have done the rest. The fact that Goyen was flying too low was decisive.

Goyen got it wrong: there can be little doubt about that. How did a pilot of such experience make such a mistake? It is this that remains the mystery of the Duke of Kent's death.

A RED EAGLE FALLING

On the overcast morning of 21 April 1918 a blood-red Fokker triplane, riddled with bullet holes, fell to earth 2 miles inside the British lines near Corbie in the Somme Valley of Flanders. It hit the ground heavily, bounced and lost a wheel, then slid to a halt close to some trenches manned by Australian troops.

The nearest witness to this rough landing was Sergeant-Major J.H. Sheridan of the 3rd Battery, Royal Artillery. He stayed watching and waiting for the pilot to emerge. Seconds passed with no sign of movement. Sheridan ran forward and looked cautiously into the cockpit. The black-helmeted pilot was slumped forward, his head supported by the butt of one of his machine-guns. A thin trail of blood trickled from his mouth, and there was blood seeping from a hole in his chest where the bullet which had gone right through his body had made its exit. Sheridan needed no second opinion to confirm that the German pilot was dead.

The credit for shooting him down went officially to Captain A. Roy Brown, of the RAF. Yet before the day was out several Australian soldiers who had fired at the German aircraft from the ground were vehemently claiming sole responsibility for the kill, and to add to the contest an announcement was made that an RE8 reconnaissance aircraft had brought the Fokker down.

Whose version of events was true and why did this single victory matter so much to the various claimants, when the credit for killing other airmen in similar circumstances was rarely argued? The first question remains unanswered – indeed unanswerable. The answer to the second lies in the identity of the dead pilot. Until that fateful day he had been a living legend, the idol of all Germany, Captain Baron Manfred von Richthofen, the Red Baron himself.

Born on 2 May 1892 at Breslau in Prussia, he was the eldest of three brothers in an aristocratic family. Horsemanship and hunting were second nature to them all. As a horseman, it was only natural for Manfred to join the 1st Regiment of Uhlan cavalry at the outbreak of war, but it was his love of the hunt that inspired him in May 1915 to be transferred into the German Flying Corps. He was accepted, and served that summer as an observer on both eastern and western fronts. During the Battle of Champagne in September he had shot down his first enemy plane, but as it fell unwitnessed in French territory the victory could not be credited officially to him.

It was not long before he applied for pilot training. 'From the beginning of my career as a pilot I had only one ambition,' he wrote later, 'and that was to fly a single-seater fighter plane.' Learning to fly at all proved a nerve-racking business. His first solo flight, on 10 October 1915, ended in a crash landing. Although he failed his first pilot's exam, he completed the course successfully by the end of the year.

Up to August 1916 Richthofen served with a two-seater squadron, based at first near Verdun before being moved for bombing and reconnaissance duties on the Russian front. He might have languished here in obscurity, but for an unexpected visit from the great Oswald Boelcke, whose leadership and tactical appreciation had established Germany as the dominant air power over Flanders. Boelcke had come looking for talented young pilots to join *Jagdstaffel 2*, the fighter squadron he was forming for the new offensive over the Somme. The eager Richthofen made a good impression on Boelcke, and three days later found himself on a west-bound train, heading towards 'the most wonderful time of my life'.

Though Boelcke was only one year his senior, Richthofen idolized him and hung on his every word. Boelcke always stressed that teamwork, not individual brilliance, was the most important element in aerial combat. So long as the team had the victory it did not matter which member of the team won it. Richthofen agreed in theory, even if the streak of arrogance in his character sometimes led him to forget it in practice – as it would on the day he died, when he forgot everything but his love of the hunt and left himself open to attack from more than one quarter.

That day was still far off when he scored his first official victory on 17 September 1916. He was one of four pilots led out by Boelcke from their base at Lagnicourt for a patrol in their new Albatros biplanes. Nearing the front, they came upon a British squadron of eight bomb-carrying BE2cs escorted by six FE2b two-seater scouts. Richthofen singled out an FE and, after one mistimed firing pass, remembered what Boelcke had taught him and slid in beneath his prey in the observer's blind spot. His close-range bullets shattered the FE's engine and mortally wounded pilot and observer. Richthofen exulted over the conquest of 'my first Englishman'.

He wrote that night to a Berlin jeweller, ordering a silver cup, 2 inches high, engraved with the date and the type of aircraft he had shot down. In the next two weeks he ordered a second trophy, then a third, so beginning a matchless, faintly macabre collection which would end only when the jeweller ran out of silver.

Richthofen was in his element now and happier than ever before. He was soon to be stunned, however, by the death of his hero, on 28 October. While flying in close formation, Boelcke's left wing brushed the undercarriage of the plane piloted by his friend Erwin Boehme. Boelcke's aircraft spiralled out of control, and he was killed on impact with the ground.

After they had recovered from the initial shock Boelcke's pupils were inspired to be worthy of their master. Manfred von Richthofen led the way, not least in the race to surpass Boelcke's final total of 40 victories, more than anyone else in the war had achieved up to that point. He was soon into double figures, and his 16th success in January 1917 made him Germany's No. 1 living ace. He was rewarded with his nation's highest military honour, the *Pour le Mérite*, popularly known as the Blue Max. He was also given his own squadron, *Jagdstaffel II*, and proved to be a more brilliant instructor and inspirational leader even than Boelcke.

His new command gave him *carte blanche* to fly whenever he wanted to. His appetite for combat was insatiable and his confidence boundless. His victory tally rose quickly into the thirites. One day, 'for no particular reason', he decided to have his Albatros painted red. 'After that,' as he wrote, 'absolutely everyone knew my red bird. In fact, even my opponents were not completely unaware of it.' The legend of the Red Baron was born.

When the rest of his squadron realized what a conspicuous target he had made of himself they all had their planes painted red as well; but each had a distinguishing splash of some other colour on the rear part of the fuselage, so only the Baron's aircraft was completely red.

April 1917 – 'Bloody April' to the Allies – was Richthofen's golden month. Out of 150 British plances shot down he accounted for 21, taking his total to 52 and racing past Boelcke's record. He felt almost ashamed to have surpassed his hero: 'I am no record-keeper. In the Flying Service records are far from our thoughts. One only fulfils one's duty.'

He went on leave on 1 May, leaving his brother Lothar in command of the squadron. Relieved by the temporary absence from the skies of *le diable rouge*, the British pilots were given new hope by the delivery of two new types of fighter, the Bristol F28 and the Sopwith Camel, which were to turn the tide of the war. The manoeuvrable little Camel would play a crucial part in the final act of the Red Baron's career.

On his return to action on 14 June, Richthofen, by now promoted to captain, found orders which formed part of a new German air strategy. Four of the old *Jagdstaffeln* were to be combined into the first *Jagdgeschwader*, a large mobile unit which, housed in tents and portable sheds, could be moved rapidly by train or lorry to any sector where it was needed most. The *Richthofen Geschwader* was soon imprinted with the stamp of its leader's personality. While the planes which had belonged to *Jagdstaffel II* remained mostly red, other pilots in the expanded squadron had theirs painted all manner of garish colours. They filled the sky like a host of gaudy dragonflies, earning from the Allies the name of 'Richthofen's Flying Circus'. The performances put on by this ruthlessly efficient fighting unit, however, were no laughing matter.

Richthofen had scored a further four victories when, near Ypres on 6 July, he had a close shave with death. A shot from a British plane at 600-foot range wounded him. The bullet drove a furrow across his scalp, splintering the bone. It was all he could do to make a forced landing before he passed out.

It was during his convalescence over the next few weeks that the Sopwith Camel began to give the Allies the upper hand. Richthofen was so concerned that he returned hurriedly to action, his head still heavily bandaged. His hopes rested much on the new Fokker triplanes, designed to climb faster and higher than the old Albatros types. The Fokker was ideal for the Baron, who liked to position himself behind his enemy. He lost no time in having his own new 'bird' painted his customary red.

As summer passed into autumn, however, his comrades saw a corresponding change in him. His talent remained intact, but his appetite for war was lost. At this time he wrote:

The battle now taking place on all fronts has become awfully serious. There is nothing left of the 'lively, merry war', as our deeds were called in the beginning. Now we must fight off despair and arm ourselves so that the enemy will not enter our country . . . I am in wretched spirits after every aerial battle. But that no doubt is an after-effect of my head wound. When I set foot on the ground again at my airfield after a flight, I go to my quarters and do not want to see anyone or hear anything.

He flew less often, devoting time to training pilots. In the six months from September 1917 to the following March he shot down only two enemy planes.

On 21 March, General von Ludendorff launched a full-scale offensive on the Western Front, the last great gamble of a nation on the brink of defeat. Recognizing the urgency of the situation, Richthofen hauled himself out of his depression by sheer will-power. For the next fortnight he was his old self again, raising his tally of victories to 78, as part of a concerted German effort which brought down hundreds of British aircraft. Then, on 8 April, just after his squadron had been moved to Cappy airfield on the Somme heavy rain set in and made flying impossible. In the following week-and-a-half of enforced idleness, Richthofen's depression returned, not helped by the news that the Allies had stemmed the German advance and were counterattacking all along the front.

On 20 April the weather was good enough for him to fly again. He promptly shot down two Sopwith Camels, to lift his score to 80, a figure unsurpassed by any other pilot. His colleagues gave a party in his honour, drinking to 'the one-man army, our leader, our teacher, and our comrade, the ace of aces'.

Richthofen had every reason to be cheerful as he walked out to his trusty red plane the next morning. It was cloudy, but an easterly breeze was keeping off the rain. In three days' time he would go on leave, to spend his 26th birthday on a hunting expedition with friends in the Black Forest. Soon he would be far away from the sights and sounds of war.

Twenty miles away, a squadron of Sopwith Camels was about to take off from Bertangles aerodrome. Its leader was a 24-year-old Canadian, Captain A. Roy Brown, a competent fighter with 12 victories to his credit. He was in a wretched state, suffering constant pain from a stomach ulcer and living on brandy and milk, unable to keep solid food down. A nervous tic twitched at the corner of his mouth. He, too, hoped to be sent on leave soon, far away from the sights and sounds of war.

One of the pilots under his command that day was an old schoolfriend, Lieutenant Wilfred May, making his first flight on active service. Brown told him to stay on the fringes of any dogfight that might develop. He could take a shot if the chance offered, but if he found himself in danger he must break away and head for home.

They had not been airborne long before Brown saw the colourful Fokkers of the *Richthofen Geschwader* attacking two RE8s over the German trenches. He led his Camels to the rescue, and there followed a whirling battle involving a dozen or more planes. Brown knew whose squadron he was up against, and the odds against his surviving the encounter. May, meanwhile, obeyed orders and stayed clear of the mêlée until he saw a stray Fokker. It seemed an easy target. He swooped after it excitedly and opened fire, missing by a wide margin. As he tried to adjust his aim his guns jammed. Furious with himself, but remembering what Brown had said, he veered away and headed for the British lines.

Richthofen, aloof from the battle and biding his time, saw the single Camel break away and decided to give chase. He put his Fokker into a shallow dive, settling in behind, effortlessly closing the gap. May was unaware of him until he heard the dread rattle of the German's machine-guns. Twisting round, he was horrified to see the hunter right on his tail. He sent his Camel into a steep turn, but there was no manoeuvre he could make that would shake off the Red Baron.

Suddenly finding himself free of the dogfight, Brown looked down for May. What he saw made him feel sick: the blood-red Fokker weaving after his friend along the Somme Valley, firing in quick bursts which ripped through the Camel's wings and sent up flurries of spray from the river just 200 feet below. Without a moment's thought, he dived down to the aid of the hapless May.

But surely he was too late? May was exhausted, and certain that his first flight in anger would be his last. 'I was a sitting duck,' he recalled; 'I was too low down between the banks to make a turn away from him. I felt that he had me cold, and I was in such a state of mind at this time that I had to restrain myself from pushing the stick forward and diving into the river, as I knew that I had had it.'

He was wrong. In the thrill of the chase, Richthofen had carried on too far. He was right over the Allied lines. On the ground, two Australians of the 24th Machine-Gun Company, Sergeant C.B. Popkin and Gunner R.F. Weston, fired a long burst as the Fokker flew low over them. Seconds later, Gunners W.J. Evans and R. Buie of the 14th Australian Field Artillery Brigade also opened fire on it with their two anti-aircraft Lewis guns. Simultaneously, Brown pulled out of his dive just above and to the right of the Fokker. Richthofen was so intent on his pursuit of May that he failed to notice Brown, who fired his twin Vickers machine-guns into the triplane's side. Only then did Richthofen look round in dismay. Brown saw his eyes glint behind the goggles for a split second, before he slumped forward in his seat. The Fokker flew on some way before making its rough landing.

Who deserved the credit for shooting down the Red Baron? The Australians, who wanted the glory when they knew the pilot's identity; or the self-effacing Canadian Roy Brown, soon to be invalided to a hospital in England. He himself felt no pride in the official recognition of his 13th victory; his only desire had been to save his friend.

One thing was certain about the Red Baron's death: he who had seemed invincible was no more. His loss, unlike Boelcke's, did not inspire his comrades to greater efforts. It dealt a devastating psychological blow to them and to his countrymen; comparable, Ludendorff thought, to the loss of 30 divisions. The end of Manfred von Richthofen, who had come to be as potent a symbol of the Fatherland as the Prussian red eagle, signified to many minds the beginning of the end of World War I.

THE *LUSITANIA*

Kapitän-Leutnant Walter Schwieger, commander of the German submarine U-20, is accused of torpedoing the Cunard liner *Lusitania*, on 7 May 1915, and thereby causing the death of 1,198 people. Among them were 128 Americans. Britain's official naval historian, Sir Julian Corbett, remarked that, 'Never had there been such a war loss at sea, never one which so violently outraged the laws of war and dictates of humanity.' Schwieger is unable to answer the charges: he was killed on 17 September 1917. Ironically, the agent of his destruction was in marked contrast to his greatest victim. Designated a 'Q-Ship', she was a 1,680-ton freighter named the *Stonecrop*. Outwardly, she looked like any other drudge of the high seas. But, when her disguise was removed, she was seen to be armed with two guns and a quartet of 200-pound howitzers. Schwieger's attack on the *Lusitania* owed little to cunning. His own demise depended upon it.

Inevitably, the German authorities protested that the 31,500-ton Cunarder had been fair game. According to the *Frankfurter Zeitung*: 'The huge steamer now at the bottom of the ocean had, as has been proved, a great quantity of war material and ammunition on board. She was moreover an enemy's vessel, for she was heavily armed. She was an auxiliary cruiser.'

Schwieger may have had similar thoughts. There was, almost certainly, a copy of the 1914 edition of *Jane's Fighting Ships* on board the submarine. In it, he would have seen a profile drawing of the liner. He would also have noted that she was listed as an armed merchant cruiser. If we are to believe the entry in his log, he fired only one torpedo. When he saw that she was carrying a great many civilians, he refrained from discharging a second. In any case, his stock was running low. He intended to conserve them for any targets that might present themselves during his voyage back to Germany.

The explosion occurred at the point just aft of the liner's bridge It did considerable damage in the engine room. On its own, however, it would not have been sufficient to sink the vessel. But the British Admiralty suggested that Schwieger was lying. In Their Lordships' version of the story, two torpedoes were fired. The second delivered the mortal blow.

But why should Schwieger have lied? One torpedo or two: it didn't much matter. His performance would be judged by his sinkings – not by his economy. Furthermore, most of the *Lusitania*'s 754 survivors were in accord with his declaration. There were, they were almost certain, two explosions, but the second seemed to have occurred within the ship.

If, then, Schwieger is to be credited with the truth, what reason had the Admiralty for inventing a second torpedo – and for sticking so tenaciously to the tale? Had they some reason for concealing the real cause of the *Lusitania*'s sinking? Was she not quite such an innocent victim as she seemed?

At the beginning of the twentieth century, it may have appeared to many people that command of the North Atlantic passenger trade was falling into German hands. They were building bigger, faster liners, and Britannia was no longer ruling these particular waves. Since they were being subsidised by the German government, it was not difficult to deduce their other purpose. In time of war, the ships could be taken over by the *Kriegsmarine* and used as raiders. This, clearly, could not remain unchallenged. In 1903, the British Admiralty handed over a considerable sum of money to the Cunard Line as a contribution towards the building of two great ships. The official reason was 'to win back for the United Kingdom the honour of having the two fastest vessels on the Atlantic.'

It may have seemed to be a nice gesture, but the Admiralty is seldom subject to such generosity. Anyone who studied the specifications would have observed that there had to be a mounting for a pair of guns on each forecastle, and that parts of the promenade decks had to be strengthened to take four guns on each side. A minimum speed of between 24 and 25 knots was stipulated and it was made clear that, in the event of hostilities, the ships would be handed over to the Royal Navy. Thus Schwieger's assessment was not unreasonable. The *Lusitania* had been built with a wartime role in mind.

The *Lusitania* and her sister, the *Mauretania*, came into service in 1907. In terms of speed, they matched up to everything that was asked of them. But there was a price: coal. Their consumption was prodigious. Had they been protected by adequate armour, the furnaces would have become even more rapacious.

Neither ship was ever used as an armed merchant cruiser. Until her demise in 1915, the *Lusitania* handled the Atlantic run. The *Mauretania* spent most of World War I at Liverpool. Her only contribution was to serve as a troopship during the Dardanelles campaign.

The rules for the treatment of merchant shipping in wartime had been laid down by the Hague Convention of 1907. The gist of them was that a hostile warship had the right to stop and search. If the vessel was unarmed, and if she was not carrying any cargo classified as contraband, she should be allowed on her way. Whatever the case, suitable provision had to be made for the safety of her crew and passengers.

That was in 1907. The submarine had yet to be recognized for the killer it turned out to be (Germany had only recently constructed her first U-boat). There were, indeed, doubts as to whether it would ever be used against merchantmen. As late as 1 January 1914, Winston Churchill said, 'I do not believe this would ever be done by a civilized power.' But it was done.

The Kaiser and Hitler had two things in common: impatience and a disregard for treaties. On 4 February 1915, the German government declared the sea around Britain as a war zone. 'From 18 February onwards,' the announcement ran, 'every enemy vessel found within this war zone will be destroyed without its always being possible to avoid danger to the crews and passengers.' And: '. . . owing to unforeseen incidents to which naval warfare is liable, it is impossible to avoid attacks being made on neutral ships in mistake for those of the enemy.' At least it was frank.

In theory, the *Lusitania* seemed to be safe against U-boat attack by reason of her considerable speed. She was far faster than any submarine yet produced. Indeed, in early 1915, she had escaped one possibly deadly encounter by making a run for it and getting out of range. But it does not seem to have occurred to anyone to wonder what might happen if, for one reason or another, the liner had to slow down.

During the first week of May 1915, *Lusitania* was berthed in New York waiting to make a return passage to Liverpool. By a coincidence, two advertisements appeared in the city's newspapers. One was placed by the Cunard Line, giving notice of the sailing and proudly proclaiming the great liner as 'the fastest and largest steamer now in Atlantic service'. The other was the work of the German Embassy in Washington. Headed, simply NOTICE!, it had this to say:

Travellers intending to embark on the Atlantic voyage are reminded that a state of war exists between Germany and her allies and Great Britain and her allies; that the zone of war includes the waters adjacent to the British Isles; that, in accordance with formal notice given by the Imperial German Government, vessels flying the flag of Great Britain, or any of her allies, are liable to destruction in those waters and that travellers sailing in the war zone on ships of Great Britain or her allies do so at their own risk.

Perhaps the Cunard advertisement was more persuasive. The stern words of the German copywriter were certainly not heeded by the 1,600 travellers who had booked their passages in the *Lusitania* and who intended to make them, war zone or no war zone. What was more remarkable was that, on the eve of departure, the millionaire Alfred Vanderbilt, Carl Frohman the theatrical producer, and nine others received telegrams warning them not to sail. They were traced back to the office of the *Providence Journal* and dismissed as a newspaper stunt in rather bad taste. It may have been, but, as it happened, the newspaper's editor was receiving payments from British Naval Intelligence. Inevitably one must ask whether the messages were sent at the behest of that organization; and, if they were, why? Was there any reason to suppose that the liner might indeed run into trouble on this particular trip? There is no answer.

As the cargo manifest suggested, she was carrying war materials, although this document was less than honest. It listed 5,000 cases of cartridges (whether for rifles or sporting guns it was not made clear), and some fulminate of mercury fuses. In fact, there were 4,527 boxes of .303 small-arms ammunition for the Royal Arsenal at Woolwich and 1,250 cases of 3.3-inch shrapnel shells (it was later indignantly denied that they contained explosive fillings). And then there was the matter of the cheese and the furs. There were 313 boxes of what purported to be cheese addressed to a dairy in Liverpool. The furs, or so the list suggested, came in 325 bales. But was this true? There is now reason to believe that these were, in fact, aliases for ill-prepared packages of gun cotton – and that these, and not a second torpedo from the U-20, caused the fatal explosion.

The first five days of the voyage were without incident until, approaching the southwest coast of Ireland, the *Lusitania* ran into fog. The master, Captain William Turner, reduced speed to 18 knots and then to 15 knots (the U-20 could accomplish 15.5 knots on the surface, 9.5 submerged). At some point, Turner received a radio message transmitted to all shipping in the vicinity. Its essence was that there were U-boats about, but it gave no details. No signal was addressed to the *Lusitania* specifically.

Captain Turner had his instructions and he tried to abide by them. He was to steer clear of all headlands by a margin of at least 5 miles. He was to follow a zigzag course, to give all ports a wide berth, to be sure that all the portholes were closed, and to keep to the centre of St George's Channel as he steamed towards the Irish Sea. Possibly he did not zigzag sufficiently, and one passenger noticed that several portholes had been left open on D Deck. He recalled thinking that this was rather strange.

On the other hand, Turner very properly doubled the watch, ordered the lifeboats to be swung out, and intended to put 12 miles between his ship and the Old Head of Kinsale on the southwest corner of Ireland.

U-boat commanders understandably favoured this patch of ocean. It covered the approaches to the Irish Sea and, indeed, to the English Channel. Consequently there were plenty of targets – either on their way to or from Southampton and London, or else Liverpool. On 6 May, the U-20 torpedoed the Harrison freighter *Candidate*. Schwieger was (for him) unusually meticulous about observing the niceties of war. The ship, assumed to be innocent, was stopped and searched. A six-pounder and two machine-guns were discovered. When, later that day, her sister, the *Centurion* came into view, she was sunk on sight.

Just before 1 p.m. on the 7th, the submarine lay submerged 12 miles off the Old Head of Kinsale. The crew was taking its lunch when in, Schwieger's words, 'a craft with very powerful engines is running above the boat'. He brought the U-20 up to periscope level and identified her, wrongly, as a small cruiser of the *Pelorus* class. In fact, she was HMS *Juno* of the *Eclipse* class hurrying back to her base at Queenstown (Cobh). The mistake was excusable: the two were very much alike.

The fog seemed to be persisting and Schwieger intended to leave the area: to move towards the Irish Sea in the hope of faring better. But then, at about 2 o'clock, the mist cleared – and there, steaming towards him, was this four-funnelled giant, immaculate in Cunard livery, but which he may have assumed to be an armed merchant cruiser. As she came closer, the captain altered course, presenting him with her flank. The target was too good to ignore; too easy to miss. He fired a torpedo, waited for a few minutes to watch the consequences, and then departed.

Although the sea was tolerably calm and land was only 12 miles away, the business of evacuating the *Lusitania* was a shambles. She sank 18 minutes after the second explosion. The din of escaping steam drowned Captain Turner's commands. The list the liner developed made it impossible to launch many of the boats. Those on one side swung out too far. Those on the other were smashed against the hull. HMS *Juno*, who might have given assistance, was well on her way back to Queenstown – ironically fleeing from the U-boat scare. There was no other vessel in sight. In the end, the only attempts to save life were made by Irish fishermen. The Royal Navy stayed at home.

The loss of the *Lusitania* so enraged Britain against Germany that it seems to have deprived the nation of logical thought. It is popularly thought to have been the reason why, on account of the 128 Americans that died (they included Vanderbilt and Frohman), the United States joined the war against Germany. But this is untrue. Nearly two years were to pass before President

Wilson sufficiently stiffened his sinews to take such a step.

Viewed with hindsight, the disaster poses a number of disturbing questions that ought to have been asked, but which seem to have escaped attention. Why, for example, was Captain Turner not given more specific warnings? A team at the Admiralty, housed in Room 40, not only intercepted German radio signals; its members had also succeeded in cracking the codes. They knew the position of just about every enemy submarine that was out on business. In some cases, they even knew the names of the commanding officers.

The naval force at Queenstown was, admittedly, small. The admiral in charge of it had been given the appointment following criticisms of the way in which he had conducted the Dover Patrol. Four aged cruisers (1897 vintage) were at his disposal and four armed yachts. On the other hand, a division of destroyers was available at Milford Haven on the far side of St George's Channel. The *Lusitania* could have been given an escort, but no escort was given. Alternatively, Captain Turner could have been instructed to proceed up the west coast of Ireland and so to Liverpool by way of the North Channel. Had he done so, he would have avoided the submarine-infested area. He received no such instructions. Then again, he might have worked up the liner to full speed after clearing the fog, and thus have made Schwieger's task more difficult.

Lord Mersey, who had headed the Board of Trade inquiry into the *Titanic*'s sinking, was charged with investigating the loss of the *Lusitania*. Turner, who survived, was exonerated of all blame. It was, Mersey remarked enigmatically, 'a damned dirty business'. To whom or what was he referring? The German U-boat arm? The fact that he knew the *Lusitania* was carrying war materials greatly in excess of those listed in the manifest? To the incompetence of the Admiralty in its handling of the situation (lack of handling might be a better way of putting it)? Or what?

The First Lord of the Admiralty, Winston Churchill, and the First Sea Lord, Admiral Sir John Fisher, were less kind to the unfortunate Turner. Fisher, in a note to Churchill, described him as 'a scoundrel' and hinted that he had 'been bribed'.

Churchill agreed. 'We shall pursue the captain without check,' he replied.

Mersey was right: there was much dirt in the business. Documents have gone missing from the Public Records Office. Records of signals that should be in the Post Office archives are not. The mystery of what happened behind the scenes in the *Lusitania* tragedy will never be completely cleared up – although Colin Simpson has gone as far as anyone can in his admirable book *Lusitania* (1972). The final grisly thought is whether the *Lusitania* was deliberately lured into the U-20's trap by Churchill: a sacrificial lamb that, once sacrified, might bring America into the war on the Allied side. After all, he did say, 'At the summit, true politics and strategy are one. The manoeuvre which brings an ally into the field is as serviceable as that which wins a great battle.' Was he thinking of the lost Cunarder? Were one liner and 1,198 lives a reasonable price to pay for the possibility of making the Triple Alliance a Quadripartite Alliance? The evidence is missing: the mystery remains.

THE HAUNTED U-BOAT

The captain of the American submarine L-2, on patrol off Cape Clear on the west coast of Ireland, could hardly believe his luck. There on the surface, well within range, a German U-boat drifted aimlessly. Through the periscope, he could read the number on her conning-tower: U-65. Quickly, he gave the order to attack.

The L-2 manoeuvred into position, opened her outer torpedo-tube doors — and then something happened that saved her the trouble of firing. With a tremendous detonation, U-65 blew up. The American captain stared in bewilderment. Who or what had intervened at the last moment to rob him of his prize? And had his eyes deceived him, or had he really seen a man standing motionless on the vessel's deck in the seconds before her destruction? If he had, no man aboard the doomed boat would have been in the least surprised. For the strange fate of U-65 was only what every crew member had been expecting: the culmination of a chain of events which had earned her the name of the 'the death-boat'.

The jinx on her could be traced back to the time of her birth, a little over two years earlier. She was built at Bruges early in 1916, one of 24 U-boats of a new design then under construction. Unlike those already in action, whose task was to patrol Belgian waters, harassing fishing fleets and disrupting Britain's supply lines, the new craft were to range farther afield, in search of rich pickings around the coasts of Britain and Ireland. They had a surface speed of 13 knots, twice as fast as their predecessors, and each of them would accommodate a crew of 34, including three officers. Conditions aboard were cramped in the extreme: the men who served on U-boats needed great courage and unusual powers of tolerance to endure being cooped up for days on end in a narrow steel tube at sea, literally breathing down one another's necks. Any outbreak of fear in that claustrophobic environment was sure to have dire consequences.

Fear, however, was far from the minds of the shipyard workers of Bruges. They would never go to sea in the U-boats they were building. But one day, as two of them stood talking, a steel girder being lowered into place for the hull of U-65 suddenly jerked and slid sideways out of its sling. With a fearful crash it fell directly on the two men, who had no time to react to the warning shouts around them. One was killed outright; the other, pinned by the legs, screamed in agony while his colleagues struggled to release him. The girder's tackle was broken, and the wretched man was trapped for an hour before they could lift the massive weight off him. He was rushed to hospital, only to die there soon afterwards.

Horrible though it had been, the fall of the girder was quickly passed off as an accident, and work resumed. A few weeks later U-65 was almost finished, and the day of her launching was at hand, when three workmen went into the engine-room to make a few final adjustments to the diesels. Minutes later, they were heard coughing and crying for help. The men who ran to see what was wrong found the sliding door in the bulkhead unaccountably jammed. Even as they tried to force it open, the anguished voices on the other side fell silent; and, when the rescuers at last broke through to the engine room, they found the men dead on the floor, asphyxiated by poisonous fumes.

Remarkably, an inquiry was unable to establish what had happened. No one could explain how the fumes had escaped, or even what kind of fumes they were. In peacetime, a more thorough investigation might have been held, and U-65 withdrawn from service; but with World War I at its height every vessel was needed, and she was hastily declared seaworthy. With any luck, the bottle broken over her bows when she was launched would fulfil its original purpose of appeasing the wrathful gods of the sea.

On a calm, clear day, with no problems on the horizon, U-65 sailed out with her sister ships for diving trials off the Scheldt estuary. Her captain was determined to start off on a successful note. Before giving the signal for her first dive, he took the precaution of sending a rating up to inspect the hatches and check that the breech of the deck-gun was closed.

What happened next was a matter of some debate. According to the bridge watch, the young man simply walked across the deck and stepped overboard, surrendering himself to the sea like a lemming calmly willing to be drowned. A boat was lowered to search for him, but no trace of his body could be found. U-65 had claimed her sixth life, and she had not yet been once under water.

A successful dive was essential now to keep the crew's spirits up. The watchmen came down from the conning-tower, the hatches were closed, and the tanks opened to let in the water which would remove the boat's positive buoyancy. Smoothly and gradually she sank, until the captain gave the command to level off at 5 fathoms. But U-65 failed to respond. She went on sinking, down and down, stopping only when she came to rest on the sea-bed. And there she stuck.

Apparently, there was a leak in one of the tanks. Compressed air was blown in to clear the water out, but still she refused to move. Minutes dragged into hours as the crew strove desperately to repair whatever had gone wrong. Fumes, perhaps due to water in the batteries, began to poison the air. For 12 hours the horror lasted, and then, almost beyond hope and for no obvious reason, she rose to the surface. The crew staggered out like drunkards, choking, sick, and gasping for oxygen — but the wonder was that they had all survived. Twelve hours was reckoned the absolute maxiumum that it was safe for a U-boat to stay submerged. If they had been trapped in that coffin-like tube minutes longer, the men would have started dropping like flies.

Surely, they thought, the worst was behind them now. They could not have been more wrong. The troubles of U-65 had scarcely begun.

After a complete overhaul at the shipyard, she was pronounced fit for service and sent off on her maiden patrol. The crew took her out to sea with trepidation in their hearts, but the trip was uneventful and she returned safely to Bruges. There she reloaded, taking on fresh supplies of food, ammunition and torpedoes. As the last of these was being lowered through the forward hatch, its warhead exploded.

When the panic and confusion had subsided, five men were found to have been killed, some inside the U-boat and some on deck. Many others had suffered grievous injuries. One of the dead men was the second officer, known to the crew as *der Schwarze* because of his dark complexion. He was by all accounts an imposing figure.

The five dead were buried in a cemetery at Wilhelmshaven, the chief German naval station. U-65 meanwhile, herself badly damaged in the blast, was towed into dry-dock to be repaired. But what had caused the torpedo to explode? The crew muttered darkly of a jinx on their vessel, while the authorities took the view that it was just another unfortunate accident. No one was prepared to consider the idea that a saboteur might be at work.

All too soon, U-65 was ready for action again. The crew, who had been enjoying an extended period of shore-leave, was summoned to assemble a few days before she was due to sail. Evening was drawing on as they trooped up the gang-plank, being counted on board by a petty officer. He was glad to see that they had all turned up — all 31 of them, including the men drafted in to replace those killed with the second officer. But wait! There was a 32nd figure, silently following the others — and it was someone he recognized, someone with a dark face . . .

The captain and his new second officer were discussing plans in the wardroom when the door was suddenly flung open. There, ashen-faced and out of breath, stood the petty officer. The captain rose, frowning angrily. What was the meaning of this interruption? Stammering, the petty officer tried to explain. He knew it sounded impossible, but he had just seen the second officer — the last second officer, he meant — the one buried at Whilhelmshaven: yes, *der Schwarze!*

The captain was a level-headed man, not easily to be convinced by such a wild story. Then again, the petty officer was not the kind of man who usually told wild stories. His cool behaviour during the near-calamitous diving trials had been an example to the rest of the crew. He was clearly not drunk; but perhaps, in the failing light, he had seen someone who looked like the dead man? No, he was adamant, it was *der Schwarze*. Besides, he was not the only witness. A rating called Petersen had seen the figure as well. Keeping cool, the captain asked for Petersen to be brought to the wardroom to give his version of events. But the petty officer explained that Petersen was up on deck, crouching behind the conning-tower and too terrified to move.

The captain, accompanied by his bewildered second officer, went up at once to speak to Petersen. In answer to the captain's questions he confirmed that he had seen *der Schwarze* walk up the gang-plank, move along deck to the bows and stand there, arms folded, gazing out to sea. He had not known that the petty officer had also seen the figure; all he knew was that he was scared out of his wits and had run to hide. When he dared to peep out again, the ghost — for what else could it be — had vanished.

One sighting could have been passed off as a hallucination, the product of one man's overwrought mind. But two? The captain was uneasy. He was no believer in ghosts, but he could believe that someone might have impersonated *der Schwarze*, playing a tasteless joke on the crew which could seriously damage their morale. Over the next two days he questioned everyone connected with U-65, but found no proof that the ghost had been a fake. Nearly all the men believed in it and were afraid – none more so that Petersen, who vanished like a ghost himself just before the vessel was due to sail. He chose to risk a deserter's punishment rather than go to sea in the vessel which he had told everyone was a 'death-boat'.

Yet many months were to pass before the jinx claimed its next victim. Against all expectations, U-65 performed well on her Channel patrols in 1917, sinking some enemy ships and evading pursuit. For the men on board, however, the Allied forces were not the only enemy. Far more powerful and insidious, wearing down their resistance day by day, ever-present among them, was the enemy within — fear.

One of the crew, a petty officer who served on the ill-fated vessel right up to the end of her penultimate patrol, later described the general standard of morale:

U-65 was never a happy ship though we were always fortunate in our officers. There was something in the atmosphere on board which made one uneasy. Perhaps, knowing her evil history, we imagined things, but I am convinced myself that she was haunted. One night at sea I saw an officer standing on deck. He was not one of us. I caught only a glimpse of him, but a shipmate who was nearer swore that he recognized our former second officer. Several of the bluejackets saw the ghost quite often, but others were unable to see it, even when it was pointed out to them standing only a few feet away.

Our last captain but one would never admit the existence of anything supernatural, but once or twice, when coming on deck, I observed him to be very agitated, and was told by the men that the ghost had been walking on the foredeck. When the captain's attention was drawn to it he pretended to see nothing and scolded the watch for being a pack of nervous fools. But afterwards I heard from a mess steward at the officers' casino that our captain openly declared his ship to be haunted by devils.

On New Year's Day 1918, U-65 cruised from Heligoland to Zeebrugge. During their stay in the Belgian port for the next ten days, the crewmen saw nothing of the ghost. They began to hope that the change of year would herald a change in their boat's fortunes. And so it did — but the change was from bad to worse.

Her next mission was to patrol the Channel off Portland, hunting down enemy merchantmen and fishing fleets. All went well until the evening of 21 January. Then, as darkness fell and gale-force winds drove clouds across the moon, U-65 had to surface to recharge her batteries. She was close to a British naval base so three watchmen were on the bridge — two ratings, one facing to port and the other to starboard, and the second officer, looking forward. Peering into the dusk, he saw showers of spray rise and fall around the bows — and in the middle a figure, standing right out on the prow. What did the fool think he was doing? The second officer cupped his hands to his mouth and shouted, warning the man to get below before he was washed overboard. Slowly the figure turned and stared back at him. It was *der Schwarze*.

By now, the other two look-outs had also seen the figure. They called frantically for the captain, and he came into the conning-tower before the ghost had faded. His blood ran cold as the dark face fixed its implacable gaze upon him. What did it mean? Was it an accusation of him for keeping the death-boat at sea, or a warning that the jinx had singled him out as its next victim? The captain saw it, and was afraid. Then he blinked, and when he looked again the apparition had gone.

Immediately, he swore the three look-outs to secrecy. On no account must the crew know what had happened. Try as he might, however, he could not keep a secret of his own altered attitude. A few days later, U-65 torpedoed a supply ship on its way to Plymouth and disabled another with gunfire. The captain had only to give the word to sink it; instead, he ordered evasive action to be taken. Was he afraid of provoking the wrath of forces beyond his ken? If so, he had started to make his peace with them too late.

His doom came like a bolt from the blue, at a time when he must have thought himself safe. Several weeks had passed and U-65 was back at Bruges, moored in a bomb-proof pen in a canal dock. The captain went cheerfully ashore to spend the evening at the officers' casino. As he walked through the streets, the air-raid siren sounded, soon followed by the crack of ack-ack fire and falling bombs. Deciding that his duty lay with U-65 — he turned round to go back. No sooner had he done so than a shell fragment flew at him like a discus, cleanly severing his head from his body.

This bizarre incident prompted the authorities to take the jinx seriously at last. A new captain was appointed — a tough, experienced submariner who was appalled to find his crew on the brink of mass hysteria. On his initiative, an official inquiry into the U-65 affair was held. High-ranking officers conducted the investigation, but all they could find out was the plain fact that most of the crew was in a state of terror. A wholesale transfer of the crew to another vessel, which was what the men wanted, was out of the question; but one by one those most demoralized were drafted to less demanding positions within the German navy.

With fresh crewmen uninhibited by old fears, it was hoped that the submarine would be free of her jinx once and for all. To be on the safe side, however, one of the investigating officers suggested calling in a priest to conduct a service of exorcism on board.

Nothing could have been more calculated to inspire terror in the new men. They had been assured there was nothing to worry about — yet here was a clergyman, commanding the evil spirits of the boat to be gone, in the name of God. So she was haunted, after all! The most hardened of them now believed all the rumours they had heard, and their morale sank lower than ever. With each patrol, their sense of impending doom deepened. The captain furiously forbade any mention of ghosts: but he was powerless to forbid the fear that possessed his men's souls.

The omens were gathering like sharks in May, when U-65 endured a harrowing voyage down the English Channel and across the Bay of Biscay. After two days at sea a torpedo-gunner named Eberhard went mad and screamed till he was bound hand and foot and given morphia to calm him. It seemed to work, and when he had quietened down he was sent on deck with a colleague for some fresh air. The moment he came up through the hatch he went berserk, took a running jump over the deck rail and was swallowed by the sea, never to be seen again.

A little later, as U-65 pitched and tossed in raging seas off Ushant, the chief engineer slipped and broke his leg. Then, while firing on a British tramp steamer with the deck-gun, one of the gun's crew was swept overboard by a huge wave and drowned.

The new captain was beginning to believe in the jinx. Like his predecessor, he adopted a policy of avoiding the enemy ships which ought to have been his prey, convinced that the malign force which seemed to hold the U-boat in its grip would use any combat encounter as an instrument of doom. 'The men were so depressed,' wrote the petty officer who survived, 'that they went about like sleep-walkers, performing their duties automatically and starting at every unusual sound.'

Their last ordeal on that trip came as they made their way home, running the gauntlet of the Straits of Dover. Three U-boats had recently been destroyed in those waters: what price U-65?

But a more mysterious fate was reserved for her. On this occasion, though detected by enemy hydrophones while submerged, and depth-charged on and off for half an hour, she came through unscathed. Then, when the captain decided it was safe to surface, Coxswain Lohmann led the look-outs up to their posts on the bridge. Before they got there, a shell splinter hurtled through the conning-tower and into Lohmann's neck, severing the jugular vein. Bloodied and very bowed, the submarine finally reached Zeebrugge. There, to his great relief, the petty officer was sent to hospital suffering from acute rheumatism. The day before the vessel was to sail again, he was visited by another officer, Wernicke by name, who brought most of his personal belongings to leave in the invalid's care. These were to be passed on to Wernicke's wife, in case . . . Neither man needed to put it into words. Both shared the feeling that the thread by which the keen-edged Damoclean sword of doom hung over U-65 was at last about to snap.

Two months passed before the petty officer heard the news he had known would come. On 31 July 1918, German naval headquarters posted U-65 missing, presumed lost. For a while it seemed that she had disappeared without a trace; then came the report of the American submarine captain who had witnessed her end on 10 July off the Irish coast. It was an end as baffling as any of the disasters that had blighted her two-year life — and could it be true that a lone figure was standing on deck, gazing out to sea, at the moment when she spontaneously blew up? Had *der Schwarze* stayed with her to the bitter end?

The cause of the explosion which destroyed U-65 was never known. One of her own torpedoes may have detonated while still in its tube; or another U-boat may have attacked her by mistake, then slunk away undetected. Perhaps it was an act of sabotage, carried out by an agent willing to lose his own life in the process; or perhaps one of the crewmen, unable to stand the strain any longer, was the agent of annihilation. All these, of course, are natural possibilities. Behind them, formless and inescapable, lurks the spectre of the supernatural.

The mystery of U-65 was thoroughly investigated after World War I by a German psychologist, Professor Hecht, who published a pamphlet on the subject. He was followed in 1932 by Hector C. Bywater, the English naval historian, who conducted his own exhaustive research into the case. Neither could offer a clear-cut solution. Though extremely sceptical Hecht was unable to prove that the ghost was a fake.

On that question the whole mystery hinges. For if the ghost was not genuine – if it was a trick, or else a hallucination arising from the crewmen's fear – then all the other disasters can be explained away as accidents, coincidences, the misfortunes of war. But if the ghost was real – what then? The terrors suffered by the men of U-65 assume a far darker complexion – dark and inscrutable as the face of *der Schwarze* himself.

WHO MINED THE *MAINE*?

Warships have for centuries represented floating 'gunpowder barrels', repositories of large amounts of explosives of many kinds, among which men work and live and sleep without fear of their environment. With proper handling, storage and vigilance, explosives are safe. At sea and in port, strict precautionary measures are enforced against carelessness and sabotage — and yet there have been not a few instances of large warships being blown to pieces without a known enemy in sight. Since the disasters have been so shatteringly complete, it cannot be certainly established whether they were accidental, or deliberately caused.

Such mysteries attend the blowing-up of no less than five Royal Naval ships during World War I: the battleship *Bulwark*, in 1914, at Sheerness, Kent, and two years later and only 5 miles from the same spot, the auxiliary minelayer *Princess Irene*; the cruiser *Natal*, in 1915 at Cromarty Firth, near Scapa Flow; two years after that, the dreadnought *Vanguard*, in Scapa Flow itself; and the monitor *Glatton* in Dover harbour, in 1918.

Each represented a dramatic and tragic loss of a warship and many lives; but none had consequences so far-reaching as the destruction in Havana harbour, Cuba, of the American cruiser *Maine*, on 15 February 1898. Whether it happened by accident or was intended, no one knows, but it was enough to start a war.

Cuba, which in recent decades has had fresh political prominence, was discovered by Christopher Columbus in that mnemonically familiar year, 1492, and was made a colony of Spain. The Monroe Doctrine, which in the nineteenth century pronounced the Americas inviolable by other nations, seemed to many people in the United States to justify their nation's taking under its wing those neighbouring territories already dominated by other powers. Since the Cuban people were in any case in revolt against the oppressive rule of their Spanish masters, this largest of the Caribbean islands seemed ripe for the purpose.

The supplying of Cuban rebels with arms did not prove

enough; it only provoked Spain to send out an even harsher overlord, Captain-General Valeriano Weyler, with a band of young thugs to put the protestors down. They held on, though, encouraged most vociferously by the sustained campaigning of one of the most powerfully irresponsible magnates in the history of the press, William Randolph Hearst, owner of influential newspapers across the United States. His *New York Journal,* in particular, stirred up animosity against Spain and trumpeted the down-trodden Cubans' cause, demanding direct American intervention.

The Spanish Prime Minister, Antonio Cánovas, recognizing the growing likelihood of such a move, promoted a bill advocating Cuban home rule. It caused much resentment in Spain, that once-mighty colonial power — and Cánovas was assassinated. This brought the prospect of America stepping up her aid to the Cuban rebels; and with the Hearst newspapers egging on their government to take Cuba over, the new Spanish premier, Sagasta, ordered the tyrant Weyler home and replaced him with a milder commander, Marshal Blanco, who had orders to smooth the way towards Cuban autonomy.

This was not enough for William Randolph Hearst and the firebrands of the Republican Party. They wanted a dramatic demonstration of America's power to make other nations toe the line, certain to prove a re-election winner for the McKinley administration, next time round.

Not all Cubans wanted home rule, either. Many had prospered under the Spaniards, while others preferred the devil they knew to the unknown one who might spring from their own midst. Spain took advantage of the divisions among Cuban sympathies, and of the helplessness of a poor, disease-stricken island people. Spanish soldiers provoked an outbreak of rioting in Havana on 15 June 1898, which they were easily able to put down, in what they believed would be seen as a show of strength. In fact, they had given the U.S.A. the excuse to take action. In classic terminology, the best interests of the Cuban people and the wish to promote friendship between nations was given as the excuse for sending out to Havana the USS *Maine.*

The cruiser's arrival on 25 January 1898 by no means heralded an attack or invasion. She exchanged the customary courtesies with the shore establishment and was conducted by a local pilot to a mooring place which met with the approval of her commanding officer, Captain Charles D. Sigsbee. Her crew was not allowed ashore.

The threat she posed was a silent one, an insult, in the eyes of the throng who watched her from the waterfront. Never mind that she lay under the harbour batteries at Morro Castle, which could have blown her out of the water at any time. Never mind that the only comings and goings between ship and shore were strictly formal, with the crew remaining pent up on board in the uncomfortable heat. Never mind that, in herself, she was unprepossessing, a second-rate warship of obsolete design, though only a few years old. If anything, this made the insult more acute; had she been the pride of the U.S. navy, the Spanish, with their own great naval history, might have felt a little complimented.

Sightseers on a ferry boat jeered her. Leaflets began circulating throughout the Spanish in Havana. One of them bore the bold heading, LONG LIVE SPAIN WITH HONOUR:

Why do you allow yourselves to be insulted in this way? If your brave and beloved Weyler had not been recalled he would have finished off the rebellious rabble who are trampling our flag and our honour. And now these Yankee pigs, who meddle in our affairs, humiliate us to the last degree with their man-of-war. Spaniards, the moment for action is come. Do not fall asleep. Let us show these vile traitors that we have not lost all our pride, and that we know how to protest with the vigour worthy of a nation such as our Spain has always been and always will be!

Death to the Americans!
Death to Autonomy!
Long Live Spain!
Long Live Weyler!

Less provocatively, Spain reciprocated America's 'friendly' gesture of sending the *Maine* to Havana by dispatching a cruiser of the Spanish navy to New York. It was a polite by pointed tit-for-tat. Her captain and officers were courteously greeted by U.S. officials, as Captain Sigsbee and his officers had been by the Havana Spanish.

For three hot, humid weeks the *Maine* rested at her mooring. Distantly, in New York and elsewhere in the United States, the trumpetings of the Hearst newspapers sounded ever louder and wilder, denouncing Spain's promise of Cuban home rule as a sham, and insisting on action without more delay. Captain Sigsbee, in his fifties, distinguished as a hydrographer but not noted for sharp discipline or running a 'tight' ship, felt that the point had been made. If one U.S. warship could lie complacently in Havana harbour without the Spanish daring to act against it, Cuba could be taken over at any chosen time.

Only the *Maine*'s crew grumbled, in their cramped, stuffy quarters, while the watchers on the shore sipped their evening drinks in the sultry heat of the evening of 15 February. One detail was different this evening, though. The warship had swung to a new posture at her mooring. As she now lay, her main armament was trained on the city and the shore fortifications.

If those who imagined any significance in this could have seen aboard, they would have found Captain Sigsbee no more urgently occupied than writing in his cabin. The crew had turned in for another restless night in the heat. The bugler had sounded 'taps' for lights-out. Suddenly the *Maine* blew up.

She went with a thunderous roar and a flash like blue lightning, vivid enough to melt the darkness for some seconds. Debris flew high into the air, to clatter and splash all around, until at last there was nothing to be heard but the cries of men in pain and fear.

There were some cheers from those ashore whose instinctive elation overrode any natural compassion. But many others cried out with concern, and there were even tears for what must undoubtedly prove to be a heavy casualty toll. Spanish and Cubans hastened to launch rescue craft, to converge on the now blazing hulk, already listing to port and going down by the head.

The water was crowded with sailors, some splashing in a

dazed attempt to swim, others floating, dead or unconscious. Captain Sigsbee had ordered the magazines flooded, but it was happening already, by natural process. Only three out of 15 ship's boats could be used. One thing Sigsbee did not neglect to do was post watchmen. For all he knew, his ship had been the target for the first strike in an outbreak of war. He had heard the gruesome cheers of those fanatics who had seen the disaster as a cause for rejoicing, and there was no knowing whether attacks on the survivors might follow.

In fact, every effort was made to save them, the rescue boats risking the danger that the main magazines, menaced by the spread of flames, might go up at any time. Sigsbee saw that danger as he and the others aboard climbed further up the steepening poop, the only part clear of the water. He gave the order to abandon ship.

There was no further explosion. With a great hissing of steam and extinguishing flame, the *Maine* was settling on the harbour-bed. Sigsbee, the last to leave her, was able to step over the side straight into a boat without getting his feet wet.

It was not until morning that an approximate count of the casualties could be made. Many men were missing, drowned or entombed in the wreck, but it was obvious that of the *Maine*'s complement of some 350 officers and men, two-thirds had died. Bodies floated ashore for days afterwards, and several survivors died of injuries.

Spanish expressions of sympathy were immediately forth-coming. Sigsbee, in his dispatch to Washington, counselled calm judgement of what had happened, though, after a day or two's consideration and exchange of opinions with his officers, he cabled to the Secretary of the Navy that he surmised that his ship's destruction had been caused by a mine, 'perhaps by accident'.

William Randolph Hearst was having no talk of accident in his newspapers. War was their demand. Every one of them carried front-page, headline accusations of Spanish treachery and murder. There were even diagrams, explaining how the deed had been done by deliberately causing the cruiser to be moored over mines able to be detonated from the Spanish shore fortress.

While responsible Americans deplored Hearst's gutter journalism, it did not necessarily lessen suspicions that the *Maine* had been mined, or even torpedoed, or perhaps sabotaged by an explosive device smuggled aboard, although Captain Sigsbee had received few visitors and had kept them under careful scrutiny. The questions were: had the detonation been accidental or deliberate? And, if deliberate, had it been a tactical blow by the Spanish, or a ruthless trick by the Cuban rebels to discredit their oppressors and provoke the United States against them?

The implications were immediately obvious to the Spanish. Genuinely, or merely going through the motions of doing the correct thing, they sought to allay American hostility by ordering a court of inquiry and sending divers down to investigate the wreck, already subsiding into the harbour mud. In their anxiety, or guilt, they spoiled the gesture by rushing out a preliminary verdict, far too quickly to have been a fully investigated and considered one, that the *Maine* could not possibly have sunk from any external cause. One reason offered was that no dead fish had been found: the harbour abounded with fish, and an explosion outside the ship would be bound to have killed hundreds. This was subsequently refuted at the Americans' own hearing, with the suggestion that the fish had probably left the harbour for the night, or had been temporarily stunned, recovered, and gone on swimming.

With hindsight, Spanish anxiety to play down the incident as quickly as possible is understandable. Spain did not want war with the United States, having nothing to gain and a great deal to lose. Equally unlikely was the possibility that planting a big enough mine or firing a torpedo could have been done by rebels without detection.

Rational-minded Americans must have recognized all of this. The hysterical exhortations of the Hearst press were not directed towards the rationally minded; besides which, there were outwardly responsible Americans who would quite welcome a war with Spain. Their powerful nation was in a mood to cut an international dash, while, as one senator was ingenuous enough to declare, a war would bring welcome stimulus to manufacturing and transport industries throughout the United States.

Nor were the Hearst newspapers the only ones clamouring for war. It was amid an atmosphere of sincere desire for revenge, and with the preconviction that the disaster must have been caused by some hostile means, that the Americans conducted their own inquiry: the practice of independent international inquiries into disputes was not much established in those days.

Witnesses from the *Maine* herself were united in one thing — there had been two explosions. The first had been minor, like a small gun going off; the one immediately following it had been cataclysmic. No one could deduce a known instance of a mine touching off a warship's magazine, but there was a first time for everything. It was equally unheard of for contact mines to be sown in a harbour, where any ship of any nationality would be equally vulnerable. There was, however, the remote-control type of mine, as depicted in the *New York Journal*'s diagram of the *Maine* sitting unsuspectingly above devices which could only be exploded by a wire contact with the shore.

Captain Sigsbee's opinion was that his ship had been led to a prepared mooring place, above mines which could be used if the cruiser should do something offensive. Had the fortuitous swing to bring the biggest guns seemingly to bear on the town caused some nervous Spaniard to press the button? Had some fanatical rebel gained access to the control and fired the mine? The possibilities were myriad, rejected or embraced according to national and individual suspicions and prejudices. The Spanish case was not helped, after their denial of the presence of any mines at all in Havana harbour, by one of their newspapers printing a boast by their Navy Secretary that there need be no fears about American warships penetrating Cuban harbours, because they were all mined in readiness, Havana in particular.

The chief alternatives to the theory that the *Maine* had been mined was that she had blown up of her own accord — that some small internal explosion had set off the fatal one. If a saboteur's explosive plant were ruled out, and there had been no obvious accident, the most likely cause remaining was spontaneous combustion of her fuel.

Six bunkers adjoined the main magazines. They had alarms and safety devices to keep a check on any build-up of heat within them. Sigsbee, the easygoing captain, left their supervision to others whose vigilance he had no reason to mistrust. There were no hot steam pipes, dangerous electric wires or exposed light fittings in the magazines. At the time of the disaster, four of the six fuel bunkers were empty, and, because the ship was moored, the power systems were working at minimal capacity.

Explosion caused from within was rejected by the American tribunal on 21 March 1898. A month later, the U.S. Minister in Spain handed in an ultimatum that Spanish occupation of Cuba must cease. Queen Cristina herself presided over the cabinet meeting at which proud old Spain determined to fight rather than give in tamely.

'How Do You Like The *Journal*'s War?' gloated Hearst's headlines when the fighting began, bringing a consequent rise in his circulation figures. It was a squalid little war, over by August, with not many casualties, not much honour, but with the Spanish fleet annihilated and the territories of the Philippines, Guam, Puerto Rica, and, of course, Cuba, Spanish possessions no longer.

In 1909 the wreck of the *Maine* was declared a hazard to shipping in Havana harbour. At great financial cost to the U.S.A. the hulk was raised, the job taking the better part of two years. One expert who examined the damaged hull declared conclusively that a small mine had gone off against it, chancing to explode a small magazine where black powder used for firing salutes was stored, which in turn had set off the great explosion. Another expert stated equally categorically that the initial explosion could not possibly have occurred outside.

Many years later, in the atomic age, a further expert, raking over old reports and unpublished details, found what to him was incontrovertible proof that the *Maine* had exploded as a result of overheating of bituminous coal which she was carrying in too close proximity to an insufficiently insulated magazine. Many other instances of such disasters have been known.

ROBERT MAXWELL: WAS HE MURDERED?

The world was stunned when, on the afternoon of 5 November 1991, media bulletins carried the news that Robert Maxwell was missing from his yacht off the Canary Islands. Some hours later follow-up bulletins announced that a body believed to be that of the publisher had been picked up from the sea by helicopter. It was difficult to comprehend that this most vital of men, who had travelled from a poverty-stricken childhood in a remote part of Europe to a pre-eminent position among the super-rich and internationally mighty, had ceased to exist. But so it proved to be.

The body was taken to the mortuary at Gran Canaria and there identified by Maxwell's widow Betty and eldest son Philip. Three Spanish doctors began a post-mortem on the following day, and organs from the body were sent to Madrid for further forensic tests. Early conclusions, later to be confirmed in the final Spanish submissions, pointed to death from natural causes – there being insufficient water in the lungs to suggest drowning. The mystery of how he had come to fall overboard remained unexplained: was it an accident, his own premeditated act, or was he pushed?

His family was anxious that his body should be buried by the Sabbath as required by Orthodox Jewish law, and hasty preparations were made for it to be flown to Israel. The 200-kilo oak casket was too large to fit into Maxwell's Gulfstream jet, and a Challenger jet had to be urgently chartered in Geneva. In Israel a second autopsy was carried out just hours prior to his interment on the Mount of Olives.

On 9 January 1992 came sensational news which strengthened speculation that Maxwell might have been murdered. The French magazine *Paris Match* revealed that three Israeli doctors who assisted at the second autopsy had become convinced that he had been brutally beaten before disappearing from the *Lady Ghislaine*.

But before we can fully appreciate the manner in which he may have died, we must go back to the beginning of the story.

Robert Maxwell was born on 10 January 1923 at Slatinske Doly, a small Ruthenian village on the Czech side of the Czechoslovak–Rumanian border – a remote area of shadowy forest between the brooding mass of the Carpathian mountains and the frontier-marking River Tisza. His father, Mechel Hock, named him Abraham Lajbi, but when the birth came to be registered the authorities insisted that he should have the Czech names of Ludvik Jan.

Great changes were taking place in this hitherto neglected part of Europe. Carpo-Ruthenia, which had belonged to Hungary up to 1919, was awarded to the new state of Czechoslovakia in 1919 by the Versailles Treaty. Traditional attitudes altered abruptly; instead of looking towards Budapest Ruthenians now shifted their gaze to Bratislava and Prague. Jan Masaryk, founding father of the new state and a liberal democrat, lifted the age-old anti-Jewish laws and granted the Jews full Czech citizenship.

The new more liberal regime made the region one of the staging-posts of eastern Europe. There had always been the natural flow of transients – Slovaks, Hungarians, Germans, Rumanians, Ukrainians, gypsies and Jews in this crossroads, but now Slatinske Doly became a transit camp for Zionists from Poland and Russia on their way to Palestine.

The new frontier also greatly encouraged smuggling. Rumania with its different and higher taxes on the slaughter of animals provided a strong incentive for the illicit shipment of horses and cattle from Ruthenia across the Tisza. Smuggling became an endemic industry and the enterprising smuggler was able to thrive.

It was into this ferment of changing attitudes and opportunities that Maxwell was born, and it was to affect his outlook for life: anything, it seemed, was possible. His childhood nevertheless was one of poverty.

Mechel was a poor Jewish peasant scratching a meagre living from the soil; now and again he was able to add a little to his income by acting as a middleman between farmer and butcher. The normal diet of the young Maxwell and his six brothers and sisters was potatoes and coarse bread, relieved at weekends and holidays by a little meat and gefilte fish. He was later to remark that he did not have a pair of shoes of his own until he was seven.

His mother Hannah came from a better family than Mechel and was fiercely ambitious for her children. She made sure that they attended regularly at the Jewish primary school and that Ludvik, her favourite, went to the synagogue daily, there to study the scriptures and learn Hebrew. His education however hardly progressed beyond the elementary stage.

But he was learning much more out of school. He was drawn to his maternal grandfather, Yaacov, who in many ways substituted for his own father. Yaacov was a much more successful dealer than Mechel, and in addition was a shrewd trader. Most of his deals were done by barter, and he could carry many transactions in his head simultaneously: there is little doubt that the future wheeler-dealer learned the tricks of the trade on the Rumanian side of the River Tisza at dead of night smuggling horses and cattle with his grandfather and watching the clever old master haggling in the moonlight. Also by the time he was in his early teens his skilful ear had picked up most of the languages of central and eastern Europe from the polyglot stream of life around him.

By the late thirties the skies were darkening over Europe. In September 1938 the Western Allies ceded the Czech Sudetenland to Germany by the Munich Agreement; in March 1939 Hitler broke the Agreement by marching into Prague and taking over the country; in the same month the German dictator transferred Ruthenia from Czech to Hungarian control, and almost immediately a company of

Hungarian troops marched into Slatinske Doly. Jews of military age were impressed into labour battalions: the shape of the future was becoming ominously clear. Maxwell's parents bought him a railway ticket to Budapest where they hoped he would be able to lose himself in the anonymity of a large city. He was just sixteen.

Maxwell has given various accounts of the ensuing months, but the most likely story is the one he later told his cousin Alex Pearl who had travelled with him to Budapest. It seems that he fell in with a group of young Czechs determined to fight for the honour of their ravished country; they left the Hungarian capital, made their way by devious and stealthy means to Zagreb in Yugoslavia, and there took ship to Palestine where they enlisted in the Czech Legion. The Legion took part in the battle of France in 1940, and disintegrated in the general Allied defeat of that disastrous summer; Maxwell was evacuated in an Egyptian ship, the *Mers-el-Kebir*, bound for Liverpool, and arrived, he said, 'with a rifle in my hand and a desire to fight the Germans': he would no doubt have felt even more strongly had he the prescience to know that except for one sister his whole family would perish in the Holocaust.

Bored with the inactivity of life in the reformed Czech Legion, he volunteered to join the Pioneer Corps and was accepted. For the next two years he strove to transform himself; he shed his boorish appearance and behaviour and donned the manners and deportment of a well-bred Englishman; he cultivated a well-rehearsed charm; and with his brilliance at languages learned to speak English with an 'upper-crust' accent. He also changed his name to Du Maurier after a brand of cigarettes popular at the time. But he had not neglected to become an excellent soldier and crack marksman so that when he applied to join a fighting unit he was accepted into the Sixth Battalion of the North Staffs Regiment. He made a particularly favourable impression on Brigadier Carthew-Yourston, who felt that his command of languages would be very usefully employed in the Intelligence (I) section of the battalion.

The brigade sailed for France on D-Day +16, landed near Arromanches, and took part in the fierce fighting around the Caen hinge and in the Falaise Gap. Paris was liberated on 25 August and Maxwell, now under the name of Jones, arrived with his unit shortly afterwards. The charming city in the first flush of liberation cast its spell over everybody: Maxwell met Elizabeth (Betty) Meynard, an attractive French girl and his future wife, and they immediately fell in love. The paternal Carthew-Yourston suggested he adopt the name of Robert Maxwell as being more suitable than the others: the erstwhile Sergeant Jones concurred. And so was born the name and the legend.

The Paris idyll lasted only a few days before Maxwell, newly commissioned, returned to the fighting. He achieved the summit of his military career by winning the Military Cross at Paarlo on the Belgian–Dutch frontier; the citation was particularly glowing and the award was made personally by Montgomery. The end of the hostilities saw him in Hamburg: Maxwell had had a 'good war'.

But although he had survived the poverty of Slatinske Doly, the Holocaust and the dangers of the battlefield the future posed a huge question-mark. Unlike the great majority of his fellow officers he had no home to return to: what was he to do? It was obvious that in the short term he would have to remain in the Army where his languages made him a much-prized possession: few British officers spoke German, and to these he could add Russian, Czech, Hungarian, Ruthenian, Polish and Rumanian. After a short period of battlefield interrogation he was posted in the rank of captain to the Control Commission – in effect the replacement of the German civilian ministries by the Army – and to that particular section known as PRISC (Public Relations and Information Services Control). Any German wishing to publish books or newspapers, put on plays or show films had to obtain permission from this important body. Maxwell was appointed Berlin's press chief: he now had a position of power and authority and one that was to afford him the opportunity of making the contacts which were to prove vital for his future.

The first friendship he formed was with Arno Scholtz, to whom he recommended the granting of a licence to publish *Der Telegraf*, which soon became the most influential newspaper in Berlin. Maxwell played an active part in this success, exhibiting an uncanny flair for locating and moving the vital spare parts in the war-torn city for keeping the presses running. The dashing young multi-lingual officer in the huge American cars soon became a well-known figure around the city. Scholtz, in gratitude for help given, introduced Maxwell to Ferdinand Springer, an introduction which was to determine the course of his subsequent career. Springer was the head of the German publishing firm of Springer Verlag, of high repute for its distinguished scientific list. Scholtz told Maxwell: 'If you help re-establish the trade, the trade will kiss your feet. . .'

In the meantime however, in March 1947, Maxwell resigned from the Control Commission and moved his headquarters to London. He had acquired the controlling interest in an import-export company formed with a fellow Czech and called Low-Bell; he bought German newspapers for sale to prisoners-of-war in Britain, collecting them at Heathrow in a huge grey Dodge, and trafficked in any commodity in short supply.

In October of that year, remembering Scholtz's advice, he returned to Germany to renew his acquaintanceship with Ferdinand Springer. Springer had built up the family publishing business to be of its class the best in Germany: his list had specialized in science and engineering, and with Germany leading the world in many fields Springer's publications were eagerly sought internationally. Among those whose first works he had published were authors of the stature of Max Born, Paul Erlich, Max Planck and Albert Einstein. Springer and his partner Tönges Lange had cleverly dispersed their stocks so that the bulk of their publications survived the bombing: they were however suffering agonies of frustration in trying to get their books and journals out of Germany to meet the demand for them abroad. The Allied customs regulations relating to exports were of nightmarish complexity, and they desperately needed someone on the outside who could distribute their publications for them.

Maxwell came to the rescue and at the same time did himself a huge favour. He had already established a firm earlier in the year for the importation of German publications (EPPAC), and it was agreed that through this agency he should own the exclusive worldwide distribution rights of Springer's journals and books. Over the next nine years their joint business was to be worth 20 million Deutschmarks. Maxwell had achieved his ambition of becoming a millionaire.

But there were to be bumps along the way. An unsuccessful attempt to revive the ailing book wholesaler Simpkin Marshall called down the wrath of the official receivers when the firm was finally wound up. All the hallmarks of the later Maxwell management style were apparent: intercompany trading, sums owed to Maxwell which were difficult to reconcile, accounting of a wildly incoherent kind.

Maxwell bounced back from this débâcle by turning with fiendish energy to Pergamon Press, a small scientific publishing firm which he had bought as Butterworth-Springer in 1951. By the end of 1957 Pergamon was publishing over one hundred journals and books per year: editorial advisers included people of the eminence of Sir John Cockroft, Sir Robert Robinson and Sir Edward Appleton. Many prominent authors accepted minimal fees for the advantage of academic prestige; yet subscriptions, based on the huge Springer mailing list to which Maxwell had access, were paid in advance. The money rolled in.

In 1969 he began to negotiate the sale of Pergamon to Leasco. Relations between Maxwell and Saul Steinberg, Leasco's precocious financial wizard, became strained however when the latter suspected that the Pergamon lily was rather too heavily gilded. A DTI investigation was ordered which condemned Maxwell's accounting and truthfulness, and concluded with the damning verdict that he was not fit to run a public company. It was the end of an extraordinary switchback of a decade during which Maxwell had also been MP for Buckingham for six years.

Again, it did not take him long to recover lost ground. Without his genius and drive the fortunes of Pergamon withered and declined, and in 1974 he was triumphantly able to buy it back at a bargain price: 'Even with your huge fees,' he gleefully told a lawyer, 'I've come out of it with a big profit.' Pergamon's health soon recovered and it boomed again: it was to remain Maxwell's flagship until he sold it to Elsevier in 1991 to meet the huge debts he was incurring elsewhere.

In 1981 he bought the ailing British Printing Corporation, and transformed terminal decline into a success story against all predictions. In 1984 he achieved one of the greatest of all his ambitions – newspaper proprietorship with its attendant aura of power and influence, by buying the Mirror Group from Reed International: the banking community, their confidence in him completely restored, lent him the money for the deal. The great Lord Northcliffe's former empire was his: grandfather Yaacov would indeed have applauded.

He took possession of the Chairman's desk at the Mirror Group building soon after midnight on 13 July, and at midday informed leaders of the print unions that if the threatened strike of the previous day had taken place he would instantly have shut all the papers down. He was determined to reverse the complex of ills that had brought the newspaper industry close to ruin, and started by a ruthless pruning of staff. The Spanish practices of the robber barons of the print unions were brought to a swift halt: and he brooked no delay in introducing the long-overdue new technology in typesetting and colour processing. More than anyone else Maxwell pioneered the transition of British national newspapers from antiquated

242

to modern production techniques; this is something on the positive side which has been lost sight of through the dark shadows cast by his disgraceful financial dealings.

If Robert Maxwell had died in 1988 posterity's view of him might have been very different. He had created successful world-wide businesses and had saved others from destruction; he had helped to transform the newspaper industry; he had headed several notable charities and by common consent had been an excellent constituency MP; he was the owner of Oxford United and Derby County football clubs; and he was the embodiment of the sort of colourful and individualistic life-style which has always endeared itself to the British: the soubriquet 'Cap'n Bob' connoted affection as much as familiarity.

Such a scenario was not to be. Throughout his life Maxwell could not leave well alone and this trait was now to become intensified in a particularly virulent way at the worst possible time. The man who had always bought cheaply and sold expensively reversed this practice; he bought prodigiously at top prices on the edge of a slump. So dramatic was this change in his pattern of behaviour as to suggest a sudden decline in his powers.

He bought the US company Macmillan for 2.6 billion dollars, and *Official Airlines Guide* for 750 million. He further tilted the balance of his main company Maxwell Communications towards the United States by buying the Berlitz language-teaching business. In the last year of his life he was increasingly beset by the double impact of the transatlantic recession and high interest rates: this did not stop him from continuing his buying spree with the purchase of the New York *Daily News*, which he advertised in characteristically dramatic fashion by sailing up the East River in his yacht the *Lady Ghislaine*.

Since his death the contortions by which, Houdini-like, he sought to escape from his mountainous debts have been fully reported in the world's press. Huge misappropriations of funds, most disgracefully from the Mirror Group and MCC Pension Funds, had taken place; the Byzantine

243

structure of his financial empire with its interlocking complex of private and public companies made it fiendishly difficult to track down the missing money now estimated at £2 billion. The anonymous Liechtenstein and Gibraltarian accounts are black holes whose secrets have yet to be revealed.

At the time that Maxwell departed for his fateful last voyage, financial nemesis was impending. The *Financial Times* was about to publish a report revealing that Maxwell's debts were double those publicly acknowledged; Goldman Sachs started to sell MCC shares when he failed to make a margin call; Seymour Hersh's book *The Samson Option*, suggesting that Maxwell was a Mossad agent, had a further effect on a jittery market. At 2.58 p.m. on 5 November, the day of the publisher's death, dealings in Maxwell company shares were suspended on the Stock Exchange.

At 6.30 a.m. on the morning of Thursday, 31 October 1991 Robert Maxwell climbed aboard a helicopter on the roof of the *Daily Mirror* building in Holborn. He had been suffering from a very heavy cold and had decided that a few days' cruising in the sun on board his yacht the *Lady Ghislaine* would restore him to fitness. The helicopter flew him to Luton where his Gulfstream jet was waiting: three and a half hours later he landed at Gibraltar, there to be greeted by Captain Angus Rankin, the yachtmaster. He was, it seems, in a good mood, and was to remain predominantly cheerful during the subsequent voyage.

The yacht set sail for Madeira at 4 p.m. and glided through the intervening 600 miles of sunlit sea to arrive at Funchal two days later. After looking round the town Maxwell, who enjoyed swimming in the nude, asked to be taken to the Desertas beach: that night the passionate and unsuccessful gambler visited the casino.

The next step was Tenerife, and the yacht made landfall at the little fishing port of Darcena Pesquera a few miles north of Santa Cruz at 10 a.m. on Monday, 4 November. Maxwell spent most of the day in relaxed and cheerful activity centred chiefly on jointly composing on the phone with his son Ian the speech he had been due to give to the Anglo-Israeli Association that night and which Ian was giving in his stead. Among his other telephone conversations was one with Samuel Pisar, an Auschwitz survivor and his French lawyer, in which jokes were exchanged about Maxwell's nomination for France's highest honour, the *Légion d'Honneur*. At almost lunch-time the yacht sailed south to Poris de Abona where Maxwell took a break for a swim.

But later calls may have served to darken his mood somewhat; these informed him of Sachs's decision to sell MCC shares, of the Swiss bank's threat to call in the Fraud Squad, and of the clamouring of two French banks for loan repayments.

By late afternoon the *Lady Ghislaine* had returned to Santa Cruz. Maxwell went ashore at 8 p.m. and was driven by a taxi-driver named Arturo Trujillo, to the Hotel Mencey, the tycoon finding the front seat of the Toyota Camry a tight fit. He ordered a green salad and hake with clams: the waiters would later say that he seemed quite calm though abstracted and apparently lost in his own thoughts. When he departed he left behind his jacket – a beige blazer – and a waiter had to run after him with it. Trujillo then drove him to El Olympo for coffee after which, there being no available entertainment within reasonable distance, Maxwell asked to be driven back to the yacht. Back on board, he instructed Rankin to put to sea for the night.

At approximately 10.15 p.m. Stewardess Lisa Kordalski went to see if Maxwell required anything further, and found him in bed wearing a night-gown – his customary attire for repose: as she was about to depart through the main stateroom door he asked her to lock that door and leave through his bathroom.

At 11 p.m. Rankin answered a satellite telephone call from the publisher's son Ian, which he connected; Ian was reporting on the Anglo-Israeli dinner of that night and, his reporting concluded, asked if his father would be returning home the following day. 'You bet,' was the reply, and these were the last words to a member of his family. His Gulfstream jet awaited him at Los Christianos on Tenerife to fly him home.

At about 4.25 a.m. the second engineer reported seeing Maxwell on deck; and about twenty minutes later he called up the bridge to complain that the air-conditioning was too high. An unbroken silence then ensued. The yacht, having sailed southward during the night from Santa Cruz around Gran Canaria and then westward to Tenerife, dropped anchor at Los Christianos at 9.45 a.m.

At 11.10 a.m. the telephone rang: it was a call from New York; Rankin put the call through to the publisher's stateroom, and getting no reply went down to investigate. Finding the door locked, he opened it with his master key: the room was empty, and on the bed lay Maxwell's folded night-gown. The yachtmaster ordered an immediate search of the vessel, and when this failed to find the publisher two more searches were urgently made. Maxwell had indeed vanished.

The first call Gus Rankin made was to Maxwell's youngest son, Kevin: this was at 11.30 a.m. An inexplicable gap of time then ensued until 12.25 p.m. when the yachtmaster dispatched a satellite news signal that Robert Maxwell was missing: the world heard the news and gasped.

The Spanish Air-Sea Rescue Service went immediately into action. Ships and planes were alerted and three helicopters began a systematic search; it was a fishing-boat, however, which reported the first sighting of a body about a hundred miles east of Tenerife: within minutes of confirmation a Superpuma helicopter began winching aboard Maxwell's 22-stone corpse. 'It was naked, stiff and floating face up, not face down which is normal,' reported a rescuer.

The body was flown to the military airport at Gando on Gran Canaria, there to be officially identified by Maxwell's widow Betty and eldest son Philip. After the identification

Betty was briefly questioned by Dr Carlos Lopez de Lamela, the local forensic director, about her husband's general health status: she revealed that he had been taking drugs to counter pulmonary oedema – a condition known to put a strain upon the heart.

The following day three pathologists, Dr Carlos Lopez de Lamela, Dr Maria Ramos and Dr Louisa Garcia Cohen carried out an autopsy: they found a little water in the lungs, a graze on the forehead, a fissure behind the ear; samples from the lung, kidney, pancreas, stomach and other vital organs were taken for dispatch to Madrid and further forensic tests. After three and a half hours they reported to Judge Luis Gutierez: the verdict was that there was no suggestion of either murder or suicide, and that death had occurred from natural causes before Maxwell fell into the sea. There was talk of 'a cardiac or cardio-vascular attack'. The central mystery of how he had gone overboard after dying from natural causes on board was dismissed as an accident. 'The initial forensic reports suggest a natural death before Mr Maxwell fell into the sea,' Gutierez told Betty Maxwell. The imprecise and vague nature of these findings drew immediate criticism from British pathologists and a flood of further questions from the hosts of assembled journalists. These were met with a shrug and the bland and unilluminating answer that 'nothing is impossible'.

Thus the field was thrown open to speculation on how precisely the publisher had come to die, and into this maelstrom of conjecture and counter-argument exploded the bombshell of the *Paris Match* revelations of 9 January, 1992.

Let us consider each of these possibilities in turn.

Natural Causes Maxwell was a prime target for a heart attack: massively overweight, he was also suffering from a chest condition known to put a strain on the heart; moreover his life-style was of an exacting intensity that would have taxed the strength of an elephant and one that made no concession to a healthy regime; above all, he was under prodigious pressure occasioned by huge debt and the sure knowledge that the reckoning was imminent and would be dire.

He was hot and uncomfortable – the message to the bridge to turn down the air-conditioning and the discarded night-gown are evidence of that; and he had been seen moving about on the lower deck at dawn. Though the ship had a solid 5½-ft barrier around the deck, there was a place near the stern where the only barrier was a thin 3-ft chrome rail strung with wire beside which the publisher often stood. If he had been at this point trying to cool off and had had a heart attack he could easily have toppled into the sea: as the spot was invisible from the bridge noboby would have seen him.

Accident Maxwell could have been standing by the low rail, had a dizzy spell, lost his balance and fallen overboard: it has been reported that the planking was moist, and footing therefore unsure. The shock of finding himself in the sea with the yacht blindly ignorant of his fate sailing away from him would have been sufficient to precipitate a heart attack.

Suicide On 21 February 1992, the *Sun* newspaper published excerpts from the report of an insurance investigator, Roger Rich, which pointed towards suicide, although there was the reservation that: 'At this stage the pathological results do not exclude other possibilities.' His conclusion was based on findings that 'the tearing and bleeding into the muscles of the back of the left shoulder and into the muscles by the spine resulted from sudden physical stress to the muscles, causing them to stretch and tear.' The injury, it is maintained, showed that Maxwell was hanging on to something – like a yacht rail – with his left hand whilst his massive pendulous weight ruptured his shoulder muscles until he finally let go and fell into the sea.

Such assertions are furiously contested by those closest to Maxwell. They maintain that he was a man who never knew when he was beaten, and point out that he could never have overcome his primitive beginnings, won an award for valour in the field, and risen time and again from the ashes of defeat and disaster to renewed achievement unless he possessed the courage of a lion: such a man would never contemplate suicide.

Moreover, it has been estimated that he could not have gone overboard later than 5.30 a.m. If he had been contemplating suicide would he have been concerned about such a mundane matter as the state of the central heating just forty-five minutes earlier?

Finally, one has to bear in mind the objective fact that the finding of the Spanish autopsy, whatever its shortcomings, maintained that there was insufficient water in the lungs to justify a verdict of suicide by drowning.

Murder On 9 January 1992 the leading French magazine *Paris Match* published the sensational news that in the opinion of three Israeli doctors and two French pathologists Maxwell was brutally beaten and may have been murdered before going overboard: the Israelis had assisted at the second autopsy carried out in Israel a few hours before he was interred on the Mount of Olives. The report was based on an 80-minute video recorded in the laboratory of the Institute for Forensic Medicine in Tel Aviv and shows in gruesome detail the operation in progress; it was illustrated with many close-ups of the dead man.

During the examination pathologists are heard making comments about a broken nose and blows to the eyes, ear and forehead.

Paris Match showed the video to two French experts. Loic le Ribault, the founder of Carne, the respected forensic laboratory, concluded: 'It is highly probable that a violent blow was struck behind the head of the victim with the use of a weapon.' He added: 'Altogether our first impressions are that these lesions were caused as a result of injury which took place before death.'

Professor Louis Roche, a pathologist and former president of the International Academy of Forensic Medicine, highlighted three major areas of bruising: 'All these lesions were caused by injury. By themselves they are not serious but they prove that injury was suffered before death.'

Dr Bartholomew Levy, one of the Israeli pathologists who carried out the second autopsy, was quoted as saying: 'Listen to me who has actually seen the body itself. I can tell you that those bruises were not made by the Holy Spirit. If Maxwell had not been beaten up he would still be alive today.'

On the strength of these and other statements the magazine concluded that Maxwell 'received numerous heavy blows, which caused many bruises and even fractured his nose and tore the ear lobe.'

These murder theories were supported by people who believed Seymour Hersh's allegations that Maxwell had been an agent for Israeli intelligence and thus a likely assassin's target.

British pathologists however dispute these opinions. Dr Peter Vanezis, head of forensic medicine and toxicology at Charing Cross and Westminster Medical School, said: 'The idea that Robert Maxwell had been subjected to a violent assault or any way beaten up before his death is, in my view, totally inaccurate.' His view is shared by Austen Gresham, the Cambridge pathologist. Both incline to the view that the publisher died from natural causes.

Dr Iain West, a Home Office pathologist who led the Israeli team, had not delivered his judgement at the time of this book going to press: he was working for British insurance companies. Maxwell's life was insured for £20 million in the event of accident or murder, so much rides on the final outcome of these medical deliberations.

The way in which Robert Maxwell came to die will remain the subject of speculation for years to come. At his death he left scores of unanswered questions to perplex and harass his erstwhile associates and the world at large; but none is so stubbornly intractable as what happened during his last few minutes on board the *Lady Ghislaine* in the early hours of Tuesday, 5 November 1991.

SELECT BIBLIOGRAPHY

WHO WAS THE MURDERER?

Dr John Bodkin Adams
Bedford, Sybille. *The Best We Can Do*. Collins, 1958
Hallworth, Rodney, and Williams, Mark. *Where There's a Will*. The Capstan Press, Jersey, 1983
Hoskins, Percy. *Two Men Were Acquitted*. Secker & Warburg, 1984

The Lindbergh Baby Kidnapping
Waller, George. *Kidnap, The Story of the Lindbergh Case*. Hamish Hamilton, 1961
Whipple, Sidney B. *The Story of Richard Bruno Hauptmann*. Heinemann, 1938
Wright, Theon. *The Search for the Lindbergh Baby*. Tower Publications, 1981

William Herbert Wallace
Goodman, Jonathan. *The Killing of Julia Wallace*. Harrap, 1969
Hussey, Robert S. *Murderer Scot-Free*. David & Charles, 1972
Wilkes, Roger. *Wallace, The Final Verdict*. The Bodley Head, 1984
Wyndham-Brown, W.F. *The Trial of William Herbert Wallace*. Gollancz, 1933

Adelaide Bartlett
Hall, Sir John. *Adelaide Bartlett*. Notable British Trial Series
Morland, Nigel. *Background to Murder*. Werner Laurie, 1955

Lizzie Borden
Pearson, Edmund. *Masterpieces of Murder*. Hutchinson, 1964
Radin, Edward. *Lizzie Borden, the Untold Story*. Gollancz, 1961
Lincoln, Victoria. *A Private Disgrace*. Putnams, 1967
Pearson, Edmund. *The Trial of Lizzie Borden*. Heinemann, 1937

Tony Mancini
Lustgarten, Edgar. *The Murderer and the Trial*. Odhams, 1960

The Axeman of New Orleans
Tallant, Robert. *Murder in New Orleans*. William Kimber, 1953

John Cartland
Cartland, Jeremy. *The Cartland File*. Linkline, 1978

Jack the Ripper
Rumbelow, Donald. *The Complete Jack the Ripper*. W.H. Allen, 1975

Zodiac
Graysmith, Robert. *Zodiac*. St. Martins/Marek, 1985

WHAT HAPPENED TO THEM?

Grey, Anthony. *The Prime Minister Was a Spy*. Weidenfeld & Nicolson, 1983
Bryson, John. *Evil Angels*. Viking, 1985
Shears, Richard. *The Dingo Baby Case*. Sphere Books, 1982
Cooke, F.B. *Single-Handed Cruising*. 1931
Kastenbaum, R. and Aisenberg, R. *The Psychology of Death*. Springer Publishing, New York, 1972
Wilson, Colin, and Seaman, Donald. *Scandal!* Weidenfeld & Nicolson, 1986

IDENTITIES: TRUE OR FALSE?

Thomas, Hugh. *The Murder of Rudolf Hess*. Hodder & Stoughton, 1979
The Verdict of the Court. Edited by Michael Hardwick. Herbert Jenkins, 1960
Machlin, Milton, and Woodfield, William Read. *Ninth Life*. Putnams, 1961
Morland, Nigel. *Patterns of Murder*. Elek, 1966
Roughhead, William. *The Trial of Oscar Slater*. Notable British Trials Series

ACCIDENTS

Ennis, John. *The Great Bombay Explosion*. Duell, Sloane and Pearce, 1959
50 Strange Mysteries of the Sea. Edited by John Canning. Souvenir Press, 1979

ENIGMAS OF AIR AND SEA

Garrett, Richard. *Flight into Mystery*. Weidenfeld & Nicolson, 1986
Barker, Ralph. *Great Mysteries of the Air*. Chatto and Windus, 1966
Garrett, Richard. *Atlantic Disaster*. Buchan and Enright, 1986
Simpson, Colin. *Lusitania*. Longman, 1972
Hardwick, Michael and Mollie. *The World's Greatest Sea Mysteries*. Odhams, 1967
Bywaters, Hector C. *Their Secret Purposes*. 1932
Beaty, David. *Strange Encounters*. Methuen, 1982
Bower, Tom. *The Outsider*. Mandarin, 1991. (The most rounded portrait of Robert Maxwell to date.)
Thompson and Delano. *Maxwell, A Portrait of Power*. Corgi, 1991
Haines, Joe. *Maxwell*. Macdonald, 1987
Hersh, Seymour. *The Samson Option*. Faber, 1991

INDEX

Figures in *italics* refer to captions.

Abel, Rudolph, 191
Adams, Arthur, 160, 161, 162, 163
Adams, Dr., 165
Allen, William J., 30
Appleton, Sir Edward, 241
Asunto, Nick, 71
Attrell, Florence, 60, 61

Ballantine, Mr Serjeant, 148, 150
Ballew, Floyd, 155, 158
Barker, Ian, QC, 125
Barritt, Coroner, 124
Barrowman, Mary, 162, 163, 165, 166
Bartlett, Adelaide Blanche, 40-9
Bartlett, Charles, 40
Bartlett, Edwin, 40-9
Bartlett, Frederick, 41
Bartlett, Mr (Edwin's father), 41, 45
Bates, Cheri Jo, 104
Belli, Melvin, 102, 103
Berkowitz, David, 104
Best, Stanley, 130
Besumer, Louis, 69, 70, 72, 74
Birkett, Norman, 62-63, 150
Birrell, Margaret, 161
Blanco, Marshal, 228
Blasco, Raymond, 82
Blunt, George, 11
Boca, Steve, 73
Bodkin Adams, Dr John, 9-17
Boelcke, Oswald, 202, 203, 204, 208
Bombay Explosion, 168-75
Borden, Abby, 50-8
Borden, Andrew Jackson, 50-8
Borden, Emma, *passim* 50, 53-8
Borden, Lizzie, 50-8, *54*
Bovill, Sir William, 148
Bowen, Dr, 51
Bradley, Leonard, 20, 22
Bradnum, Julia, 11
Brighton Trunk Murders, 59-66
Broadribb, Ted, 107
Brown, Captain A. Roy, 201, 206, 207
Buie, Gunner R., 207

Bushaw, Elaine, 155
Byung-in, Captain Chun, 184-191
Baywater, Hector C., 225

Cameron, Professor James, 81, 125
Camps, Francis, 11
Cánovas, Antonia, 228
Capone, Al, 24, 30
Carlson, William 73
Carthew-Yourston, Brigadier, 238, 239
Cartland, Elizabeth, 80, 82
Cartland, Jeremy, 76-84
Cartland, Professor John Basil, 76-84
Casey, Charles, 96
Castro, Tom, 145, 146, 147, 150 *see also*
    Orton, Arthur
Cavill, Florence, 11
Chamberlain, Aidan, 121
Chamberlain, Alice Lynne 'Lindy',
    121-7
Chamberlain, Azaria, 121-7
Chamberlain, Michael, *passim* 121-6
Chamberlain, Reagan, 121
Chapman, Annie, 86
Chessman, Caryl Whittier, 154-9
Churchill, Sir Winston, 140, 211,
    215-16
Clarence, Prince Albert, Duke of, 93,
    94-95
Clarke, Edward, 46
Close, Alan, 34
Cockburn, Lord, 150
Cockroft, Sir John, 241
Cohen, Dr Louisa Garcia, 247
Coleridge, Sir John, 148, 149-50
Condon, Dr John F., *passim* 25-9
Cook, David, 166
Coombs, Norman, 172, 173
Corbett, Sir Julian, 209
Cortimiglia, Charles, 71, 72
Cortimiglia, Rosie, 71, 72, 73
Crowhurst, Donald, 128-133
Cruti, Mr, 68
Czech Legion, 238

Deedman, Ronald, 180

de Lamela, Dr Carlos Lopez, 247
Delaune, Frederick, 76
Delmas, Andŕe, 81
'Dingo Baby', 121-7
Doggett, Mrs, 43, 44
Dominici, Gaston, 78
Dowding, Annie, 11
Downs, James, 11, 13
Doyle, Sir Arthur Conan, 166-7
Druitt, Montague John, 93
Drummond, Sir Jack, 78
Duckworth, Chief Inspector, 165
Du Maurier, Mr, (Robert Maxwell), 238
Dunbar, Jim, 103
Duncan, Sir Oliver, 78
Dyson, Rev. George *passim* 42-8

Eddowes, Catherine, 88
Evans, Gunner, W.J., 207

Farraday, David, 96
Ferrin, Darlene Elizabeth, 97, 98
Fisch, Isidor, 28
Fisher, Admiral Sir John, 215
Forbes, Colin, 155
Fort Stikine, s.s., 168-74
Fox, Charles, 164
Freedman, Dr Laurence, 104
Fricke, Charles, 157
Frohman, Carl, 212, 214

Gaute, J.H.H., 37
Genusa, Frank, 73
Gibbes, Mr, 145, 146
Gibson, Janet, 79, 82
Gilchrist, Marion, 160-7
Gillespie, Marjorie, 113, 119
Gow, Betty, 23, 26, 30
Goyen, *passim* 193-200
Gresham, Austen, 250
Grey, Anthony, *passim* 114-20
Gull, Sir William, 93, 94
Gutierez, Judge Luis, 247

Hales, John, 195
Hallworth, Rodney, 130, 131
Hamilton, Duke of, 136, 137

Hannam, Herbert, 13, 14, 16
Harden, Donald, 98
Harrington, Hiram, 52
Harrington, Special Officer, 52
Hartnell, Bryan, 99, 100, 101, 103
Hauptmann, Bruno Richard, 27-30
Haushofer, Albrecht, 135, 136, 138
Haushofer, Karl, 138
Hearst, William Randolph, 228, 230, 231, 232, 233, 234
Hecht, Professor, 225-6
Heggs, Christopher, 81
Hemmerde, G.E., 35
Henderson, William, 169, 174
Herbert, Irene, 11
Hersh, Seymour, 244, 250
Hess, Rudolf, 134-43
Hesse, Ilse, 135, 138, 140
Hill, Dr Ian, 20
Himmler, Heinrich, 139-40
Hitler, Adolf, 135, 140, 211, 237
Ho, Andy, 108, 109
Hoby, Alan, 107
Hock, Abraham Lajbi, (Robert Maxwell), 236
Hock, Hannah, 237
Hock, Ludvik Jan, (Robert Maxwell), 236
Hock, Mechel, 236, 237
Hoffman, Harold, 28, 29
Holt, Harold, 113-20
Horn, Alfred, 137, 138
Hullett, 'Bobbie', 9-10, 12
Hullett, Jack, 10, 11
Hullett, Theodora, 11
Hurlburt, Frank, 153

Isner, Heinz, 18, 21

Jack, Andrew, 198, 200
Jack the Ripper, 70, 85-95
Jenson, Bettilou, 96
Johnson, Regina, 152, 155, 157, 158
Johnson, John, 33, 34
Johnston, Mrs, 34
Jones, Sergeant, (Robert Maxwell), 239
Jordano, Frank, 71, 72, 73, 74

Jordano, Iorlando, 71, 72, 73, 74
Junio, Mme, 163
Juno, HM, 214

Kaden, Helmut, 136
Kaye, Violette, 59-66
Kelly, Mary Jeanette, 90, 91, 92, 94
Kennedy, Dr, 197-8
Kent, Prince George Edward
  Alexander, Duke of, 192, 193, 194,
  195, 199, 200
Kilgour, Annabella, 11, 14
Knowles, David, 154, 159
Knox-Johnson, Robin, 130, 131, 133
Koehler, Arthur, 26
Kordalski, Lisa, 245
Korean Airlines Flight 007, 183-91
Krikorian, Grigoire, 79, 82
Kuhl, Joy, 125, 126

L-2 submarine, 217
Lady Ghislaine, 236, 243, 244, 245, 250
Lambie, Helen *passim* 160-7
Lange, Tönges, 240
Lassetter, Michael, 78
Lauman, Sarah, 73
Lawrence, Geoffrey, 15-16
Lea, Jarnigan, 152, 153, 155
Leach, Dr Alfred, 44, 45, 48
le Ribault, Loic, 249
Lescher, Joe, 154
Levy, Dr Bartholomew, 250
Lindbergh, Charles, 23, 24, 25, 26, 30
Lindbergh, Charles Junior 'Buster',
  23, 26, 29
Liu, Yim ('Mr Wong'), 118
Lloyd, Lily, 38
Lohman, Coxswain, 225
Lombard, Mâitre, 80
Lowe, Harriet, 69, 75
Lowther, J.A., 195
Ludendorff, General von, 205, 208
Lundblad, Leslie, 97
Lusitania, 163, 165, 209-16
Lynch, Dr Roche, 63

MacBrayne, Duncan, 165
McCorkindale, Donny, 107, 108, 110
McDonald, Larry, 184, 190

MacFall, Professor J.E.W., 34
Macnaghten, Sir Melville, 87, 90, 93
Mageau, Michael Renault, 97
Maggio, Andrew, 67
Maggio, Jake, 67
Maggio, Joe, 67, 68, 74
Maggio, Mrs, 67, 68, 74
Maine, USS, 227-34
Mancini, Tony, 59-66
Manningham-Buller, Sir Reginald, 14
Mao Tse-tung, 117
Marina, Princess, of Greece, 192, 195
Mark, Sir Robert, 83
Marshall, June, 78
Martin, Ray, 127
Masaryk, Jan, 236
Matters, Leonard, 91-2
Matthews, Alice, 43, 45
Maxwell, Elizabeth, (Betty), 235, 239,
  246, 247
Maxwell, Ian, 245
Maxwell, Kevin, 246
Maxwell, Philip, 235, 246
Maxwell, Robert, 235-250
  adoption of this name, 239
May, Robert, 154
May, Wilfred, 206, 207
Menzies, Robert, 116, 118
Mers-el-Kebir, 238
Mersey, Lord, 215
Meynard, Elizabeth, (Betty), 239
Meza, Mary Alice, 153, 154, 155, 158
Miller, Clara, 11
Mills, Christine, 106-12
Mills, Freddie, 106-12
M'Lean, Allan, 162
Moitessier, Bernard, 131
Moorgate Crash, 176-82
Morland, Nigel, 35, 47
Morrell, Edith, 11, 13, 14-15, 16
Morrison, David, 197
Morrison, Hugh, 197
Morse, John Vinnicum, 50, 52, 53-4, 55
Mortimer, Emily, 11
Moseley, T.L., 193, 199
Muirhead, Mr Justice, 126
Mumfre, Joseph, 74
Munro, Hector, 38

Naismith, Alexander, 169, 170, 172, 173, 174
Newson, Leslie, 180-2
Nicholls, Mary Ann, 85, 86, 87

Oberst, Brinley, 172
Obitz, Theodore, 68
Olson, Harold, 29-30
Olson, Roy, 30
Orton, Arthur, 147, 149, 150 151 see also Castro, Tom
Orton, George, 149
Owens, Thomas, 56

Page, Ron, 82, 83
Paget, Sir James, 49
Parkes, John, 39
Parry, Gordon, 37, 38
Paul, David, 179, 180, 181
Pearl, Alex, 238
Pepitone, Mike, 73, 74
Pepitone, Mrs, 73, 74
Pergamon Press, 241
Pintsch, Karlheinz, 136, 140
Pisar, Samuel, 245
Polydeskis, Henrico, 81
Popkin, C.B., 207
Powers, Francis Gary, 191
Prince, Mary, 11
Prince, Sidney, 11
Pyper, Detective-inspector, 164

Ramos, Dr Maria, 247
Randall, Nurse, 16
Rankin, Angus, 244, 245, 246
Read, Leonard 'Nipper', 110, 111-112
Reagan, Ronald, 187, 190
'Red Baron' see Richthofen, Captain Baron Manfred von
Red Light Bandit, 152-9
Rich, Roger, 248
Richthofen, Captain Baron Manfred von, 201-8
Robinson, Dr Ann, 130, 181
Robinson, John, 66
Robinson, Sir Robert, 241
Roche, Professor Louis, 249
Romano, Joseph, 70, 71, 74
Romano, Mary, 70, 71

Roman, Pauline, 70, 71, 75
Rose, Alec, 129
Rosetti, Mr, 68
Russell, Miss, 52

Sachs, Goldman, 244, 245
Sadler, Colonel, 173
Salisbury, Lord, 94
Schellenberg, Walter, 139, 140
Schiambra, Tony, 68
Schneider, Edward, 70
Schneider, Mrs Edward, 70, 74
Scholtz, Arno, 240
Schwieger, Walter, 209, 210, 214
Sharpe, Violet, 26
Shepard, Cecilia, 99-100, 101
Sheridan, J.H., 201
Sickert, Walter, 95
Sigsbee, Captain Charles D., 229-34 passim
Sinclair, Sir Archibald, 192
Slater, Oscar (Leschziner), 162-7
Smith, Emma, 86
Solomons, Jack, 110
Sommerville, Dr A.C., 10
Son, First Officer, 187, 189, 190
Spilsbury, Sir Bernard, 63
Springer, Ferdinand, 240
Steinberg, Saul, 241
Stephen, James Kenneth, 94
Stewart, Alan, 113, 119
Stine, Paul, 101, 102
Stone, Gerald, 153, 155, 158
Stonecrop, 209
Stride, Elizabeth, 90
Stronach, Nurse, 15, 16
Strutt, The Hon. Michael, 195
Sturgess, Desmond, 125
Sullivan, Bridget, 50-2, 53, 55-6

Tabram, Martha, 86
Teignmouth, Electron, 131
Terranova, Charles, 155, 158, 159
Tetley, Nigel, 130, 131
Tichborne, Dowager Lady, 144-50 passim
Tichborne, Sir James, 145
Tichborne, Sir Roger Charles, 144, 145, 146, 148

Tichborne, Claimant, 144-151
Trench, John, 166
Trujillo, Arturo, 245
Turner, William, 213, 214, 215

U-20 submarine, 209, 213, 214, 216
U-65 submarine, 217-26

Vanderbilt, Alfred, 212, 214
Venezis, Dr Peter, 250

Waisler, Melvin, 154
Wallace, Amy, 36
Wallace, Joseph, 36
Wallace, Julia, 31-9
Wallace, William Herbert, 31-9
Ware, Amy, 11, 13

Warren, Sir Charles, 90
Wernicke (naval officer), 225
West, Dr Iain, 250
West, Rebecca, 140
Weston, Janice, 18-22
Weston, R.F., 207
Weston, Tony, 18, 19, 21
Weyler, Valeriano, 228, 229
Whittington-Egan, Richard, 37
Whitton, Matilda, 11
Wilentz, David, 29
Wright, Sir Denis, 79
Wright, Mr Justice, 35

Zanca, John, 69
'Zodiac', 96-105